# BARRON'S

# TOEIC®

## PRACTICE EXAMS

## 3RD EDITION

**Lin Lougheed**
Ed.D., Teachers College
Columbia University

### BARRON'S

**Photo Credits**

All photos are courtesy of Shutterstock.com

## IMPORTANT
## NEW TOEIC

In some countries, there will be a "new" TOEIC. After May 2016, there will be a different TOEIC administered in certain countries. Japan and Korea will be the first countries to administer the new TOEIC. The TOEIC will change in other countries over the next few years. Please visit the ETS TOEIC website (*www.ets.org/toeic*) for dates when the test will change in your country.

The new TOEIC will have the same question types as the old TOEIC plus some new question types.

Tests A and B are in the new format in this book. However, all six tests in this book will be helpful for all test takers.

## AUDIO AND AUDIOSCRIPTS

The MP3 files and audioscripts for all listening segments can be found online at
*http://barronsbooks.com/tp/toeic/audio/*

*All inquiries should be addressed to:*
Barron's Educational Series, Inc.
250 Wireless Boulevard
Hauppauge, New York 11788
**www.barronseduc.com**

*Library of Congress Catalog Card Number: 2016957048*

ISBN: 978-1-4380-7727-7

PRINTED IN THE UNITED STATES OF AMERICA
9 8 7 6 5 4 3 2 1

**10%**
**POST-CONSUMER WASTE**
Paper contains a minimum of 10% post-consumer waste (PCW). Paper used in this book was derived from certified, sustainable forestlands.

# Contents

# Introduction

◤◥◤◥◤◥◤◥◤◥◤◥◤◥◤◥◤◥◤◥◤◥◤◥◤◥

## WHAT IS THE TOEIC LISTENING AND READING EXAM?

The **TOEIC** (Test of English for International Communication) **Listening and Reading** measures your ability to understand spoken and written English in a variety of real-world situations. The listening comprehension section is divided into four parts with a total of 100 questions, and the reading comprehension section is divided into three parts, also with a total of 100 questions.

> Audioscripts for Parts 1–4 of each test can be found beginning on page 345. If you do not have access to the MP3 files, please refer to the audioscripts when prompted to listen to an audio passage.

In some countries, there will be a "new" TOEIC. After May 2016, there will be a different TOEIC administered in certain countries. Japan and Korea will be the first countries to have the new TOEIC. The TOEIC will change in other countries over the next few years. Please visit the ETS TOEIC website (*ets.org/toeic*) for dates in your country.

The new TOEIC will have the same number of questions overall although the number of questions in each part will change slightly. The new TOEIC will also have the same question types as the old TOEIC, as well as some new question types.

These charts show the differences between the old and new versions of the TOEIC.

| TOEIC | | | | NEW TOEIC | | |
|---|---|---|---|---|---|---|
| **Section 1: Listening Comprehension** **Time: Approximately 45 minutes** | | | | **Section 1: Listening Comprehension** **Time: Approximately 45 minutes** | | |
| Part | Name | Number of Questions | | Part | Name | Number of Questions |
| 1 | Photographs | 10 | | 1 | Photographs | 6 |
| 2 | Question-Response | 30 | | 2 | Question-Response | 25 |
| 3 | Conversations (10) | 30 | | 3 | Conversations (13) with and without a visual image | 39 |
| 4 | Talks (10) | 30 | | 4 | Talks (10) with and without a visual image | 30 |

| TOEIC | | | | NEW TOEIC | | |
|---|---|---|---|---|---|---|
| **Section 2: Reading**<br>**Time: 75 minutes** | | | | **Section 2: Reading**<br>**Time: 75 minutes** | | |
| Part | Name | Number of Questions | | Part | Name | Number of Questions |
| 5 | Incomplete Sentences | 40 | | 5 | Incomplete Sentences | 30 |
| 6 | Text Completion (4) | 12 | | 6 | Text Completion (4) | 16 |
| 7 | Reading Comprehension | | | 7 | Reading Comprehension | |
| | ■ Single Passages | 28 | | | ■ Single Passages | 29 |
| | ■ Double passages | 20 | | | ■ Multiple passages | 25 |

## HOW TO USE THIS BOOK

This book has four complete current version TOEIC tests and two complete new version TOEIC tests. You can use this book to familiarize yourself with the Listening and Reading sections of the TOEIC test. Whether you will take the old version of the test or the new version, studying both types of practice tests will help you prepare. All of the item types in the old version are used in the new version. You can use the tests in this book for extra practice when taking a TOEIC preparation course or when studying on your own. You can also use this book to supplement the activities in other Barron's TOEIC preparation materials.

Start by taking the first test. Try to simulate a real test experience. Set aside two hours without interruptions. When you are finished, use the answer key to check your answers. Determine the areas where you need to improve the most. Do you need to improve your language skills, test-taking skills, or vocabulary?

You can improve your language skills and test-taking skills by studying *Barron's TOEIC*. You can improve your vocabulary by studying *Barron's Essential Words for the TOEIC*.

As you continue to study, take another test every month (or week, or two weeks) to see how much you have learned and where you still need to improve.

In addition to studying specifically for the test, you can improve your performance on the TOEIC by working to develop your English language skills in general. You need to make some time available every day to study English. You need to sign a TOEIC Study Contract.

## TOEIC LISTENING AND READING STUDY CONTRACT

You must make a commitment to study English. Sign a contract with yourself. A contract is a legal document that establishes procedures. You should not break a contract—especially a contract with yourself.

■ Print your name below on the first line.
■ Write how much time you will spend each week studying English on the following lines. Think about how much time you have to study every day and every week. Make your schedule realistic.
■ Sign your name and date the contract on the last line.
■ At the end of each week, add up your hours. Did you meet the requirements of your contract?

```
┌─────────────────────────────────────────────────┐
│                                                 │
│         TOEIC LISTENING AND READING             │
│              STUDY CONTRACT                     │
│                                                 │
│   I, _____, promise to study for the TOEIC. I will begin │
│   my study with Barron's Practice Tests for the TOEIC Listening and Reading, │
│   and I will also study English on my own.      │
│                                                 │
│   I understand that to improve my English I need to spend time on English. │
│                                                 │
│   I promise to study English _____ hours a week. │
│                                                 │
│   I will spend _____ hours a week listening to English. │
│                                                 │
│   I will spend _____ hours a week writing English. │
│                                                 │
│   I will spend _____ hours a week speaking English. │
│                                                 │
│   I will spend _____ hours a week reading English. │
│                                                 │
│   This is a contract with myself. I promise to fulfill the terms of this contract. │
│                                                 │
│   _____      _____ │
│   Signed                    Date                │
│                                                 │
└─────────────────────────────────────────────────┘
```

## SELF-STUDY ACTIVITIES

Here are some ways you can study English on your own. Check the ones you plan to try. Add some of your own ideas.

## Internet-Based Self-Study Activities

### LISTENING

☐ Podcasts on the Internet
☐ News websites: CNN, BBC, NBC, ABC, CBS
☐ Movies in English
☐ YouTube
☐ _____
☐ _____

### SPEAKING

☐ Use Skype to talk to English speakers
☐ _____
☐ _____

## WRITING

- ☐ Write e-mails to website contacts
- ☐ Write a blog
- ☐ Leave comments on blogs
- ☐ Post messages in a chat room
- ☐ Use Facebook and Twitter
- ☐ _____
- ☐ _____

## READING

- ☐ Read news and magazine articles online
- ☐ Do web research on topics that interest you
- ☐ Follow blogs that interest you
- ☐ _____
- ☐ _____

# Other Self-Study Activities

## LISTENING

- ☐ Listen to CNN and BBC on the radio
- ☐ Watch movies and TV in English
- ☐ Listen to music in English
- ☐ _____
- ☐ _____

## SPEAKING

- ☐ Describe what you see and do out loud
- ☐ Practice speaking with a conversation buddy
- ☐ _____
- ☐ _____

## WRITING

- ☐ Write a daily journal
- ☐ Write a letter to an English speaker
- ☐ Make lists of the things you see every day
- ☐ Write descriptions of your family and friends
- ☐ _____
- ☐ _____

## READING

- ☐ Read newspapers and magazines in English
- ☐ Read books in English
- ☐ _____
- ☐ _____

## Examples of Self-Study Activities

You can use websites, books, newspapers, movies, and TV programs to practice reading, writing, speaking, and listening in English.

- Read about it.
- Paraphrase and write about it.
- Give a talk or presentation about it.
- Record or make a video of your presentation
- Listen to or watch what you recorded.  Write down your presentation.
- Correct your mistakes.
- Do it all again.

### PLAN A TRIP

Go to *www.cntraveler.com*

 Choose a city, choose a hotel, go to that hotel's website and choose a room, and then choose some sites to visit (*reading*). Write a report about the city. Tell why you want to go there. Describe the hotel and the room you will reserve. Tell what sites you plan to visit and when. Where will you eat? How will you get around?

Now write a letter to someone recommending this place (*writing*). Pretend you have to give a lecture on your planned trip (*speaking*). Make a video of yourself talking about this place. Then watch the video and write down what you said. Correct any mistakes you made and record the presentation again. Then choose another city and do all of this again.

### SHOP FOR AN ELECTRONIC PRODUCT

Go to *www.cnet.com*

 Choose an electronic product and read about it (*reading*). Write a report about the product. Tell why you want to buy one. Describe its features.

Now write a letter to someone recommending this product (*writing*). Pretend you have to give a talk about this product (*speaking*). Make a video of yourself talking about this product. Then watch the video and write down what you said. Correct any mistakes you made and record the presentation again. Then choose another product and do all of this again.

### DISCUSS A BOOK OR A CD

Go to *www.amazon.com*

 Choose a book, CD, or another product. Read the product description and reviews (*reading*). Write a report about the product. Tell why you want to buy one or why it is interesting to you. Describe its features.

Now write a letter to someone recommending this product (*writing*). Pretend you have to give a talk about this product (*speaking*). Make a video of yourself talking about this product. Then watch the video and write down what you said. Correct any mistakes you made and record the presentation again. Then choose another product and do all of this again.

## DISCUSS ANY SUBJECT

Go to *http://simple.wikipedia.org/wiki/Main_Page*

 This website is written in simple English. Pick any subject and read the entry (*reading*). Write a short essay about the topic (*writing*). Give a presentation about it (*speaking*). Record the presentation. Then watch the video and write down what you said. Correct any mistakes you made and record the presentation again. Choose another topic and do all of this again.

## DISCUSS ANY EVENT

Go to *http://news.google.com*

 Google News has a variety of links. Pick one event and read the articles about it (*reading*). Write a short essay about the event (*writing*). Give a presentation about it (*speaking*). Record the presentation. Then watch the video and write down what you said. Correct any mistakes you made and record the presentation again. Then choose another event and do all of this again.

## REPORT THE NEWS

Listen to an English language news report on the radio, TV, or online at sites such as *www.npr.org* (*listening*). Take notes as you listen. Write a summary of what you heard (*writing*).

Pretend you are a news reporter. Use the information from your notes to report the news (*speaking*). Record the presentation. Then watch the video and write down what you said. Correct any mistakes you made and record the presentation again. Then listen to another news program and do all of this again.

## EXPRESS AN OPINION

Read a letter to the editor in the newspaper (*reading*). Write a letter in response in which you say whether or not you agree with the opinion expressed in the first letter. Explain why (*writing*). Pretend you have to give a talk explaining your opinion (*speaking*). Record yourself giving the talk. Then watch the video and write down what you said. Correct any mistakes you made and record the presentation again. Then read another letter to the editor and do all of this again.

## REVIEW A BOOK OR MOVIE

Read a book (*reading*). Think about your opinion of the book. What did you like about it? What didn't you like about it? Who would you recommend it to and why? Pretend you are a book reviewer for a newspaper. Write a review of the book with your opinion and recommendations (*writing*).

Give an oral presentation about the book. Explain what the book is about and what your opinion is (*speaking*). Record yourself giving the presentation. Then watch the video and write down what you said. Correct any mistakes you made and record the presentation again. Then read another book and do all of this again.

You can do this same activity after watching a movie (*listening*).

## SUMMARIZE A TV SHOW

Watch a TV show in English (*listening*). Take notes as you listen. After watching, write a summary of the show (*writing*).

Use your notes to give an oral summary of the show. Explain the characters, setting, and plot (*speaking*). Record yourself speaking. Then watch the video and write down what you said. Correct any mistakes you made and record the presentation again. Then watch another TV show and do all of this again.

## LISTEN TO A LECTURE

Listen to an academic or other type of lecture on the Internet. Go to any of the following or similar sites and look for lectures on topics that are of interest to you:

*http://lecturefox.com*

*http://podcasts.ox.ac.uk*

*http://freevideolectures.com*

*www.ted.com/talks*

Listen to a lecture and take notes as you listen. Listen again to check and add to your notes (*listening*). Use your notes to write a summary of the lecture (*writing*).

Pretend you have to give a lecture on the same subject. Use your notes to give your lecture (*speaking*). Record yourself as you lecture. Then watch the video and write down what you said. Correct any mistakes you made and record the lecture again. Then listen to another lecture and do this again.

> These Barron's TOEIC books will help you prepare for the TOEIC. They provide focused practice for each part of the TOEIC.
>
> *Barron's TOEIC*
> *Barron's Essential Words for the TOEIC*

# CORRECT ANSWER CHART

When you finish a practice test, write the number of your correct answers in each part. This will show you where you need to improve.

| Listening Comprehension | Goal | Exam 1 | Exam 2 | Exam 3 | Exam 4 | Exam A | Exam B |
|---|---|---|---|---|---|---|---|
| Part 1 Photographs | 10 | | | | | | |
| Part 2 Question-Response | 30 | | | | | | |
| Part 3 Conversations | 30 | | | | | | |
| Part 4 Talks | 30 | | | | | | |

| Reading | Goal | Exam 1 | Exam 2 | Exam 3 | Exam 4 | Exam A | Exam B |
|---|---|---|---|---|---|---|---|
| Part 5 Incomplete Sentences | 40 | | | | | | |
| Part 6 Text Completion | 12 | | | | | | |
| Part 7 Reading Comprehension | 48 | | | | | | |

# ANSWER SHEET
## TOEIC Practice Exam 1

**LISTENING COMPREHENSION**

### Part 1: Photographs

1. Ⓐ Ⓑ Ⓒ Ⓓ    4. Ⓐ Ⓑ Ⓒ Ⓓ    7. Ⓐ Ⓑ Ⓒ Ⓓ    10. Ⓐ Ⓑ Ⓒ Ⓓ
2. Ⓐ Ⓑ Ⓒ Ⓓ    5. Ⓐ Ⓑ Ⓒ Ⓓ    8. Ⓐ Ⓑ Ⓒ Ⓓ
3. Ⓐ Ⓑ Ⓒ Ⓓ    6. Ⓐ Ⓑ Ⓒ Ⓓ    9. Ⓐ Ⓑ Ⓒ Ⓓ

### Part 2: Question-Response

11. Ⓐ Ⓑ Ⓒ    19. Ⓐ Ⓑ Ⓒ    27. Ⓐ Ⓑ Ⓒ    35. Ⓐ Ⓑ Ⓒ
12. Ⓐ Ⓑ Ⓒ    20. Ⓐ Ⓑ Ⓒ    28. Ⓐ Ⓑ Ⓒ    36. Ⓐ Ⓑ Ⓒ
13. Ⓐ Ⓑ Ⓒ    21. Ⓐ Ⓑ Ⓒ    29. Ⓐ Ⓑ Ⓒ    37. Ⓐ Ⓑ Ⓒ
14. Ⓐ Ⓑ Ⓒ    22. Ⓐ Ⓑ Ⓒ    30. Ⓐ Ⓑ Ⓒ    38. Ⓐ Ⓑ Ⓒ
15. Ⓐ Ⓑ Ⓒ    23. Ⓐ Ⓑ Ⓒ    31. Ⓐ Ⓑ Ⓒ    39. Ⓐ Ⓑ Ⓒ
16. Ⓐ Ⓑ Ⓒ    24. Ⓐ Ⓑ Ⓒ    32. Ⓐ Ⓑ Ⓒ    40. Ⓐ Ⓑ Ⓒ
17. Ⓐ Ⓑ Ⓒ    25. Ⓐ Ⓑ Ⓒ    33. Ⓐ Ⓑ Ⓒ
18. Ⓐ Ⓑ Ⓒ    26. Ⓐ Ⓑ Ⓒ    34. Ⓐ Ⓑ Ⓒ

### Part 3: Conversations

41. Ⓐ Ⓑ Ⓒ Ⓓ    49. Ⓐ Ⓑ Ⓒ Ⓓ    57. Ⓐ Ⓑ Ⓒ Ⓓ    65. Ⓐ Ⓑ Ⓒ Ⓓ
42. Ⓐ Ⓑ Ⓒ Ⓓ    50. Ⓐ Ⓑ Ⓒ Ⓓ    58. Ⓐ Ⓑ Ⓒ Ⓓ    66. Ⓐ Ⓑ Ⓒ Ⓓ
43. Ⓐ Ⓑ Ⓒ Ⓓ    51. Ⓐ Ⓑ Ⓒ Ⓓ    59. Ⓐ Ⓑ Ⓒ Ⓓ    67. Ⓐ Ⓑ Ⓒ Ⓓ
44. Ⓐ Ⓑ Ⓒ Ⓓ    52. Ⓐ Ⓑ Ⓒ Ⓓ    60. Ⓐ Ⓑ Ⓒ Ⓓ    68. Ⓐ Ⓑ Ⓒ Ⓓ
45. Ⓐ Ⓑ Ⓒ Ⓓ    53. Ⓐ Ⓑ Ⓒ Ⓓ    61. Ⓐ Ⓑ Ⓒ Ⓓ    69. Ⓐ Ⓑ Ⓒ Ⓓ
46. Ⓐ Ⓑ Ⓒ Ⓓ    54. Ⓐ Ⓑ Ⓒ Ⓓ    62. Ⓐ Ⓑ Ⓒ Ⓓ    70. Ⓐ Ⓑ Ⓒ Ⓓ
47. Ⓐ Ⓑ Ⓒ Ⓓ    55. Ⓐ Ⓑ Ⓒ Ⓓ    63. Ⓐ Ⓑ Ⓒ Ⓓ
48. Ⓐ Ⓑ Ⓒ Ⓓ    56. Ⓐ Ⓑ Ⓒ Ⓓ    64. Ⓐ Ⓑ Ⓒ Ⓓ

### Part 4: Talks

71. Ⓐ Ⓑ Ⓒ Ⓓ    79. Ⓐ Ⓑ Ⓒ Ⓓ    87. Ⓐ Ⓑ Ⓒ Ⓓ    95. Ⓐ Ⓑ Ⓒ Ⓓ
72. Ⓐ Ⓑ Ⓒ Ⓓ    80. Ⓐ Ⓑ Ⓒ Ⓓ    88. Ⓐ Ⓑ Ⓒ Ⓓ    96. Ⓐ Ⓑ Ⓒ Ⓓ
73. Ⓐ Ⓑ Ⓒ Ⓓ    81. Ⓐ Ⓑ Ⓒ Ⓓ    89. Ⓐ Ⓑ Ⓒ Ⓓ    97. Ⓐ Ⓑ Ⓒ Ⓓ
74. Ⓐ Ⓑ Ⓒ Ⓓ    82. Ⓐ Ⓑ Ⓒ Ⓓ    90. Ⓐ Ⓑ Ⓒ Ⓓ    98. Ⓐ Ⓑ Ⓒ Ⓓ
75. Ⓐ Ⓑ Ⓒ Ⓓ    83. Ⓐ Ⓑ Ⓒ Ⓓ    91. Ⓐ Ⓑ Ⓒ Ⓓ    99. Ⓐ Ⓑ Ⓒ Ⓓ
76. Ⓐ Ⓑ Ⓒ Ⓓ    84. Ⓐ Ⓑ Ⓒ Ⓓ    92. Ⓐ Ⓑ Ⓒ Ⓓ    100. Ⓐ Ⓑ Ⓒ Ⓓ
77. Ⓐ Ⓑ Ⓒ Ⓓ    85. Ⓐ Ⓑ Ⓒ Ⓓ    93. Ⓐ Ⓑ Ⓒ Ⓓ
78. Ⓐ Ⓑ Ⓒ Ⓓ    86. Ⓐ Ⓑ Ⓒ Ⓓ    94. Ⓐ Ⓑ Ⓒ Ⓓ

# ANSWER SHEET
## TOEIC Practice Exam 1

## READING

### Part 5: Incomplete Sentences

101. Ⓐ Ⓑ Ⓒ Ⓓ    111. Ⓐ Ⓑ Ⓒ Ⓓ    121. Ⓐ Ⓑ Ⓒ Ⓓ    131. Ⓐ Ⓑ Ⓒ Ⓓ
102. Ⓐ Ⓑ Ⓒ Ⓓ    112. Ⓐ Ⓑ Ⓒ Ⓓ    122. Ⓐ Ⓑ Ⓒ Ⓓ    132. Ⓐ Ⓑ Ⓒ Ⓓ
103. Ⓐ Ⓑ Ⓒ Ⓓ    113. Ⓐ Ⓑ Ⓒ Ⓓ    123. Ⓐ Ⓑ Ⓒ Ⓓ    133. Ⓐ Ⓑ Ⓒ Ⓓ
104. Ⓐ Ⓑ Ⓒ Ⓓ    114. Ⓐ Ⓑ Ⓒ Ⓓ    124. Ⓐ Ⓑ Ⓒ Ⓓ    134. Ⓐ Ⓑ Ⓒ Ⓓ
105. Ⓐ Ⓑ Ⓒ Ⓓ    115. Ⓐ Ⓑ Ⓒ Ⓓ    125. Ⓐ Ⓑ Ⓒ Ⓓ    135. Ⓐ Ⓑ Ⓒ Ⓓ
106. Ⓐ Ⓑ Ⓒ Ⓓ    116. Ⓐ Ⓑ Ⓒ Ⓓ    126. Ⓐ Ⓑ Ⓒ Ⓓ    136. Ⓐ Ⓑ Ⓒ Ⓓ
107. Ⓐ Ⓑ Ⓒ Ⓓ    117. Ⓐ Ⓑ Ⓒ Ⓓ    127. Ⓐ Ⓑ Ⓒ Ⓓ    137. Ⓐ Ⓑ Ⓒ Ⓓ
108. Ⓐ Ⓑ Ⓒ Ⓓ    118. Ⓐ Ⓑ Ⓒ Ⓓ    128. Ⓐ Ⓑ Ⓒ Ⓓ    138. Ⓐ Ⓑ Ⓒ Ⓓ
109. Ⓐ Ⓑ Ⓒ Ⓓ    119. Ⓐ Ⓑ Ⓒ Ⓓ    129. Ⓐ Ⓑ Ⓒ Ⓓ    139. Ⓐ Ⓑ Ⓒ Ⓓ
110. Ⓐ Ⓑ Ⓒ Ⓓ    120. Ⓐ Ⓑ Ⓒ Ⓓ    130. Ⓐ Ⓑ Ⓒ Ⓓ    140. Ⓐ Ⓑ Ⓒ Ⓓ

### Part 6: Text Completion

141. Ⓐ Ⓑ Ⓒ Ⓓ    144. Ⓐ Ⓑ Ⓒ Ⓓ    147. Ⓐ Ⓑ Ⓒ Ⓓ    150. Ⓐ Ⓑ Ⓒ Ⓓ
142. Ⓐ Ⓑ Ⓒ Ⓓ    145. Ⓐ Ⓑ Ⓒ Ⓓ    148. Ⓐ Ⓑ Ⓒ Ⓓ    151. Ⓐ Ⓑ Ⓒ Ⓓ
143. Ⓐ Ⓑ Ⓒ Ⓓ    146. Ⓐ Ⓑ Ⓒ Ⓓ    149. Ⓐ Ⓑ Ⓒ Ⓓ    152. Ⓐ Ⓑ Ⓒ Ⓓ

### Part 7: Reading Comprehension

153. Ⓐ Ⓑ Ⓒ Ⓓ    165. Ⓐ Ⓑ Ⓒ Ⓓ    177. Ⓐ Ⓑ Ⓒ Ⓓ    189. Ⓐ Ⓑ Ⓒ Ⓓ
154. Ⓐ Ⓑ Ⓒ Ⓓ    166. Ⓐ Ⓑ Ⓒ Ⓓ    178. Ⓐ Ⓑ Ⓒ Ⓓ    190. Ⓐ Ⓑ Ⓒ Ⓓ
155. Ⓐ Ⓑ Ⓒ Ⓓ    167. Ⓐ Ⓑ Ⓒ Ⓓ    179. Ⓐ Ⓑ Ⓒ Ⓓ    191. Ⓐ Ⓑ Ⓒ Ⓓ
156. Ⓐ Ⓑ Ⓒ Ⓓ    168. Ⓐ Ⓑ Ⓒ Ⓓ    180. Ⓐ Ⓑ Ⓒ Ⓓ    192. Ⓐ Ⓑ Ⓒ Ⓓ
157. Ⓐ Ⓑ Ⓒ Ⓓ    169. Ⓐ Ⓑ Ⓒ Ⓓ    181. Ⓐ Ⓑ Ⓒ Ⓓ    193. Ⓐ Ⓑ Ⓒ Ⓓ
158. Ⓐ Ⓑ Ⓒ Ⓓ    170. Ⓐ Ⓑ Ⓒ Ⓓ    182. Ⓐ Ⓑ Ⓒ Ⓓ    194. Ⓐ Ⓑ Ⓒ Ⓓ
159. Ⓐ Ⓑ Ⓒ Ⓓ    171. Ⓐ Ⓑ Ⓒ Ⓓ    183. Ⓐ Ⓑ Ⓒ Ⓓ    195. Ⓐ Ⓑ Ⓒ Ⓓ
160. Ⓐ Ⓑ Ⓒ Ⓓ    172. Ⓐ Ⓑ Ⓒ Ⓓ    184. Ⓐ Ⓑ Ⓒ Ⓓ    196. Ⓐ Ⓑ Ⓒ Ⓓ
161. Ⓐ Ⓑ Ⓒ Ⓓ    173. Ⓐ Ⓑ Ⓒ Ⓓ    185. Ⓐ Ⓑ Ⓒ Ⓓ    197. Ⓐ Ⓑ Ⓒ Ⓓ
162. Ⓐ Ⓑ Ⓒ Ⓓ    174. Ⓐ Ⓑ Ⓒ Ⓓ    186. Ⓐ Ⓑ Ⓒ Ⓓ    198. Ⓐ Ⓑ Ⓒ Ⓓ
163. Ⓐ Ⓑ Ⓒ Ⓓ    175. Ⓐ Ⓑ Ⓒ Ⓓ    187. Ⓐ Ⓑ Ⓒ Ⓓ    199. Ⓐ Ⓑ Ⓒ Ⓓ
164. Ⓐ Ⓑ Ⓒ Ⓓ    176. Ⓐ Ⓑ Ⓒ Ⓓ    188. Ⓐ Ⓑ Ⓒ Ⓓ    200. Ⓐ Ⓑ Ⓒ Ⓓ

# TOEIC Practice Exam 1

## LISTENING COMPREHENSION

In this section of the test, you will have the chance to show how well you understand spoken English. There are four parts to this section, with special directions for each part. You will find the Answer Sheet for Practice Exam 1 on pages 9–10. Detach it from the book and use it to record your answers. Check your answers using the Answer Key on pages 44–45 and see the Answers Explained beginning on page 47.

## Part 1: Photographs

**Track 2**

**Directions:** You will see a photograph. You will hear four statements about the photograph. Choose the statement that most closely matches the photograph and fill in the corresponding oval on your answer sheet.

**Example**

Now listen to the four statements.

Sample Answer
Ⓐ Ⓑ Ⓒ Ⓓ

Statement (B), "She's reading a magazine," best describes what you see in the picture. Therefore, you should choose answer (B).

---

**TIP**

If you do not have access to the MP3 files, please use the audioscripts beginning on page 345. You can also download the MP3 files and audioscripts from *http://barronsbooks.com/tp/toeic/audio/*

1.

4.

2.

5.

3.

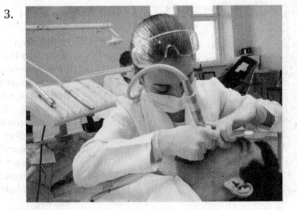

6.

7.

8.

9.

10.

## Part 2: Question-Response

**Directions:** You will hear a question and three possible responses. Choose the response that most closely answers the question and fill in the corresponding oval on your answer sheet.

Track 3

**Example**

Now listen to the sample question.

You will hear:

How is the weather?

You will also hear:

(A) It's raining.
(B) He's fine, thanks.
(C) He's my boss.

The best response to the question *How is the weather?* is choice (A), *It's raining*. Therefore, you should choose answer (A).

11. Mark your answer on your answer sheet.

12. Mark your answer on your answer sheet.

13. Mark your answer on your answer sheet.

14. Mark your answer on your answer sheet.

15. Mark your answer on your answer sheet.

16. Mark your answer on your answer sheet.

17. Mark your answer on your answer sheet.

18. Mark your answer on your answer sheet.

19. Mark your answer on your answer sheet.

20. Mark your answer on your answer sheet.

21. Mark your answer on your answer sheet.

22. Mark your answer on your answer sheet.

23. Mark your answer on your answer sheet.

24. Mark your answer on your answer sheet.

25. Mark your answer on your answer sheet.

26. Mark your answer on your answer sheet.

27. Mark your answer on your answer sheet.

28. Mark your answer on your answer sheet.

29. Mark your answer on your answer sheet.

30. Mark your answer on your answer sheet.

31. Mark your answer on your answer sheet.

32. Mark your answer on your answer sheet.

33. Mark your answer on your answer sheet.

34. Mark your answer on your answer sheet.

35. Mark your answer on your answer sheet.

36. Mark your answer on your answer sheet.

37. Mark your answer on your answer sheet.

38. Mark your answer on your answer sheet.

39. Mark your answer on your answer sheet.

40. Mark your answer on your answer sheet.

## Part 3: Conversations

**Directions:** You will hear a conversation between two people. You will see three questions on each conversation and four possible answers. Choose the best answer to each question and fill in the corresponding oval on your answer sheet.

Track 4

41. What time will they leave for the airport?
    (A) 2:00
    (B) 2:05
    (C) 3:00
    (D) 4:30

42. How will they get to the airport?
    (A) Bus
    (B) Car
    (C) Taxi
    (D) Subway

43. Where will the speakers meet?
    (A) The airport
    (B) The woman's office
    (C) The man's office
    (D) The subway station

44. Where does this conversation take place?
    (A) A store
    (B) An office
    (C) A post office
    (D) A bank

45. What is the man looking for?
    (A) Envelopes
    (B) Printers
    (C) Paper
    (D) Money

46. What does the woman offer to do?
    (A) Take something off the shelf
    (B) Suggest a new style
    (C) Place an order
    (D) Count the man's money

47. What will the man be doing at 11:00 tomorrow morning?
    (A) Talking with Mr. Lee
    (B) Meeting with the accountants
    (C) Writing a letter
    (D) Eating lunch

48. What does Mr. Lee want to discuss?
    (A) A phone call
    (B) A marketing plan
    (C) The meeting agenda
    (D) The accounts

49. What does the woman want to know?
    (A) The time that the man can meet with Mr. Lee
    (B) The name of the place where the man will eat lunch
    (C) The name of the man's accountant
    (D) Mr. Lee's phone number

50. When will the copies be ready?
    (A) Before lunch
    (B) This afternoon
    (C) Tonight
    (D) Tomorrow morning

51. What are the extra copies for?
    (A) New additions to the mailing list
    (B) Replacements for lost copies
    (C) The man's personal files
    (D) The office employees

52. What does the woman ask the man for?
    (A) Lunch
    (B) Files
    (C) Addresses
    (D) Labels

53. Who is the man, most likely?
    (A) An office assistant
    (B) A hotel manager
    (C) A travel agent
    (D) A tour guide

54. How many nights does the woman want to stay at the hotel?
    (A) 1
    (B) 2
    (C) 3
    (D) 4

55. What does the woman ask the man to do?
    (A) Read a book
    (B) Make a phone call
    (C) Go sightseeing
    (D) Type some reports

56. What's the weather like?
    (A) Foggy
    (B) Snowy
    (C) Rainy
    (D) Clear

57. How does Jack probably get to work?
    (A) He walks.
    (B) He drives.
    (C) He takes the train.
    (D) He rides the subway.

58. What will the man be doing at two o'clock?
    (A) Taking the train
    (B) Reading a report
    (C) Meeting with someone
    (D) Waiting for Jack

59. Where does the man want to go?
    (A) Her office
    (B) The post office
    (C) The library
    (D) A park

60. Where is it?
    (A) Two blocks from the parking lot
    (B) Across the street from the bank
    (C) Straight ahead
    (D) On a corner

61. What does the woman say about the library?
    (A) It has Wi-Fi.
    (B) It's free to use.
    (C) It has a lot of space.
    (D) It doesn't cost anything to park there.

62. Why is the man excited?
    (A) He found a lost item.
    (B) He's going to a banquet.
    (C) He's employee of the year.
    (D) The woman is speaking with him.

63. When is the banquet?
    (A) September
    (B) October
    (C) November
    (D) December

64. What does the woman offer to do?
    (A) Help the man prepare his talk
    (B) Serve at the banquet
    (C) Give the man a party
    (D) Go to the bank

65. What does the woman want to do?
    (A) Get something to eat
    (B) Buy clothes
    (C) Make a phone call
    (D) Drink coffee

66. What is the problem?
    (A) Prices are too high.
    (B) The man's phone is broken.
    (C) The woman is angry with the man.
    (D) Places are closed because it's late.

67. How will the man pay?
    (A) Check
    (B) Money order
    (C) Credit card
    (D) Cash

68. Who is the woman shopping for?
    (A) Herself
    (B) Her husband
    (C) Her brother
    (D) Her boss

69. What color suit does the woman want?
    (A) White
    (B) Beige
    (C) Blue
    (D) Black

70. What does the man say about the suit?
    (A) It costs less than other suits.
    (B) It's a good color for a summer suit.
    (C) It's inexpensive for such a good suit.
    (D) It isn't available in other stores.

## Part 4: Talks

Track 5

**Directions:** You will hear a talk given by a single speaker. You will see three questions on each talk, each with four possible answers. Choose the best answer to each question and fill in the corresponding oval on your answer sheet.

71. What will happen in five minutes?
(A) Passengers will get on the train.
(B) The train will leave for New York.
(C) Tickets will go on sale.
(D) The store will open.

72. Who can ride this train?
(A) Anyone who has a ticket.
(B) Anyone who has a reservation.
(C) Anyone who can find a seat.
(D) Anyone who is age 16 or older.

73. What should passengers do with their luggage?
(A) Check it.
(B) Show it to the gate agent.
(C) Put it on the overhead rack.
(D) Leave it beside the track.

74. What kind of a business is Prescott?
(A) Accountants
(B) Party-planning service
(C) Bank
(D) Credit card company

75. What should a caller press to speak to a customer service representative?
(A) 3
(B) 4
(C) 5
(D) 6

76. What can a caller do by pressing 0?
(A) Open an account
(B) Transfer funds
(C) Place an order
(D) Hear the menu again

77. When do people often lack energy?
(A) In the morning
(B) During lunch
(C) In the afternoon
(D) At the end of the day

78. What does the speaker recommend to maintain energy?
(A) Have lunch
(B) Drink coffee
(C) Eat sugar
(D) Take a walk

79. How often should this be done?
(A) Once an hour
(B) Every 5 minutes
(C) Every 45 minutes
(D) Two times a day

80. What kind of business is Magruder's?
(A) A computer training center
(B) An office furniture store
(C) An electronics store
(D) A bookseller

81. What is suggested about Magruder's?
(A) It is a new business.
(B) It is going out of business.
(C) It sells high-quality products.
(D) It has several locations.

82. What will happen at Magruder's this month?
(A) Prices will be discounted.
(B) There will be a party for customers.
(C) New products will be offered.
(D) It will be redecorated.

83. What is being offered?
    (A) Computer repair service
    (B) Computer technician training course
    (C) Computer-based employment service
    (D) Computers and related equipment

84. How much does it cost?
    (A) $200
    (B) $600
    (C) $2,000
    (D) $6,000

85. How can one take advantage of the offer?
    (A) Go online
    (B) Visit the office
    (C) Call on the phone
    (D) Send a letter

86. How is the weather today?
    (A) Snowing
    (B) Raining
    (C) Clear
    (D) Windy

87. What does the speaker suggest listeners do?
    (A) Put on shorts and sandals
    (B) Report accidents
    (C) Take the train
    (D) Stay home

88. When will the weather change?
    (A) This afternoon
    (B) This evening
    (C) Tonight
    (D) Tomorrow morning

89. What is the main purpose of this talk?
    (A) To present a map of a hotel
    (B) To explain a conference schedule
    (C) To introduce workshop speakers
    (D) To describe a conference registration
        process

90. Who is Lucille Snow, most likely?
    (A) A business expert
    (B) The hotel manager
    (C) The conference organizer
    (D) A computer programmer

91. Where will refreshments be served?
    (A) In the conference room
    (B) At the restaurant
    (C) In the garden
    (D) On the patio

92. What is the problem?
    (A) A train station is closed.
    (B) Buses can't run.
    (C) Parking is not available.
    (D) The curb is broken.

93. What is the cause of the problem?
    (A) Rain
    (B) Construction
    (C) Crowds
    (D) Traffic

94. How long will the problem last?
    (A) 2 weeks
    (B) 3 weeks
    (C) 4 weeks
    (D) 5 weeks

95. How many countries will the president visit
    on his tour?
    (A) 2
    (B) 4
    (C) 5
    (D) 10

96. What will the president talk about with
    national leaders?
    (A) Economics
    (B) Leadership
    (C) War
    (D) Science

97. What will the president do when his trip is over?
    (A) Attend a banquet
    (B) Receive an award
    (C) Eat at a restaurant
    (D) Go to the beach

98. What opportunity is offered?
    (A) A meeting
    (B) A workshop
    (C) A train ride
    (D) A shopping trip

99. When will it happen?
    (A) Next Monday
    (B) At the end of the week
    (C) In September
    (D) Next month

100. What should people bring?
    (A) A computer
    (B) A camera
    (C) Some lunch
    (D) The list

# READING

In this section of the test, you will have the chance to show how well you understand written English. There are three parts to this section, with special directions for each part.

**YOU WILL HAVE ONE HOUR AND FIFTEEN MINUTES
TO COMPLETE PARTS 5, 6, AND 7 OF THE TEST.**

## Part 5: Incomplete Sentences

> **Directions:** You will see a sentence with a missing word. Four possible answers follow the sentence. Choose the best answer to the question and fill in the corresponding oval on your answer sheet.

101. The document you requested is ready and _____ sent to your office as soon as possible.
  (A) will be
  (B) were
  (C) have been
  (D) were being

102. The _____ businessperson knows that appearance is important and always dresses appropriately.
  (A) success
  (B) succeed
  (C) successful
  (D) succession

103. If you are interested in the position, please _____ your résumé to the Human Resources office before the end of the week.
  (A) compose
  (B) revise
  (C) apply
  (D) submit

104. The report wasn't particularly useful since several key pieces of information were _____ from it.
  (A) omit
  (B) omitted
  (C) omitting
  (D) omission

105. If the road conditions don't improve by tomorrow, then we _____ the trip.
  (A) will cancel
  (B) have canceled
  (C) canceled
  (D) cancel

106. You can always count on Ms. Cho, as she is one of our most _____ employees.
  (A) depend
  (B) depending
  (C) dependable
  (D) dependence

107. After working at the company for a year, Mr. Jones received a _____ from assistant manager to manager.
  (A) promissory
  (B) promptness
  (C) prominent
  (D) promotion

108. The office was in excellent condition when we moved in because the former _____ was very tidy.
  (A) occupy
  (B) occupied
  (C) occupant
  (D) occupancy

109. No one on the team will be able to go home _____ this work is finished.
  (A) if
  (B) until
  (C) since
  (D) because

110. Just walk _____ that door and you will see the copy machine on the other side.
  (A) under
  (B) around
  (C) between
  (D) through

111. There were several qualified candidates for the job, but we could _____ only one.
  (A) chose
  (B) chosen
  (C) choose
  (D) choice

112. In order to be _____ to the building, you must show proper identification.
  (A) admitted
  (B) emitted
  (C) remitted
  (D) submitted

113. If you need to make a call, you can use the phone that's on that table _____ my desk.
  (A) inside
  (B) outside
  (C) beside
  (D) reside

114. It is a bit scary riding this elevator because it _____ at such a rapid rate.
  (A) decreases
  (B) descends
  (C) devalues
  (D) diminishes

115. In order to keep an accurate record of your work hours, _____ your time card when you arrive and when you leave.
  (A) punch
  (B) punches
  (C) punched
  (D) punching

116. As soon as the paychecks _____, the office manager will distribute them to the staff.
  (A) arrived
  (B) arrive
  (C) arriving
  (D) will arrive

117. Ms. Wilson was fired _____ she always arrived late and never finished her work on time.
  (A) unless
  (B) though
  (C) because
  (D) however

118. Our boss is very organized and tidy and _____ that we keep the office neat.
  (A) consists
  (B) persists
  (C) resists
  (D) insists

119. _____ Mr. Lee works very hard and always meets his deadlines, he still hasn't been given a promotion.
  (A) Since
  (B) Even
  (C) Despite
  (D) Although

120. He _____ an employee of this company ever since he first started working.
  (A) is
  (B) was
  (C) has been
  (D) will be

121. The walls are in bad shape and will require _____ before we can begin painting them.
    (A) preparation
    (B) preparatory
    (C) preparer
    (D) prepare

122. If we had worked through the night, we _____ have finished the report on time.
    (A) should
    (B) might
    (C) must
    (D) will

123. It is necessary to have at least one advanced degree in order to _____ in today's job market.
    (A) compete
    (B) compile
    (C) compose
    (D) comprise

124. Because so few people showed _____ for the meeting, we decided to postpone it to a later date.
    (A) through
    (B) down
    (C) off
    (D) up

125. Our corporate headquarters are located on a hill high _____ the city with a spectacular view of the entire valley.
    (A) beyond
    (B) above
    (C) next to
    (D) across from

126. If you wish to speak with the director, you have to _____ an appointment first.
    (A) call
    (B) invite
    (C) schedule
    (D) receive

127. Customers don't necessarily resist paying more for a product if they feel the _____ is high.
    (A) quality
    (B) quantity
    (C) quantify
    (D) qualify

128. We _____ all employees of this company to arrive at the office on time every day.
    (A) hope
    (B) deem
    (C) intend
    (D) expect

129. All expenses must be approved _____ the department head at the beginning of each month.
    (A) by
    (B) to
    (C) for
    (D) from

130. The next staff meeting will _____ in the large conference room on Friday morning at 10:00.
    (A) go to
    (B) take place
    (C) attend
    (D) adjourn

131. We _____ proceed with this project according to the specifications we received from the client.
    (A) have
    (B) had to
    (C) have to
    (D) will have

132. This _____ is probably the most important one you'll make, so think it over carefully.
    (A) decidedly
    (B) decisive
    (C) decision
    (D) decide

133. We're trying to keep the electric bill down, so please _____ off the lights before you leave the office.
     (A) turn
     (B) turned
     (C) turning
     (D) will turn

134. Leading economists have predicted the prices will continue to _____ during the second half of the year.
     (A) growth
     (B) raise
     (C) up
     (D) rise

135. The books that he showed us at the meeting _____ not really pertinent to our discussion.
     (A) was
     (B) were
     (C) is
     (D) did

136. Mr. Kim is not a particularly interesting speaker, and several people fell asleep _____ his lecture.
     (A) although
     (B) while
     (C) because
     (D) during

137. We plan to add a number of new positions to our staff because our business is _____ quite rapidly.
     (A) sizing
     (B) bulging
     (C) expanding
     (D) inducing

138. The building _____ with lots of large windows on all sides to receive passive solar energy.
     (A) design
     (B) designed
     (C) was designed
     (D) was designing

139. We have high _____ for the new line of products and hope that we won't be disappointed.
     (A) expectations
     (B) expectancy
     (C) expects
     (D) expect

140. Please don't ask for personal information about our employees, as we keep that information _____.
     (A) consequential
     (B) confidential
     (C) conservative
     (D) considerate

## Part 6: Text Completion

> **Directions:** You will see four passages, each with three blanks. Under each blank are four answer options. Choose the word or phrase that best completes the statement.

Questions 141–143 refer to the following newspaper article.

The Evergreen Department Store has been hit hard by the current recession. Sales have been _____ at a rapid rate. "Fewer and fewer customers are

141. (A) decreasing
(B) increasing
(C) stabilizing
(D) advertising

coming into the store," says Violet Dupree, floor manager at Evergreen. Ms. Dupree explained that earnings during the past fiscal year were the worst the store had ever seen since it opened for business 25 years ago. She went on to say, "The worst part of it is that we have had to _____ a number

142. (A) train
(B) lay off
(C) take on
(D) interview

of fine employees." Job loss is becoming a more widespread problem as the recession deepens, and applications for unemployment _____ are on

143. (A) beneficiaries
(B) benefactors
(C) beneficial
(D) benefits

the rise. Evergreen is just one more in a long list of local businesses that have been falling victim to the current economic crisis.

Questions 144–146 refer to the following letter.

April 21, 20--

Martha Dinsmore
Pet Supply Company
3774 State Street
Westminister, VA 22901

Dear Ms. Dinsmore,

This is to serve as a letter of recommendation for Andrew Richardson, a former employee of my company, PT, Inc. Mr. Richardson _____ for my company

144. (A) works
     (B) worked
     (C) has worked
     (D) is working

for three years, from June of 20-- until he left to continue his university studies two years ago. Mr. Richardson was a great asset to my company. He always fulfilled his responsibilities in a careful and thorough manner. He was also extremely _____. We could always count on him to do what he promised

145. (A) punctual
     (B) prepared
     (C) reliable
     (D) organized

to do. He was eager to pursue professional development opportunities and attended a number of training workshops while employed by PT. His upbeat personality was also a great _____ addition to our workplace. I think

146. (A) addend
     (B) additive
     (C) addendum
     (D) addition

everyone on the PT staff would agree that it was indeed a pleasure to work with him. I highly recommend Mr. Richardson for the position he has applied for at your company. If you have any questions, please don't hesitate to contact me.

Sincerely,

*Patricia Thompson*

Patricia Thompson
President

**STORE POLICY REGARDING RETURNED MERCHANDISE**

Customer satisfaction is our top priority. If you are dissatisfied with your purchase for any reason, you may return it to the store for a full _____,

147. (A) refund
(B) refusal
(C) referral
(D) restoration

no questions asked, providing the following conditions are met:

- The item is returned with its original packaging intact.
- The item is accompanied by the store receipt.
- The item is returned within 30 days of purchase.

Customers returning items after 30 days but within 90 days of purchase or without _____ original packaging will receive store credit. We are

148. (A) its
(B) his
(C) their
(D) your

sorry but we cannot accept returns on items after 90 days of the purchase date or _____ a store receipt. Any questions about the return policy

149. (A) apart
(B) either
(C) neglecting
(D) without

should be directed to the Management Office.

Misty View Office Complex has several office spaces for rent. Misty View is _____ located near several bus lines and is just a short,

150. (A) convenient
(B) convenience
(C) conveniently
(D) conventionally

five-block walk from the subway station. Your clients who drive will never have to worry about finding a place to park. Misty View has _____

151. (A) scarce
(B) ample
(C) covered
(D) underground

visitor parking. Tenant parking is also available for an additional monthly fee. Rents start at $2 per square foot, all utilities included. Six-month, one-year, and five-year leases are available. _____ this opportunity to locate

152. (A) Miss
(B) You don't miss
(C) Don't miss
(D) Shouldn't miss

your business in the city's prime office building. Call our leasing office today to make an appointment to visit Misty View and find out why it has become the city's most desirable business location.

TOEIC PRACTICE EXAM 1

## Part 7: Reading Comprehension

> **Directions:** You will see single and double reading passages followed by several questions. Each question has four answer choices. Choose the best answer to the question and fill in the corresponding oval on your answer sheet.

Questions 153–154 refer to the following advertisement.

# Mary's Lunch, Inc.

You work hard, and you deserve good food. Mary's Lunch, Inc. provides everything from snacks to four-course dinners for your conference, meeting, office party, or any other business occasion. We deliver to most downtown locations.

Menu choices can be viewed on our website: www.maryslunch.com. Our planning consultants can help you plan your next event and will explain our pricing system. Simply call 987-3722 or stop by our office during normal business hours.

153. What kind of business is advertised?
  (A) Kitchen supply
  (B) Grocery store
  (C) Catering
  (D) Restaurant

154. How can someone planning an event get prices for food?
  (A) Go to his or her office any evening
  (B) Go to his or her next event
  (C) Call a consultant
  (D) Check online

Questions 155–156 refer to the following invoice.

**Newforth Office Renovators**
P.O. Box 17
Newforth, MA 01253

December 16, 20--
Invoice #004

Client name:
Williams and Drivers Law Offices
34 Highland Ave., Suite 5
Newforth, MA 01253

Painting, 2 rooms:                $500
Carpentry repair work:           $750
Total due:                      $1,250

Previous account balance: $600
Paid in full. Thank you!

The work described herein covers work completed during the month of November. Please pay the entire amount by the end of next month.

*Thank you for your business.*

155. What does $600 represent on this invoice?
(A) The payment due on this invoice
(B) The remaining funds in the account
(C) The amount billed on invoice #003
(D) The previous funds in the account before this invoice

156. When is the bill due?
(A) November 30
(B) December 16
(C) December 31
(D) January 31

Questions 157–158 refer to the following notice.

BECAUSE OF THE HOLIDAY, WEEKEND PARKING REGULATIONS WILL BE IN EFFECT THROUGHOUT THE CITY ALL DAY TOMORROW. THERE WILL BE NO CHARGE FOR PARKING IN METERED PARKING PLACES; HOWEVER, DOWNTOWN PUBLIC PARKING GARAGES WILL BE CLOSED. SUBWAYS AND BUSES WILL FOLLOW THE SUNDAY SCHEDULE, AND WEEKEND FARES AND SENIOR CITIZEN DISCOUNTS WILL BE IN EFFECT ALL DAY. CONSTRUCTION ON THE GREEN RIVER BRIDGE WILL BE SUSPENDED, BUT THE BRIDGE WILL REMAIN CLOSED.

157. What will be free tomorrow?
(A) Metered parking
(B) Garage parking
(C) Subway fares
(D) Bridge use

158. Why will this be free?
(A) It's the weekend.
(B) It's a holiday.
(C) There is construction.
(D) The bridge is closed.

Boris Lutz of Greenfield recently won the Good Citizen Prize for service to the local community. The prize is given annually at the Greenfield Bank to a bank employee who has demonstrated good citizenship by contributing to community projects in some way. The purpose is to promote community goodwill and acknowledge bank employees' contributions to the greater Greenfield community. Lutz, a teller at the Simsbury Village branch of the bank, received the honor from his bank coworkers. "Boris has always given generously of his time to community groups," explained his supervisor, Doris Wilson. "We thought it was about time his contributions were acknowledged. We at the bank are all so pleased that he is this year's winner." This is the second year the prize has been given. Last year the honor went to Maria Pendleton, assistant to the bank's president.

159.  What did Boris Lutz get?
   (A)  A bank account
   (B)  A promotion
   (C)  An assistant
   (D)  An award

160.  What is Boris Lutz's job?
   (A)  Office assistant
   (B)  Bank teller
   (C)  Community organizer
   (D)  Mayor of Greenfield

161.  How do Boris Lutz's coworkers feel about him?
   (A)  He's a helpful community member.
   (B)  He's a model employee.
   (C)  He's easy to get along with.
   (D)  He's their favorite colleague.

Questions 162–164 refer to the following advertisement.

---

### ATTENTION!

Babcock is now hiring for positions in a variety of locations. We have fantastic opportunities available for writers, editors, and proofreaders. See below for a partial list of currently available positions.

Visit the Careers page on our website to find out more and to apply for any of these positions. To access a particular job posting, copy and paste the job number into the search field on the Careers page. Or, browse through the list of available positions. When you find a position for which you are qualified, complete the online job application. You may also attach your resume. Letters of recommendation are not required at this point. Please do not call the office. All job application information is included on the website.

Now hiring:
Proofreader. Job #4882
Requires two years' experience OR proof of relevant training.

Assistant Editor. Job #6874
No previous experience required. Must have a degree in English, journalism, or a related field.

Editorial Intern. Job #5822
No previous experience required. Current college student preferred.

Staff Writer. Job #5773
Requires minimum of three years' experience in a similar position.

---

162. What kind of business is Babcock probably engaged in?
    (A) Training
    (B) Publishing
    (C) Career counseling
    (D) Internet services

163. How can someone apply for a job at Babcock?
    (A) Visit the website
    (B) Call the office
    (C) Mail a résumé
    (D) Write a letter

164. Which of the advertised jobs requires previous experience?
    (A) Proofreader
    (B) Assistant Editor
    (C) Editorial Intern
    (D) Staff Writer

Questions 165–168 refer to the following article.

Park and Smith, a financial planning company based in Lakeview, has opened a branch office in downtown Salem in the building owned by the Salem Office Properties real estate company. Park and Smith is taking over office space formerly occupied by the law offices of James Robertson. The space had been vacant for a year and a half. The new Park and Smith office was open for business as of yesterday. Greta Park, president of Park and Smith, says that her company chose the Salem location because of a rising demand for financial planning services in the area. "Salem is a growing community," she explained, "and the town's citizens are becoming more affluent. It is just the type of community where services such as ours are needed." Park and Smith closed its branch offices in Johnstown and Freeburg at the end of last year. These communities are close enough to Lakeview to be served by the main office there, Ms. Park explained, but having an office in Salem will facilitate expanding services to the entire eastern part of the state. The branch's opening comes just a few months after the opening of the PD Miller stock brokerage firm at the Salem Center office complex.

165. What kind of a business is Smith and Park?
(A) Financial planning
(B) Law office
(C) Real estate
(D) Stock brokerage

166. When did Park and Smith open its branch office in Salem?
(A) Yesterday
(B) A few months ago
(C) At the end of last year
(D) A year and a half ago

167. Why did Smith and Park open a branch office in Salem?
(A) They closed their other branch offices.
(B) It's close to the main office.
(C) There is a need for their services there.
(D) The rent is reasonable.

168. The word *facilitate* in line 25 is closest in meaning to _____.
(A) fund
(B) assist
(C) impede
(D) upgrade

Questions 169–172 refer to the following letter.

To the Editor:

I read with great concern the report in your newspaper this morning about the plans of the Holbrook Manufacturing Company to build a factory in this city. The project has received strong support from the city council, based on their belief that Holbrook will bring a significant number of jobs to our area and boost the local economy. Apparently, they are blind to the reality. Holbrook is well known for its innovative manufacturing methods, which are largely automated. Because of this, very little manual labor is required. Holbrook's system generally requires highly skilled technicians, who would likely come here from other places to work at the factory. There will be few, if any, jobs for local citizens. What do we get in return for this? A large, unsightly building that will require the destruction of natural areas and throw pollution into our air and water. The city council must approve Holbrook's project before they begin construction of the factory. Holbrook's board of directors, eager to break ground on the project as early as next month, have urged the city council to move forward with their vote, and it will take place tomorrow night rather than two weeks from now, as originally planned. This gives even less time for council members to develop an informed opinion. I strongly urge them not to bow to the pressure of Holbrook and to vote against the proposed project.

Sincerely,

Henry Judson

169. Why did Henry Judson write this letter?
   (A) To protest a new factory
   (B) To analyze the economy
   (C) To explain sources of pollution
   (D) To get elected to the city council

170. What kind of people generally work at Holbrook?
   (A) Manual laborers
   (B) Blind people
   (C) Trained specialists
   (D) Economists

171. When will the city council vote on the Holbrook project?
   (A) This morning
   (B) Tomorrow night
   (C) Two weeks from now
   (D) Early next month

172. The word *unsightly* in line 11 is closest in meaning to _____.
   (A) attractive
   (B) enormous
   (C) costly
   (D) ugly

## SAFETY INSTRUCTIONS

To avoid personal injury or property damage, follow these safety instructions when using this product:

- Keep product away from radiators and other heat sources and in a place where air can circulate freely around it.
- Do not make or receive calls while standing in or near water, such as a sink, bathtub, or swimming pool.
- Do not place furniture or other items on top of the power cord.
- Do not apply excess force when dialing. This could result in permanent damage to the buttons.
- Disconnect product from electrical outlet before cleaning. Do not use liquid cleaners and do not immerse product in water. Instead, wipe thoroughly and gently with a damp cloth.
- Avoid using product during an electrical storm.
- If repair work is required, contact the manufacturer at the phone number listed on the front cover of this manual.

173. What kind of product are these instructions for?
(A) Power cord
(B) Telephone
(C) Bathtub
(D) Radiator

174. What should the customer do if the product stops working properly?
(A) Get in touch with the company that produced it
(B) Clean the product thoroughly
(C) Return the product to the store
(D) Look for instructions in the manual

175. When should the product not be used?
(A) During a thunderstorm
(B) Before unplugging it
(C) When air is not circulating
(D) After an electrical power loss

176. What do the instructions say about cleaning the product?
(A) Use liquid soap.
(B) Scrub it hard.
(C) Unplug it first.
(D) Dip it in water.

Questions 177–180 refer to the following article.

Andrew Peterson, president of the Mount Auburn Bank, announced yesterday afternoon that Jolene Simmons has been appointed as the bank's new director of human resources. Ms. Simmons has more than 20 years' experience in the banking industry. After completing her undergraduate degree, she worked for Halt and Levin, a local accounting firm. She left the firm after several years and started her banking career as a teller at the Windsor Bank. She eventually worked her way up to a position as branch manager at the Riverside branch of that institution. Two years ago, she left that job to pursue a master's degree in human resource management at State University, which she completed last month. "She comes to us highly recommended both by her previous employers and by her instructors at the university," says Mr. Peterson. Ms. Simmons will begin her new job at the beginning of next year.

177. What was Ms. Simmons's most recent job?
(A) Human Resources Assistant
(B) Accountant
(C) Branch Manager
(D) University Instructor

178. Where did Ms. Simmons work as a teller?
(A) Mount Auburn Bank
(B) Halt and Levin Bank
(C) Windsor Bank
(D) Riverside Bank

179. When did Ms. Simmons complete her graduate degree?
(A) Twenty years ago
(B) Two years ago
(C) A year ago
(D) A month ago

180. The word *previous* in line 9 is closest in meaning to _____.
(A) former
(B) preferred
(C) future
(D) professional

Questions 181–185 refer to the following schedule and e-mail.

### Business Association Conference
Friday, May 15 • San Francisco, CA
#### Schedule of Presentations and Workshops

| Time | Place | Event | Presenter |
|------|-------|-------|-----------|
| 8:30–9:00 | Auditorium | Opening Remarks | Raymond Larkins |
| 9:15–10:15 | Conference Rooms | Room A: Business Law | Myra Johnson |
| | | Room B: Hiring Practices | Joe Rizzoli |
| 10:30–11:30 | Conference Rooms | Room A: The Future of Business | Sam Choi |
| | | Room B: Effective Management | Mary Kim |
| 11:30–12:30 | Exhibit Hall | Exhibits | Various |
| 12:30–1:45 | Lunch | Dining Room | n/a |
| 2:00–4:00 | Conference Rooms | Room A: Contract Negotiation | Raymond Larkins |
| | | Room B: Local business tour* | Ellen Peters |

*Tour participants will gather in Room B, then proceed together to the hotel parking lot, where the tour bus will be waiting.

---

To: Raymond Larkins
From: Myra Johnson
Sent: May 8, 20--, 10:00
Subject: Meeting at conference

Hi, Raymond,

I will be flying to San Francisco to attend the Business Association Conference next Friday, and I understand you will be there, too. I was hoping we could have a chance to meet sometime during the day Friday for about 30 minutes. I think we should take the opportunity to go over the project in person. Let me know when would be a good time for you. I will be giving a workshop on business law, but other than that my schedule is flexible. Anytime before 6:00 would work for me. I can't stay later than that since I'm driving to Sacramento in the evening and don't want to arrive there too late. A colleague will be signing his book at a store there, and I want to attend. I'm looking forward to your presentation on contracts. I wouldn't miss that for anything. Perhaps we could have our meeting immediately afterward. Let me know what works best for you.

Myra

181. How will Myra get to San Francisco?
   (A) Bus
   (B) Plane
   (C) Train
   (D) Car

182. What does Myra want to discuss with Raymond?
   (A) A workshop
   (B) A contract
   (C) A project
   (D) A law

183. What time is Myra NOT available to meet with Raymond?
   (A) 9:15
   (B) 10:30
   (C) 11:30
   (D) 2:00

184. Where will Myra probably be at 2:30 on the day of the conference?
   (A) In the auditorium
   (B) In Room A
   (C) In Room B
   (D) In the hotel parking lot

185. What will Myra do on Friday night?
   (A) Meet with Raymond
   (B) Sign a contract
   (C) Give a workshop
   (D) Attend a book signing

Questions 186–190 refer to the following two letters.

July 30, 20--

David Mendez
Director of Marketing
The Grover Company
1809 Lyme Road
Newland, IL

Dear Mr. Mendez,

I have heard that there is an opening for a researcher in the Marketing Department, and my supervisor, Marla Petrowski, suggested that I contact you about applying for it. I have worked at Grover for three years now as an office assistant in the Accounting Department. I previously worked for a year at a small marketing firm called R-J Associates. That is the only marketing job experience I have, but I have a degree in marketing, which I completed last month. Now I would like to get a position in my field. Through my years working at Grover, I have become quite familiar with the way this company works, and I feel that I would have a great deal to offer Grover's Marketing Department.

I am enclosing my resume and could also provide you with letters of reference from my university professors. Thank you for your attention. I look forward to hearing from you.

Sincerely,

Sylvia Krim

Sylvia Krim

August 8, 20--

Sylvia Krim
Accounting Department
The Grover Company
1809 Lyme Road
Newland, IL

Dear Ms. Krim,

Thank you for your letter expressing interest in applying for the position in the Marketing Department. I have spoken with Ms. Petrowski, who highly recommends you for the job. I have also shown your credentials to our head researcher, and we both agree that you would be a good asset to our department. Unfortunately, the position you are interested in is not an entry-level job. We generally require at least twice the amount of marketing job experience that you have, as a minimum, for that type of position. Although you appear to have a good reference from your former employer, we feel that you are not yet qualified for the job. However, I anticipate that we will have an opening for a marketing assistant, possibly as soon as September. I will let you know when that position becomes available in case you might be interested in applying for it. I hope you will. In the meantime, please accept my best wishes for your continued success.

Sincerely,

David Mendez

David Mendez
Director of Marketing

186. What job is Ms. Krim interested in applying for?
(A) Marketing Assistant
(B) Researcher
(C) Office Assistant
(D) Accountant

187. When did Ms. Krim finish her degree in marketing?
(A) June
(B) July
(C) August
(D) September

188. Who recommends Ms. Krim for the job?
(A) The director of marketing
(B) A university professor
(C) The head researcher
(D) Her supervisor

189. How many years of experience are required for the job she wants?
(A) One
(B) Two
(C) Three
(D) Four

190. What will Mr. Mendez do?
(A) Hire Ms. Krim right away
(B) Check Ms. Krim's credentials
(C) Speak with Ms. Krim's former employer
(D) Notify Ms. Krim when a position is available

Questions 191–195 refer to the following memo and e-mail.

---

**MEMO**

To:            All personnel
From:        Marvin McLean, Office Manager
Re:            Workplace safety workshop
Date:        November 17

On December 7, a workshop on workplace safety will be offered by Elvira Walters of the National Workplace Safety Commission. The workshop will take place in Conference Room 2 from 9:30 to 11:30. This workshop is required for all department heads and recommended for all staff members. Please let me know before November 22 if you plan to attend. Also, please let me know if you cannot attend at this time but are still interested. If there is enough interest, we will offer the workshop again at a later date. Finally, because the end of the year is fast approaching, let me take this opportunity to remind everyone that attendance at a minimum of three staff development workshops per year is required of all personnel. A schedule of upcoming workshops is posted outside my office.

---

To:            marvin_mclean@zipsys.com
From:        sandy_bayliss@zipsys.com
Sent:        18 November 20--, 11:40
Subject:    safety workshop

Hi, Marvin,
I am very much interested in next month's workshop on workplace safety that was mentioned in the memo you sent out yesterday. I would like to attend it, so please put me on the list. After this workshop, I will have fulfilled my attendance requirement for this year. I would like you to know that I have found each workshop I attended to be very informative and worthwhile. Also, I would like to apologize in advance because I will probably arrive about 15 minutes late to the workplace safety workshop. I have to be downtown early that morning for a breakfast meeting, but it shouldn't last much past 9:00, and then I can catch the subway to the office. I hope a slightly late arrival won't be a problem.
Thanks.
Sandy

---

191. Who has to attend the workshop?
 (A) All staff members
 (B) The security officer
 (C) Department heads
 (D) The office manager

192. When did Sandy Bayliss write her e-mail message?
 (A) November 17
 (B) November 18
 (C) November 22
 (D) December 7

193. What time will Sandy Bayliss probably arrive at the workshop?
 (A) 9:00
 (B) 9:15
 (C) 9:30
 (D) 9:45

194. How many workshops has Sandy Bayliss already attended this year?
 (A) One
 (B) Two
 (C) Three
 (D) Four

195. Where will Sandy's breakfast meeting take place?
 (A) At Marvin McLean's office
 (B) At her office
 (C) Downtown
 (D) In Conference Room 2

## NOTICE OF WARRANTY
### Paper Eater 2000 Deluxe Office Paper Shredder

*Paper Eater, Inc. warrants to the original purchaser of this product that it is free from defects for one year from the date of purchase. We will repair any manufacturing defects, or if we deem repair to be impracticable, we will replace the entire product with a new one. Repair or replacement are guaranteed only when the product has not been mishandled and has been used according to our instructions. Products that have been dropped or thrown or to which any item other than paper, such as staples, paper clips, or pieces of plastic, have been introduced are not covered by the terms of this warranty.*

*When returning a product for repair, please enclose it in its original packaging and include a purchase receipt and the model number. Customers will be charged for any repairs outside the limits of this warranty.*

April 1, 20--

Customer Service Department
Paper Eater, Inc.
17 Main Street
Harlowe's Junction, OH 43327

Dear Customer Service,

I was excited about my recent purchase of a Paper Eater 2000 Deluxe Office Paper Shredder. Many sensitive financial reports come through my office, so a reliable and durable paper shredder is a necessity for me. I chose the Paper Eater 2000 Deluxe because I read many good reviews of it online and in consumer magazines. At first it lived up to its reputation, shredding large volumes of paper without a glitch. At one point, I even spilled a box of paper clips into it, but that didn't appear to slow it down. Then last week it completely stopped, and I have not been able to get it going again. I have to say I am not pleased about this at all. I have owned this machine only since the beginning of February. I would expect that a machine with such a good reputation would last a good deal longer. I am returning the machine herewith, wrapped up in a brand new box. The receipt, including place and date of purchase and the machine's model number, are enclosed. Please send me my refund as soon as possible. Thank you.

Sincerely,

*Arnold Ahern*

Arnold Ahern

196. When did the customer buy his paper shredder?
    (A) A week ago
    (B) A month ago
    (C) Two months ago
    (D) One year ago

197. What does the customer shred in his paper shredder?
    (A) Financial reports
    (B) Magazines
    (C) Receipts
    (D) Product instructions

198. How does the customer feel about the paper shredder now?
    (A) Excited
    (B) Dissatisfied
    (C) Pleased
    (D) Sensitive

199. What did the customer neglect to include when returning the shredder?
    (A) The receipt
    (B) The model number
    (C) The refund form
    (D) The original packaging

200. How will the customer service department probably respond?
    (A) They will issue a refund.
    (B) They will replace the product.
    (C) They will deny the customer's request.
    (D) They will sell the customer a new product.

# ANSWER KEY
## Practice Exam 1

## LISTENING COMPREHENSION

### Part 1: Photographs

1. **C**
2. **B**
3. **D**
4. **A**
5. **A**
6. **D**
7. **C**
8. **B**
9. **A**
10. **D**

### Part 2: Question-Response

11. **A**
12. **B**
13. **C**
14. **B**
15. **C**
16. **A**
17. **A**
18. **C**
19. **B**
20. **A**
21. **C**
22. **A**
23. **B**
24. **C**
25. **B**
26. **B**
27. **A**
28. **A**
29. **C**
30. **B**
31. **A**
32. **A**
33. **C**
34. **A**
35. **B**
36. **B**
37. **C**
38. **A**
39. **C**
40. **B**

### Part 3: Conversations

41. **C**
42. **D**
43. **B**
44. **A**
45. **A**
46. **C**
47. **B**
48. **B**
49. **A**
50. **D**
51. **D**
52. **C**
53. **A**
54. **C**
55. **B**
56. **A**
57. **B**
58. **C**
59. **B**
60. **D**
61. **D**
62. **C**
63. **B**
64. **A**
65. **A**
66. **D**
67. **D**
68. **B**
69. **D**
70. **C**

### Part 4: Talks

71. **A**
72. **B**
73. **C**
74. **C**
75. **D**
76. **D**
77. **C**
78. **D**
79. **A**
80. **B**
81. **D**
82. **A**
83. **B**
84. **C**
85. **A**
86. **A**
87. **D**
88. **D**
89. **B**
90. **A**
91. **D**
92. **A**
93. **B**
94. **B**
95. **C**
96. **A**
97. **D**
98. **B**
99. **D**
100. **A**

## READING

### Part 5: Incomplete Sentences

| | | | | | | | |
|---|---|---|---|---|---|---|---|
| 101. | A | 111. | C | 121. | A | 131. | C |
| 102. | C | 112. | A | 122. | B | 132. | C |
| 103. | D | 113. | C | 123. | A | 133. | A |
| 104. | B | 114. | B | 124. | D | 134. | D |
| 105. | A | 115. | A | 125. | B | 135. | B |
| 106. | C | 116. | B | 126. | C | 136. | D |
| 107. | D | 117. | C | 127. | A | 137. | C |
| 108. | C | 118. | D | 128. | D | 138. | C |
| 109. | B | 119. | D | 129. | A | 139. | A |
| 110. | D | 120. | C | 130. | B | 140. | B |

### Part 6: Text Completion

| | | | | | | | |
|---|---|---|---|---|---|---|---|
| 141. | A | 144. | B | 147. | A | 150. | C |
| 142. | B | 145. | C | 148. | C | 151. | B |
| 143. | D | 146. | D | 149. | D | 152. | C |

### Part 7: Reading Comprehension

| | | | | | | | |
|---|---|---|---|---|---|---|---|
| 153. | C | 165. | A | 177. | C | 189. | B |
| 154. | C | 166. | A | 178. | C | 190. | D |
| 155. | C | 167. | C | 179. | D | 191. | C |
| 156. | D | 168. | B | 180. | A | 192. | B |
| 157. | A | 169. | A | 181. | B | 193. | D |
| 158. | B | 170. | C | 182. | C | 194. | B |
| 159. | D | 171. | B | 183. | A | 195. | C |
| 160. | B | 172. | D | 184. | B | 196. | C |
| 161. | A | 173. | B | 185. | D | 197. | A |
| 162. | B | 174. | A | 186. | B | 198. | B |
| 163. | A | 175. | A | 187. | A | 199. | D |
| 164. | D | 176. | C | 188. | D | 200. | C |

# TEST SCORE CONVERSION TABLE

Count your correct responses. Match the number of correct responses with the corresponding score from the Test Score Conversion Table (below). Add the two scores together. This is your Total Estimated Test Score. As you practice taking the TOEIC model tests, your scores should improve. Keep track of your Total Estimated Test Scores.

| # Correct | Listening Score | Reading Score | # Correct | Listening Score | Reading Score | # Correct | Listening Score | Reading Score | # Correct | Listening Score | Reading Score |
|---|---|---|---|---|---|---|---|---|---|---|---|
| 0 | 5 | 5 | 26 | 110 | 65 | 51 | 255 | 220 | 76 | 410 | 370 |
| 1 | 5 | 5 | 27 | 115 | 70 | 52 | 260 | 225 | 77 | 420 | 380 |
| 2 | 5 | 5 | 28 | 120 | 80 | 53 | 270 | 230 | 78 | 425 | 385 |
| 3 | 5 | 5 | 29 | 125 | 85 | 54 | 275 | 235 | 79 | 430 | 390 |
| 4 | 5 | 5 | 30 | 130 | 90 | 55 | 280 | 240 | 80 | 440 | 395 |
| 5 | 5 | 5 | 31 | 135 | 95 | 56 | 290 | 250 | 81 | 445 | 400 |
| 6 | 5 | 5 | 32 | 140 | 100 | 57 | 295 | 255 | 82 | 450 | 405 |
| 7 | 10 | 5 | 33 | 145 | 110 | 58 | 300 | 260 | 83 | 460 | 410 |
| 8 | 15 | 5 | 34 | 150 | 115 | 59 | 310 | 265 | 84 | 465 | 415 |
| 9 | 20 | 5 | 35 | 160 | 120 | 60 | 315 | 270 | 85 | 470 | 420 |
| 10 | 25 | 5 | 36 | 165 | 125 | 61 | 320 | 280 | 86 | 475 | 425 |
| 11 | 30 | 5 | 37 | 170 | 130 | 62 | 325 | 285 | 87 | 480 | 430 |
| 12 | 35 | 5 | 38 | 175 | 140 | 63 | 330 | 290 | 88 | 485 | 435 |
| 13 | 40 | 5 | 39 | 180 | 145 | 64 | 340 | 300 | 89 | 490 | 445 |
| 14 | 45 | 5 | 40 | 185 | 150 | 65 | 345 | 305 | 90 | 495 | 450 |
| 15 | 50 | 5 | 41 | 190 | 160 | 66 | 350 | 310 | 91 | 495 | 455 |
| 16 | 55 | 10 | 42 | 195 | 165 | 67 | 360 | 320 | 92 | 495 | 465 |
| 17 | 60 | 15 | 43 | 200 | 170 | 68 | 365 | 325 | 93 | 495 | 470 |
| 18 | 65 | 20 | 44 | 210 | 175 | 69 | 370 | 330 | 94 | 495 | 480 |
| 19 | 70 | 25 | 45 | 215 | 180 | 70 | 380 | 335 | 95 | 495 | 485 |
| 20 | 75 | 30 | 46 | 220 | 190 | 71 | 385 | 340 | 96 | 495 | 490 |
| 21 | 80 | 35 | 47 | 230 | 195 | 72 | 390 | 350 | 97 | 495 | 495 |
| 22 | 85 | 40 | 48 | 240 | 200 | 73 | 395 | 355 | 98 | 495 | 495 |
| 23 | 90 | 45 | 49 | 245 | 210 | 74 | 400 | 360 | 99 | 495 | 495 |
| 24 | 95 | 50 | 50 | 250 | 215 | 75 | 405 | 365 | 100 | 495 | 495 |
| 25 | 100 | 60 | | | | | | | | | |

Number of Correct Listening Responses _____ = Listening Score _____

Number of Correct Reading Responses _____ = Reading Score _____

Total Estimated Test Score _____

# ANSWERS EXPLAINED

## Listening Comprehension

### PART 1: PHOTOGRAPHS

1. **(C)** A group of businesspeople at a conference table are clapping their hands; they have probably just finished listening to a presentation. Choice (A) misidentifies the action they are doing with their hands. Choice (B) identifies the glasses that are on the table, but no one is filling them. Choice (D) refers to the movement of their hands, but they are *applauding* not *waving*.

2. **(B)** People are carrying umbrellas and the street looks wet, so it's a rainy day. Choice (A) confuses similar-sounding words *rain* and *train*. Choice (C) correctly identifies the umbrellas but not their location. Choice (D) correctly identifies the action of the people but not their location.

3. **(D)** A dentist is working on or examining a patient's teeth. Choice (A) confuses the dentist's drill in the photo with a carpenter's drill. Choice (B) misidentifies the position of the patient. Choice (C) correctly identifies the gloves, but misidentifies the person wearing them.

4. **(A)** A man and a woman are looking at a house under construction and the woman is pointing to it, so they must be talking about it. Choice (B) identifies the incomplete window in the house, but there is no glass in it yet, so it can't be closed. Choice (C) refers to the plans in their hands, but they are referring to the plans, not printing them. Choice (D) confuses similar-sounding words *house* and *mouse*.

5. **(A)** The plane is at the airport, not up in the air, so it has already landed. Choice (B) uses the associated word *passengers*, but there are none in the photo. Choice (C) confuses similar-sounding words *plane* and *train*. Choice (D) uses the associated word *pilot*, but there isn't one in the photo.

6. **(D)** A couple is looking at clothes in a store window. Choice (A) correctly identifies the hats in the photo, but they are on the people's heads, not in their hands. Choice (B) mentions the window, but it is not broken. Choice (C) mentions the people's bags, but the bags are in their hands, not in the car.

7. **(C)** A man in business attire is standing and talking to a group of people also dressed in business attire—his colleagues. Choice (A) confuses similar-sounding words *talking* and *walking*. Choice (B) confuses *business suit* with *bathing suit*. Choice (D) misidentifies the man's action; he is *gesturing* with his hands, not *looking out* a window.

8. **(B)** This is a sidewalk café and chairs and tables are placed outside on the sidewalk. Choice (A) correctly identifies the people as customers, but they are *outside*, not *inside*. Choice (C) uses the associated word *waiter*. Choice (D) misidentifies the location of the tables.

9. **(A)** A woman is holding a newspaper and looking at it. Choice (B) confuses similar-sounding words *reading* and *eating*. Choice (C) correctly identifies the action, *looking*, but confuses *newspaper* with *new shoes*. Choice (D) associates reporting the *news* with *newspaper*.

10. **(D)** Cars on a highway are moving under a highway bridge. Choice (A) uses the associated word *truck*, but no trucks are visible. Choice (B) is incorrect because the bridge crosses a highway, not a river. Choice (C) is incorrect because there is a lot of traffic on the highway.

## PART 2: QUESTION-RESPONSE

11. **(A)** This answers the question *What time?* Choice (B) confuses the meaning of the word *program*. Choice (C) repeats the word *begin*.

12. **(B)** This answers the question about possession. Choice (A) confuses the meaning of the word *coat*. Choice (C) confuses similar-sounding words *coat* and *note*.

13. **(C)** The mention of rain prompts the second speaker to offer an umbrella. Choice (A) confuses similar-sounding words *rain* and *again*. Choice (B) uses the wrong pronoun (*he* instead of *it*).

14. **(B)** *On your desk* answers the question *Where?* Choice (A) confuses *new* and *newspaper*. Choice (C) associates *newspaper* with *read*.

15. **(C)** This answers the question *How many?* Choice (A) incorrectly uses future tense to answer a past tense question. Choice (B) confuses *showed up* with *showed*.

16. **(A)** *My boss* answers the question *Who?* Choice (B) confuses *assignment* with the similar-sounding phrase *signed it*. Choice (C) answers the question *When?*

17. **(A)** This answers the question *How long?* Choice (B) repeats the word *long*. Choice (C) uses the wrong pronoun (*she* instead of *it*) and confuses the meaning of the word *last*.

18. **(C)** The complaint about the warm room prompts the speaker to offer to open a window. Choice (A) repeats the phrase *in here*. Choice (B) confuses *warm* with the similar-sounding word *warned*.

19. **(B)** *No* answers the tag question *isn't it?* Choice (A) repeats the word *desk*. Choice (C) repeats the phrase *by the door*.

20. **(A)** *In an hour* answers the question *When?* Choice (B) confuses *arrive* with the similar-sounding word *drive*. Choice (C) answers the question *How?*

21. **(C)** *Mr. Kim* answers the question *Who?* Choice (A) associates *phone* with *call*. Choice (B) repeats the word *phone*.

22. **(A)** *Silver* and *black* answer the question about color. Choice (B) repeats the word *car*. Choice (C) would answer a question about the age of the car, not its color.

23. **(B)** This answers the question *Where?* Choice (A) repeats the words *copy machine*. Choice (C) repeats the word *find*.

24. **(C)** The mention of being hungry prompts the second speaker to suggest a lunch break. Choice (A) confuses similar-sounding words *hungry* and *hurry*. Choice (B) confuses similar-sounding words *hungry* and *angry*.

25. **(B)** This explains the reason for the lateness. Choice (A) confuses similar-sounding words *late* and *eight*. Choice (C) uses present continuous with a future meaning to answer a past tense question.

26. **(B)** This answers the question about a place to eat. Choice (A) associates *eat* with *food.* Choice (C) confuses similar-sounding words *eat* and *heat.*

27. **(A)** This is a logical response to a remark about how long the trip will take. Choice (B) repeats the word *airport.* Choice (C) associates *airport* with *fly.*

28. **(A)** *Not much* answers the question *How much?* Choice (B) confuses *cost* with the similar-sounding word *lost.* Choice (C) repeats the word *computer.*

29. **(C)** *Friday* answers the question *What day?* Choice (A) confuses the meaning of the word *meeting.* Choice (B) confuses similar-sounding words *meeting* and *seating.*

30. **(B)** This answers the question *Who?* Choice (A) confuses similar-sounding words *dinner* and *thinner.* Choice (C) associates *dinner* with *ate.*

31. **(A)** This answers the yes-no question about the building. Choice (B) repeats the word *building.* Choice (C) repeats the word *work.*

32. **(A)** This answers the question about possession. Choices (B) and (C) repeat parts of the word *briefcase.*

33. **(C)** This answers the yes-no question about the letters. Choice (A) confuses similar-sounding words *letters* and *later.* Choice (B) associates *letters* with *envelopes.*

34. **(A)** Feeling sick is the reason for not being at the office. Choice (B) repeats the word *office.* Choice (C) confuses *yesterday* with similar-sounding words *day* and *today.*

35. **(B)** This is a logical response to the comment about the hotel. Choice (A) confuses similar-sounding words *hotel* and *tell.* Choice (C) associates *hotel* with *reservation.*

36. **(B)** *The subway* answers the question about how to get *downtown.* Choice (A) repeats part of the word *downtown.* Choice (C) confuses the meaning of the word *get.*

37. **(C)** *Tomorrow* answers the question *When?* Choice (A) associates *call* with *phone.* Choice (B) confuses the meaning of the word *call.*

38. **(A)** This explains Tom's problem. Choice (B) confuses *matter* with the similar-sounding word *chatter.* Choice (C) answers a yes-no question, not a *What?* question.

39. **(C)** *Hot tea* answers the question about a drink. Choice (A) associates *drink* with *glass.* Choice (B) confuses similar-sounding words *drink* and *think.*

40. **(B)** *Across the street* answers the question *Where?* Choice (A) confuses similar-sounding words *car* and *card.* Choice (C) associates *car* with *drive.*

## PART 3: CONVERSATIONS

41. **(C)** The man suggests that they leave at 3:00 and the woman agrees. Choices (A) and (B) confuse the similar-sounding words *due* and *two.* Choice (D) is the time the plane will arrive.

42. **(D)** The woman suggests going by subway and the man agrees. Choice (A) confuses the similar-sounding words *bus* and *but.* Choice (B) confuses the similar-sounding words *car* and *far.* Choice (C) is what the woman says they shouldn't do.

43. **(B)** The man says he will meet the woman at her office. Choice (A) is where they will go together. Choice (C) repeats the word *office*. Choice (D) is also where they will go together.

44. **(A)** The envelopes are in aisle 6 and they are on sale, both situations that suggest this is a store. Choice (B) associates *envelopes, printers,* and *ink* with an office. Choice (C) associates *envelope* with a post office. Choice (D) associates *save money* with a bank.

45. **(A)** The man asks where the envelopes are. Choices (B) and (C) are confused with the printer paper that is on the shelf near the envelopes. Choice (D) repeats the word *money*.

46. **(C)** The woman says she will order more envelopes if the man can't find the style he wants on the shelf. Choice (A) repeats the word *shelf*. Choice (B) repeats the word *style*. Choice (D) confuses *count* with the similar-sounding word *discount* and repeats the word *money*.

47. **(B)** This is what the man says he will be doing at that time. Choice (A) is what Mr. Lee wants. Choice (C) confuses *later* with the similar-sounding word *letter*. Choice (D) is what the man will do after his meeting with the accountants.

48. **(B)** The woman says that Mr. Lee wants to go over the marketing plan. Choice (A) is confused with the phone call between Mr. Lee and the woman about making the appointment. Choice (C) is confused with the meeting that the man will be at. Choice (D) is confused with the accountants who will be at the meeting.

49. **(A)** The woman is preparing to call Mr. Lee to make an appointment for the man. She asks him: *What time would be best for you?* Choice (B) repeats the word *lunch*. Choice (C) repeats the word *accountant*. Choice (D) is related to the fact that the woman is about to call Mr. Lee, but she never asks for his phone number.

50. **(D)** This is when the woman says the copies will be ready. Choice (A) is when the woman got the originals. Choice (B) is when the man wants them. Choice (C) confuses *right* with the similar-sounding word *night*.

51. **(D)** The woman says she is making 10 extra copies *for the office staff and file*. Choice (A) is related to the discussion of mailing the copies. Choice (B) is not mentioned. Choice (C) repeats *file*, but it is the office file that is referred to.

52. **(C)** This is what the woman asks for. Choice (A) repeats the word *lunch*, which is related to when the woman got the originals. Choices (B) and (D) repeat things the woman mentioned, but she didn't ask the man for them.

53. **(A)** The man is making hotel arrangements for the woman and is typing reports, so he is probably an office assistant. Choice (B) repeats the word *hotel*. Choices (C) and (D) are related to the discussion of hotel arrangements.

54. **(C)** The man has reserved two nights at the hotel and the woman asks him to add one more. Choice (A) is not mentioned. Choice (B) is the number of nights the man has reserved. Choice (D) confuses the number 4 with the word *for*.

55. **(B)** The woman asks the man to call the hotel back and add one more night to her reservation. Choice (A) confuses the meaning of the word *book*. Choice (C) is what the woman wants to do while she is at the hotel. Choice (D) is what the man is doing now.

56. **(A)** The woman mentions the *thick fog*. Choice (B) confuses similar-sounding words *know* and *snow*. Choice (C) confuses similar-sounding words *train* and *rain*. Choice (D) is how the man hopes the weather will be soon.

57. **(B)** Jack will be late because of heavy traffic, so he probably drives to work. Choices (A), (C), and (D) are methods of transportation that aren't affected by traffic.

58. **(C)** The man says, *I have to get to a 2:00 meeting*. Choice (A) is how the woman got to work. Choice (B) confuses similar-sounding words *meeting* and *reading*. Choice (D) repeats the name Jack, the man who is late for work.

59. **(B)** The man asks for directions to the post office. Choice (A) repeats the word *office*. Choice (C) is near the post office. Choice (D) confuses *parking lot* with *park*.

60. **(D)** The woman says, *you'll see it on the corner*. Choice (A) repeats *two blocks* and *parking lot*. Choice (B) is incorrect because it is *next to* not *across the street from* the bank. Choice (C) repeats the first part of the directions.

61. **(D)** The woman suggests using the library parking lot because there is space there and it's free. Choice (A) is often true of libraries but isn't mentioned here. Choice (B) repeats the word *free*. Choice (C) repeats the word *space*.

62. **(C)** This is the news the man is telling the woman about. Choice (A) confuses *found out* with *found*. Choice (B) is true but it is not the reason for the man's excitement. Choice (D) confuses *speech* with s*peaking*.

63. **(B)** The woman says that it is September now and the banquet is next month. Choice (A) is the current month. Choices (C) and (D) sound similar to *September*.

64. **(A)** The woman says, *I could help you write your speech . . . .* Choice (B) confuses similar-sounding words *deserve* and *serve*. Choice (C) confuses similar-sounding words *part* and *party*. Choice (D) confuses similar-sounding words *banquet* and *bank*.

65. **(A)** The woman is hungry and looking for a place to eat. Choice (B) confuses similar-sounding words *closed* and *clothes*. Choice (C) is what the man says he will do. Choice (D) associates *café* with *coffee*.

66. **(D)** The speakers are looking for a café that stays open late because the restaurant they wanted to go to has closed for the night. Choice (A) is associated with the discussion of how to pay. Choice (B) is not likely because the man offers to make a phone call. Choice (C) confuses similar-sounding words *hungry* and *angry*.

67. **(D)** The man says he has cash and will pay. Choice (A) confuses the meaning of the word *check*. Choice (B) confuses the meaning of the word *order*. Choice (C) is mentioned by the woman, but the man says he doesn't have this.

68. **(B)** The woman says she is looking for a business suit for her husband. Choice (A) is who the woman says she isn't shopping for. Choice (C) confuses *another* with the similar-sounding word *brother*. Choice (D) is mentioned, but not as the recipient of the suit.

69. **(D)** This is the color suit the woman says she wants. Choices (A), (B), and (C) are the colors of the summer suits that the woman rejects.

70. **(C)** After telling the price, the man says, *You couldn't get a suit like this for less than that*. Choice (A) repeats the word *less*. Choice (B) is confused with the man's mention of the different colors of the summer suits. Choice (D) is confused with *You couldn't get a suit like this*, but the man is really talking about the price, not the availability.

## PART 4: TALKS

71. **(A)** The speaker says that the train *will begin boarding* in five minutes. Choice (B) is mentioned but is not what will happen in five minutes. Choice (C) repeats the word *tickets*. Choice (D) confuses the meaning of the word *store*.

72. **(B)** The speaker says it is an *all-reserved train* and that passengers should check to make sure they have a reservation. Choice (A) repeats the word *ticket*. Choice (C) is possible but not mentioned. Choice (D) repeats *16*, the number of the train.

73. **(C)** This is the instruction the speaker gives. Choice (A) is confused with *check your ticket*. Choice (B) is what should be done with tickets. Choice (D) confuses similar-sounding words *rack* and *track*.

74. **(C)** At Prescott, a customer can open an account, transfer funds, order checks, and apply for a loan, so it is a bank. Choice (A) confuses *account* with *accountants*. Choice (B) confuses the meaning of the word *party*. Choice (D) repeats the word *credit card*.

75. **(D)** The recording says to press 6 to speak with a customer service representative. Choice (A) is the number to press to ask questions about an existing account. Choice (B) is the number to press to order new checks. Choice (C) is the number to press to apply for a loan.

76. **(D)** The recording says to press zero in order to hear the menu again. Choice (A) is what the caller can do by pressing one. Choice (B) is what the caller can do by pressing two. Choice (C) is what the caller can do by pressing four.

77. **(C)** The speaker says that this is often a problem *after lunch*, that is, in the afternoon. Choice (A) is when people feel energetic. Choice (B) repeats the word *lunch*. Choice (D) is confused with *until the workday ends*.

78. **(D)** The speaker says to *take a brisk walk*. Choice (A) repeats the word *lunch*. Choices (B) and (C) are things the speaker says not to do.

79. **(A)** The speaker says to do this every hour. Choice (B) is how long it should be done. Choice (C) sounds similar to *for five minutes*. Choice (D) is not mentioned.

80. **(B)** Magruder's sells desks, computer stands, filing cabinets, and other types of office furniture. Choice (A) repeats the word *computer*. Choice (C) associates *computer* with *electronics*. Choice (D) associates *bookshelves* with *bookseller*.

81. **(D)** The speaker says, *Magruder's is closing its uptown branch*, implying that there are other branches. Choice (A) is not likely since the business already has a branch that is closing. Choice (B) is confused with the information that a branch is closing, but that isn't the entire business. Choice (C) is incorrect because the quality of the listed products is not mentioned.

82. **(A)** The speaker says, *Everything is marked down 65% off its usual price.* Choice (B) is not mentioned. Choice (C) is confused with the list of sale products mentioned. Choice (D) is not mentioned.

83. **(B)** The ad is for the Computer Training Institute, where people are trained as computer technicians. Choice (A) is what you can learn to do in the training course. Choice (C) is confused with the employment service offered to graduates of the training course. Choice (D) is what students in the training course learn to repair.

84. **(C)** The ad mentions this as the cost of the six-month course. Choice (A) sounds similar to the correct answer. Choices (B) and (D) sound similar to the length of the course—six months.

85. **(A)** Listeners are told to visit a website to sign up for the course. Choice (B) repeats the word *office.* Choice (C) confuses similar-sounding words *all* and *call.* Choice (D) is not mentioned.

86. **(A)** The speaker says that snow is falling. Choice (B) confuses similar-sounding words *train* and *rain.* Choices (C) and (D) are how the weather will be tomorrow.

87. **(D)** The speaker says, *don't go out.* Choice (A) is what the speaker says not to do. Choice (B) is confused with *accidents have been reported.* Choice (C) is confused with *commuter trains are experiencing delays.*

88. **(D)** The weather will be clear tomorrow. Choices (A), (B), and (C) are all times when the snow will continue to fall.

89. **(B)** The speaker explains where and when workshops and other conference activities will take place. Choice (A) refers to the different places in the hotel that are mentioned. Choice (C) refers to the workshop speaker who is mentioned. Choice (D) is not mentioned.

90. **(A)** Lucille Snow is the guest speaker at a conference put on by the Business Owners Association, so she is probably some kind of business expert. Choice (B) is associated with the location of the conference. Choice (C) is who the speaker probably is. Choice (D) is associated with the computer software demonstration that is mentioned.

91. **(D)** The speaker says that refreshments will be enjoyed outside on the patio. Choice (A) is where workshops will take place. Choice (B) is where lunch will be served. Choice (C) is confused with the name of the place where lunch will be served, the *Garden Restaurant.*

92. **(A)** The speaker says, *Park Street Station is closed.* Choice (B) is incorrect because the speaker says that bus service is available. Choice (C) confuses the meaning of the word *park* and repeats the word *available.* Choice (D) repeats the word *curb.*

93. **(B)** This is the problem the speaker mentions. Choice (A) confuses similar-sounding words *train* and *rain.* Choice (C) repeats the word *crowd.* Choice (D) repeats the word *traffic.*

94. **(B)** The speaker says that the station will reopen in three weeks. Choice (A) confuses similar-sounding words *due* and *two.* Choice (C) confuses the word *for* with the number *four.* Choice (D) is not mentioned.

95. **(C)** The president will take a *five-nation tour*. Choice (A) confuses the word *to* with the number *two*. Choice (B) confuses the word *for* with the number *four*. Choice (D) is the number of days his trip will last.

96. **(A)** The president will *discuss the current economic situation.* Choice (B) confuses *leaders* with *leadership.* Choice (C) confuses similar-sounding words *where* and *war.* Choice (D) is confused with the scientists who will be at the banquet.

97. **(D)** The president will take a few days of rest at his beach house. Choice (A) is something he will do during his trip. Choice (B) is confused with the awards he will give at the banquet. Choice (C) confuses similar-sounding words *rest* and *restaurant.*

98. **(B)** The speaker is offering the opportunity to attend a management training workshop. Choice (A) is where the opportunity is announced. Choice (C) confuses the meaning of the word *train.* Choice (D) confuses *workshop* with *shop.*

99. **(D)** This is when the speaker says the workshop is offered. Choice (A) confuses similar-sounding words *month* and *Monday.* Choice (B) is when the speaker wants to hear from all those wishing to attend. Choice (C) confuses *December,* when the workshop will take place, with the similar-sounding word *September.*

100. **(A)** This is what the speaker says people will need to bring. Choice (B) is mentioned but not as something to bring. Choice (C) will be provided. Choice (D) refers to the list of attendees the speaker will make.

## Reading

### PART 5: INCOMPLETE SENTENCES

101. **(A)** *As soon as possible* usually implies the future. In addition, *document* is a singular noun and Choice (A) is the only choice that agrees with a singular noun. Choices (B), (C), and (D) are all plural verbs.

102. **(C)** This is the adjective form, used to describe the noun *businessperson.* Choices (A) and (D) are nouns. Choice (B) is a verb.

103. **(D)** *Submit* means *present* or *give.* Choices (A) and (B) are things you might do to a résumé—*compose* means *write* and *revise* means *correct*—but they don't fit the context. Choice (C) is not used with the word *résumé.* You *apply* for a *job* by *submitting a résumé.*

104. **(B)** This is a passive voice sentence and uses the past participle form of the verb. Choice (A) is the simple present or base form. Choice (C) is the present participle. Choice (D) is the noun form.

105. **(A)** A future real conditional sentence uses future tense in the main clause. Choice (B) is present perfect. Choice (C) is simple past. Choice (D) is simple present.

106. **(C)** This is the adjective form, used to describe the noun *employees.* Choice (A) is a present tense or base form verb. Choice (B) is a present participle verb. Choice (D) is a noun.

107. **(D)** A *promotion* is an advancement at a job. Choices (A), (B), and (C) look similar to the correct answer but have meanings that don't fit the context.

108. **(C)** This is the noun form referring to a person in the position of subject of the clause. Choice (A) is a verb. Choice (B) is a past tense verb. Choice (D) is a noun but refers to a situation, not a person.

109. **(B)** *Until* introduces the time clause, which tells us when the action in the main clause, *go home*, will occur. Choice (A) introduces a condition, which would not make sense with the negative idea of the main clause. Choices (C) and (D) introduce a reason that, again, would not make sense with the negative idea of the main clause.

110. **(D)** *Through* means to move from one side to the other. Choices (A), (B), and (C) are not logical for the context of a door.

111. **(C)** The base form of the verb follows the modal *could*. Choice (A) is past tense. Choice (B) is past participle. Choice (D) is a noun.

112. **(A)** *Admitted* means to *be let in*. Choices (B), (C), and (D) all look similar to the correct answer but have very different meanings.

113. **(C)** *Beside* means *next to*. Choices (A), (B), and (D) look similar to the correct answer but do not fit the context of the sentence.

114. **(B)** *Descends* means *goes down*. Choices (A), (C), and (D) all have the meaning of *goes down* but are not used to describe the motion of an elevator.

115. **(A)** This is an imperative verb, telling the listener what to do. Choice (B) is simple present tense. Choice (C) is simple past tense. Choice (D) is present participle.

116. **(B)** A future time clause uses a present tense verb. Choice (A) is past tense. Choice (C) is the present participle form. Choice (D) is future tense.

117. **(C)** *Because* indicates a cause-and-effect relationship between the two events. Choice (A) introduces a condition. Choices (B) and (D) imply contrast.

118. **(D)** *Insists* in this context means *requires*. Choices (A), (B), and (C) look similar to the correct answer but have very different meanings.

119. **(D)** *Although* implies a contrast between the two clauses; one would expect hard-working Mr. Lee to get a promotion, but he hasn't gotten one. Choice (A) indicates a cause-and-effect relationship. Choice (B) could be used with *though* but cannot stand alone in this sentence. Choice (C) needs to be followed by a gerund, not a clause.

120. **(C)** This is a present perfect verb used to describe an action that started in the past and continues into the present. Choice (A) is simple present tense. Choice (B) is past tense. Choice (D) is future tense.

121. **(A)** A noun form is needed as the object of the verb *require*. Choice (B) is an adjective. Choice (C) is a noun but refers to a person, so it does not fit the context. Choice (D) is a verb.

122. **(B)** This is a past tense unreal conditional and requires a modal, either *would* or *might* as part of the verb in the main clause. Choices (A), (C), and (D) are all modals but are not used with unreal past tense conditionals.

123. **(A)** *Compete* means *perform well against others*. Choices (B), (C), and (D) look similar to the correct answer but have meanings that don't fit the context of the sentence.

124. **(D)** *Show up* means *appear* or *arrive*. (A), (B), and (C) cannot be logically used in this sentence.

125. **(B)** *Above* is a preposition of place that means *over* and refers to something that is *high* or *up*. Choice (A) means *past*. Choice (C) means *at the side*. Choice (D) means *on the opposite side*.

126. **(C)** *Schedule an appointment* means the same as *make an appointment*. Choices (A), (B), and (D) are not normally used together with the word *appointment*.

127. **(A)** *Quality* is a noun meaning *excellence* or *high value*. Choices (B) and (C) look similar to the correct answer but have different meanings. Choice (D) is a verb, not a noun.

128. **(D)** *Expect* means *require* in this context. Choices (A), (B), and (C) have meanings that don't fit the context of the sentence.

129. **(A)** In a passive-voice sentence, *by* introduces the performer of the action. Choices (B), (C), and (D) are not used in this position in a passive-voice sentence.

130. **(B)** *Take place* means *happen*. Choices (A), (C), and (D) are words that might be used when talking about a meeting but they don't fit the meaning of the sentence.

131. **(C)** *Have to* plus the base form of a verb indicates necessity. Choices (A) and (D) lack the word *to*. Choice (B) is past tense so cannot be used in this sentence about the present.

132. **(C)** A noun is required to act as the subject of the sentence. Choice (A) is an adverb. Choice (B) is an adjective. Choice (D) is a verb.

133. **(A)** This is an imperative verb, telling the listener what to do. Choice (B) is past tense. Choice (C) is present participle or a gerund. Choice (D) is future tense.

134. **(D)** *Rise* is a verb that means *go up*. Choice (A) is a verb. Choice (B) is a transitive verb—it requires an object. Choice (C) is an adverb.

135. **(B)** *Were* agrees with the plural noun *books*. Choices (A) and (C) are singular. Choice (D) is an auxiliary verb and cannot be used without a main verb.

136. **(D)** *During* is a preposition, placed before a noun, describing when the people fell asleep. Choices (A), (B), and (C) are used to introduce a clause.

137. **(C)** *Expanding* means *growing*. Choices (A), (B), and (C) have meanings that don't fit the context.

138. **(C)** The subject of the sentence, *the building*, received the action, so a passive-voice verb is required. Choices (A), (B), and (D) are all active-voice forms.

139. **(A)** A noun is needed to act as the object of the verb *have*. Choice (B) is a noun but has a meaning that doesn't fit the context of the sentence. Choices (C) and (D) are verbs.

140. **(B)** *Confidential* means *private* or *secret*. Choices (A), (C), and (D) look similar to the correct answer but don't fit the context of the sentence.

## PART 6: TEXT COMPLETION

141. **(A)** We know that sales are *decreasing*, or going down, because fewer customers are coming into the store. Choice (B) is the opposite meaning. Choice (C) means *staying the same*. Choice (D) is related to sales but doesn't fit the context.

142. **(B)** The store has had to *lay off*, or fire, employees because business has been so bad. Choices (A) and (D) are things they might do with new employees. Choice (C) means *hire*, the opposite of the correct answer.

143. **(D)** Unemployed people might seek *benefits*, or assistance, from the government. Choice (A) refers to people who receive benefits. Choice (B) refers to people who help others. Choice (C) is an adjective describing things that are good or helpful.

144. **(B)** This is a simple past tense verb used to describe an action that was completed in the past, two years ago. Choice (A) is simple present. Choice (C) is present perfect. Choice (D) is also present tense.

145. **(C)** We know that Mr. Richardson is reliable because the next sentence says, *We could always count on him.* Choices (A), (B), and (D) are also good qualities for an employee but do not fit the context.

146. **(D)** An *addition* is something that is added; in this case, Mr. Richardson's positive personality added good feelings to the workplace. The other choices are related in meaning but have more specific uses. Choice (A) is a mathematical term. Choice (B) is used to refer to substances added to improve products. Choice (C) is used to refer to information added to publications or documents.

147. **(A)** A *refund* is a return of money, which is what customers hope for when they return purchases. Choices (B), (C), and (D) look similar to the correct answer but don't fit the context.

148. **(C)** *Their* refers to the third person plural noun *items*. Choices (A) and (B) refer to a third person singular noun. Choice (D) is second person.

149. **(D)** *Without* is a preposition referring to something that is missing or absent. Choices (A), (B), and (C) are not prepositions.

150. **(C)** The adverb form is used to modify the adjective *located*. Choice (A) is an adjective. Choice (B) is a noun. Choice (D) is an adverb but belongs to a different word family and has a completely different meaning.

151. **(B)** *Ample* means *plentiful*. Choice (A) is opposite in meaning, so it isn't logical here. Choices (C) and (D) could be used to describe parking but don't fit the context.

152. **(C)** This is an imperative verb form telling readers what to do. Choice (A) could be imperative but is affirmative, so it isn't logical here. Choice (B) mentions the subject and is simple present tense, not imperative. Choice (D) isn't imperative, so it requires mention of the subject.

## PART 7: READING COMPREHENSION

153. **(C)** This business offers to provide food for conferences, meetings, and office parties, so it is a catering business. Choices (A), (B), and (D) are also businesses involving food but are not the correct answer.

154. **(C)** The ad says that consultants will explain the pricing system, and to call in order to speak with one. Choice (A) is incorrect because the ad says to visit the office during normal business hours, which implies daytime, not evening, hours. Choice (B) repeats the word *event*, but nowhere is going to an event mentioned. Choice (D) is how to see menu choices.

155. **(C)** On an invoice, *previous account balance* refers to the amount due on a previous invoice. Since this amount was paid in full, it hasn't been added to the amount due on the current invoice. Choice (A) is incorrect because the amount due on this invoice appears next to *total due*. Choices (B) and (D) use words from the invoice but are not the correct answer.

156. **(D)** The bill asks for payment by the end of next month. Because the bill has a December date, January is the next month. Choice (A) is the end of the month when the work was done. Choice (B) is the date on the bill. Choice (C) is the end of the current month.

157. **(A)** *There will be no charge* for metered parking means *it will be free*. Choice (B) is incorrect because parking garages will be closed. Choice (C) is incorrect because there will be fares for subway rides—weekend fares. Choice (D) is incorrect because the bridge will be closed.

158. **(B)** The free parking is *because of the holiday*. Choice (A) describes the type of parking regulations and fares that will be in effect during the holiday. Choices (C) and (D) are mentioned but are not the reason for free parking.

159. **(D)** Boris Lutz won a prize, or award. Choice (A) is associated with his place of work—a bank. Choice (B) confuses the meaning of *promote* as it is used here—to promote, or encourage, goodwill. Choice (C) is confused with Maria Pendleton's job.

160. **(B)** The article states that Lutz is a teller at the Simsbury Village branch of the bank. Choice (A) repeats the word *assistant*, which describes Maria Pendleton's job. Choice (C) repeats the word *community*. Choice (D) repeats the name of the town, *Greenfield*.

161. **(A)** Boris's coworkers gave him the Good Citizen Prize, and his supervisor says he "has always given generously of his time to community groups." Choice (B) repeats the word *employee*. Choices (C) and (D) are compatible with the good feelings about Boris expressed in the article, but they are never mentioned.

162. **(B)** The company wants to hire writers, editors, and proofreaders, so it is probably a publishing company.

163. **(A)** The ad directs job hunters to visit the company's website. Choice (B) is what job hunters are asked not to do. Choice (C) repeats the word *résumé*, but the ad does not say to mail a résumé, it says to attach one to the online application. Choice (D) repeats the word *letter* as in *letters of recommendation*, which are not required.

164. **(D)** This job requires three years' experience. Choice (A) mentions experience, but training can replace it. Choices (B) and (C) say that previous experience is not required.

165. **(A)** The company type is stated in the first sentence. Choice (B) is confused with the previous tenant of the office. Choice (C) is confused with the type of company that owns the office building. Choice (D) is confused with the other company that opened recently nearby.

166. **(A)** The article says, *The new Park and Smith office was open for business as of yesterday.* Choice (B) is when the stock brokerage office opened. Choice (C) is when the company closed other branch offices. Choice (D) is confused with how long the office space had been vacant.

167. **(C)** The company president says, *It is just the type of community where services such as ours are needed.* Choice (A) is true but not the reason they opened an office in Salem. Choice (B) is confused with the reason why the other branch offices were closed. Choice (D) is associated with renting a new office but not mentioned.

168. **(B)** The word *facilitate* means *to make something happen more easily.* Choices (A), (C), and (D) don't fit the meaning of the sentence.

169. **(A)** Henry Judson explains several reasons why he doesn't like the factory and urges the city council members to vote against it. Choices (B), (C), and (D) repeat words used in the letter but are not the correct answer.

170. **(C)** Henry Judson explains that the company usually hires highly skilled technicians. Choice (A) is the type of person who does not usually work at Holbrook. Choice (B) repeats the word *blind* out of context. Choice (D) is related to the word *economy* but is not mentioned.

171. **(B)** This is when Henry Judson says the vote will take place. Choice (A) is when he read the newspaper article. Choice (C) was the original schedule for the vote. Choice (D) is when the company wants to begin construction of the factory.

172. **(D)** *Unsightly* means *ugly*—Henry Judson does not like the looks of the proposed building. Choice (A) is the opposite of the correct meaning. Choices (B) and (C) are words that could be used to describe a building but are not the correct answer.

173. **(B)** The instructions mention making calls and dialing, so the product is a telephone. Choices (A), (C), and (D) are mentioned but are not the correct answer.

174. **(A)** The customer is asked to contact the manufacturer by phone for repair work. Choice (B) is explained but not in connection with repair. Choices (C) and (D) repeat words used in the text.

175. **(A)** According to the instructions, the product should not be used during an electrical, or thunder, storm. Choices (B) and (C) are mentioned but are not related to the question. Choice (D) repeats the word *electrical.*

176. **(C)** The instructions say to disconnect the product from the electrical outlet. Choices (A), (B), and (D) are mentioned as things not to do when cleaning the product.

177. **(C)** She was branch manager at the Riverside branch of the Windsor bank until two years ago, and she has been a student since then. Choice (A) is confused with the new

job she will be taking on—human resources director. Choice (B) is confused with her first job, at an accounting firm. Choice (D) is confused with *her instructors at the university*, who recommended her for her new job.

178. **(C)** This is where Ms. Simmons began her banking career. Choice (A) is the location of her new job. Choice (B) is confused with the name of the accounting firm where she used to work. Choice (D) is confused with the name of the branch of the Windsor bank where she was manager.

179. **(D)** According to the article, Ms. Simmons completed her degree last month. Choice (A) is when she began her banking career. Choice (B) is when she began working on her master's degree. Choice (C) is not mentioned.

180. **(A)** *Previous* means *former*, and this sentence refers to Ms. Simmons's employers from before. Choices (B), (C), and (D) don't fit the meaning of the sentence.

181. **(B)** Myra writes that she will be flying to San Francisco, so she plans to go by plane. Choice (A) is confused with the bus that will be available for the tour. Choice (C) is not mentioned. Choice (D) is confused with Myra's plan to drive to Sacramento after the conference.

182. **(C)** Myra wants to *go over the project* with Raymond. Choice (A) is confused with the workshops at the conference. Choice (B) is related to the topic of Raymond's workshop. Choice (D) is related to the topic of Myra's workshop.

183. **(A)** Myra will not be available to meet with Raymond while she is giving her workshop on business law, which will take place at 9:15. Choices (B) and (C) are the beginning and ending times of the following workshop session. Choice (D) is the beginning time of the afternoon workshop session.

184. **(B)** According to her e-mail, Myra plans to attend the workshop given by Raymond, which takes place from 2:00 to 4:00. Choices (A), (C), and (D) are places where other conference events will take place.

185. **(D)** Myra will drive to Sacramento to attend a colleague's book signing. Choice (A) is what she wants to do during the day on Friday. Choice (B) repeats the words *sign* and *contract* out of context. Choice (C) is what she will do Friday morning.

186. **(B)** There is an opening for a researcher in the Marketing Department, and this is the position Ms. Krim wants to apply for. Choice (A) is the position Mr. Mendez suggests she apply for. Choice (C) is her current position. Choice (D) is related to the department she currently works in.

187. **(A)** Ms. Krim says that she finished her degree *last month*. Her letter is dated July, so last month would be June. Choice (B) is the date of her letter. Choice (C) is the date of Mr. Mendez's letter. Choice (D) is when the marketing assistant job may be open.

188. **(D)** Ms. Petrowski, who is Ms. Krim's supervisor, recommends her for the job. Choices (A), (B), and (C) are other people mentioned in the letters.

189. **(B)** Ms. Krim has one year of experience in marketing and Mr. Mendez says that twice that amount is required. Choice (A) is the amount of experience Ms. Krim has. Choice (C) is the number of years she has worked in the accounting department. Choice (D) is not mentioned.

190. **(D)** Mr. Mendez writes that he anticipates that a new position will become available and that he will let Ms. Krim know about it. Choice (A) is what Ms. Krim wants him to do. Choices (B) and (C) are things he has already done.

191. **(C)** The workshop is required for department heads. Choice (A) is the people for whom it is recommended, but not required. Choice (B) is related to the topic—safety—of the workshop. Choice (D) is the person who wrote the memo.

192. **(B)** Sandy Bayliss refers to the memo of *yesterday*, which is dated November 17. Choice (A) is the date the memo was written. Choice (C) is the deadline for signing up for the workshop. Choice (D) is the date of the workshop.

193. **(D)** The workshop begins at 9:30 and she will arrive fifteen minutes late. Choice (A) is when her breakfast meeting will end. Choice (B) is fifteen minutes after the breakfast meeting. Choice (C) is the time the meeting will begin.

194. **(B)** Three workshops are required and this workshop will complete her requirement, so she has already attended two.

195. **(C)** She says that she has to be downtown for a breakfast meeting. Choice (A) refers to the office manager, who wrote the memo. Choice (B) repeats the word *office*. Choice (D) is where the workshop will take place.

196. **(C)** He bought it at the beginning of February and wrote the letter at the beginning of April. Choice (A) is when the shredder stopped working. Choice (B) is not mentioned. Choice (D) is confused with the length of the warranty.

197. **(A)** The customer says that he needs a paper shredder because of the sensitive financial reports that come to his office. Choice (B) is where he read reviews of the product. Choices (C) and (D) are items mentioned in the warranty notice.

198. **(B)** The customer says that he is *not pleased* about it. Choice (A) is how he felt when he bought it. Choice (C) repeats the word *pleased*. Choice (D) is the word used to describe the financial reports.

199. **(D)** The customer wrapped up the shredder in a *brand new box*, instead of in its original packaging as requested in the warranty notice. Choices (A) and (B) are things that he did include. Choice (C) is related to his request for a refund, but a refund form is not requested by the company.

200. **(C)** The refund request is outside the limits of the warranty because the customer spilled a box of paper clips into the product. Choice (A) is what the customer requests. Choice (B) is what is done in cases of manufacturing defects. Choice (D) is not mentioned.

# ANSWER SHEET
## TOEIC Practice Exam 2

**LISTENING COMPREHENSION**

### Part 1: Photographs

1. Ⓐ Ⓑ Ⓒ Ⓓ    4. Ⓐ Ⓑ Ⓒ Ⓓ    7. Ⓐ Ⓑ Ⓒ Ⓓ    10. Ⓐ Ⓑ Ⓒ Ⓓ
2. Ⓐ Ⓑ Ⓒ Ⓓ    5. Ⓐ Ⓑ Ⓒ Ⓓ    8. Ⓐ Ⓑ Ⓒ Ⓓ
3. Ⓐ Ⓑ Ⓒ Ⓓ    6. Ⓐ Ⓑ Ⓒ Ⓓ    9. Ⓐ Ⓑ Ⓒ Ⓓ

### Part 2: Question-Response

11. Ⓐ Ⓑ Ⓒ    19. Ⓐ Ⓑ Ⓒ    27. Ⓐ Ⓑ Ⓒ    35. Ⓐ Ⓑ Ⓒ
12. Ⓐ Ⓑ Ⓒ    20. Ⓐ Ⓑ Ⓒ    28. Ⓐ Ⓑ Ⓒ    36. Ⓐ Ⓑ Ⓒ
13. Ⓐ Ⓑ Ⓒ    21. Ⓐ Ⓑ Ⓒ    29. Ⓐ Ⓑ Ⓒ    37. Ⓐ Ⓑ Ⓒ
14. Ⓐ Ⓑ Ⓒ    22. Ⓐ Ⓑ Ⓒ    30. Ⓐ Ⓑ Ⓒ    38. Ⓐ Ⓑ Ⓒ
15. Ⓐ Ⓑ Ⓒ    23. Ⓐ Ⓑ Ⓒ    31. Ⓐ Ⓑ Ⓒ    39. Ⓐ Ⓑ Ⓒ
16. Ⓐ Ⓑ Ⓒ    24. Ⓐ Ⓑ Ⓒ    32. Ⓐ Ⓑ Ⓒ    40. Ⓐ Ⓑ Ⓒ
17. Ⓐ Ⓑ Ⓒ    25. Ⓐ Ⓑ Ⓒ    33. Ⓐ Ⓑ Ⓒ
18. Ⓐ Ⓑ Ⓒ    26. Ⓐ Ⓑ Ⓒ    34. Ⓐ Ⓑ Ⓒ

### Part 3: Conversations

41. Ⓐ Ⓑ Ⓒ Ⓓ    49. Ⓐ Ⓑ Ⓒ Ⓓ    57. Ⓐ Ⓑ Ⓒ Ⓓ    65. Ⓐ Ⓑ Ⓒ Ⓓ
42. Ⓐ Ⓑ Ⓒ Ⓓ    50. Ⓐ Ⓑ Ⓒ Ⓓ    58. Ⓐ Ⓑ Ⓒ Ⓓ    66. Ⓐ Ⓑ Ⓒ Ⓓ
43. Ⓐ Ⓑ Ⓒ Ⓓ    51. Ⓐ Ⓑ Ⓒ Ⓓ    59. Ⓐ Ⓑ Ⓒ Ⓓ    67. Ⓐ Ⓑ Ⓒ Ⓓ
44. Ⓐ Ⓑ Ⓒ Ⓓ    52. Ⓐ Ⓑ Ⓒ Ⓓ    60. Ⓐ Ⓑ Ⓒ Ⓓ    68. Ⓐ Ⓑ Ⓒ Ⓓ
45. Ⓐ Ⓑ Ⓒ Ⓓ    53. Ⓐ Ⓑ Ⓒ Ⓓ    61. Ⓐ Ⓑ Ⓒ Ⓓ    69. Ⓐ Ⓑ Ⓒ Ⓓ
46. Ⓐ Ⓑ Ⓒ Ⓓ    54. Ⓐ Ⓑ Ⓒ Ⓓ    62. Ⓐ Ⓑ Ⓒ Ⓓ    70. Ⓐ Ⓑ Ⓒ Ⓓ
47. Ⓐ Ⓑ Ⓒ Ⓓ    55. Ⓐ Ⓑ Ⓒ Ⓓ    63. Ⓐ Ⓑ Ⓒ Ⓓ
48. Ⓐ Ⓑ Ⓒ Ⓓ    56. Ⓐ Ⓑ Ⓒ Ⓓ    64. Ⓐ Ⓑ Ⓒ Ⓓ

### Part 4: Talks

71. Ⓐ Ⓑ Ⓒ Ⓓ    79. Ⓐ Ⓑ Ⓒ Ⓓ    87. Ⓐ Ⓑ Ⓒ Ⓓ    95. Ⓐ Ⓑ Ⓒ Ⓓ
72. Ⓐ Ⓑ Ⓒ Ⓓ    80. Ⓐ Ⓑ Ⓒ Ⓓ    88. Ⓐ Ⓑ Ⓒ Ⓓ    96. Ⓐ Ⓑ Ⓒ Ⓓ
73. Ⓐ Ⓑ Ⓒ Ⓓ    81. Ⓐ Ⓑ Ⓒ Ⓓ    89. Ⓐ Ⓑ Ⓒ Ⓓ    97. Ⓐ Ⓑ Ⓒ Ⓓ
74. Ⓐ Ⓑ Ⓒ Ⓓ    82. Ⓐ Ⓑ Ⓒ Ⓓ    90. Ⓐ Ⓑ Ⓒ Ⓓ    98. Ⓐ Ⓑ Ⓒ Ⓓ
75. Ⓐ Ⓑ Ⓒ Ⓓ    83. Ⓐ Ⓑ Ⓒ Ⓓ    91. Ⓐ Ⓑ Ⓒ Ⓓ    99. Ⓐ Ⓑ Ⓒ Ⓓ
76. Ⓐ Ⓑ Ⓒ Ⓓ    84. Ⓐ Ⓑ Ⓒ Ⓓ    92. Ⓐ Ⓑ Ⓒ Ⓓ    100. Ⓐ Ⓑ Ⓒ Ⓓ
77. Ⓐ Ⓑ Ⓒ Ⓓ    85. Ⓐ Ⓑ Ⓒ Ⓓ    93. Ⓐ Ⓑ Ⓒ Ⓓ
78. Ⓐ Ⓑ Ⓒ Ⓓ    86. Ⓐ Ⓑ Ⓒ Ⓓ    94. Ⓐ Ⓑ Ⓒ Ⓓ

# ANSWER SHEET
## TOEIC Practice Exam 2

## READING

### Part 5: Incomplete Sentences

101. Ⓐ Ⓑ Ⓒ Ⓓ       111. Ⓐ Ⓑ Ⓒ Ⓓ       121. Ⓐ Ⓑ Ⓒ Ⓓ       131. Ⓐ Ⓑ Ⓒ Ⓓ
102. Ⓐ Ⓑ Ⓒ Ⓓ       112. Ⓐ Ⓑ Ⓒ Ⓓ       122. Ⓐ Ⓑ Ⓒ Ⓓ       132. Ⓐ Ⓑ Ⓒ Ⓓ
103. Ⓐ Ⓑ Ⓒ Ⓓ       113. Ⓐ Ⓑ Ⓒ Ⓓ       123. Ⓐ Ⓑ Ⓒ Ⓓ       133. Ⓐ Ⓑ Ⓒ Ⓓ
104. Ⓐ Ⓑ Ⓒ Ⓓ       114. Ⓐ Ⓑ Ⓒ Ⓓ       124. Ⓐ Ⓑ Ⓒ Ⓓ       134. Ⓐ Ⓑ Ⓒ Ⓓ
105. Ⓐ Ⓑ Ⓒ Ⓓ       115. Ⓐ Ⓑ Ⓒ Ⓓ       125. Ⓐ Ⓑ Ⓒ Ⓓ       135. Ⓐ Ⓑ Ⓒ Ⓓ
106. Ⓐ Ⓑ Ⓒ Ⓓ       116. Ⓐ Ⓑ Ⓒ Ⓓ       126. Ⓐ Ⓑ Ⓒ Ⓓ       136. Ⓐ Ⓑ Ⓒ Ⓓ
107. Ⓐ Ⓑ Ⓒ Ⓓ       117. Ⓐ Ⓑ Ⓒ Ⓓ       127. Ⓐ Ⓑ Ⓒ Ⓓ       137. Ⓐ Ⓑ Ⓒ Ⓓ
108. Ⓐ Ⓑ Ⓒ Ⓓ       118. Ⓐ Ⓑ Ⓒ Ⓓ       128. Ⓐ Ⓑ Ⓒ Ⓓ       138. Ⓐ Ⓑ Ⓒ Ⓓ
109. Ⓐ Ⓑ Ⓒ Ⓓ       119. Ⓐ Ⓑ Ⓒ Ⓓ       129. Ⓐ Ⓑ Ⓒ Ⓓ       139. Ⓐ Ⓑ Ⓒ Ⓓ
110. Ⓐ Ⓑ Ⓒ Ⓓ       120. Ⓐ Ⓑ Ⓒ Ⓓ       130. Ⓐ Ⓑ Ⓒ Ⓓ       140. Ⓐ Ⓑ Ⓒ Ⓓ

### Part 6: Text Completion

141. Ⓐ Ⓑ Ⓒ Ⓓ       144. Ⓐ Ⓑ Ⓒ Ⓓ       147. Ⓐ Ⓑ Ⓒ Ⓓ       150. Ⓐ Ⓑ Ⓒ Ⓓ
142. Ⓐ Ⓑ Ⓒ Ⓓ       145. Ⓐ Ⓑ Ⓒ Ⓓ       148. Ⓐ Ⓑ Ⓒ Ⓓ       151. Ⓐ Ⓑ Ⓒ Ⓓ
143. Ⓐ Ⓑ Ⓒ Ⓓ       146. Ⓐ Ⓑ Ⓒ Ⓓ       149. Ⓐ Ⓑ Ⓒ Ⓓ       152. Ⓐ Ⓑ Ⓒ Ⓓ

### Part 7: Reading Comprehension

153. Ⓐ Ⓑ Ⓒ Ⓓ       165. Ⓐ Ⓑ Ⓒ Ⓓ       177. Ⓐ Ⓑ Ⓒ Ⓓ       189. Ⓐ Ⓑ Ⓒ Ⓓ
154. Ⓐ Ⓑ Ⓒ Ⓓ       166. Ⓐ Ⓑ Ⓒ Ⓓ       178. Ⓐ Ⓑ Ⓒ Ⓓ       190. Ⓐ Ⓑ Ⓒ Ⓓ
155. Ⓐ Ⓑ Ⓒ Ⓓ       167. Ⓐ Ⓑ Ⓒ Ⓓ       179. Ⓐ Ⓑ Ⓒ Ⓓ       191. Ⓐ Ⓑ Ⓒ Ⓓ
156. Ⓐ Ⓑ Ⓒ Ⓓ       168. Ⓐ Ⓑ Ⓒ Ⓓ       180. Ⓐ Ⓑ Ⓒ Ⓓ       192. Ⓐ Ⓑ Ⓒ Ⓓ
157. Ⓐ Ⓑ Ⓒ Ⓓ       169. Ⓐ Ⓑ Ⓒ Ⓓ       181. Ⓐ Ⓑ Ⓒ Ⓓ       193. Ⓐ Ⓑ Ⓒ Ⓓ
158. Ⓐ Ⓑ Ⓒ Ⓓ       170. Ⓐ Ⓑ Ⓒ Ⓓ       182. Ⓐ Ⓑ Ⓒ Ⓓ       194. Ⓐ Ⓑ Ⓒ Ⓓ
159. Ⓐ Ⓑ Ⓒ Ⓓ       171. Ⓐ Ⓑ Ⓒ Ⓓ       183. Ⓐ Ⓑ Ⓒ Ⓓ       195. Ⓐ Ⓑ Ⓒ Ⓓ
160. Ⓐ Ⓑ Ⓒ Ⓓ       172. Ⓐ Ⓑ Ⓒ Ⓓ       184. Ⓐ Ⓑ Ⓒ Ⓓ       196. Ⓐ Ⓑ Ⓒ Ⓓ
161. Ⓐ Ⓑ Ⓒ Ⓓ       173. Ⓐ Ⓑ Ⓒ Ⓓ       185. Ⓐ Ⓑ Ⓒ Ⓓ       197. Ⓐ Ⓑ Ⓒ Ⓓ
162. Ⓐ Ⓑ Ⓒ Ⓓ       174. Ⓐ Ⓑ Ⓒ Ⓓ       186. Ⓐ Ⓑ Ⓒ Ⓓ       198. Ⓐ Ⓑ Ⓒ Ⓓ
163. Ⓐ Ⓑ Ⓒ Ⓓ       175. Ⓐ Ⓑ Ⓒ Ⓓ       187. Ⓐ Ⓑ Ⓒ Ⓓ       199. Ⓐ Ⓑ Ⓒ Ⓓ
164. Ⓐ Ⓑ Ⓒ Ⓓ       176. Ⓐ Ⓑ Ⓒ Ⓓ       188. Ⓐ Ⓑ Ⓒ Ⓓ       200. Ⓐ Ⓑ Ⓒ Ⓓ

# TOEIC Practice Exam 2

## LISTENING COMPREHENSION

In this section of the test, you will have the chance to show how well you understand spoken English. There are four parts to this section, with special directions for each part. You will find the Answer Sheet for Practice Exam 2 on pages 63–64. Detach it from the book and use it to record your answers. Check your answers using the Answer Key on pages 100–101 and see the Answers Explained beginning on page 103.

## Part 1: Photographs

Track 6

**Directions:** You will see a photograph. You will hear four statements about the photograph. Choose the statement that most closely matches the photograph and fill in the corresponding oval on your answer sheet.

**Example**

Now listen to the four statements.

Sample Answer
Ⓐ Ⓑ Ⓒ Ⓓ

Statement (B), "She's reading a magazine," best describes what you see in the picture. Therefore, you should choose answer (B).

**TIP**

If you do not have access to the MP3 files, please use the audioscripts beginning on page 358. You can also download the MP3 files and audioscripts from *http:// barronsbooks. com/tp/toeic/ audio/*

1.

4.

2.

5.

3.

6.

7.

8.

9.

10.

## Part 2: Question-Response

11.   Mark your answer on your answer sheet.

12.   Mark your answer on your answer sheet.

13.   Mark your answer on your answer sheet.

14.   Mark your answer on your answer sheet.

15.   Mark your answer on your answer sheet.

16.   Mark your answer on your answer sheet.

17.   Mark your answer on your answer sheet.

18.   Mark your answer on your answer sheet.

19.   Mark your answer on your answer sheet.

20.   Mark your answer on your answer sheet.

21.   Mark your answer on your answer sheet.

22.   Mark your answer on your answer sheet.

23.   Mark your answer on your answer sheet.

24.   Mark your answer on your answer sheet.

25.   Mark your answer on your answer sheet.

26.   Mark your answer on your answer sheet.

27.   Mark your answer on your answer sheet.

28.   Mark your answer on your answer sheet.

29.   Mark your answer on your answer sheet.

30.   Mark your answer on your answer sheet.

31.   Mark your answer on your answer sheet.

32.   Mark your answer on your answer sheet.

33.   Mark your answer on your answer sheet.

34.   Mark your answer on your answer sheet.

35.   Mark your answer on your answer sheet.

36.   Mark your answer on your answer sheet.

37.   Mark your answer on your answer sheet.

38.   Mark your answer on your answer sheet.

39.   Mark your answer on your answer sheet.

40.   Mark your answer on your answer sheet.

TOEIC PRACTICE EXAM 2

## Part 3: Conversations

Track 8

**Directions:** You will hear a conversation between two people. You will see three questions on each conversation and four possible answers. Choose the best answer to each question and fill in the corresponding oval on your answer sheet.

41. What does the man tell the woman?
    (A) He can wait for her after the meeting.
    (B) He'll call her after the meeting.
    (C) He can't be at the meeting.
    (D) He'll arrive late to the meeting.

42. Why is the woman calling a meeting?
    (A) To check the accounts
    (B) To explain the late paychecks
    (C) To announce a pay raise
    (D) To discuss next week's work

43. How does the man feel about the situation?
    (A) Supportive of the woman's plan
    (B) Happy that a problem will be discussed
    (C) Bothered because the situation has occurred before
    (D) Mad that he has to attend so many meetings

44. Where does this conversation take place?
    (A) At a restaurant
    (B) On an airplane
    (C) In a movie theater
    (D) On a train

45. What's the weather like?
    (A) Clear
    (B) Cloudy
    (C) Windy
    (D) Snowy

46. What will happen in a half an hour?
    (A) The movie will begin.
    (B) Food will be served.
    (C) Tickets will be collected.
    (D) The schedule will be updated.

47. What does the woman want to do?
    (A) Move a piece of furniture
    (B) Clean the window
    (C) Find a broom
    (D) Fix a table

48. Why can't the man help her do it?
    (A) He's at a workshop.
    (B) He's late for an appointment.
    (C) He's busy with work.
    (D) He hurt his back.

49. What does the woman decide to do?
    (A) Do the job herself
    (B) Pay someone to help her
    (C) Ask Samantha to help her
    (D) Wait for the man to be available

50. What will the man buy?
    (A) Gloves
    (B) Hats
    (C) Scarves
    (D) Bags

51. What color will he take?
    (A) Red
    (B) White
    (C) Brown
    (D) Black

52. How much will he pay?
    (A) $15.00
    (B) $15.50
    (C) $16.50
    (D) $50.00

53. When does the man need the copies?
    (A) By noon
    (B) This morning
    (C) Tomorrow
    (D) On Tuesday

54. Why can't the woman make the copies now?
    (A) She's too busy.
    (B) He wants too many.
    (C) It's very late.
    (D) The stapler is broken.

55. What does the woman agree to do?
    (A) Make a few extra copies
    (B) Finish the copies by morning
    (C) Put aside her other copying jobs
    (D) Bring the copies to the conference

56. What does the woman want to do?
    (A) Buy something
    (B) See Mr. Lee
    (C) Go on a trip
    (D) Make an appointment

57. Where is Mr. Lee?
    (A) Out of town
    (B) Downtown
    (C) At home
    (D) In his office

58. What does the man suggest that the woman do?
    (A) Come by later
    (B) Call back next week
    (C) Provide her contact information
    (D) Leave the office right away

59. Where does the man have to go?
    (A) To work
    (B) To computer class
    (C) To the train station
    (D) To a doctor's appointment

60. Where is the woman's car?
    (A) In the garage
    (B) Across the street
    (C) In the park
    (D) Downtown

61. What does the woman warn the man about?
    (A) The time
    (B) The traffic
    (C) The weather
    (D) The car engine

62. Why did Ms. Jones leave the office early?
    (A) To catch a train
    (B) To go to a meeting
    (C) To avoid bad traffic
    (D) To work on a report

63. What is the woman surprised about?
    (A) Ms. Jones missed their appointment.
    (B) Ms. Jones didn't answer her phone.
    (C) The report is already finished.
    (D) The office is closed.

64. What is the weather like?
    (A) Hot
    (B) Rainy
    (C) Snowy
    (D) Cold

65. What did the woman send the man?
    (A) Books
    (B) Reports
    (C) Photocopies
    (D) Photographs

66. How long does the man suggest waiting?
    (A) For three days
    (B) Until Friday
    (C) Until Thursday
    (D) Since Monday

67. What does the woman want to do now?
    (A) Report the package as lost
    (B) Resend the package
    (C) Make more copies
    (D) Wait another day

68. What does the woman invite the man to do?
    (A) Play golf
    (B) Play tennis
    (C) Go dancing
    (D) Have dinner

69. Why doesn't the man want to do it?
    (A) He needs to go to the bank.
    (B) He doesn't have a ticket.
    (C) He has to write a letter.
    (D) He's too tired.

70. Where will the man be tonight?
    (A) At the club
    (B) At the park
    (C) At the hotel
    (D) At the restaurant

## Part 4: Talks

Track 9

**Directions:** You will hear a talk given by a single speaker. You will see three questions on each talk, each with four possible answers. Choose the best answer to each question and fill in the corresponding oval on your answer sheet.

71. When can a customer speak with a technician?
    (A) Between 4:00 and 7:00
    (B) Between 2:00 and 4:00
    (C) Any time before 7:00
    (D) Any time of day

72. How can a caller make an appointment?
    (A) Call back after 7:00
    (B) Go online
    (C) Press 2
    (D) Visit the office

73. What can a caller do by pressing 3?
    (A) Speak with Tech Support
    (B) Buy a new computer
    (C) Get information about a bill
    (D) Hear the menu again

74. What will Dr. Swanson talk about?
    (A) Small business
    (B) Tourism
    (C) Customer relations
    (D) Book promotion

75. What will happen after the talk?
    (A) Refreshments will be served.
    (B) There will be a book sale.
    (C) Dr. Swanson will sign books.
    (D) Another speaker will talk.

76. When will the next lecture take place?
    (A) Tomorrow evening
    (B) Next Thursday
    (C) In a week
    (D) Next month

77. What product is being advertised?
    (A) Chairs
    (B) Desks
    (C) Phones
    (D) Computers

78. Where would this product be used?
    (A) Home
    (B) Office
    (C) Theater
    (D) Classroom

79. How much is the discount?
    (A) 15%
    (B) 16%
    (C) 20%
    (D) 50%

80. What is the weather like today?
    (A) Sunny
    (B) Cold
    (C) Rainy
    (D) Cloudy

81. What is suggested about the weather?
    (A) It changes frequently.
    (B) It is unusually warm.
    (C) It often rains this time of year.
    (D) It has been dry for a long time.

82. When will the weather change?
    (A) This morning
    (B) This afternoon
    (C) Tonight
    (D) On Sunday

83. Who is the talk for?
  (A) Parents
  (B) Tourists
  (C) Business travelers
  (D) Restaurant owners

84. What does the speaker recommend eating?
  (A) Salty or sweet food
  (B) A big breakfast
  (C) Fast food
  (D) Dessert

85. Why is this recommended?
  (A) It's fast.
  (B) It's cheap.
  (C) It's healthful.
  (D) It's convenient.

86. What should a caller do in an emergency?
  (A) Speak with the office staff
  (B) Call another dentist
  (C) Ask for Dr. Elizabeth Pekar
  (D) Visit the office immediately

87. What time does the office close on Saturday?
  (A) 12:00
  (B) 4:00
  (C) 7:30
  (D) 9:00

88. Why should a caller leave a message?
  (A) To ask about the office schedule
  (B) To order dental supplies
  (C) To speak with the doctor
  (D) To make an appointment

89. Who would be most interested in the advertised event?
  (A) Career counselors
  (B) City employees
  (C) Hotel managers
  (D) Job seekers

90. What costs $10?
  (A) City maps
  (B) A newspaper
  (C) Entry to the event
  (D) A book of advice

91. What should people bring to the event?
  (A) Tickets
  (B) Résumés
  (C) Newspapers
  (D) Applications

92. Where would this announcement be heard?
  (A) On a plane
  (B) On a train
  (C) On a boat
  (D) On a bus

93. What does the speaker suggest about the trip?
  (A) They will arrive late at the destination.
  (B) They will encounter some dangers.
  (C) The traffic will be light.
  (D) The weather will be nice.

94. What can be seen out the window?
  (A) A line of houses
  (B) A nature scene
  (C) A view of the city
  (D) A group of clouds

95. What is the problem?
  (A) Banks are closed.
  (B) Water mains broke.
  (C) Streets are flooded.
  (D) Rush hour traffic is heavy.

96. What are citizens asked to do?
  (A) Stop using their cars
  (B) Call the police
  (C) Clear up the area
  (D) Avoid the downtown area

97. When will the situation improve?
    (A) Today
    (B) Tonight
    (C) By Saturday
    (D) Next month

_____

98. What can guests do at the Lakeside Resort?
    (A) Ride horses
    (B) Play tennis
    (C) Go biking
    (D) Play golf

99. How much does the special weekend package cost?
    (A) $100
    (B) $700
    (C) $1,100
    (D) $1,500

100. When is the resort closed?
    (A) February–March
    (B) April–May
    (C) September–November
    (D) December–January

# READING

In this section of the test, you will have the chance to show how well you understand written English. There are three parts to this section, with special directions for each part.

**YOU WILL HAVE ONE HOUR AND FIFTEEN MINUTES
TO COMPLETE PARTS 5, 6, AND 7 OF THE TEST.**

## Part 5: Incomplete Sentences

> **Directions:** You will see a sentence with a missing word. Four possible answers follow the sentence. Choose the best answer to the question and fill in the corresponding oval on your answer sheet.

101. Mr. Chan considered _____ some money in the new company but decided that it was too much of a risk.
    (A) investing
    (B) inputting
    (C) introducing
    (D) inducting

102. If we had made a point of leaving the house on time, we _____ the plane.
    (A) wouldn't have missed
    (B) wouldn't miss
    (C) won't have missed
    (D) won't miss

103. The completed expense reports must be turned _____ to the accounting office before the end of the month.
    (A) off
    (B) on
    (C) up
    (D) in

104. Samantha worked very hard and put in a lot of overtime hours because she wanted a salary _____.
    (A) improvement
    (B) expansion
    (C) raise
    (D) growth

105. They brought extra chairs into the room _____ they expected a large number of people to attend the meeting.
    (A) although
    (B) since
    (C) however
    (D) nevertheless

106. We have been asked not to walk _____ the lobby today because it's being painted.
    (A) beside
    (B) between
    (C) around
    (D) through

107. Traffic _____ our taxi so much that by the time we got to the train station, the train had already left.
    (A) delayed
    (B) postponed
    (C) inhibited
    (D) annoyed

108. Dr. Smith is a well-respected expert of international renown, and she has _____ experience in her field.
    (A) extend
    (B) extends
    (C) extensive
    (D) extension

109. _____ he graduated from the university, he got a job at a good company.
   (A) Following
   (B) Later
   (C) After
   (D) Next

110. If you don't want to get stuck in a traffic jam, you should avoid _____ during rush hour.
   (A) drive
   (B) driving
   (C) to drive
   (D) driven

111. Once you start using the new software, you will be able to do your work much more _____.
   (A) easy
   (B) easily
   (C) easier
   (D) easement

112. The director asked us to have the report completed _____ 5:00 today at the latest.
   (A) until
   (B) after
   (C) to
   (D) by

113. Since they came to us with such an _____ offer, signing the contract was an easy decision.
   (A) attract
   (B) attracted
   (C) attraction
   (D) attractive

114. Currently they _____ lower prices than any of their competitors.
   (A) are offering
   (B) to offer
   (C) did offer
   (D) offered

115. The government will _____ new price controls on the industry next year.
   (A) impose
   (B) compose
   (C) repose
   (D) suppose

116. They will spend most of next week interviewing candidates before they _____ who to hire.
   (A) decide
   (B) are deciding
   (C) will decide
   (D) decided

117. We had two different experts examine the equipment, but neither of them could _____ the source of the problem.
   (A) presume
   (B) achieve
   (C) release
   (D) detect

118. The new designs submitted for the state highway development project _____ highly confidential.
   (A) is
   (B) are
   (C) do
   (D) was

119. The weekly staff meetings begin at 8:30 sharp, and everyone is expected to arrive _____.
   (A) promptness
   (B) promote
   (C) promptly
   (D) prompt

120. In order to avoid the inconvenience of missed appointments, the office will send you _____ two days before your appointment date.
   (A) an agenda
   (B) a reminder
   (C) an alert
   (D) a memento

121. _____ we've hired several temporary employees, we are still having a hard time getting all the work done on time.
    (A) Because
    (B) Since
    (C) Although
    (D) Despite

122. As soon as Robert's contract _____, he will have to look for another job.
    (A) expires
    (B) expects
    (C) exposes
    (D) expands

123. I _____ eat at expensive restaurants because I don't have a lot of extra money.
    (A) always
    (B) often
    (C) usually
    (D) seldom

124. The storm caused a lot of damage to the building and we had to buy new _____ for many of the windows.
    (A) glass
    (B) glasses
    (C) glassy
    (D) glassine

125. If we _____ more time, we would be able to do a more thorough job.
    (A) would have
    (B) will have
    (C) have
    (D) had

126. You should _____ with your boss before committing yourself to such a time-consuming project.
    (A) will speak
    (B) speak
    (C) speaking
    (D) spoken

127. They are leaving by car early tomorrow morning and expect _____ in Denver before noon.
    (A) arrive
    (B) to arrive
    (C) arriving
    (D) will arrive

128. It is not easy to get a position at that company because they are very _____ about who they hire.
    (A) prospective
    (B) enthusiastic
    (C) selective
    (D) explicit

129. My boss has given me some really excellent _____ about dealing with difficult clients.
    (A) advice
    (B) advise
    (C) advisory
    (D) adverse

130. It is hoped that the extended store hours will _____ more evening shoppers to the mall.
    (A) embrace
    (B) contain
    (C) attract
    (D) acquire

131. I don't recommend buying that model of car because it is _____ cheap nor reliable.
    (A) not
    (B) both
    (C) either
    (D) neither

132. We need to buy a more _____ photocopier because the one we have now is always breaking down.
    (A) unique
    (B) durable
    (C) affordable
    (D) contemporary

133. We are using this space only _____ until the renovations on our new office are completed.
   (A) temporarily
   (B) alternately
   (C) partially
   (D) timely

134. We decided that the office didn't suit our needs because it was not very _____.
   (A) space
   (B) spaced
   (C) spacious
   (D) spaciousness

135. Last month's customer satisfaction survey _____ several areas where we could improve our services.
   (A) combined
   (B) unfolded
   (C) enlarged
   (D) revealed

136. Of all the people who applied for the position, Mr. Sato is the _____.
   (A) qualified
   (B) more qualified
   (C) most qualified
   (D) qualification

137. I think the new rug will look much more attractive _____ that table.
   (A) bottom
   (B) under
   (C) down
   (D) floor

138. We agreed that hiring an outside accountant to _____ the company's financial records would be a good idea.
   (A) audit
   (B) audition
   (C) auditory
   (D) auditorium

139. We will have the building _____ by a construction specialist before we close the deal.
   (A) inspect
   (B) inspected
   (C) inspects
   (D) to inspect

140. Ms. Lee _____ with us only since November but she is already familiar with most of our projects.
   (A) works
   (B) worked
   (C) is working
   (D) has been working

## Part 6: Text Completion

**Directions:** You will see four passages, each with three blanks. Under each blank are four answer options. Choose the word or phrase that best completes the statement.

Questions 141–143 refer to the following passage.

### Your Paycheck

Checks _____ on a biweekly basis by department heads. Arrangements can

141. (A) distribute
    (B) distributed
    (C) are distributed
    (D) are distributing

be made with the Accounting Department to have checks mailed to the employee's home address instead, if desired. Each employee should review the check stub carefully. _____ contains a breakdown of all deductions, including state

142. (A) It
    (B) He
    (C) She
    (D) They

and local taxes, retirement fund contributions, and insurance payments. Any inaccuracies should be reported to the Accounting Department as soon as possible. Every effort will be made to correct any errors in a timely manner. The Human Resources Department conducts monthly workshops that explain in detail how each paycheck deduction is calculated. Anyone interested in _____

143. (A) assisting
    (B) attending
    (C) accessing
    (D) approving

a workshop should contact the Human Resources Department.

To:     All office staff
From:   Rita Johnson
Re:     Employee Appreciation Banquet
Date:   March 15, 20--

It's time to start planning for the _____ Employee Appreciation

144. (A) daily
     (B) monthly
     (C) annual
     (D) biannual

Banquet. I know you all look forward to this every spring. As you know, the winner of the Employee of the Year Award is chosen by the staff. Please get your nominations to me before the end of this month. The winner will be announced on the night of the banquet.

I have received your comments and complaints and have been looking into a new _____ for this year's banquet. We are hoping to hold it at

145. (A) location
     (B) program
     (C) decoration
     (D) entertainment

the Hamilton Hotel. The rooms there are large, and the hotel is conveniently accessible by public transportation.

I have also paid attention to your comments about the food and will work with the hotel chef to develop a menu that provides a variety of choices. Please _____ me know if you have any further suggestions

146. (A) allow
     (B) leave
     (C) tell
     (D) let

regarding this year's banquet.

Dear Customer,

Your Quimby Bank Certificate of Deposit (CD), number 005589403, will mature on January 12 with a value of $5,095.86. If you _____ no action,

147. (A)  take
     (B)  taken
     (C)  taking
     (D)  will take

your CD will automatically renew for another six months and will earn the interest rate in effect on January 12. The following reinvestment options are also available to you.

1. An Authorization to Renew Form is _____ with this letter. If you

   148. (A)  enclose
        (B)  encloses
        (C)  enclosed
        (D)  enclosing

   wish to add funds to your CD, simply complete and return the form to us no later than five business days before the maturity date.

2. Quimby Bank Investment Advisers are available to discuss your financial situation with you. They can help you understand how a CD and other investment options can fit in with your overall financial plan. Call the Quimby Bank Customer Service Office to _____ an appointment.

   149. (A)  make up
        (B)  put in
        (C)  turn on
        (D)  set up

Thank you for banking with Quimby.

Sincerely,

*Ramona Higgins*

Ramona Higgins
Vice President

## City Bus Lines
## Notice of Fare Increases and Schedule Changes

**Fare Increases**

As of May 31 there will be a 25% increase in all bus fares on the City Bus Lines. The normal fare will go up to $2.50 during regular hours and $3.50 during rush hour. Senior citizens possessing a valid City Bus Line Senior Citizen Identification Card will be _____ $1.25 to ride the bus

150. (A) paid
    (B) charged
    (C) reimbursed
    (D) compensated

during regular hours and $2.00 during rush hour.

**Schedule Changes**

The number 42 bus, which _____ leaves the train station every

151. (A) promptly
    (B) usually
    (C) currently
    (D) previously

half hour, will leave the train station every 45 minutes as of May 31.

The number 56 bus, serving the Greensville neighborhood, will no longer run as of May 31.

Any questions or concerns _____ these changes should be directed to

152. (A) refusing
    (B) regaining
    (C) referring
    (D) regarding

the City Bus Lines Office of Public Relations.

## Part 7: Reading Comprehension

**Directions:** You will see single and double reading passages followed by several questions. Each question has four answer choices. Choose the best answer to the question and fill in the corresponding oval on your answer sheet.

Questions 153–154 refer to the following advertisement.

# SALE! SALE! SALE!

**Grover's Office Supply Store announces its annual winter sale!**

**All paper items are on sale, with discounts from 15% to 25% off our already low prices.**

**Sale ends Saturday.**

Join our Frequent Buyer's Club and save even more. Stop by the manager's desk for an application. Once we have your contact information in our computer files, you will receive notices of special sales and discounts available to Frequent Buyer's Club members only.

*Grover's Office Supply Store.*
*Supplying your office with all its paper needs.*

153. Which of the following items are most likely on sale?
(A) Envelopes
(B) Desks
(C) Filing cabinets
(D) Computers

154. How can a customer become a member of the Frequent Buyer's Club?
(A) Visit the store before Saturday
(B) Speak with the manager
(C) Send a request by mail
(D) Contact the club president

## Norwich Office Towers
## Maintenance and Cleaning Department
## Notice of Painting and Repair Work

*The west bank elevators will be closed for routine maintenance and repair starting Monday, August 17. Tenants and visitors are asked to use the east bank elevators or the west or east stairs during this time. The west bank elevators will be back in operation on Monday, August 24, at which time the east bank elevators will be closed. All elevator maintenance and repair work should be completed by the end of the month. Stairs and hallways will be painted during the months of September and October. A complete painting schedule will be posted before September 1.*

155. What will the elevators be closed for?

(A) Painting

(B) Repair

(C) Cleaning

(D) Rescheduling

156. How long will the work on all elevators take?

(A) One week

(B) Two weeks

(C) One month

(D) Two months

Questions 157–158 refer to the following instructions.

1. Remove the back cover, using a small screwdriver to loosen the screw.

2. Remove batteries and replace with two new AAA batteries. Use the + and – signs to position them correctly. Dispose of used batteries properly.

3. Replace the cover and tighten the screw with the screwdriver.

4. Reset the time using the side buttons.

The GMX 200 is guaranteed to keep time accurately for one full year from date of purchase. Should it malfunction in any way during this time period, your money will be refunded in full.

157. What are these instructions for?

(A) Repairing a cover

(B) Setting the date

(C) Getting a refund

(D) Changing the batteries

158. What is the GMX 200?

(A) A calendar

(B) A screwdriver

(C) A clock

(D) A garbage disposal

Questions 159–161 refer to the following article.

The International Experience Project (IEP) provides young professionals with the opportunity to gain work experience abroad. IEP was founded by Margery Wilson four years ago. "When I graduated from college," she explained, "my dream was to work abroad for one or two years, learn another language, and experience living in another country. I knew I wanted to do this, but I didn't know how to find a job abroad. That was six years ago. At that time, there were no businesses that specialized in helping job seekers like myself. So I decided to start my own."

Since its beginnings, IEP has provided jobs for several thousand young professionals in countries all around the world. Knowing a foreign language helps, says Wilson, but it isn't a prerequisite for all jobs. In fact, many of the companies that provide employment for her clients also provide language training. IEP finds jobs for people in all fields, from economics to science to teaching. "All you need is a college degree, an interest in other countries, and an adventurous spirit," says Wilson.

159. What kind of business is IEP?
(A) An employment agency
(B) A travel agency
(C) A language school
(D) A teacher training school

160. How long ago was IEP started?
(A) One year
(B) Two years
(C) Four years
(D) Six years

161. What is a requirement for using IEP's services?
(A) Foreign language skills
(B) Experience living abroad
(C) A science background
(D) A college degree

Questions 162–164 refer to the following advertisement.

---

**For Sale**

Fully equipped convenience store on North Main Street close to downtown. Annual sales of $2,198,456. Sells snacks, groceries, newspapers, gasoline, etc. Ample customer parking behind. Spacious two-bedroom owner's apartment on second floor. Asking $750,000. Includes building and grounds, all equipment, and $85,000 in inventory. No brokers, please. Shown by appointment only. Call Maria at White Horse Realty—243-8674.

---

162. What is above the store?
   (A) A place to live
   (B) A snack bar
   (C) A place for equipment
   (D) An office

163. How much is the store being sold for?
   (A) $85,000
   (B) $750,000
   (C) $835,000
   (D) $2,198,456

164. The word *inventory* in line 4 is closest in meaning to _____.
   (A) rents
   (B) accounts
   (C) furnishings
   (D) merchandise

Questions 165–168 refer to the following article.

The Clear Sound Communications takeover of local telephone service, which was originally welcomed with great optimism, now seems to be heading down the road toward disaster. Ever since Clear Sound bought out the FreeTel Company just under six months ago, it has experienced loss of income, loss of customers, and, perhaps worst of all, the loss of its reputation as a company that delivers on its promises.

When Clear Sound came into the area, it promised that all its telephone customers would have access to high-speed Internet service by the end of the year. Not only has the company failed to deliver on this promise, but customers who are receiving Clear Sound Internet service have expressed great dissatisfaction with it. "The connection goes out all the time. You just can't count on it when you need it," a Clear Sound customer complained at a town meeting last week. Customers have also claimed that repair service is slow and overpriced. Clear Sound, on the other hand, claims that such problems are minor and not widespread. "Every company experiences an adjustment period," explained Richard Whittier, Clear Sound public relations officer. "Before one more year has passed, you can be certain that all operations will be running smoothly and customers will be 100% satisfied," he said.

165. When did Clear Sound take over the FreeTel Company?
   (A) Early last week
   (B) A little less than six months ago
   (C) A little more than six months ago
   (D) Near the end of the year

166. What kind of company is Clear Sound?
   (A) Telephone only
   (B) Telephone and Internet
   (C) Delivery service
   (D) Transportation

167. How do Clear Sound customers currently feel about the company?
   (A) Pleased
   (B) Optimistic
   (C) Unhappy
   (D) Bored

168. The word *minor* in paragraph 2, line 13 is closest in meaning to _____.
   (A) small
   (B) common
   (C) expected
   (D) important

Questions 169–172 refer to the following article.

Green Garden Café recently opened downtown and is offering a variety of handcrafted sandwiches, along with homemade soups and ice cream. All food served at the café is made from pure organic ingredients. Sandwiches are made with 100% whole-grain bread, which is baked in the café's kitchen.

Diners are lining up to try Green Garden's sandwiches for breakfast, lunch, and dinner. "One of our best sellers is our breakfast sandwich," explains café owner Melissa Whitehead. "It's not your typical bacon-and-cheese concoction. Instead, we combine eggs with fresh vegetables and serve it on fresh-baked bread. Customers can't seem to get enough of it."

You won't find the usual ham, turkey, or roast beef sandwich among the café's offered fare. In fact, all the food they serve is 100% vegetarian. Their sandwiches are filled with fresh vegetables, locally made cheese, or a combination of both. "Customers enjoy our soups and ice cream, but what they really come here for are the sandwiches," says Whitehead. "That's our most popular item."

Give the Green Garden Café a try next time you are downtown. You won't be disappointed. The café is open six days a week: Monday–Friday from 9 A.M. to 9 P.M. and Saturday from 11 A.M. to 4 P.M.

169. What is true of the soups at Green Garden?
(A) They are made with organic ingredients.
(B) They are the most popular item.
(C) They come from a factory.
(D) They contain bacon.

170. The word *concoction* in paragraph 2, line 4 is closest in meaning to _____.
(A) flavor
(B) combination
(C) ingredient
(D) meal

171. Which of the following sandwiches can you get at the Green Garden Café?
(A) Cheese and bacon
(B) Ham and turkey
(C) Cheese and vegetable
(D) Roast beef

172. According to Whitehead, why do most customers go to the Green Garden Café?
(A) Because it recently opened
(B) For the fresh-baked bread
(C) Because it's downtown
(D) For the sandwiches

Questions 173–176 refer to the following article.

A job interview is your chance to make a good impression on a potential employer, and the way you dress is an important part of the impression you make. It is not an occasion to show how fashionably you can dress. Rather, it is the time to present yourself as a serious professional who conveys a sense of confidence. The colors you wear help to give this impression. Choose dark colors such as black, navy blue, or charcoal gray, and stay away from warm browns and greens. In addition to a dark color, the suit you wear should have a conservative, neatly tailored cut.

Don't forget to pay attention to details. Your accessories are an important part of your overall look. For men this means wearing ties with simple patterns and quiet colors. Also, men should not wear any type of jewelry, even of the highest quality gold or silver, except for a wristwatch or tie clip. Women should wear plain earrings. Matching necklaces or bracelets are permissible as long as they are not gaudy or loud.

Finally, make sure your feet are dressed as well as the rest of you. Avoid any kind of fancy footwear. Your footwear should look neat and fit you comfortably. You may think that no one will look at your feet, but if you wear super-high heels, garish buckles, or bright colors on your shoes, you are calling attention to them in a way you don't want.

173. Who is this article for?
(A) Tailors
(B) Job hunters
(C) Fashion designers
(D) Clothing retailers

174. Why are dark colors recommended?
(A) They feel warmer.
(B) They are fashionable.
(C) They look professional.
(D) They show off accessories.

175. What kind of accessories are recommended?
(A) Plain and quiet
(B) Loud and gaudy
(C) Gold and silver
(D) Patterned and colorful

176. What kind of shoes should be worn?
(A) Brightly colored
(B) Comfortable
(C) High heeled
(D) Fancy

## INFORMATION FOR VISITORS

### GETTING AROUND

- Two major bus routes, No. 34 and No. 56, pass in front of the building. Bus schedules and bus route maps are available at the front desk.
- The Market Mall subway station is five blocks away. Subway maps and information are available at the subway station.
- Taxis are available at the taxi stand near the main entrance.

### MEALS

- A full-service restaurant and a café are just off the main lobby. Daily breakfast at the café is included with the price of your room.
- Ask at the front desk for a listing of local restaurants.

### SHOPPING

- Market Mall, the city's premier shopping mall, is five blocks away. Whether you are looking for clothes, jewelry, books, gifts, linens, or office supplies, you are sure to find it at the Market Mall.
- The downtown shopping district, famous for its elegant fashion boutiques, is just three miles away. The downtown district is served by the No. 34 bus line.
- A pharmacy and grocery store are just across the street.

### TOURISM

- The city boasts a number of fine museums, including the National History Museum and the Museum of Fine Arts. The Sun Tours Travel Company offers bus tours of historic locations around the city. Please ask at the front desk for more information.
- Hotel guests are entitled to a discount at the City Aquarium. Get your discount coupon at the front desk.

### EMERGENCIES

In case of emergency, dial 01 for the hotel manager.

177. Where would you find this information sheet?
    (A) In a hotel
    (B) In a tourist agency
    (C) In a shopping mall
    (D) In an office building

178. What is five blocks away?
    (A) A pharmacy
    (B) A café
    (C) A subway station
    (D) A taxi stand

179. What can you buy in the shopping district?
    (A) Books
    (B) Office supplies
    (C) Clothes
    (D) Linens

180. Where can you probably buy cough medicine?
    (A) In the shopping district
    (B) Across the street
    (C) In the lobby
    (D) At the Market Mall

**HELP WANTED**

Busy downtown law firm seeks certified paralegal to assist three attorneys. Duties include legal research, assisting with documents, providing legal information to clients, some word processing. Requires minimum of two years' paralegal experience and word processing and database skills. Knowledge of French or Spanish desirable. Send resume and names of three references before June 1 to Martha Lee, P.O. Box 7, Williamsburg, MA 01234. No phone calls, please. We will contact you to make an appointment for an interview.

May 8, 20--

Martha Lee
P.O. Box 7
Williamsburg, MA 01234

Dear Ms. Lee,

I am writing in response to your ad in yesterday's paper for a certified paralegal. I have recently completed a paralegal training course and received my certificate last March. I am looking for a job in a small downtown firm. I am proficient with the commonly used word processing and database programs. I have a working knowledge of French and will be taking a Spanish course starting June 15. My job experience includes three years as an office assistant at an architectural firm. I have not worked for the past year, as I was busy with my paralegal training course.

I would really enjoy the opportunity to work at a firm such as yours. I am enclosing my resume and would be happy to provide you with letters of reference. I look forward to meeting with you soon.

Sincerely,

James Jones

181. When did the job ad appear in the newspaper?
    (A) May 7
    (B) May 8
    (C) June 1
    (D) June 15

182. What is one of the duties of the advertised job?
    (A) Interviewing clients
    (B) Working on legal documents
    (C) Answering phone calls
    (D) Making appointments

183. What job requirement does James Jones NOT meet?
    (A) Paralegal certificate
    (B) Knowledge of a foreign language
    (C) Computer software skills
    (D) Paralegal work experience

184. Where did James Jones work before?
    (A) At a Spanish school
    (B) At a law office
    (C) At an architectural firm
    (D) At a French company

185. What did James Jones include with his letter?
    (A) His paralegal course diploma
    (B) His résumé
    (C) His French certificate
    (D) His letters of reference

## Computer Training Center

### CLASS SCHEDULE

**Word Processing Basics**
Section 1: M, W 1–3
Section 2: T, Th 6–8

**Advanced Word Processing**
Section 1: W, F 9–12

**Database Basics**
Section 1: M, W 4–6
Section 2: Saturday, 9–1

**Advanced Database**
Section 1: M, W 1–3

### INFORMATION FOR STUDENTS

- You may choose either section 1 or section 2 of any course.
- All courses last three months.
- Course fees are $300 for courses meeting four hours a week, and $500 for courses meeting six hours a week. Materials fees are $25 for word processing classes and $45 for database classes.
- Register online by visiting our website, www.computertrainingcenter.com, or call us at 456-8874.

---

To: marvinpeabody@nzinc.com
From: samsilliman@nzinc.com
Sent: 21 September 20--, 9:35
Subject: computer training

Marvin,

I am attaching the latest schedule from the Computer Training Center. As we have discussed in person, your computer skills are not quite up to par and you would benefit from taking one of these courses. We also discussed the fact that your first-year employee probationary status is still in effect and that you are required to take some training courses during this time. Please sign up for one of these courses as soon as possible. I would encourage you to choose a beginning word processing class, as your skills in that area are woefully lacking. You have a good knowledge of database software, though you could benefit from an advanced-level class if that is what interests you most. The choice, of course, is up to you, but I recommend word processing. In choosing your class schedule, please remember that you must be present at our weekly staff meetings (Wednesday afternoons at 2:00). As soon as you have decided on a course and schedule, please contact Elizabeth Mortimer in the Human Resources Department and she will take care of the registration process for you. We at NZ, Inc. will, of course, take care of all the fees. All you have to do is attend the classes. Please e-mail me as soon as you are registered for a course.
Sam Silliman

186. Which class will Marvin probably take?
    (A) Word Processing Basics, Section 1
    (B) Word Processing Basics, Section 2
    (C) Database Basics, Section 2
    (D) Advanced Database, Section 1

187. How will Marvin register for the class?
    (A) By visiting the training center website
    (B) By calling the training center
    (C) By talking with the human resources officer
    (D) By e-mailing Sam Silliman

188. How much will Marvin pay for his course?
    (A) $0
    (B) $300
    (C) $325
    (D) $545

189. Who is Sam Silliman?
    (A) The Computer Training Center manager
    (B) Elizabeth Mortimer's employee
    (C) A computer instructor
    (D) Marvin's supervisor

190. How long has Marvin been working at NZ, Inc.?
    (A) Exactly three months
    (B) Less than one year
    (C) A little more than a year
    (D) For several years

We are starting an Internship Program in Information Technology. We will offer 10 internships for undergraduate and graduate students as well as for recent graduates who have finished their degrees within the last 12 months. All of the interns will receive an hourly salary plus a bonus at the end of the internship.

The first internships will begin on June 1. They will last for a minimum of two months.

Every intern will work on projects with a supervisor. These projects include Networking, Business Software, and Computer Maintenance—Crash Prevention. Applicants who speak a second language are encouraged to apply and will be assigned to our special Global Communications project.

First preference will be given to employees' children and relatives. The application deadline is April 15. Write to interns@excel.com to learn more about the internships and to request an application.

| From: | Jon Samuels [Jon@gomail.com] |
|---|---|
| To: | Excel Company [interns@excel.com] |
| Sent: | Friday, April 1, 20--   1:29 P.M. |
| Subject: | Application for Internship Program |

I would like to learn more about the Internship Program in Information Technology. My mother, who works as an electrical engineer at your company, told me about this opportunity.

   I am a junior at National University. Although my major is business administration, I am also interested in information technology and am considering studying this subject in graduate school. Can business majors apply for the internship?

   I will be leaving for a trip to Korea in May to visit relatives and brush up on my second language, Korean. I won't return from my trip until four days after the first internships begin. Could I start my internship then? I can work until the beginning of September.

   If I qualify for the internship, please send me an application as soon as possible, as well as any other information I may need.

Thank you.

191. What qualification does Jon have that will give him preference over other applicants?
    (A) His mother works for the company.
    (B) He is majoring in business administration.
    (C) He speaks Korean.
    (D) He took classes in electrical engineering.

192. How long does Jon have to complete his application?
    (A) 2 weeks
    (B) 3 weeks
    (C) 2 months
    (D) 12 months

193. What does Jon want to study in graduate school?
    (A) Business administration
    (B) Information technology
    (C) Communications
    (D) Korean language

194. What project will Jon probably be assigned to work on?
    (A) Networking
    (B) Business Software
    (C) Computer Maintenance
    (D) Global Communications

195. When does Jon want to start his internship?
    (A) May 1
    (B) June 1
    (C) June 5
    (D) September 4

Questions 196–200 refer to the following fax and price sheet.

**FAX TRANSMISSION   FAX TRANSMISSION · FAX TRANSMISSION**

Linton Systems, Inc.
154 North Washington Street
Bradford, NY

To:      Cosmo Catering Company
         17 River Road
         Bradford, NY

From:    Elaine Conway
         Office Manager

Date:    August 30

We are planning an all-day conference for October 15 and will need catering services for lunch. We expect around 40–45 people to attend. Some will be vegetarian, but we will also want some meat dishes available. We would need you to provide dishes and silverware, but we will use our own tables and chairs. Please fax menus, prices, and ordering information. Thank you.

**Cosmo Catering Company
Menu and Price List**

**Lunch Buffets**

| Option 1 | Option 2 | Option 3 |
|---|---|---|
| 1 chicken entrée | 1 chicken entrée | 2 vegetarian entrées |
| 1 meat entrée | 1 meat entrée | 1 meat entrée |
| salad | 1 vegetarian entrée | salad |
| 2 desserts | salad | 2 desserts |
|  | 3 desserts |  |

*Prices*

Up to 25 people— Option 1: $250
                 Option 2: $350
                 Option 3: $200

Up to 50 people— Option 1: $500
                 Option 2: $700
                 Option 3: $400

Up to 100 people— Option 1: $1,000
                  Option 2: $1,400
                  Option 3: $800

*Above prices include all dishes and silverware, tablecloths and napkins (white only), and setup and takedown.
*Tables and chairs are available for $2 per person.
Orders must be accompanied by a 25% deposit, local checks only. The remainder is due on the date of service.
Credit cards and cash are not accepted.

*Discounts*
• All orders placed a month in advance will receive a 10% discount.
• Use your own dishes and silverware and receive a 15% discount.

196. What would be the cost of the Option 2
buffet for 100 people, with tables and
chairs?
(A) $800
(B) $1,000
(C) $1,400
(D) $1,600

197. Which lunch buffets would meet Elaine
Conway's needs?
(A) Options 1 and 2
(B) Options 2 and 3
(C) Options 1, 2, and 3
(D) Option 2 only

198. What does Elaine Conway have to do to
get a 10% discount?
(A) Pay with cash
(B) Rent tables and chairs
(C) Use her own silverware
(D) Order before September 15

199. What does she have to send with her
order?
(A) Her credit card number
(B) Choice of tablecloth color
(C) A check for the deposit
(D) A dessert order

200. If she chooses Option 2, how much
would she pay, without discounts?
(A) $350
(B) $700
(C) $790
(D) $1,400

## LISTENING COMPREHENSION

### Part 1: Photographs

| | | |
|---|---|---|
| 1. **B** | 4. **D** | 7. **B** | 9. **D** |
| 2. **C** | 5. **A** | 8. **C** | 10. **D** |
| 3. **A** | 6. **C** | | |

### Part 2: Question-Response

| | | | |
|---|---|---|---|
| 11. **A** | 19. **C** | 27. **C** | 35. **A** |
| 12. **C** | 20. **A** | 28. **B** | 36. **C** |
| 13. **B** | 21. **B** | 29. **B** | 37. **A** |
| 14. **B** | 22. **B** | 30. **A** | 38. **B** |
| 15. **C** | 23. **C** | 31. **C** | 39. **B** |
| 16. **A** | 24. **B** | 32. **B** | 40. **B** |
| 17. **C** | 25. **A** | 33. **B** | |
| 18. **A** | 26. **A** | 34. **A** | |

### Part 3: Conversations

| | | | |
|---|---|---|---|
| 41. **D** | 49. **C** | 57. **A** | 65. **D** |
| 42. **B** | 50. **A** | 58. **C** | 66. **B** |
| 43. **C** | 51. **D** | 59. **D** | 67. **A** |
| 44. **B** | 52. **B** | 60. **B** | 68. **B** |
| 45. **A** | 53. **C** | 61. **C** | 69. **D** |
| 46. **B** | 54. **A** | 62. **C** | 70. **C** |
| 47. **A** | 55. **B** | 63. **A** | |
| 48. **D** | 56. **B** | 64. **B** | |

### Part 4: Talks

| | | | |
|---|---|---|---|
| 71. **D** | 79. **A** | 87. **A** | 95. **C** |
| 72. **C** | 80. **A** | 88. **C** | 96. **D** |
| 73. **C** | 81. **D** | 89. **D** | 97. **C** |
| 74. **A** | 82. **D** | 90. **C** | 98. **B** |
| 75. **B** | 83. **C** | 91. **B** | 99. **B** |
| 76. **D** | 84. **B** | 92. **A** | 100. **A** |
| 77. **A** | 85. **C** | 93. **D** | |
| 78. **B** | 86. **B** | 94. **B** | |

# ANSWER KEY
## Practice Exam 2

**READING**

**Part 5: Incomplete Sentences**

| | | | |
|---|---|---|---|
| 101. **A** | 111. **B** | 121. **C** | 131. **D** |
| 102. **A** | 112. **D** | 122. **A** | 132. **B** |
| 103. **D** | 113. **D** | 123. **D** | 133. **A** |
| 104. **C** | 114. **A** | 124. **A** | 134. **C** |
| 105. **B** | 115. **A** | 125. **D** | 135. **D** |
| 106. **D** | 116. **A** | 126. **B** | 136. **C** |
| 107. **A** | 117. **D** | 127. **B** | 137. **B** |
| 108. **C** | 118. **B** | 128. **C** | 138. **A** |
| 109. **C** | 119. **C** | 129. **A** | 139. **B** |
| 110. **B** | 120. **B** | 130. **C** | 140. **D** |

**Part 6: Text Completion**

| | | | |
|---|---|---|---|
| 141. **C** | 144. **C** | 147. **A** | 150. **B** |
| 142. **A** | 145. **A** | 148. **C** | 151. **C** |
| 143. **B** | 146. **D** | 149. **D** | 152. **D** |

**Part 7: Reading Comprehension**

| | | | |
|---|---|---|---|
| 153. **A** | 165. **B** | 177. **A** | 189. **D** |
| 154. **B** | 166. **B** | 178. **C** | 190. **B** |
| 155. **B** | 167. **C** | 179. **C** | 191. **A** |
| 156. **B** | 168. **A** | 180. **B** | 192. **A** |
| 157. **D** | 169. **A** | 181. **A** | 193. **B** |
| 158. **C** | 170. **B** | 182. **B** | 194. **D** |
| 159. **A** | 171. **C** | 183. **D** | 195. **C** |
| 160. **C** | 172. **D** | 184. **C** | 196. **D** |
| 161. **D** | 173. **B** | 185. **B** | 197. **B** |
| 162. **A** | 174. **C** | 186. **B** | 198. **D** |
| 163. **B** | 175. **A** | 187. **C** | 199. **C** |
| 164. **D** | 176. **B** | 188. **A** | 200. **B** |

# TEST SCORE CONVERSION TABLE

Count your correct responses. Match the number of correct responses with the corresponding score from the Test Score Conversion Table (below). Add the two scores together. This is your Total Estimated Test Score. As you practice taking the TOEIC model tests, your scores should improve. Keep track of your Total Estimated Test Scores.

| # Correct | Listening Score | Reading Score | # Correct | Listening Score | Reading Score | # Correct | Listening Score | Reading Score | # Correct | Listening Score | Reading Score |
|---|---|---|---|---|---|---|---|---|---|---|---|
| 0 | 5 | 5 | 26 | 110 | 65 | 51 | 255 | 220 | 76 | 410 | 370 |
| 1 | 5 | 5 | 27 | 115 | 70 | 52 | 260 | 225 | 77 | 420 | 380 |
| 2 | 5 | 5 | 28 | 120 | 80 | 53 | 270 | 230 | 78 | 425 | 385 |
| 3 | 5 | 5 | 29 | 125 | 85 | 54 | 275 | 235 | 79 | 430 | 390 |
| 4 | 5 | 5 | 30 | 130 | 90 | 55 | 280 | 240 | 80 | 440 | 395 |
| 5 | 5 | 5 | 31 | 135 | 95 | 56 | 290 | 250 | 81 | 445 | 400 |
| 6 | 5 | 5 | 32 | 140 | 100 | 57 | 295 | 255 | 82 | 450 | 405 |
| 7 | 10 | 5 | 33 | 145 | 110 | 58 | 300 | 260 | 83 | 460 | 410 |
| 8 | 15 | 5 | 34 | 150 | 115 | 59 | 310 | 265 | 84 | 465 | 415 |
| 9 | 20 | 5 | 35 | 160 | 120 | 60 | 315 | 270 | 85 | 470 | 420 |
| 10 | 25 | 5 | 36 | 165 | 125 | 61 | 320 | 280 | 86 | 475 | 425 |
| 11 | 30 | 5 | 37 | 170 | 130 | 62 | 325 | 285 | 87 | 480 | 430 |
| 12 | 35 | 5 | 38 | 175 | 140 | 63 | 330 | 290 | 88 | 485 | 435 |
| 13 | 40 | 5 | 39 | 180 | 145 | 64 | 340 | 300 | 89 | 490 | 445 |
| 14 | 45 | 5 | 40 | 185 | 150 | 65 | 345 | 305 | 90 | 495 | 450 |
| 15 | 50 | 5 | 41 | 190 | 160 | 66 | 350 | 310 | 91 | 495 | 455 |
| 16 | 55 | 10 | 42 | 195 | 165 | 67 | 360 | 320 | 92 | 495 | 465 |
| 17 | 60 | 15 | 43 | 200 | 170 | 68 | 365 | 325 | 93 | 495 | 470 |
| 18 | 65 | 20 | 44 | 210 | 175 | 69 | 370 | 330 | 94 | 495 | 480 |
| 19 | 70 | 25 | 45 | 215 | 180 | 70 | 380 | 335 | 95 | 495 | 485 |
| 20 | 75 | 30 | 46 | 220 | 190 | 71 | 385 | 340 | 96 | 495 | 490 |
| 21 | 80 | 35 | 47 | 230 | 195 | 72 | 390 | 350 | 97 | 495 | 495 |
| 22 | 85 | 40 | 48 | 240 | 200 | 73 | 395 | 355 | 98 | 495 | 495 |
| 23 | 90 | 45 | 49 | 245 | 210 | 74 | 400 | 360 | 99 | 495 | 495 |
| 24 | 95 | 50 | 50 | 250 | 215 | 75 | 405 | 365 | 100 | 495 | 495 |
| 25 | 100 | 60 | | | | | | | | | |

Number of Correct Listening Responses _____ = Listening Score _____

Number of Correct Reading Responses _____ = Reading Score _____

Total Estimated Test Score _____

# ANSWERS EXPLAINED

## Listening Comprehension

### PART 1: PHOTOGRAPHS

1. **(B)** This is a street scene on a snowy day. Choice (A) correctly identifies the parked car but not its location. Choice (C) associates *driving* with *car* and confuses similar sounds *snow* and *slow*. Choice (D) misidentifies what is *white*—it is *snow*, not *flowers*.

2. **(C)** A man talks about information on a blackboard while an audience listens—a professor lecturing his class. Choice (A) identifies an object in the photo—lights—but there is no janitor. Choice (B) refers to the students' books that are shown in the photo. Choice (D) refers to the blackboard.

3. **(A)** A ship holding freight is sitting in port. Choice (B) uses associated words *passenger* and *deck*. Choice (C) is incorrect because the boat is in port, not at sea. Choice (D) uses the associated word *captain*.

4. **(D)** A scientist is examining liquid in a test tube. Choice (A) refers to the liquid in the test tube, but no one is drinking it. Choice (B) refers to the scientist's mask, but she is wearing it, not removing it. Choice (C) refers to the scientist's gloves, which she is wearing, not washing.

5. **(A)** Two laptops are sitting open on a coffee table. Choice (B) refers to the curtains, which are open, not closed. Choice (C) is incorrect because it is the woman, not the man, who has a magazine. Choice (D) is incorrect because the woman is looking at her magazine, not at the man.

6. **(C)** A woman in a grocery store is picking out apples, so we can assume she plans to buy them. Choice (A) confuses similar-sounding words *fruit* and *suit*. Choice (B) refers to the apples, but they are in a store, not on a tree. Choice (D) misidentifies the action—she is *selecting* fruit not *cleaning* it.

7. **(B)** Two men shake hands as two women look on. Choice (A) confuses *drinking glasses* with *eyeglasses*, which one of the men is wearing. Choice (C) confuses similar-sounding words *smiling* and *filing*. Choice (D) refers to the stairs in the background, but no one is climbing them.

8. **(C)** Two people are looking at paintings hanging on a museum wall. Choice (A) is incorrect because they are already inside the museum. Choice (B) confuses the meaning of the word *pictures* (paintings or photos). Choice (D) refers to the bench in the photo, but no one is sitting on it.

9. **(D)** Two houses are separated by a fence. Choice (A) is incorrect because there are no people in the photo painting the fence. Choice (B) is incorrect because the fence is shorter, not taller, than the houses. Choice (C) is incorrect because there are no bushes in the photo.

10. **(D)** A tired businessman is lying on a bed. Choice (A) refers to the jacket that is lying across his arm and that he has probably just taken off. Choice (B) refers to the briefcase he is holding in his hand but not opening. Choice (C) confuses similar-sounding words *lying on* and *trying on*.

### PART 2: QUESTION-RESPONSE

11. **(A)** This is the common, polite response when meeting someone. Choices (B) and (C) confuse the meaning of the word *meeting*.

12. **(C)** This answers the yes/no question about where Mr. Kim works. Choice (A) repeats the word *here*. Choice (B) associates *worker* with *work*.

13. **(B)** This explains the reason for not opening the door. Choice (A) confuses similar-sounding words *door* and *more*. Choice (C) confuses similar-sounding words *door* and *floor*.

14. **(B)** This answers the question about possession. Choice (A) repeats the word *car*. Choice (C) associates *car* with *drive*.

15. **(C)** This answers the question about time. Choice (A) uses the wrong pronoun (*she* instead of *they*) and incorrectly uses future tense to answer a past tense question. Choice (B) confuses similar-sounding words *arrive* and *five*.

16. **(A)** This explains what the speaker forgot. Choice (B) confuses similar-sounding words *forget* and *get* and associates *something* with *anything*. Choice (C) confuses similar-sounding words *forget* and *get* and repeats the word *something*.

17. **(C)** This answers the question *Where?* Choice (A) repeats the word *stop*. Choice (B) associates *bus* with *ride*.

18. **(A)** This answers the question *How often?* Choice (B) would answer the question *Where?* Choice (C) confuses similar-sounding words *meeting* and *reading*.

19. **(C)** This is the information the question asks for—an address. Choice (A) associates *moved to a new house* with *address*, but doesn't answer the question. Choice (B) confuses similar-sounding words *address* and *dress*.

20. **(A)** This answers the question about phone calls. Choice (B) confuses similar-sounding words *call* and *cold* and *out* and *outside*. Choice (C) repeats the word *call* and incorrectly uses future tense to answer a past tense question.

21. **(B)** A steak and some salad are what the speaker wants to eat for dinner. Choice (A) associates *dinner* with cook. Choice (C) confuses similar-sounding words *dinner* and *thinner*.

22. **(B)** The word *ten* answers the question *How many?* Choice (A) associates *books* with *read*. Choice (C) confuses similar-sounding words *books* and *looks*.

23. **(C)** *August* answers the question *When?* Choice (A) would answer the question *Where?* Choice (B) confuses similar-sounding words *vacation* and *station*.

24. **(B)** This explains the reason for not coming to lunch. Choice (A) confuses similar-sounding words *lunch* and *punch*. Choice (C) associates *lunch* with *restaurant*.

25. **(A)** Paper and envelopes are what the speaker needs from the store. Choice (B) confuses similar-sounding words *store* and *four*. Choice (C) associates *store* with *shopping*.

26. **(A)** The phrase *in my desk drawer* answers the question *Where?* Choice (B) associates *pens* with *ink*. Choice (C) repeats the word *pen*.

27. **(C)** The mention of rain prompts the second speaker to suggest an umbrella. Choice (A) confuses similar-sounding words *might* and *night* and repeats the word *soon*. Choice (B) confuses similar-sounding words *rain* and *train* and *soon* and *noon*.

28. **(B)** This describes the coat. Choice (A) repeats the word *coat*. Choice (C) explains the reason for having a coat but doesn't answer the question.

29. **(B)** This is a logical response to a complaint about a warm room. Choice (A) confuses similar-sounding words *warm* and *warn*. Choice (C) confuses the meaning of the word *room*.

30. **(A)** This tells where, or how close, the subway station is. Choice (B) confuses similar-sounding words *close* and *clothes*. Choice (C) repeats the word *station*.

31. **(C)** This answers the question *Where?* Choice (A) confuses *newspaper* with the similar-sounding words *new paper*. Choice (B) associates *newspaper* with *read*.

32. **(B)** *Tennis* answers the question about a favorite sport. Choice (A) confuses similar-sounding words *sport* and *port*. Choice (C) confuses similar-sounding words *favorite* and *favor*.

33. **(B)** The first speaker liked the movie and the second speaker agrees. Choice (A) confuses the related words *interesting* and *interested* and repeats the word *movies*. Choice (C) confuses similar-sounding words *movie* and *moving*.

34. **(A)** *On your desk* answers the question *Where?* Choice (B) associates *package* with *mail*. Choice (C) confuses similar-sounding words *package* and *packed*.

35. **(A)** This explains why the speaker wasn't at the workshop. Choice (B) confuses the compound word *workshop* with the two separate words *work* and *shop*. Choice (C) repeats the word *Friday*.

36. **(C)** *The whole staff* answers the question *Who?* Choice (A) confuses similar-sounding words *meeting* and *greeting*. Choice (B) repeats the word *meeting*.

37. **(A)** This answer responds to the statement about looking hungry by explaining the reason for being hungry (*I didn't have breakfast . . .*). Choice (B) confuses similar-sounding words *hungry* and *hurry*. Choice (C) confuses the meaning of the word *look*.

38. **(B)** This answers the question *Where?* Choice (A) confuses similar-sounding words *live* and *leave*. Choice (C) confuses similar-sounding words *live* and *give*.

39. **(B)** *This afternoon* answers the question *When?* Choice (A) would answer the question *How many?* Choice (C) repeats the words *copies*.

40. **(B)** The second speaker doesn't need more paper because there is already enough. Choice (A) repeats the word *paper*. Choice (C) associates *paper* with *write*.

## PART 3: CONVERSATIONS

41. **(D)** The man says, *I'll probably be about 15 minutes late.* Choice (A) confuses similar-sounding words *late* and *wait*. Choice (B) repeats the word *call*. Choice (C) is the opposite of what he says—*I can be there.*

42. **(B)** The woman says she wants to explain the situation, which is the delayed pay-checks. Choice (A) uses the word *check* out of context and confuses *accounts* with *accounting department*. Choice (C) repeats the word *pay*. Choice (D) repeats the phrase *next week*.

43. **(C)** The man says, *this has happened before*, and, *I can't pretend not to be annoyed about it*, meaning he is bothered by the situation. Choice (A) is plausible but not mentioned. Choice (B) confuses similar-sounding words *happen* and *happy*. Choice (D) confuses similar-sounding words *bad* and *mad*.

44. **(B)** The woman asks how long the flight will last, so she has to be on an airplane. Choice (A) associates restaurant with food. Choices (C) and (D) are both associated with *ticket*.

45. **(A)** The man says that it is a *cloudless*, meaning *clear*, day. Choice (B) confuses *cloudless* with *cloudy*. Choice (C) confuses *window* with the similar-sounding word *windy*. Choice (D) confuses *know* with the similar-sounding word *snow*.

46. **(B)** The man says, *We'll begin food service in about half an hour.* Choice (A) repeats the word *movie*. Choice (C) repeats the word *ticket*. Choice (D) repeats the word *schedule*.

47. **(A)** The woman asks the man to help her move a desk. Choice (B) repeats the word *window*. Choice (C) confuses *room* with the similar-sounding word *broom*. Choice (D) confuses *table* with the similar-sounding word *able*.

48. **(D)** The man explains that he hurt his back and can't lift heavy things. Choice (A) is where Samantha is. Choice (B) confuses *wait* with the similar-sounding word *late*. Choice (C) repeats the word *work*.

49. **(C)** The man suggests asking Samantha for help, and the woman agrees. Choices (A) and (B) are plausible but not mentioned. Choice (D) is incorrect because she will wait for Samantha, not the man, to be available.

50. **(A)** This is what the man says he is looking for and will take. Choices (B) and (C) are things the woman offers to sell him. Choice (D) is what the woman will put the gloves in.

51. **(D)** This is the color the man says he will take. Choice (A) confuses similar-sounding words *said* and *red*. Choice (B) confuses similar-sounding words *right* and *white*. Choice (C) confuses similar-sounding words *down* and *brown*.

52. **(B)** This is the price the woman gives. Choices (A), (C), and (D) all sound similar to the correct answer.

53. **(C)** He wants them for the conference tomorrow morning. Choice (A) confuses similar-sounding words *soon* and *noon*. Choice (B) repeats the word *morning*. Choice (D) confuses similar-sounding words *today* and *Tuesday*.

54. **(A)** The woman says that it is a busy day and she has several other jobs to do. Choice (B) repeats the phrase *too many*. Choice (C) confuses similar-sounding words *collated* and *late*. Choice (D) confuses related words *stapled* and *stapler*.

55. **(B)** The man asks if the copies can be ready by *tomorrow morning* and the woman agrees to do that. Choice (A) is plausible but not mentioned. Choice (C) refers to the

*three jobs ahead of you* mentioned by the woman, but she doesn't say she will put them aside. Choice (D) repeats the word *conference*.

56. **(B)** This is what the woman says she wants to do. Choice (A) confuses homonyms *by* and *buy*. Choice (C) is what Mr. Lee is doing. Choice (D) is what the man asks the woman about.

57. **(A)** The man says that Mr. Lee is out of town. Choice (B) confuses *out of town* with *downtown*. Choice (C) confuses similar-sounding words *phone* and *home*. Choice (D) repeats the word *office*.

58. **(C)** The man asks the woman to leave her name and phone number so that Mr. Lee can call her when he returns. Choice (A) repeats the phrase *come by*. Choice (B) mentions when Mr. Lee will return, *next week*, but the man suggests that Mr. Lee, not the woman, will call. Choice (D) confuses the meaning of the word *leave*, and also repeats the word *office*.

59. **(D)** The man is afraid he'll be late for his doctor's appointment downtown. Choice (A) is not mentioned. Choice (B) is where the woman will go later. Choice (C) confuses similar-sounding words *rain* and *train*.

60. **(B)** This is where the woman says her car is. Choice (A) is where the man thinks the car is. Choice (C) confuses the meaning of the word *park*. Choice (D) is where the man has to go.

61. **(C)** The woman says, *Drive carefully. It looks like it might rain.* Choice (A) is what the man is already worried about. Choice (B) associates *car* with *traffic*. Choice (D) is a plausible reason for the *drive carefully* warning but is not mentioned.

62. **(C)** Ms. Jones wanted to avoid the bad traffic caused by the rain. Choice (A) confuses similar-sounding words *rain* and *train*. Choice (B) refers to the meeting she was supposed to have with the woman this afternoon. Choice (D) refers to the report that was to be discussed at the meeting.

63. **(A)** The woman is surprised that Ms. Jones has left the office because *She knew we had a meeting this afternoon.* Choice (B) refers to the fact that the woman plans to call Ms. Jones, but she hasn't done so yet, we don't know whether or not she will answer the phone. Choice (C) is not likely because the meeting was for working on the report. Choice (D) is incorrect because the speakers are in the office.

64. **(B)** Ms. Jones left the office early because of the rain. Choice (A) confuses similar-sounding words *not* and *hot*. Choice (C) confuses similar-sounding words *know* and *snow*. Choice (D) confuses similar-sounding words *call* and *cold*.

65. **(D)** This is what the woman says she mailed. Choice (A) confuses similar-sounding words *books* and *look*. Choice (B) repeats the word *report* out of context. Choice (C) confuses *photographs* with *photocopies*.

66. **(B)** The man says, . . . *today's only Thursday. Let's just wait another day* . . . . Choice (A) is confused with *three days ago*, when the woman mailed the photos. Choice (C) is the day of the conversation. Choice (D) is the day the woman mailed the photos.

67. **(A)** This is what the woman says she thinks she should do. Choices (B) and (D) are what the man suggests. Choice (C) repeats the word *copies*.

68. **(B)** The woman asks the man to play tennis at the park. Choice (A) is what the man did in the morning. Choices (C) and (D) are what the man and woman will do tonight, but these are plans already in place and not what she is inviting him to do now.

69. **(D)** The man says that he is *wiped out,* or very tired. Choice (A) confuses similar-sounding words *banquet* and *bank.* Choice (B) refers to the tickets the man bought for the banquet. Choice (C) confuses similar-sounding words *better* and *letter.*

70. **(C)** The man will attend the banquet at the hotel. Choice (A) is where the man played golf. Choice (B) is where the woman will play tennis. Choice (D) confuses similar-sounding words *rest* and *restaurant.*

## PART 4: TALKS

71. **(D)** Technicians are available *24 hours a day, seven days a week,* so a caller can speak with one any time he likes. Choices (A), (B), and (C) all sound similar to *24 hours a day, seven days a week.*

72. **(C)** The recording says to press 2 to make an appointment. Choice (A) is confused with *seven days a week,* which is when the business is open. Choice (B) is confused with *stay on the line,* which is the way to speak with Tech Support. Choice (D) repeats the word *office.*

73. **(C)** The recording says to press 3 for billing questions. Choice (A) is what happens if the caller stays on the line. Choice (B) is what happens if the caller presses 1. Choice (D) is what happens if the caller presses zero.

74. **(A)** Dr. Swanson will talk about small business (the topic of her book). Choice (B) is confused with the book promotion tour. Choice (C) is the topic of next month's lecture. Choice (D) is confused with the book promotion tour.

75. **(B)** The speaker says that books *will be available for sale.* Choice (A) is what the speaker says will not happen. Choice (C) uses the word *sign* out of context. Choice (D) repeats the words *speaker* and *talk.*

76. **(D)** The speaker says, *Don't miss next month's lecture.* Choice (A) repeats the word *evening.* Choice (B) repeats the word *Thursday.* Choice (C) is not mentioned.

77. **(A)** The EZ Sit chair is the product advertised. Choices (B), (C), and (D) repeat other words mentioned, but they are not the product advertised for sale.

78. **(B)** This product is advertised to be used in an office. Choice (A) confuses *phone* with the similar-sounding word *home.* Choice (C) associates *show* with *theater* by confusing the meaning of the word *show* (*showroom* in the advertisement). Choice (D) confuses *roomy* with *classroom.*

79. **(A)** This is the discount mentioned. Choices (B) and (D) sound similar to the correct answer. Choice (C) is confused with the date the discount offer ends—*May 20th.*

80. **(A)** The announcer says that there will be *plenty of sunshine.* Choice (B) refers to the cold front coming in on the weekend. Choices (C) and (D) are how the weather will be on Sunday.

81. **(D)** The announcer mentions a *drought*, or period of dry weather, and later says, *Don't despair. Change is in the air,* implying that the dry period has gone on long enough for people to be eager for a change. Choice (A) repeats the word *change*. Choice (B) is associated with the mention of the temperature, but there is no implication that it is unusual. Choice (C) repeats *rain*, the weather prediction for Sunday.

82. **(D)** The announcer predicts rain on Sunday. Choices (A) and (B) repeat words used in the talk. Choice (C) is confused with *overnight*.

83. **(C)** The speaker addresses the talk to people who *travel frequently for business*. Choice (A) mentions people who are often concerned about nutrition, the theme of the talk. Choice (B) associates travel with tourists. Choice (D) repeats the word *restaurants*.

84. **(B)** The speaker says, to *make sure to eat a big breakfast*. Choices (A), (C), and (D) are foods that the speaker implies are not healthful.

85. **(C)** A big breakfast is the speaker's solution to the problem of maintaining a healthful diet while traveling. Choices (A), (B), and (D) are reasons one might choose less healthful foods.

86. **(B)** The caller is instructed to dial another number to contact the on-call dentist. Choice (A) is what the caller can do by leaving a message. Choice (C) mentions the name of the dentist whose office this is. Choice (D) repeats different words from the recording.

87. **(A)** The office is open from 9:00 A.M. until noon on Saturday. Choice (B) is the time it closes on weekdays. Choice (C) is the time it opens on weekdays. Choice (D) is the time it opens on Saturdays.

88. **(C)** The speaker says, *If you would like to speak with the doctor . . . please leave a message.* Choice (A) doesn't make sense because the speaker tells the schedule. Choice (B) repeats the word *dental*, but the speaker never mentions supplies. Choice (D) can be done by calling back during office hours.

89. **(D)** The event is a job fair where job seekers can find out about job opportunities and pass out their résumés. Choice (A) repeats the word *career*. Choice (B) repeats the word *city*. Choice (C) repeats the word *hotel*.

90. **(C)** The speaker says, *Admission is just ten dollars.* Choice (A) repeats the word *city*, which is part of the name of the event (Center City Job Fair). Choice (B) repeats the word *newspaper*. Choice (D) is associated with the topics of the seminars, which are all about advice for job seekers.

91. **(B)** Attendees are advised to bring copies of their résumé. Choice (A) is available at the door. Choice (C) is where the event was mentioned. Choice (D) is available at the event.

92. **(A)** The speaker mentions *flight* and *flying*, so it is a plane. Choice (B) confuses similar-sounding words *rain* and *plane*. Choice (C) associates *sailing* with *boat*. Choice (D) confuses similar-sounding words *us* and *bus*.

93. **(D)** The speaker mentions the *threatening rain clouds* have *cleared up, smooth sailing,* and *bright, sunny skies.* Choice (A) repeats the word *destination*. Choice (B) associates *threatening* with *dangers*. Choice (C) is related to the topic of travel but is not mentioned.

94. **(B)** The speaker mentions a view of a lake with mountains in the distance. Choice (A) confuses similar-sounding words *pine* and *line*. Choice (C) repeats the word *city*. Choice (D) repeats the word *clouds*.

95. **(C)** The report is about flooding caused by heavy rains and the overflowing river. Choice (A) confuses the meaning of the word *banks*. Choice (B) confuses the meaning of the word *main*. Choice (D) repeats the words *rush* and *heavy* and associates *driving* with *traffic*.

96. **(D)** The report says, *citizens are asked to stay away from downtown*. Choice (A) is incorrect because citizens are warned to *drive with caution*, not avoid driving all together. Choice (B) repeats the word *police*. Choice (C) repeats the word *clear*.

97. **(C)** The speaker says, . . . *the floods should recede by the weekend*. Choice (A) confuses similar-sounding words *few days* and *today*. Choice (B) confuses similar-sounding words *night* and *tonight*. Choice (D) repeats the word *month*.

98. **(B)** This is one of the activities mentioned. Choice (A) confuses *course* with the similar-sounding word *horse*. Choice (C) confuses *hiking* with the similar-sounding word *biking*. Choice (D) confuses the meaning of the word *course* (four-course meal) by associating it with *golf* (golf course).

99. **(B)** This is the price mentioned. Choice (A) repeats the word *one*. Choice (C) confuses similar-sounding numbers *seven* and *eleven*. Choice (D) is confused with the date when the weekend package offer begins.

100. **(A)** The resort is open April through January, so it is closed in February and March. Choice (B) is the months when the weekend package is offered. Choice (C) confuses *December* with the similar-sounding months *September* and *November*. Choice (D) is when the winter vacation specials are available.

## Reading

### PART 5: INCOMPLETE SENTENCES

101. **(A)** *Invest* means to put money into a business with the hope of getting a profit. Choices (B), (C), and (D) have meanings that don't fit the context.

102. **(A)** This is a past unreal conditional sentence, which requires a past conditional verb in the main clause. Choice (B) is present conditional. Choice (C) is future perfect. Choice (D) is simple future.

103. **(D)** *Turned in* means *submitted*. Choices (A), (B), and (C) cannot be used in this context.

104. **(C)** *Raise* is the word commonly used to refer to an increase in salary. Choices (A), (B), and (D) all mean *better* or *bigger* but are not used when talking about a salary.

105. **(B)** *Since* means *because*. They needed a lot of chairs because they expected a lot of people. Choices (A), (C), and (D) are not logical in this context.

106. **(D)** *Through* means *pass from one end to the other*. People are asked not to enter the lobby at all while it is being painted. Choices (A), (B), and (C) do not have the meaning of entering or being inside a place.

107. **(A)** *Delay* means *make late.* Choices (B), (C), and (D) have meanings that don't fit the context.

108. **(C)** This is an adjective used to describe the noun *experience.* Choices (A) and (B) are verbs. Choice (D) is a noun.

109. **(C)** *After* at the beginning of the time clause tells us that the action in the main clause happened after the action in the time clause. Choices (A), (B), and (D) all have meanings similar to *after* but cannot be used to introduce a time clause.

110. **(B)** The verb *avoid* is followed by a gerund. Choice (A) is the base or present tense form. Choice (C) is the infinitive form. Choice (D) is the past participle.

111. **(B)** This is an adverb of manner used to describe how you will work. Choices (A) and (C) are adjectives. Choice (D) is a noun.

112. **(D)** *By* in this sentence means *before.* Choices (A) and (C) don't make sense in this sentence. Choice (B) is the opposite of the correct meaning.

113. **(D)** This is an adjective used to describe the noun *offer.* Choices (A) and (B) are verbs. Choice (C) is a noun.

114. **(A)** This is a present continuous verb used to describe an action that is taking place *currently,* or now. Choice (B) is the infinitive form. Choice (C) is a past tense form. Choice (D) is a past tense form.

115. **(A)** *Impose* means to *require* or *force upon.* Choice (B), (C), and (D) look similar to the correct answer but do not fit the context of the sentence.

116. **(A)** The present tense form of the verb is used in a future time clause. Choice (B) is present continuous. Choice (C) is future. Choice (D) is simple past.

117. **(D)** *Detect* means *discover.* Choices (A), (B), and (C) have meanings that don't fit the context.

118. **(B)** The plural verb form *are* agrees with the plural subject *designs.* Choices (A) and (D) are singular forms. Choice (C) doesn't make sense in this sentence.

119. **(C)** This is an adverb of manner used to describe the verb *arrive.* Choice (A) is a noun. Choice (B) is a verb and belongs to a different word family. Choice (D) is an adjective.

120. **(B)** A *reminder* is a notice to help someone remember something. Choices (A), (C), and (D) have meanings that don't fit the context.

121. **(C)** *Although* shows a contrast between the two clauses. Choices (A) and (B) are used to show a cause-and-effect relationship. Choice (D) is normally followed by a noun, not by a clause.

122. **(A)** *Expires* means *ends.* Choices (B), (C), and (D) look similar to the correct answer but cannot be used in this context.

123. **(D)** *Seldom* means *almost never.* Choices (A), (B), and (C) are all opposite in meaning.

124. **(A)** This is a non-count noun referring to *glass* as a material. Choice (B) is a plural count noun referring to *drinking glasses* or *eyeglasses.* Choice (C) is an adjective. Choice (D) looks similar to the other choices but has a different meaning.

125. **(D)** This is an unreal conditional in the present tense, so a past tense verb is required in the *if* clause. Choice (A) is the verb form for the main clause. Choice (B) is future tense. Choice (C) is present tense.

126. **(B)** The modal *should* is followed by the base form of the verb. Choice (A) is future tense. Choice (C) is present participle or a gerund. Choice (D) is past participle.

127. **(B)** The verb *expect* is followed by an infinitive verb. Choice (A) is base form or present tense. Choice (C) is present participle or a gerund. Choice (D) is future tense.

128. **(C)** *Selective* means *careful about choosing*. Choices (A), (B), and (D) have meanings that don't fit the context.

129. **(A)** *Advice* is a noun; in this sentence it is the object of the verb *has given*. Choice (B) is a verb. Choices (C) and (D) are adjectives.

130. **(C)** *Attract* means *draw* or *bring*. Choices (A), (B), and (D) have meanings that don't fit the context.

131. **(D)** This is the correct word to use in a sentence with *nor*. Choices (A), (B), and (C) are not used with *nor*.

132. **(B)** *Durable* means *strong* or *long-lasting*. Choices (A), (C), and (D) have meanings that don't fit the context.

133. **(A)** *Temporarily* means *not permanently* or *for a short time*. Choices (B), (C), and (D) have meanings that don't fit the context.

134. **(C)** This is an adjective used to describe the noun *office*. Choice (A) is a noun or a verb. Choice (B) is a past tense verb. Choice (D) is a noun.

135. **(D)** *Revealed* means *showed* or *made public*. Choices (A), (B), and (C) have meanings that don't fit the context.

136. **(C)** This is a superlative adjective used with *the* to compare Mr. Sato to everyone else in a group. Choice (A) is a simple adjective form. Choice (B) is a comparative adjective. Choice (D) is a noun.

137. **(B)** This is a preposition of place describing the position of the rug. Choices (A) and (D) are nouns. Choice (C) is an adverb.

138. **(A)** *Audit* is a verb that tells what the accountant will do. Choices (B) and (D) are nouns. Choice (C) is an adjective.

139. **(B)** This is a past participle verb used to complete the passive causative form, *have inspected,* meaning, *We will ask another person to inspect.* Choice (A) is the base form or present tense. Choice (C) is present tense. Choice (D) is an infinitive.

140. **(D)** This present perfect verb form is used to describe an action that began in the past and continues to the present. Choice (A) is simple present. Choice (B) is simple past. Choice (C) is present continuous.

## PART 6: TEXT COMPLETION

141. **(C)** A passive-voice word is required in this sentence. The action is performed *by department heads.* Choices (A), (B), and (D) are all active-voice forms.

142. **(A)** The singular third person pronoun *It* refers to the *check stub* mentioned in the previous sentence. Choices (B) and (C) are also singular third person pronouns, but they are used to refer to people, not things. Choice (D) is a plural pronoun.

143. **(B)** *Attend* means *go to* or *be present at.* Choices (A), (C), and (D) look similar to the correct answer but have different meanings.

144. **(C)** This banquet takes place once a year in the spring, so it is *annual.* Choice (A) means *once a day.* Choice (B) means *once a month.* Choice (D) means *once every two years.*

145. **(A)** The writer is discussing the place, or *location,* for the banquet. Choices (B), (C), and (D) are all things that may be part of a banquet, but they are not the topic of this paragraph.

146. **(D)** *Let know* means *inform.* Choices (A), (B), and (C) cannot combine with *know* to have this meaning.

147. **(A)** A present tense verb is used in an *if* clause that refers to a future action. Choice (B) is past participle. Choice (C) is the present participle or gerund form. Choice (D) is future tense.

148. **(C)** This is a passive-voice sentence, so the past participle form of the verb is required. Choices (A) and (B) are present tense active-voice forms. Choice (D) is a gerund.

149. **(D)** *Set up* in this context means *arrange.* Choices (A), (B), and (C) have meanings that don't fit the context.

150. **(B)** This is a passive-voice sentence. Senior citizens *will be charged,* or *asked to pay* a fare. Choices (A), (C), and (D) all have the meaning of receiving money rather than paying it.

151. **(C)** *Currently* means *now.* This sentence explains the schedule that is in effect now and will change in the future. Choice (A) means *on time.* Choice (B) means *frequently.* Choice (D) means *before.*

152. **(D)** *Regarding* means *about.* Choices (A), (B), and (C) look similar to the correct answer but do not fit the context.

## PART 7: READING COMPREHENSION

153. **(A)** The ad says that paper items are on sale, so that would include envelopes. Choice (B) is confused with the mention of the *manager's desk.* Choices (C) and (D) are confused with the mention of the *computer files.*

154. **(B)** Customers are asked to go to the manager's desk for an application. Choice (A) is confused with the day the sale ends. Choice (C) is confused with the notifications that club members will receive by mail. Choice (D) is confused with *contact information.*

155. **(B)** The elevators will be closed for maintenance and repair. Choice (A) is what will be done later on in the stairs and hallways. Choice (C) is not mentioned. Choice (D) is confused with the mention of the painting schedule.

156. **(B)** The work will begin August 17 and be completed by the end of the month, which is two weeks. Choice (A) repeats the word *week*. Choices (C) and (D) repeat the word *month*.

157. **(D)** The instructions explain how to put new batteries into the GMX 200. Choice (A) repeats the word *cover*, which needs to be removed in order to change the batteries. Choice (B) is confused with *date of purchase*. Choice (C) is mentioned but is not the purpose of the instructions.

158. **(C)** The product is guaranteed to keep time accurately, so it is a clock. Choice (A) is confused with the mention of a date. Choice (B) is used to change the batteries. Choice (D) is confused with *dispose of used batteries properly*.

159. **(A)** IEP is an agency that helps people find jobs in other countries. Choice (B) is confused with the topic of going to other countries, something a travel agency might help people do. Choice (C) is something IEP specifically does not provide. Choice (D) repeats the words *teacher* and *training*.

160. **(C)** The article says that IEP was founded four years ago. Choices (A) and (B) are confused with the amount of time Margery Wilson wanted to spend abroad. Choice (D) is confused with how long ago Margery Wilson graduated from college.

161. **(D)** The service is for young professionals, people who normally have a college degree, and Margery Wilson says: *All you need is a college degree . . . .* Choice (A) is something that is mentioned as not required. Choice (B) is what will be gained by using the agency's services. Choice (C) is something a client might have but isn't required.

162. **(A)** An apartment for the owner to live in is on the second floor. Choice (B) is confused with the snacks that are sold in the store. Choice (C) is confused with the equipment that is being sold with the store. Choice (D) is something that might be above a store, but it is not mentioned in the ad.

163. **(B)** The asking price is $750,000. Choice (A) is what the inventory is worth. Choice (C) is the sum of the asking price plus the value of the inventory. Choice (D) is the volume of sales.

164. **(D)** *Inventory* means *merchandise*, or the stock of items available for sale. Choices (A), (B), and (C) are all things that might be associated with the sale of a business but are not the correct answer.

165. **(B)** *Just under* means the same as *a little less than*. Choice (A) is confused with when the town meeting was held (*last week*). Choice (C) misinterprets the meaning of *just under*. Choice (D) is confused with *by the end of the year*, which is when the company promised to have high-speed Internet service for everyone.

166. **(B)** Clear Sound has telephone customers and also provides high-speed Internet access. Choice (A) is only part of what the company does. Choice (C) is confused with *delivers on its promises*. Choice (D) is not mentioned.

167. **(C)** Customers have *expressed great dissatisfaction* and they have complained, so they are unhappy. Choice (A) is the opposite of the correct answer. Choice (B) is confused with *welcomed with great optimism*, which is how people felt at first. Choice (D) is not mentioned.

168. **(A)** *Minor* means *small* or *unimportant*. Choices (B), (C), and (D) do not mean the same as *minor*.

169. **(A)** All food at the café is made with organic ingredients, so that would include the soups. Choice (B) is incorrect because sandwiches are the most popular item. Choice (C) is incorrect because the soups are homemade. Choice (D) is incorrect because all the food at the café is vegetarian.

170. **(B)** *Concoction* means *combination*. Choices (A), (C), and (D) are all related to the topic of food, but they do not have the same meaning as *concoction*.

171. **(C)** Both cheese and vegetables are mentioned as sandwich ingredients. Choices (A), (B), and (D) all contain meat, which is not served at this vegetarian café.

172. **(D)** Whitehead is quoted as saying . . . what they really come here for are the sandwiches. Choices (A), (B), and (C) all correctly describe the café but are not the reason mentioned by Whitehead.

173. **(B)** The article explains how to make a good impression at a job interview, so it is for job hunters. Choices (A), (C), and (D) are all related to the topic of clothes but are not who the article is for.

174. **(C)** The first paragraph discusses wearing dark colors to give a professional impression. Choice (A) is confused with the description of browns and greens. Choice (B) is what is mentioned as being not important. Choice (D) repeats the word *accessories*, which are discussed later, but not in relation to suit colors.

175. **(A)** Simple, quiet ties and plain earrings are recommended. Choices (B), (C), and (D) are all things that are specifically not recommended.

176. **(B)** Shoes that fit comfortably are recommended. Choices (A), (C), and (D) are all things that are specifically not recommended.

177. **(A)** The sheet contains information that would be of interest to a hotel guest. In addition, it mentions breakfast being included in the price of the room and a hotel manager, so it is information for hotel guests. Choice (B) is confused with the mention of tourism. Choice (C) is confused with the mention of a shopping mall. Choice (D) is a place where some of this information might be useful, but it is not the correct answer.

178. **(C)** The Market Mall subway station is five blocks from the hotel. Choices (A), (B), and (D) are other places mentioned in the information sheet.

179. **(C)** The downtown shopping district is famous for its fashion, or clothing, boutiques. Choices (A), (B), and (D) are all things that can be bought at the Market Mall.

180. **(B)** You can probably buy any kind of medicine at the pharmacy across the street. Choices (A), (C), and (D) are other places mentioned in the information sheet.

181. **(A)** The letter is dated May 8 and refers to the ad in *yesterday's paper,* so the ad appeared the day before May 8. Choice (B) is the date on the letter. Choice (C) is not mentioned. Choice (D) is the date James Jones's Spanish class begins.

182. **(B)** The ad mentions *assisting with documents* as one of the paralegal's duties. Choice (A) is incorrect because the duty is described as *providing legal information to clients,* not getting information from them, as in an interview. Choice (C) is confused with the

request *No phone calls, please.* Choice (D) is confused with the line *We will contact you to make an appointment.*

183. **(D)** James Jones has work experience at an architectural firm, not as a paralegal, and the ad requested paralegal experience. Choices (A), (B), and (C) are all qualifications that he possesses.

184. **(C)** James Jones worked for three years at an architectural firm. Choice (A) is confused with the Spanish class he will be taking. Choice (B) is where he wants to work now. Choice (D) is confused with his knowledge of French.

185. **(B)** He mentions enclosing his résumé. Choice (A) is something we can assume he has, but he doesn't say anything about enclosing it. Choice (C) is incorrect because even though he mentions knowing French, he never mentions a French certificate. Choice (D) is something he offers to send later.

186. **(B)** The courses recommended for Marvin are beginning word processing (Word Processing Basics) and Advanced Database. Of these, only Word Processing Basics, Section 2 fits his schedule because of his weekly meeting on Wednesdays at 2:00. Choices (A) and (D) are the courses that don't fit his schedule. Choice (C) is not recommended for Marvin because he already has a good knowledge of database programs.

187. **(C)** Sam Silliman tells Marvin that someone in the Human Resources Department will complete the registration process for him. Choices (A) and (B) are suggested on the course schedule materials. Choice (D) is what Sam Silliman wants Marvin to do after he has registered.

188. **(A)** Marvin will pay nothing himself because NZ, Inc. will pay all his fees for him. Choice (B) is the cost of a four-hour class. Choice (C) is the cost of a four-hour class plus materials. Choice (D) is the cost of a six-hour class plus materials.

189. **(D)** Sam Silliman is responsible for Marvin fulfilling the requirements of his probationary employment and other duties, so he must be Marvin's supervisor. Choices (A) and (C) are incorrect because Sam Silliman works for NZ, Inc., not for the Computer Training Center. Choice (B) is incorrect because Sam Silliman does not work in the Human Resources Department.

190. **(B)** Sam Silliman points out that Marvin's *first-year employee probationary status is still in effect*, which means that he has been there for less than one year. Choice (A) is incorrect because we don't know exactly how long he has been working there. Choices (C) and (D) are incorrect because he is still in his first year of employment.

191. **(A)** Jon's mother works as an electrical engineer at the company, and the ad says that preference will be given to employees' children. Choices (B) and (C) are true about Jon but are not things that will give him preference. Choice (D) is confused with Jon's mother's profession.

192. **(A)** Jon's e-mail is dated April 1, and the application deadline is April 15. Choice (B) is not mentioned. Choice (C) is confused with the minimum length of the internships. Choice (D) is confused with the maximum time following graduation that a person can apply to become an intern.

193. **(B)** Jon is thinking about studying information technology. Choice (A) is what he is studying now as an undergraduate. Choice (C) is confused with the Global Communications project. Choice (D) is confused with Jon's second language.

194. **(D)** Interns who speak a second language will be assigned to the Global Communications project. Choices (A), (B), and (C) are other projects that interns may be assigned to.

195. **(C)** June 1 is when the first internships start, and Jon wants to start when he returns from Korea, four days after that. Choice (A) is confused with when Jon will go to Korea. Choice (B) is when the first internships start. Choice (D) is confused with when Jon wants to finish his internship.

196. **(D)** The Option 2 buffet for 100 people costs $1,400, and tables and chairs for 100 people cost $200. Choice (A) is the cost of the Option 3 buffet. Choice (B) is the cost of the Option 1 buffet. Choice (C) is the cost of the Option 2 buffet without tables and chairs.

197. **(B)** She wants both vegetarian and meat entrées, and Options 2 and 3 both include those. Choices (A) and (C) are incorrect because Option 1 doesn't include a vegetarian entrée. Choice (D) is incorrect because Option 2 is not the only choice that has both vegetarian and meat entrées.

198. **(D)** She would have to order a month before her conference date of October 15. Choice (A) is incorrect because the business does not accept cash. Choice (B) is something the customer has to pay extra for. Choice (C) offers a 15% discount.

199. **(C)** Orders must be accompanied by a 25% deposit, payable by check. Choice (A) is incorrect because credit cards are not accepted. Choice (B) is incorrect because there is no tablecloth color choice; they are all white. Choice (D) is included in all the options.

200. **(B)** She expects 40–45 people, so she would pay the price for up to 50 people. Choice (A) is the price for up to 25 people. Choice (C) is the price for up to 50 people plus tables and chairs, but she will use her own tables and chairs. Choice (D) is the price for up to 100 people.

# ANSWER SHEET
## TOEIC Practice Exam 3

**LISTENING COMPREHENSION**

### Part 1: Photographs

1. Ⓐ Ⓑ Ⓒ Ⓓ    4. Ⓐ Ⓑ Ⓒ Ⓓ    7. Ⓐ Ⓑ Ⓒ Ⓓ    10. Ⓐ Ⓑ Ⓒ Ⓓ
2. Ⓐ Ⓑ Ⓒ Ⓓ    5. Ⓐ Ⓑ Ⓒ Ⓓ    8. Ⓐ Ⓑ Ⓒ Ⓓ    9. Ⓐ Ⓑ Ⓒ Ⓓ
3. Ⓐ Ⓑ Ⓒ Ⓓ    6. Ⓐ Ⓑ Ⓒ Ⓓ    9. Ⓐ Ⓑ Ⓒ Ⓓ

### Part 2: Question-Response

11. Ⓐ Ⓑ Ⓒ    19. Ⓐ Ⓑ Ⓒ    27. Ⓐ Ⓑ Ⓒ    35. Ⓐ Ⓑ Ⓒ
12. Ⓐ Ⓑ Ⓒ    20. Ⓐ Ⓑ Ⓒ    28. Ⓐ Ⓑ Ⓒ    36. Ⓐ Ⓑ Ⓒ
13. Ⓐ Ⓑ Ⓒ    21. Ⓐ Ⓑ Ⓒ    29. Ⓐ Ⓑ Ⓒ    37. Ⓐ Ⓑ Ⓒ
14. Ⓐ Ⓑ Ⓒ    22. Ⓐ Ⓑ Ⓒ    30. Ⓐ Ⓑ Ⓒ    38. Ⓐ Ⓑ Ⓒ
15. Ⓐ Ⓑ Ⓒ    23. Ⓐ Ⓑ Ⓒ    31. Ⓐ Ⓑ Ⓒ    39. Ⓐ Ⓑ Ⓒ
16. Ⓐ Ⓑ Ⓒ    24. Ⓐ Ⓑ Ⓒ    32. Ⓐ Ⓑ Ⓒ    40. Ⓐ Ⓑ Ⓒ
17. Ⓐ Ⓑ Ⓒ    25. Ⓐ Ⓑ Ⓒ    33. Ⓐ Ⓑ Ⓒ
18. Ⓐ Ⓑ Ⓒ    26. Ⓐ Ⓑ Ⓒ    34. Ⓐ Ⓑ Ⓒ

### Part 3: Conversations

41. Ⓐ Ⓑ Ⓒ Ⓓ    49. Ⓐ Ⓑ Ⓒ Ⓓ    57. Ⓐ Ⓑ Ⓒ Ⓓ    65. Ⓐ Ⓑ Ⓒ Ⓓ
42. Ⓐ Ⓑ Ⓒ Ⓓ    50. Ⓐ Ⓑ Ⓒ Ⓓ    58. Ⓐ Ⓑ Ⓒ Ⓓ    66. Ⓐ Ⓑ Ⓒ Ⓓ
43. Ⓐ Ⓑ Ⓒ Ⓓ    51. Ⓐ Ⓑ Ⓒ Ⓓ    59. Ⓐ Ⓑ Ⓒ Ⓓ    67. Ⓐ Ⓑ Ⓒ Ⓓ
44. Ⓐ Ⓑ Ⓒ Ⓓ    52. Ⓐ Ⓑ Ⓒ Ⓓ    60. Ⓐ Ⓑ Ⓒ Ⓓ    68. Ⓐ Ⓑ Ⓒ Ⓓ
45. Ⓐ Ⓑ Ⓒ Ⓓ    53. Ⓐ Ⓑ Ⓒ Ⓓ    61. Ⓐ Ⓑ Ⓒ Ⓓ    69. Ⓐ Ⓑ Ⓒ Ⓓ
46. Ⓐ Ⓑ Ⓒ Ⓓ    54. Ⓐ Ⓑ Ⓒ Ⓓ    62. Ⓐ Ⓑ Ⓒ Ⓓ    70. Ⓐ Ⓑ Ⓒ Ⓓ
47. Ⓐ Ⓑ Ⓒ Ⓓ    55. Ⓐ Ⓑ Ⓒ Ⓓ    63. Ⓐ Ⓑ Ⓒ Ⓓ
48. Ⓐ Ⓑ Ⓒ Ⓓ    56. Ⓐ Ⓑ Ⓒ Ⓓ    64. Ⓐ Ⓑ Ⓒ Ⓓ

### Part 4: Talks

71. Ⓐ Ⓑ Ⓒ Ⓓ    79. Ⓐ Ⓑ Ⓒ Ⓓ    87. Ⓐ Ⓑ Ⓒ Ⓓ    95. Ⓐ Ⓑ Ⓒ Ⓓ
72. Ⓐ Ⓑ Ⓒ Ⓓ    80. Ⓐ Ⓑ Ⓒ Ⓓ    88. Ⓐ Ⓑ Ⓒ Ⓓ    96. Ⓐ Ⓑ Ⓒ Ⓓ
73. Ⓐ Ⓑ Ⓒ Ⓓ    81. Ⓐ Ⓑ Ⓒ Ⓓ    89. Ⓐ Ⓑ Ⓒ Ⓓ    97. Ⓐ Ⓑ Ⓒ Ⓓ
74. Ⓐ Ⓑ Ⓒ Ⓓ    82. Ⓐ Ⓑ Ⓒ Ⓓ    90. Ⓐ Ⓑ Ⓒ Ⓓ    98. Ⓐ Ⓑ Ⓒ Ⓓ
75. Ⓐ Ⓑ Ⓒ Ⓓ    83. Ⓐ Ⓑ Ⓒ Ⓓ    91. Ⓐ Ⓑ Ⓒ Ⓓ    99. Ⓐ Ⓑ Ⓒ Ⓓ
76. Ⓐ Ⓑ Ⓒ Ⓓ    84. Ⓐ Ⓑ Ⓒ Ⓓ    92. Ⓐ Ⓑ Ⓒ Ⓓ    100. Ⓐ Ⓑ Ⓒ Ⓓ
77. Ⓐ Ⓑ Ⓒ Ⓓ    85. Ⓐ Ⓑ Ⓒ Ⓓ    93. Ⓐ Ⓑ Ⓒ Ⓓ
78. Ⓐ Ⓑ Ⓒ Ⓓ    86. Ⓐ Ⓑ Ⓒ Ⓓ    94. Ⓐ Ⓑ Ⓒ Ⓓ

# ANSWER SHEET
# TOEIC Practice Exam 3

## READING

### Part 5: Incomplete Sentences

101. Ⓐ Ⓑ Ⓒ Ⓓ
102. Ⓐ Ⓑ Ⓒ Ⓓ
103. Ⓐ Ⓑ Ⓒ Ⓓ
104. Ⓐ Ⓑ Ⓒ Ⓓ
105. Ⓐ Ⓑ Ⓒ Ⓓ
106. Ⓐ Ⓑ Ⓒ Ⓓ
107. Ⓐ Ⓑ Ⓒ Ⓓ
108. Ⓐ Ⓑ Ⓒ Ⓓ
109. Ⓐ Ⓑ Ⓒ Ⓓ
110. Ⓐ Ⓑ Ⓒ Ⓓ

111. Ⓐ Ⓑ Ⓒ Ⓓ
112. Ⓐ Ⓑ Ⓒ Ⓓ
113. Ⓐ Ⓑ Ⓒ Ⓓ
114. Ⓐ Ⓑ Ⓒ Ⓓ
115. Ⓐ Ⓑ Ⓒ Ⓓ
116. Ⓐ Ⓑ Ⓒ Ⓓ
117. Ⓐ Ⓑ Ⓒ Ⓓ
118. Ⓐ Ⓑ Ⓒ Ⓓ
119. Ⓐ Ⓑ Ⓒ Ⓓ
120. Ⓐ Ⓑ Ⓒ Ⓓ

121. Ⓐ Ⓑ Ⓒ Ⓓ
122. Ⓐ Ⓑ Ⓒ Ⓓ
123. Ⓐ Ⓑ Ⓒ Ⓓ
124. Ⓐ Ⓑ Ⓒ Ⓓ
125. Ⓐ Ⓑ Ⓒ Ⓓ
126. Ⓐ Ⓑ Ⓒ Ⓓ
127. Ⓐ Ⓑ Ⓒ Ⓓ
128. Ⓐ Ⓑ Ⓒ Ⓓ
129. Ⓐ Ⓑ Ⓒ Ⓓ
130. Ⓐ Ⓑ Ⓒ Ⓓ

131. Ⓐ Ⓑ Ⓒ Ⓓ
132. Ⓐ Ⓑ Ⓒ Ⓓ
133. Ⓐ Ⓑ Ⓒ Ⓓ
134. Ⓐ Ⓑ Ⓒ Ⓓ
135. Ⓐ Ⓑ Ⓒ Ⓓ
136. Ⓐ Ⓑ Ⓒ Ⓓ
137. Ⓐ Ⓑ Ⓒ Ⓓ
138. Ⓐ Ⓑ Ⓒ Ⓓ
139. Ⓐ Ⓑ Ⓒ Ⓓ
140. Ⓐ Ⓑ Ⓒ Ⓓ

### Part 6: Text Completion

141. Ⓐ Ⓑ Ⓒ Ⓓ
142. Ⓐ Ⓑ Ⓒ Ⓓ
143. Ⓐ Ⓑ Ⓒ Ⓓ

144. Ⓐ Ⓑ Ⓒ Ⓓ
145. Ⓐ Ⓑ Ⓒ Ⓓ
146. Ⓐ Ⓑ Ⓒ Ⓓ

147. Ⓐ Ⓑ Ⓒ Ⓓ
148. Ⓐ Ⓑ Ⓒ Ⓓ
149. Ⓐ Ⓑ Ⓒ Ⓓ

150. Ⓐ Ⓑ Ⓒ Ⓓ
151. Ⓐ Ⓑ Ⓒ Ⓓ
152. Ⓐ Ⓑ Ⓒ Ⓓ

### Part 7: Reading Comprehension

153. Ⓐ Ⓑ Ⓒ Ⓓ
154. Ⓐ Ⓑ Ⓒ Ⓓ
155. Ⓐ Ⓑ Ⓒ Ⓓ
156. Ⓐ Ⓑ Ⓒ Ⓓ
157. Ⓐ Ⓑ Ⓒ Ⓓ
158. Ⓐ Ⓑ Ⓒ Ⓓ
159. Ⓐ Ⓑ Ⓒ Ⓓ
160. Ⓐ Ⓑ Ⓒ Ⓓ
161. Ⓐ Ⓑ Ⓒ Ⓓ
162. Ⓐ Ⓑ Ⓒ Ⓓ
163. Ⓐ Ⓑ Ⓒ Ⓓ
164. Ⓐ Ⓑ Ⓒ Ⓓ

165. Ⓐ Ⓑ Ⓒ Ⓓ
166. Ⓐ Ⓑ Ⓒ Ⓓ
167. Ⓐ Ⓑ Ⓒ Ⓓ
168. Ⓐ Ⓑ Ⓒ Ⓓ
169. Ⓐ Ⓑ Ⓒ Ⓓ
170. Ⓐ Ⓑ Ⓒ Ⓓ
171. Ⓐ Ⓑ Ⓒ Ⓓ
172. Ⓐ Ⓑ Ⓒ Ⓓ
173. Ⓐ Ⓑ Ⓒ Ⓓ
174. Ⓐ Ⓑ Ⓒ Ⓓ
175. Ⓐ Ⓑ Ⓒ Ⓓ
176. Ⓐ Ⓑ Ⓒ Ⓓ

177. Ⓐ Ⓑ Ⓒ Ⓓ
178. Ⓐ Ⓑ Ⓒ Ⓓ
179. Ⓐ Ⓑ Ⓒ Ⓓ
180. Ⓐ Ⓑ Ⓒ Ⓓ
181. Ⓐ Ⓑ Ⓒ Ⓓ
182. Ⓐ Ⓑ Ⓒ Ⓓ
183. Ⓐ Ⓑ Ⓒ Ⓓ
184. Ⓐ Ⓑ Ⓒ Ⓓ
185. Ⓐ Ⓑ Ⓒ Ⓓ
186. Ⓐ Ⓑ Ⓒ Ⓓ
187. Ⓐ Ⓑ Ⓒ Ⓓ
188. Ⓐ Ⓑ Ⓒ Ⓓ

189. Ⓐ Ⓑ Ⓒ Ⓓ
190. Ⓐ Ⓑ Ⓒ Ⓓ
191. Ⓐ Ⓑ Ⓒ Ⓓ
192. Ⓐ Ⓑ Ⓒ Ⓓ
193. Ⓐ Ⓑ Ⓒ Ⓓ
194. Ⓐ Ⓑ Ⓒ Ⓓ
195. Ⓐ Ⓑ Ⓒ Ⓓ
196. Ⓐ Ⓑ Ⓒ Ⓓ
197. Ⓐ Ⓑ Ⓒ Ⓓ
198. Ⓐ Ⓑ Ⓒ Ⓓ
199. Ⓐ Ⓑ Ⓒ Ⓓ
200. Ⓐ Ⓑ Ⓒ Ⓓ

# TOEIC Practice Exam 3

## LISTENING COMPREHENSION

In this section of the test, you will have the chance to show how well you understand spoken English. There are four parts to this section, with special directions for each part. You will find the Answer Sheet for Practice Exam 3 on pages 119–120. Detach it from the book and use it to record your answers. Check your answers using the Answer Key on pages 156–157 and see the Answers Explained beginning on page 159.

## Part 1: Photographs

**Track 10**

**Directions:** You will see a photograph. You will hear four statements about the photograph. Choose the statement that most closely matches the photograph and fill in the corresponding oval on your answer sheet.

**Example**

Now listen to the four statements.

Sample Answer

ⓐ ⓑ ⓒ ⓓ

Statement (B), "She's reading a magazine," best describes what you see in the picture. Therefore, you should choose answer (B).

**TIP**

If you do not have access to the MP3 files, please use the audioscripts beginning on page 371. You can also download the MP3 files and audioscripts from *http:// barronsbooks. com/tp/toeic/ audio/*

1.

2.

3.

4.

5.

6.

7.

8.

9.

10.

## Part 2: Question-Response

Track 11

**Directions:** You will hear a question and three possible responses. Choose the response that most closely answers the question and fill in the corresponding oval on your answer sheet.

**Example**

Now listen to the sample question.

You will hear:

How is the weather?

You will also hear:

(A)  It's raining.
(B)  He's fine, thanks.
(C)  He's my boss.

The best response to the question *How is the weather?* is choice (A), *It's raining*. Therefore, you should choose answer (A).

11.  Mark your answer on your answer sheet.

12.  Mark your answer on your answer sheet.

13.  Mark your answer on your answer sheet.

14.  Mark your answer on your answer sheet.

15.  Mark your answer on your answer sheet.

16.  Mark your answer on your answer sheet.

17.  Mark your answer on your answer sheet.

18.  Mark your answer on your answer sheet.

19.  Mark your answer on your answer sheet.

20.  Mark your answer on your answer sheet.

21.  Mark your answer on your answer sheet.

22.  Mark your answer on your answer sheet.

23.  Mark your answer on your answer sheet.

24.  Mark your answer on your answer sheet.

25.  Mark your answer on your answer sheet.

26.  Mark your answer on your answer sheet.

27.  Mark your answer on your answer sheet.

28.  Mark your answer on your answer sheet.

29.  Mark your answer on your answer sheet.

30.  Mark your answer on your answer sheet.

31.  Mark your answer on your answer sheet.

32.  Mark your answer on your answer sheet.

33.  Mark your answer on your answer sheet.

34.  Mark your answer on your answer sheet.

35.  Mark your answer on your answer sheet.

36.  Mark your answer on your answer sheet.

37.  Mark your answer on your answer sheet.

38.  Mark your answer on your answer sheet.

39.  Mark your answer on your answer sheet.

40.  Mark your answer on your answer sheet.

## Part 3: Conversations

**Directions:** You will hear a conversation between two people. You will see three questions on each conversation and four possible answers. Choose the best answer to each question and fill in the corresponding oval on your answer sheet.

Track 12

41. What does the woman want to do?
    (A) See a TV show
    (B) Go to the movies
    (C) Take a walk
    (D) Read a book

42. Why does the man say he can't do this?
    (A) He has to catch a plane.
    (B) He wants to go to bed early.
    (C) He doesn't have tickets.
    (D) He is working late.

43. What does the man say he will do?
    (A) Buy a few flowers
    (B) Leave work early
    (C) Meet the woman at 9:00
    (D) Buy the tickets

44. Why does the man want to meet with the woman?
    (A) To have lunch
    (B) To work on a report
    (C) To discuss his health
    (D) To point out some problems

45. Where will they meet?
    (A) At the man's office
    (B) In a conference room
    (C) At a restaurant
    (D) Downtown

46. What does the woman have to do tomorrow afternoon?
    (A) See her doctor
    (B) Go out of town
    (C) Buy a new gown
    (D) Attend a conference

47. Where does this conversation take place?
    (A) In a store
    (B) In an office
    (C) In an elevator
    (D) In an apartment

48. Who is the woman visiting?
    (A) A college friend
    (B) A work colleague
    (C) Her brother
    (D) The man

49. What is the man's opinion of the building?
    (A) He likes it.
    (B) It's a bad building.
    (C) It's too close to the shops.
    (D) He feels sad in it.

50. What does the man want to do?
    (A) Reserve a meeting room
    (B) Make a new schedule
    (C) Serve a luncheon
    (D) Order a book

51. What time will he finish?
    (A) 8:00
    (B) 10:00
    (C) 11:00
    (D) 1:00

52. What does the woman ask him to do?
    (A) Set up for the luncheon
    (B) Work that morning
    (C) Find a new place
    (D) Put the chairs back

53. What will be cleaned today?
    (A) The conference room
    (B) The hallways
    (C) The office
    (D) The front door

54. What does the woman suggest about the office cleaning?
    (A) It won't be done well.
    (B) It's difficult to schedule.
    (C) It's been delayed too long.
    (D) It will take a long time.

55. What will the woman do next week?
    (A) Give a workshop
    (B) Go shopping
    (C) Serve a lunch
    (D) Make a schedule

56. Why is the woman going to Chicago?
    (A) To see relatives
    (B) To take a vacation
    (C) To take care of business
    (D) To visit friends

57. How long does the trip take by train?
    (A) 2 hours
    (B) 4 hours
    (C) 9 hours
    (D) 16 hours

58. Why does the woman prefer the train to the plane?
    (A) She's afraid of planes.
    (B) The train is more interesting.
    (C) She has lots of time.
    (D) The plane is expensive.

59. Why is the local post office closed?
    (A) It's Sunday.
    (B) The hour is late.
    (C) It's a holiday.
    (D) The weather is bad.

60. How far away is the main post office?
    (A) Two blocks
    (B) Four blocks
    (C) A little less than a mile
    (D) More than a mile

61. How will the man get to the post office?
    (A) Walking
    (B) Bus
    (C) Taxi
    (D) Driving

62. Who does the man eat lunch with?
    (A) Nobody
    (B) The woman
    (C) His assistant
    (D) His officemates

63. Where does the man eat lunch?
    (A) At a café
    (B) At his desk
    (C) In the park
    (D) In the cafeteria

64. What does the woman do during her lunch break?
    (A) She returns to her apartment.
    (B) She telephones her friends.
    (C) She takes a walk.
    (D) She drinks coffee.

65. What does the woman request?
    (A) A room key
    (B) A bigger room
    (C) An extra night
    (D) Help with her suitcase

66. What does the woman want to do now?
    (A) Park her car
    (B) Have dinner
    (C) Go to the bank
    (D) Take a walk

67. What is the weather like?
    (A) Warm
    (B) Snowy
    (C) Rainy
    (D) Cool

---

68. Where does this conversation take place?
    (A) A travel agency
    (B) A train station
    (C) A hotel
    (D) A bank

69. What does the woman want to do?
    (A) Check the schedule
    (B) Find out the time
    (C) Find the gate
    (D) Make a reservation

70. What does the woman need help with?
    (A) Her book
    (B) Her ticket
    (C) Her check
    (D) Her suitcase

## Part 4: Talks

**Directions:** You will hear a talk given by a single speaker. You will see three questions on each talk, each with four possible answers. Choose the best answer to each question and fill in the corresponding oval on your answer sheet.

Track 13

71. What time does the office open?
    (A) 7:00 A.M.
    (B) 9:00 A.M.
    (C) 11:00 P.M.
    (D) 2:00 P.M.

72. How can a caller open an account?
    (A) Visit during office hours
    (B) Press 0
    (C) Stay on the line
    (D) Press 3

73. What can a caller do by pressing 2?
    (A) Leave a message
    (B) Ask a question about a bill
    (C) Hear the message in Spanish
    (D) Speak with a customer service representative

74. What is the main purpose of this talk?
    (A) To give traffic information
    (B) To give driving directions
    (C) To report on road repair work
    (D) To describe areas of interest in the city

75. What is being repaired?
    (A) A tunnel
    (B) A highway
    (C) A bridge
    (D) A park

76. When will the repairs be finished?
    (A) May
    (B) September
    (C) November
    (D) December

77. What kind of job does this school train for?
    (A) Law office assistant
    (B) Computer researcher
    (C) Customer service representative
    (D) Career counselor

78. How many months does the course last?
    (A) Two
    (B) Four
    (C) Five
    (D) Six

79. How can someone get an application?
    (A) Visit the office
    (B) Call the school
    (C) Go online
    (D) Send a letter

80. Where would this announcement be heard?
    (A) Train station
    (B) Boat dock
    (C) Airport
    (D) Bus station

81. What are passengers asked to do now?
    (A) Wait near the back
    (B) Remove their coats
    (C) Check their tickets
    (D) Go to the gate

82. Who will get on first?
    (A) Passengers for Honolulu
    (B) Passengers with children
    (C) Passengers with luggage
    (D) Passengers in rows 30–35

83. What is indicated about the event?
    (A) It happens once a year.
    (B) It is usually free.
    (C) It takes place indoors.
    (D) It is not suitable for children.

84. When will the event take place?
    (A) Next month
    (B) In 15 days
    (C) On June 15
    (D) Next year

85. What will happen on Thursday night?
    (A) There will be dancing.
    (B) Games will be free.
    (C) Food will be served.
    (D) A concert will be performed.

86. Why will airport workers go on strike?
    (A) They are working in freezing cold conditions.
    (B) They are having problems with passengers.
    (C) They won't get their salary increase.
    (D) They don't have a contract.

87. When will the strike begin?
    (A) Immediately
    (B) Tomorrow afternoon
    (C) Next week
    (D) In two months

88. Where will union leaders and airline officials meet?
    (A) In the mayor's office
    (B) At a hotel
    (C) In a boardroom
    (D) At the airport

89. What is suggested about the fourth car from the rear?
    (A) It is colder than the other cars.
    (B) It is a good place to work undisturbed.
    (C) It is for first-class passengers only.
    (D) It has a modern design.

90. What is not allowed anywhere on the train?
    (A) Laptop computers
    (B) Loud sounds
    (C) Cell phones
    (D) Smoking

91. What will happen in 15 minutes?
    (A) Drinks will be sold.
    (B) Food service will end.
    (C) The weather will get cold.
    (D) The rear car will be closed.

92. What kind of show will take place at the theater?
    (A) A concert
    (B) A dog show
    (C) A musical play
    (D) A puppet show

93. What costs $24?
    (A) A ticket for the evening show
    (B) A ticket for the afternoon show
    (C) A ticket for the front row
    (D) A ticket for a child

94. How can tickets be reserved?
    (A) Call back later
    (B) Visit the theater
    (C) Send an e-mail
    (D) Leave a message

95. What is the weather like now?
    (A) Sunny
    (B) Cloudy
    (C) Rainy
    (D) Dry

96. What will the low temperature be tonight?
    (A) 15
    (B) 50
    (C) 60
    (D) 80

97. What does the announcer recommend doing this week?
    (A) Work in the garden.
    (B) Go to the beach.
    (C) Read a book.
    (D) Cook a good meal.

98. Who is the guest speaker?
    (A) An actor
    (B) A filmmaker
    (C) A mountain climber
    (D) An equipment salesperson

99. How much does the book cost?
    (A) $4
    (B) $13
    (C) $30
    (D) $32

100. What will happen next month?
    (A) There will be a talk on diving.
    (B) A film will be shown.
    (C) There won't be a program.
    (D) Books will be discounted.

# READING

In this section of the test, you will have the chance to show how well you understand written English. There are three parts to this section, with special directions for each part.

**YOU WILL HAVE ONE HOUR AND FIFTEEN MINUTES
TO COMPLETE PARTS 5, 6, AND 7 OF THE TEST.**

## Part 5: Incomplete Sentences

**Directions:** You will see a sentence with a missing word. Four possible answers follow the sentence. Choose the best answer to the question and fill in the corresponding oval on your answer sheet.

101. The instructions indicate that applications must be submitted to the personnel office _____ May 31.
   (A) no later than
   (B) ahead
   (C) beforehand
   (D) in advance

102. Since we are already almost over budget, we will have to _____ strictly to avoid overspending this month.
   (A) economy
   (B) economize
   (C) economist
   (D) economical

103. Last night's storm was a big surprise because it so _____ snows in this part of the country.
   (A) unlikely
   (B) rarely
   (C) barely
   (D) uneasily

104. After a long search, we finally found the _____ equipment in the closet of an unused office.
   (A) discovered
   (B) anticipated
   (C) missing
   (D) outdated

105. In the end, they decided to cancel the meeting because less than half the staff showed _____.
   (A) through
   (B) down
   (C) up
   (D) off

106. If you need any help filling out the forms, _____ somebody at the front desk for assistance.
   (A) to ask
   (B) asking
   (C) asks
   (D) ask

107. We will need to think _____ in order to find a good solution to this problem.
   (A) creatively
   (B) creative
   (C) created
   (D) creator

108. This office is _____ than our old one, but we are paying top dollar to rent it.
   (A) space
   (B) spacious
   (C) more spacious
   (D) the most spacious

109. Dr. Chin, _____ book you have been enjoying so much, works in the office opposite mine.
   (A) who
   (B) that
   (C) whom
   (D) whose

110. We moved the company offices last month, and they are now located _____ Oakdale Avenue.
   (A) at
   (B) on
   (C) in
   (D) to

111. I really enjoy the work that I do, _____ I have a hard time getting along with my colleagues.
   (A) but
   (B) and
   (C) as
   (D) or

112. We returned the table to the store because we discovered a small _____ on the surface.
   (A) accent
   (B) inlay
   (C) flaw
   (D) pattern

113. Roberta _____ to take on some extra duties while her supervisor was out of town.
   (A) lengthened
   (B) interfered
   (C) extended
   (D) consented

114. I will need these documents for the meeting tomorrow, so please have them on my desk _____ 8:00.
   (A) before
   (B) between
   (C) until
   (D) during

115. Once we _____ that his credentials were in order, we went ahead and offered him the job.
   (A) validated
   (B) ascertained
   (C) required
   (D) exposed

116. The _____ of our manufacturing process has saved the company a lot of money.
   (A) simplification
   (B) simplify
   (C) simply
   (D) simple

117. Ms. Lee _____ moving ahead with the project without waiting for the client to approve the recommended changes.
   (A) supposed
   (B) assumed
   (C) proposed
   (D) predicted

118. We are proud of the fact that everyone employed by this office _____ a professional degree.
   (A) has
   (B) have
   (C) to have
   (D) is having

119. After a brief discussion, they agreed _____ the contract as it was written, without making any further changes.
   (A) accept
   (B) to accept
   (C) accepting
   (D) acceptance

120. It is better for the economy to buy things that are produced _____ rather than bringing in products from far away.
   (A) local
   (B) localize
   (C) locally
   (D) location

121. If you _____ your reservations earlier, you would have gotten on the flight you wanted.
(A) made
(B) had made
(C) have made
(D) would have made

122. Because over half the staff was going to the convention, the manager let everyone _____ the office early.
(A) left
(B) to leave
(C) leaves
(D) leave

123. The number of people who ask questions at the end of the lecture _____ always quite astonishing.
(A) be
(B) are
(C) were
(D) is

124. You can sign the document now, _____ you can speak to an attorney first if you prefer.
(A) and
(B) but
(C) or
(D) nor

125. You will find that document you have been looking for _____ the papers on my desk.
(A) along
(B) among
(C) almost
(D) alone

126. He might _____ a discount if he pays for his ticket before next week.
(A) get
(B) gets
(C) will get
(D) going to get

127. In the absence of the director, Mr. Kane has agreed to _____ this month's staff meeting.
(A) include
(B) accept
(C) present
(D) conduct

128. After listening to his thorough _____, I had no problems understanding how to use the software.
(A) explains
(B) explained
(C) explanation
(D) explanatory

129. He had a good reputation among his colleagues and was _____ as a very fair boss as well.
(A) regarded
(B) registered
(C) regulated
(D) regretted

130. We will review your application and schedule an interview _____ you have submitted all your paperwork.
(A) while
(B) prior to
(C) as soon as
(D) during which

131. She earns more money than her coworkers _____ she works a lot of overtime hours.
(A) although
(B) because
(C) despite
(D) nevertheless

132. _____ writing articles, the job also involves editing and proofreading the newsletter and keeping the subscriber list up to date.
    (A) By
    (B) Beside
    (C) Between
    (D) Besides

133. _____ the lack of publicity, there was quite a large crowd at the event.
    (A) Because of
    (B) Despite
    (C) Although
    (D) During

134. The list of registered guests _____ sitting on the manager's desk.
    (A) have
    (B) were
    (C) are
    (D) is

135. Mr. Sato _____ here for many years and is one of our most knowledgeable employees.
    (A) is working
    (B) used to work
    (C) has been working
    (D) will have worked

136. Both _____ must sign the contract in the presence of a lawyer.
    (A) clauses
    (B) parties
    (C) signals
    (D) provisions

137. We can't work on a solution until we _____ the source of the problem.
    (A) internalize
    (B) indemnify
    (C) identity
    (D) identify

138. We discussed _____ a temporary assistant to help out with the extra work.
    (A) hire
    (B) hired
    (C) hiring
    (D) to hire

139. The keynote speaker is a well-known and respected journalist, and his articles are _____ read.
    (A) widely
    (B) mostly
    (C) famously
    (D) normally

140. The _____ of this business is a result of a lot of hard work and some solid financial support.
    (A) success
    (B) successful
    (C) succeed
    (D) successfully

## Part 6: Text Completion

**Directions:** You will see four passages, each with three blanks. Under each blank are four answer options. Choose the word or phrase that best completes the statement.

Questions 141–143 refer to the following notice.

### DISPUTING A BILL

If you have reason to believe that an item on your bill is wrong or if you need more information about any part of your bill, please contact us by writing to the Customer Service address shown on the front of this statement. We must hear from _____ within 90 days of the date on the statement. When

141. (A) us
     (B) him
     (C) you
     (D) it

writing to us about your bill, please include your name and account number and a complete description and explanation of the error you claim. You will not have to pay the amount in question while we are _____ your claim.

142. (A) investigating
     (B) interrogating
     (C) insuring
     (D) invalidating

We need to receive your explanation in writing, however. If you have any questions about the procedure, please telephone the Customer Service office for _____ with making your claim.

143. (A) assists
     (B) assisted
     (C) assistants
     (D) assistance

February 6, 20--

To Whom It May Concern:

This is to serve as a letter of reference for Ms. Alicia Maldonado, who worked for us from January until November of last year. During her time with us, Ms. Maldonado proved herself to be a reliable and responsible worker. We _____ always count on her to get the job done well

144. (A) can
     (B) could
     (C) could have
     (D) could never

and on time. She acquired many job skills while working with us and was capable of taking on more responsibilities. In fact, I planned to give her a _____ but, unfortunately for us, she decided to leave the

145. (A) demotion
     (B) promotion
     (C) probation
     (D) detention

company for personal reasons. I understand that her husband's company transferred him to a position in another city. We miss Ms. Maldonado's contributions to our work and were very sorry to see her go.

I believe Ms. Maldonado would be a great _____ to any company.

146. (A) hindrance
     (B) attendant
     (C) asset
     (D) position

Sincerely,

*Maria Taylor*

Maria Taylor

TOEIC PRACTICE EXAM 3

Questions 147–149 refer to the following memo.

To:       All Personnel
From:    Simon Shumlin, Office Manager
Re:       Office Supply Requests

As of today, a new policy regarding the distribution of office supplies has been instituted. Unlimited entry to the supply closet is no longer allowed. Any staff member requiring supplies must make a request using the new Office Supply Request Form, available from my office. The form _____ completely and include the signature of the department

147. (A) must be filled out
     (B) must filling out
     (C) must to fill out
     (D) must fill out

head. Supplies requested by 3:00 P.M. Friday will be distributed by my assistant the _____ Monday.

148. (A) previous
     (B) following
     (C) foregoing
     (D) prior

We believe that this policy is the best way to ensure that everyone will have the supplies that they need available when they need them. Thank you for your _____.

149. (A) consolation
     (B) condemnation
     (C) corporation
     (D) cooperation

Many people are interested in making their homes and offices more environmentally friendly. However, they hesitate to put in alternative energy systems such as solar panels because of the high cost of installation. Alternative energy systems may actually be more _____ than is commonly believed. In looking for

150. (A) effective
(B) affordable
(C) polluting
(D) popular

ways to reduce costs, it is important to start with a thorough energy analysis of your home or office. An energy expert can help you _____ how much power you actually need.

151. (A) assess
(B) assesses
(C) assessing
(D) will assess

Reducing your power needs may be as _____ as buying a

152. (A) simplicity
(B) simplify
(C) simply
(D) simple

few energy-efficient appliances. With reduced energy needs, you may be able to install a smaller alternative energy system, thus saving hundreds of dollars.

## Part 7: Reading Comprehension

> **Directions:** You will see single and double reading passages followed by several questions. Each question has four answer choices. Choose the best answer to the question and fill in the corresponding oval on your answer sheet.

Questions 153–154 refer to the following advertisement.

### Office Space Available
### 815 Enfield Street

This suite of offices is conveniently located close to downtown and major bus lines. The 3,000-square-foot floor plan has lots of potential, with space for ten offices, two conference rooms, and a large reception area. Large windows make it pleasant and sunny. Ample tenant and customer parking is in the rear of the building. Contract includes minor renovations to be made at the owner's expense prior to move-in; new tenant chooses paint and carpet colors. Call now for an appointment to see this incredible space. Melissa Soto Rental Agency, 637-2120.

153. What is true of the space for rent?
   (A) It is dark.
   (B) It will be painted.
   (C) It has a new carpet.
   (D) It doesn't include parking.

154. Who should potential tenants call to see the space?
   (A) The owner
   (B) The contractor
   (C) The rental agent
   (D) The current tenant

---

### Information for Building Visitors

All visitors must register at the Security Desk when entering the building. You will receive a visitor's badge. Keep it visible at all times while in the building. The security officer on duty will notify the office you are visiting, and an escort will be sent down to meet you. Please wait for your escort by the elevators. Badges are not required in the lobby and ground-floor cafeteria, which are open to the public.

The cafeteria and lobby area close at 6:30 P.M., and the security officer goes off duty at 7:00 P.M. All visitors must be out of the building before the security officer goes off duty. Exceptions to this rule must be arranged beforehand. For more information, speak with the security manager during normal office hours, 9:00 A.M. to 5:00 P.M.

---

155. What must visitors do while in the building?
    (A) Wear a visitor's badge
    (B) Stay with the escort
    (C) Avoid the cafeteria
    (D) Remain in the lobby

156. What time should visitors leave the building?
    (A) After 9:00 A.M.
    (B) Before 5:00 P.M.
    (C) At 6:30 P.M.
    (D) Before 7:00 P.M.

Shelley Hallowell of Fairfield has been hired as the general manager for the new Harlequin Hotel in Fairfield's West Park district. Ms. Hallowell will assume her new position a month before the hotel's scheduled opening next September.

Ms. Hallowell returned to Fairfield last year after a five-year stint in the Fiji Islands as a tour guide. She held a temporary position between January and May of this year as a consultant to the local tourism board. Before moving to Fiji, she worked locally as an office assistant while studying for her degree. She is a graduate of the Hotel and Hospitality School of Fairfield.

"Ms. Hallowell has a great deal to offer our business. We feel very fortunate to have a person of her caliber working with us," said George Larue, co-owner of the Harlequin Hotel.

157. When will Ms. Hallowell begin her new job?
(A) January
(B) May
(C) August
(D) September

158. What was Ms. Hallowell's most recent job?
(A) Hotel manager
(B) Tourism consultant
(C) School instructor
(D) Office assistant

159. What did Ms. Hallowell do in the Fiji Islands?
(A) She was a student.
(B) She vacationed.
(C) She owned a hotel.
(D) She led tours.

**Edgemont Residents**
**Scrap Metal and Electronics Collection**
**Saturday, October 10, 9 A.M.–3 P.M.**

Residents of the Town of Edgemont can bring their scrap metal and unwanted electronics and household appliances to the Town Recycling Center on the above date and time. This event is for town residents only. A Town of Edgemont recycling permit must be displayed on the lower right-hand side of your car's windshield to participate in this event. Permits are available at the Town Hall for $20. The following items can be recycled for free:

• computers
• computer monitors
• printers
• fax machines
• VCR and DVD players

There will be a $30 charge per item for the following items:

• air conditioners
• refrigerators
• freezers

Only the above-mentioned items can be recycled on this date. For information on recycling hazardous wastes such as paint, gasoline, solvents, etc., please contact the Town Hall.

160. What is required for participating in this recycling event?
(A) A permit
(B) $30
(C) A driver's license
(D) A computer

161. Which of the following items will not be accepted for recycling at this event?
(A) Old refrigerators
(B) Computer printers
(C) Paint in metal cans
(D) Used fax machines

162. The word *displayed* in line 8 is closest in meaning to _____.
(A) shown
(B) hidden
(C) purchased
(D) submitted

Questions 163–165 refer to the following advertisement.

**Are You Looking for Work?**

Advertise your skills where they will be noticed.

*Job Wanted* ads in the *City Times* are seen by the thousands of employers throughout the metropolitan area who read our paper daily.

This month, a 10-line classified ad is free for job seekers* in the Monday–Friday editions of the *City Times*.

Take advantage of this one time offer now. Send an e-mail with your ad copy and phone number to jobads@citytimes.com. Ads must be received by Saturday for inclusion in the following week's editions.

*This offer is available to *City Times* subscribers only. All others will be charged the normal fees.

163. What is being advertised?
(A) A job
(B) Skills training
(C) Advertising space
(D) A newspaper subscription

164. What should be included in the e-mail?
(A) A charge card number
(B) A telephone number
(C) A résumé
(D) Money

165. When should the e-mail be sent?
(A) Monday
(B) Friday
(C) By Saturday
(D) Monday or Friday

Questions 166–168 refer to the following memo.

**MEMO**

To:       All personnel
From:    K. Takubo, Human Resources Manager
Date:     March 3, 20--
Subject: Discount on bus passes

We are pleased to announce that, because of an agreement we have made with the City Office of Public Transportation, as of next month discounted bus passes will be available to all company employees. The passes are good for two weeks of unlimited travel on any bus in the city bus system and can be purchased from us with a 25% discount. This means that instead of paying the normal price of $50, you will be charged just $37.50 for a two-week pass. We hope this will encourage more of you to come to work by bus instead of driving.

If you are interested in purchasing a discounted bus pass on a regular basis, you can download a Bus Pass Request Form from the company website. E-mail the completed form to your supervisor by March 24, and you will receive your first bus pass by e-mail before March 31. The cost will appear as a deduction on your first April paycheck. Your first bus pass will be valid from April 1 through April 15.

166. How much will company employees pay for a bus pass?
(A) $7.50
(B) $25
(C) $37.50
(D) $50

167. How can a company employee request a discounted bus pass?
(A) Ask the Office of Public Transportation
(B) Call up the bus company
(C) Send a memo to the Human Resources Office
(D) Submit a form to her supervisor

168. How will a company employee pay for the discounted bus pass?
(A) It will be deducted from the employee's bank account.
(B) The employee must provide a credit card number.
(C) It will be taken out of the employee's salary.
(D) The employee must write a check.

Questions 169–172 refer to the following advertisement.

We at the First Main Street Bank are expanding our services to help your business grow. For more than a century, we have been proudly providing the local business community with a full range of banking services, including small-business loans, special accounts, financial management services, and more. Now we are offering for the first time our free online business banking service, bringing you the convenience of paying telephone and utility bills, managing your payroll and accounts, real-time transactions, and more, all online. It's easy to set up and easy to use. Stop by any First Main Street branch to talk with the accounts manager about using online banking services to enhance your business banking experience. Call the main office at 438-0832 to find the location of a First Main Street Bank branch near you.

169. What is this advertisement announcing?
(A) A new service
(B) A new manager
(C) A new branch
(D) A new type of account

170. How can customers find out more about it?
(A) Call the main office
(B) Go online
(C) Read a brochure
(D) Visit the bank

171. How long has the bank been in business?
(A) Close to 10 years
(B) A little more than 10 years
(C) Almost 100 years
(D) More than 100 years

172. The word *enhance* in line 11 is closest in meaning to _____.
(A) begin
(B) improve
(C) finance
(D) simplify

To the Editor:

I read with great interest the article in your paper yesterday about the growing traffic problems in our region and how the planned construction work on a new Millers River Bridge will exacerbate the problem over the coming months. Proponents of building a new bridge, which is scheduled to begin next month and be completed within two years, claim that it will greatly alleviate the traffic problem in that part of the city once it is completed. In my opinion, that solution will be temporary at best. Allow me to propose another idea. For the past four years, a group of city planners, transportation experts, and others have been hard at work on a plan for a light rail system to serve our region. Of course, construction of a region-wide light rail train system would require a far greater investment than construction of a bridge, but it would serve a far larger percentage of our population and the effects on our traffic problems would be more far-reaching and permanent.

As discussed in yesterday's article, the new, bigger Millers River Bridge will carry more traffic than the old one, serving one small part of the city. The bridge has been artistically designed and will add beauty to our city landscape. These are small returns, in my opinion, for the expense city taxpayers will incur for the bridge construction. Clearly, investment in a regional light rail system is a better idea for our future.

Sincerely,

David Spaulding

David Spaulding

173. Why did David Spaulding write this letter?
(A) To complain about the traffic problem
(B) To support a new light rail system
(C) To explain bridge construction
(D) To report on a city planners meeting

174. What did David Spaulding do yesterday?
(A) Read the newspaper
(B) Visited the new bridge
(C) Rode on a light rail train
(D) Met with transportation experts

175. When will the new bridge be completed?
(A) Next month
(B) In several months
(C) In two years
(D) In four years

176. What is David Spaulding's opinion of the new bridge?
(A) It's not a good solution.
(B) It won't look beautiful.
(C) It will be too big.
(D) It won't cost too much.

Many people are not aware that plane trips pose several health hazards. This is of particular concern for business travelers who fly frequently. The more often you travel, the greater the health risk becomes. One problem with planes is that the air in the cabin is constantly recirculated. This means that instead of breathing fresh air from the outside, you breathe the same air over and over again, along with all the other passengers. This exposes you to colds, flu, or any other contagious disease that another passenger may have brought on board. You can protect yourself by making sure you get plenty of Vitamin C in the days before your flight. While on the plane, drink a lot of water. The dryness of the cabin air enhances your susceptibility to disease. Maintaining a general state of good health by eating right, exercising regularly, and getting enough sleep is also important.

Long flights pose another sort of health problem. Being forced to sit for a long time in the same position is bad for your circulation. It is particularly dangerous for people who are at risk for blood clots and other circulatory problems. You can lessen the risk by getting up from your seat every hour or so and taking a walk down the aisle. Standing up and moving around even for just a few minutes will improve your circulation and help you feel more comfortable.

Your business obligations may not allow you to fly less frequently or take shorter flights. These recommendations will help you look out for your health while traveling.

177. Who is this article for?
(A) Flight attendants
(B) Businesspeople
(C) Airline companies
(D) Doctors

178. Which of the following problems with flying is discussed in the article?
(A) Sickness
(B) Bad food
(C) Plane crashes
(D) Uncomfortable seats

179. What is advised in the article?
(A) Don't exercise.
(B) Stay seated.
(C) Don't fly frequently.
(D) Take vitamins.

180. The word *obligations* in paragraph 3, line 1 is closest in meaning to _____.
(A) trips
(B) duties
(C) budgets
(D) managers

## NATIONAL RAILWAY SYSTEMS
### SCHEDULE: PIKESVILLE-WINSTON

| DEPART PIKESVILLE | ARRIVE WINSTON | DEPART WINSTON | ARRIVE PIKESVILLE |
|---|---|---|---|
| 5:30 A.M.* | 8:45 A.M. | 6:45 A.M.* | 10:00 A.M. |
| 7:45 A.M. | 11:00 A.M. | 8:15 A.M. | 11:30 A.M. |
| 9:30 A.M. | 12:45 P.M. | 10:15 A.M. | 1:30 P.M. |
| 2:30 P.M.* | 5:45 P.M. | 1:45 P.M.* | 5:00 P.M. |
| 4:14 P.M. | 7:30 P.M. | 3:30 P.M. | 6:45 P.M. |

*WEEKDAYS ONLY

### FARE INFORMATION
WEEKDAYS: $55 EACH WAY
WEEKENDS: $43 EACH WAY

To:       henry_rollins@pikesvillepaper.com
From:     monica_kowalski@pikesvillepaper.com
Sent:     2 March 20--, 12:45
Subject:  train and hotel reservations

Henry,

Please arrange my train ticket and hotel room for the paper producer's conference in Winston next week. It begins on Wednesday with a luncheon, so I will need to arrive before noon. But please don't put me on one of those early, early trains. You know how I hate to get up too early. The conference is at the High Tower Hotel, but don't get me a room there. I'd prefer to stay at the Inn at Winston. Ask for a room with a view of the park. Book it for Wednesday and Thursday nights. I'll stay Friday night with my cousins, who live in town. Book my ticket home for Saturday. Any afternoon train will do.

Thanks.
Monica

181. What time will Monica probably leave Pikesville on Wednesday?
    (A) 5:30 A.M.
    (B) 7:45 A.M.
    (C) 9:30 A.M.
    (D) 11:00 A.M.

182. What is the purpose of Monica's trip to Winston?
    (A) To tour a paper-production facility
    (B) To spend time with her cousins
    (C) To attend a conference
    (D) To have lunch

183. Where does Monica want to stay on Wednesday night?
    (A) The High Tower Hotel
    (B) The Inn at Winston
    (C) Her cousins' house
    (D) At home

184. What time will she arrive home on Saturday?
    (A) 11:30 A.M.
    (B) 1:30 P.M.
    (C) 5:00 P.M.
    (D) 6:45 P.M.

185. How much will Monica's round-trip ticket cost?
    (A) $43
    (B) $55
    (C) $98
    (D) $110

TOEIC PRACTICE EXAM 3

Edward Peters
President
Whispering Pines Inn and Resort
P.O. Box 65
Upper River, New Brunswick
Canada

Dear Mr. Peters,

I am writing in regard to my recent stay at Whispering Pines. I have spent my annual summer vacation there for the past four or five years and have always enjoyed it. The comfortable accommodations and delicious menu are a big attraction for me. This year, however, the resort seemed to be lacking in the area of customer service. I enjoyed my three daily meals that came with my room. However, when on the last day of my stay I decided to try out the inn's high tea, I had a disappointing experience. The food was delicious, but the waitress was sullen and rude. Also, this year I decided to take golf lessons instead of my usual tennis lessons. I am a complete beginner and the instructor had no patience with me. He yelled at my mistakes and made me feel very uncomfortable. Despite these issues, I am not thinking about vacationing elsewhere. I plan to return to Whispering Pines and may even try another golf lesson. However, Whispering Pines is a high-quality resort, and I thought you should know about these things.

Sincerely,

Mary Kim

Mary Kim

**Whispering Pines Inn and Resort**
**P.O. Box 65**
**Upper River, New Brunswick**
**Canada**

Mary Kim
1165 Putnam Avenue
Croton, NY

Dear Ms. Kim,

I was very sorry to hear about your recent unpleasant experience at the Whispering Pines Inn and Resort. As you know from your previous stays at Whispering Pines, we do everything possible to ensure the comfort of our guests and are widely known for our excellent accommodations and five-star menu. I sincerely regret the problems you had with your meal and your instructor. I will be in contact with the manager of the inn to discuss these issues. In the meantime, please accept the enclosed coupon. It entitles you to the same special meal you enjoyed on your last day, and I am sure next time you will have a better experience. I am glad to hear that you plan on being our guest again. You may be interested to know that in addition to golf and tennis, next year we will be adding a system of hiking trails and an indoor pool. We look forward to seeing you again at Whispering Pines.

Sincerely,

*Edward Peters*

Edward Peters
President

186. Why did Ms. Kim write the letter?
(A) To complain about some employees
(B) To praise the accommodations
(C) To ask about the menu
(D) To make reservations

187. How often does Ms. Kim visit Whispering Pines?
(A) Every week
(B) Every month
(C) Every year
(D) Every four or five years

188. What will Mr. Peters do about Ms. Kim's letter?
(A) Redo the menu
(B) Add hiking trails
(C) Fire an instructor
(D) Speak to the manager

189. What can Ms. Kim get with the coupon Mr. Peters sent?
(A) High tea
(B) Three daily meals
(C) A golf lesson
(D) A room at the inn

190. What will Ms. Kim probably do on her next summer vacation?
(A) Hike
(B) Give up golf
(C) Return to Whispering Pines
(D) Go to another resort

Business Fashions
Fall Catalog                                          p. 35

**Men's Dress Shirts.** Solid color. Item #387
These comfortable yet elegant shirts are made of
100% combed cotton.
Colors: white, cream, light blue, light green.
Sizes  S M L XL. $55

**Men's Dress Shirts.** Striped. Item #387A
Same as above, but with a thin stripe over a solid
background color.
Colors: red on white, blue on white, green on cream,
brown on cream.
Sizes  S M L XL. $65

**Striped Ties.** Item #765
These stylish ties with a jaunty stripe are made of
imported silk.
Colors: burgundy red/navy blue, moss green/navy blue,
moss green/golden yellow, black/bright red.
$30

**Cashmere Sweaters.** Item #521
You'll feel oh-so-comfortable in these sweaters made
of 100% genuine cashmere with a chic V neck.
Colors: burgundy red, charcoal gray, midnight black.
$150

| Description | Color | Size | Item No. | Quantity | Price |
|---|---|---|---|---|---|
| men's dress shirt-striped | blue/white | L | 387A | 2 | $110 |
| silk tie | red/blue | | 765 | 3 | $90 |
| cashmere sweater | black | L | 521 | 1 | $150 |
| | | | | | |
| | | | | | |
| | | | | sub total | $350 |
| | | | | shipping | |
| | | | | total | |

Payment Method*: __X__ check ____ credit card

Credit card number _____

Shipping Charges: for orders up to $200—$12.50
for orders up to $400—$20.00
for orders over $400—no charge

Please allow six weeks for delivery.
*Cash and money orders not accepted.

Send Order to

Bill Simpson
P.O. Box 78
Ardmore, IL

191. Which item is available in only three colors?
(A) Solid color shirts
(B) Striped shirts
(C) Ties
(D) Sweaters

192. What mistake did Mr. Simpson make with his shirt order?
(A) He didn't specify a size.
(B) He ordered a color that isn't available.
(C) He forgot the item number.
(D) He wrote the wrong price.

193. How many ties did Mr. Simpson order?
(A) 1
(B) 2
(C) 3
(D) 4

194. How much should Mr. Simpson pay for shipping?
(A) $0
(B) $12.50
(C) $20
(D) $22.50

195. How will Mr. Simpson pay for his order?
(A) Cash
(B) Check
(C) Credit card
(D) Money order

## Nugent, Inc.
## Professional Development Reimbursement Policy

All Nugent employees are encouraged to take advantage of professional development opportunities that are relevant to their work. Nugent sponsors a number of professional development workshops each year, and there are also many opportunities available outside the company, including classes at the local community college, at the City Computer Training Center, and at other local institutions. Information on these and other professional development opportunities is available from the Human Resources Office.

Nugent employees are entitled to 100% reimbursement for money spent on professional development. Please note that the reimbursement is for tuition and fees only. Travel, food, and other personal expenses are the responsibility of the employee. To receive reimbursement, please obtain Form 1276 from the Human Resources Office or download one from the Nugent, Inc. website. The form must be authorized by the employee's supervisor and submitted to the Human Resources Office within one month of the last day of the class or workshop attended. Forms that are submitted late or incomplete will not result in reimbursement.

**1276**

## Nugent, Inc.
## Professional Development Reimbursement Form

**Name:** Muriel Hicks    **Department:** Marketing

**Title of Workshop:** Intensive French    **Location:** City Language Academy

**Dates:** August 6–August 10

**Describe how this training is relevant to your work.** We are getting more French-speaking clients from Quebec. Everyone in my department is being encouraged to learn the language.

**Cost:** I spent $350 for the class plus a $20 registration fee. Also my bus fare totaled $45.

**Authorizing signature:** Eleanor Lee

196. How can a Nugent employee find
out about professional development
opportunities?
(A) From the Human Resources Office
(B) From his or her supervisor
(C) From the Nugent, Inc. website
(D) From a training specialist

197. Where did Muriel Hicks take a class?
(A) Nugent
(B) A language school
(C) The local community college
(D) The City Computer Training Center

198. How much money will be reimbursed
to Ms. Hicks?
(A) $45
(B) $350
(C) $370
(D) $415

199. Who is Eleanor Lee?
(A) A workshop organizer
(B) A human resources officer
(C) A French instructor
(D) Ms. Hicks's supervisor

200. What is the last date Ms. Hicks can submit
her reimbursement form?
(A) August 6
(B) August 10
(C) September 6
(D) September 10

# ANSWER KEY
## Practice Exam 3

## LISTENING COMPREHENSION

### Part 1: Photographs

| | | | |
|---|---|---|---|
| 1. **A** | 4. **B** | 7. **D** | 9. **B** |
| 2. **B** | 5. **B** | 8. **C** | 10. **C** |
| 3. **D** | 6. **A** | | |

### Part 2: Question-Response

| | | | |
|---|---|---|---|
| 11. **A** | 19. **B** | 27. **A** | 35. **A** |
| 12. **B** | 20. **C** | 28. **C** | 36. **C** |
| 13. **C** | 21. **C** | 29. **B** | 37. **B** |
| 14. **B** | 22. **A** | 30. **A** | 38. **A** |
| 15. **C** | 23. **A** | 31. **B** | 39. **B** |
| 16. **A** | 24. **B** | 32. **C** | 40. **C** |
| 17. **C** | 25. **C** | 33. **B** | |
| 18. **A** | 26. **B** | 34. **B** | |

### Part 3: Conversations

| | | | |
|---|---|---|---|
| 41. **B** | 49. **A** | 57. **D** | 65. **C** |
| 42. **D** | 50. **A** | 58. **B** | 66. **D** |
| 43. **C** | 51. **B** | 59. **C** | 67. **A** |
| 44. **B** | 52. **D** | 60. **D** | 68. **B** |
| 45. **A** | 53. **B** | 61. **C** | 69. **C** |
| 46. **A** | 54. **C** | 62. **A** | 70. **D** |
| 47. **C** | 55. **A** | 63. **B** | |
| 48. **B** | 56. **A** | 64. **C** | |

### Part 4: Talks

| | | | |
|---|---|---|---|
| 71. **A** | 79. **C** | 87. **C** | 95. **A** |
| 72. **D** | 80. **C** | 88. **B** | 96. **B** |
| 73. **B** | 81. **D** | 89. **B** | 97. **C** |
| 74. **A** | 82. **B** | 90. **D** | 98. **C** |
| 75. **C** | 83. **A** | 91. **A** | 99. **D** |
| 76. **B** | 84. **A** | 92. **C** | 100. **C** |
| 77. **A** | 85. **D** | 93. **B** | |
| 78. **D** | 86. **C** | 94. **D** | |

## READING

### Part 5: Incomplete Sentences

| | | | | | | | |
|---|---|---|---|---|---|---|---|
| 101. | A | 111. | A | 121. | B | 131. | B |
| 102. | B | 112. | C | 122. | D | 132. | D |
| 103. | B | 113. | D | 123. | D | 133. | B |
| 104. | C | 114. | A | 124. | C | 134. | D |
| 105. | C | 115. | B | 125. | B | 135. | C |
| 106. | D | 116. | A | 126. | A | 136. | B |
| 107. | A | 117. | C | 127. | D | 137. | D |
| 108. | C | 118. | A | 128. | C | 138. | C |
| 109. | D | 119. | B | 129. | A | 139. | A |
| 110. | B | 120. | C | 130. | C | 140. | A |

### Part 6: Text Completion

| | | | | | | | |
|---|---|---|---|---|---|---|---|
| 141. | C | 144. | B | 147. | A | 150. | B |
| 142. | A | 145. | B | 148. | B | 151. | A |
| 143. | D | 146. | C | 149. | D | 152. | D |

### Part 7: Reading Comprehension

| | | | | | | | |
|---|---|---|---|---|---|---|---|
| 153. | B | 165. | C | 177. | B | 189. | A |
| 154. | C | 166. | C | 178. | A | 190. | C |
| 155. | A | 167. | D | 179. | D | 191. | D |
| 156. | D | 168. | C | 180. | B | 192. | D |
| 157. | C | 169. | A | 181. | B | 193. | C |
| 158. | B | 170. | D | 182. | C | 194. | C |
| 159. | D | 171. | D | 183. | B | 195. | B |
| 160. | A | 172. | B | 184. | D | 196. | A |
| 161. | C | 173. | B | 185. | C | 197. | B |
| 162. | A | 174. | A | 186. | A | 198. | C |
| 163. | C | 175. | C | 187. | C | 199. | D |
| 164. | B | 176. | A | 188. | D | 200. | D |

# TEST SCORE CONVERSION TABLE

Count your correct responses. Match the number of correct responses with the corresponding score from the Test Score Conversion Table (below). Add the two scores together. This is your Total Estimated Test Score. As you practice taking the TOEIC model tests, your scores should improve. Keep track of your Total Estimated Test Scores.

| # Correct | Listening Score | Reading Score | # Correct | Listening Score | Reading Score | # Correct | Listening Score | Reading Score | # Correct | Listening Score | Reading Score |
|---|---|---|---|---|---|---|---|---|---|---|---|
| 0 | 5 | 5 | 26 | 110 | 65 | 51 | 255 | 220 | 76 | 410 | 370 |
| 1 | 5 | 5 | 27 | 115 | 70 | 52 | 260 | 225 | 77 | 420 | 380 |
| 2 | 5 | 5 | 28 | 120 | 80 | 53 | 270 | 230 | 78 | 425 | 385 |
| 3 | 5 | 5 | 29 | 125 | 85 | 54 | 275 | 235 | 79 | 430 | 390 |
| 4 | 5 | 5 | 30 | 130 | 90 | 55 | 280 | 240 | 80 | 440 | 395 |
| 5 | 5 | 5 | 31 | 135 | 95 | 56 | 290 | 250 | 81 | 445 | 400 |
| 6 | 5 | 5 | 32 | 140 | 100 | 57 | 295 | 255 | 82 | 450 | 405 |
| 7 | 10 | 5 | 33 | 145 | 110 | 58 | 300 | 260 | 83 | 460 | 410 |
| 8 | 15 | 5 | 34 | 150 | 115 | 59 | 310 | 265 | 84 | 465 | 415 |
| 9 | 20 | 5 | 35 | 160 | 120 | 60 | 315 | 270 | 85 | 470 | 420 |
| 10 | 25 | 5 | 36 | 165 | 125 | 61 | 320 | 280 | 86 | 475 | 425 |
| 11 | 30 | 5 | 37 | 170 | 130 | 62 | 325 | 285 | 87 | 480 | 430 |
| 12 | 35 | 5 | 38 | 175 | 140 | 63 | 330 | 290 | 88 | 485 | 435 |
| 13 | 40 | 5 | 39 | 180 | 145 | 64 | 340 | 300 | 89 | 490 | 445 |
| 14 | 45 | 5 | 40 | 185 | 150 | 65 | 345 | 305 | 90 | 495 | 450 |
| 15 | 50 | 5 | 41 | 190 | 160 | 66 | 350 | 310 | 91 | 495 | 455 |
| 16 | 55 | 10 | 42 | 195 | 165 | 67 | 360 | 320 | 92 | 495 | 465 |
| 17 | 60 | 15 | 43 | 200 | 170 | 68 | 365 | 325 | 93 | 495 | 470 |
| 18 | 65 | 20 | 44 | 210 | 175 | 69 | 370 | 330 | 94 | 495 | 480 |
| 19 | 70 | 25 | 45 | 215 | 180 | 70 | 380 | 335 | 95 | 495 | 485 |
| 20 | 75 | 30 | 46 | 220 | 190 | 71 | 385 | 340 | 96 | 495 | 490 |
| 21 | 80 | 35 | 47 | 230 | 195 | 72 | 390 | 350 | 97 | 495 | 495 |
| 22 | 85 | 40 | 48 | 240 | 200 | 73 | 395 | 355 | 98 | 495 | 495 |
| 23 | 90 | 45 | 49 | 245 | 210 | 74 | 400 | 360 | 99 | 495 | 495 |
| 24 | 95 | 50 | 50 | 250 | 215 | 75 | 405 | 365 | 100 | 495 | 495 |
| 25 | 100 | 60 | | | | | | | | | |

Number of Correct Listening Responses _____ = Listening Score _____

Number of Correct Reading Responses _____ = Reading Score _____

Total Estimated Test Score _____

# ANSWERS EXPLAINED

## Listening Comprehension

### PART 1: PHOTOGRAPHS

1. **(A)** A group of scientists in lab coats is gathered around a microscope. Choice (B) confuses *microscope* with *telescope*. Choice (C) correctly identifies the action, *examining*, but not the people. Choice (D) correctly identifies an object, *coats*, but no one is hanging them up.

2. **(B)** There is a sofa in front of the bookshelves with an open book lying on it. Choice (A) is incorrect because some of the bookshelves are full. Choice (C) is incorrect because there is no man in the photo. Choice (D) is incorrect because there is no table in the photo.

3. **(D)** A taxi cab is moving down a crowded street. Choice (A) uses the associated word *drivers*, but none are visible in the photo. Choice (B) refers to the cars, but they are moving, not parked. Choice (C) confuses *taxi* with *taxman*.

4. **(B)** Several businesspeople are gathered around a table discussing something. Choices (A), (C), and (D) all use words that sound similar to *meeting*.

5. **(B)** Passengers are seated on an airplane. Choice (A) confuses similar-sounding words *plane* and *rain*. Choice (C) is incorrect because the aisle is empty, not crowded. Choice (D) associates bookstore with the *books* that some passengers are reading.

6. **(A)** Two businessmen are standing on steps shaking hands with each other. Choice (B) misidentifies the action they are doing with their hands. Choice (C) identifies the stairs, but the men are not walking up them. Choice (D) identifies the railing, but no one is holding on to it.

7. **(D)** A waiter is carrying a tray holding a glass and a cup. Choice (A) associates *drinks* with *glass* and *cup*. Choice (B) associates *tea* with *cup*. Choice (C) associates *drinking* with *glass* and confuses similar-sounding words *waiter* and *water*.

8. **(C)** An auto mechanic is working under the hood of a car. Choice (A) mentions a type of car *van*, but misidentifies the action. Choice (B) associates *car* with *passenger*. Choice (D) associates *car* with *driver*.

9. **(B)** A young woman is in a library next to some shelves filled with books. Choice (A) confuses similar-sounding words *books* and *cooks*. Choice (C) identifies the location, but the library is clearly open since the young woman is there. Choice (D) incorrectly identifies the woman's action—she is reading, not writing.

10. **(C)** A man in a storehouse is using a lift to put heavy items on a high shelf. Choice (A) identifies the shelf, but no one is fixing it. Choice (B) identifies the boxes on the shelf, but no one is opening them. Choice (D) identifies the man's action, but not his location.

### PART 2: QUESTION-RESPONSE

11. **(A)** This answers the question about time. Choice (B) repeats the word *time*. Choice (C) answers a future tense question with the past tense.

12. **(B)** The speaker explains when Mr. Kim will *be back*, meaning *return*, from his vacation. Choice (A) confuses *vacation* with the similar-sounding word s*tation*. Choice (C) uses the wrong pronoun, *she* instead of *he*, to refer to *Mr. Kim*.

13. **(C)** The first speaker doesn't have a pen, so the second speaker offers one. Choice (A) associates *pen* with *write*. Choice (B) confuses *pen* with the similar-sounding word *open*.

14. **(B)** The phrase *in this closet* answers the question *Where?* Choice (A) confuses *coat* with the similar-sounding word *boat*. Choice (C) confuses *put* with *bought*.

15. **(C)** *Two* answers the question *How many?* Choice (A) confuses *buy* with the homonym *by*. Choice (B) answers *How much?*

16. **(A)** The word *friend* answers the question *Who?* Choice (B) associates *lunch* with *restaurant*. Choice (C) associates *lunch* with *hungry*.

17. **(C)** *Thirty minutes* answers the question *How long?* Choice (A) confuses *meeting* with the similar-sounding word *reading*. Choice (B) answers *How often* and repeats the word *last*.

18. **(A)** The second speaker wants to leave the store because it is crowded. Choice (B) confuses *store* with the similar-sounding word *more*. Choice (C) confuses *crowded* with the similar-sounding word *cloudy*.

19. **(B)** *Five years* answers the question *How long?* Choice (A) repeats the words *work* and *here*. Choice (C) repeats the word *here*.

20. **(C)** The second speaker suggests getting the carpet cleaned because the first speaker thinks it looks dirty. Choice (A) confuses similar-sounding words *books* and *looks* and *carpet* and *car*. Choice (B) confuses similar-sounding words *carpet* and *car*.

21. **(C)** *Two hundred dollars* answers the question *How much?* Choice (A) confuses similar-sounding words *train* and *rain*. Choice (B) would answer *How long?*

22. **(A)** This answers the question about the days the bank is open. Choice (B) confuses similar-sounding words *today* and *day*. Choice (C) associates *bank* with *account*.

23. **(A)** This explains why Ms. Lee isn't here. Choice (B) confuses homonyms *here* and *hear*. Choice (C) confuses similar-sounding words *here* and *her*.

24. **(B)** *A five-minute walk* answers the question *How far?* Choice (A) associates *restaurant* with *food*. Choice (C) associates r*estaurant* with *ate*.

25. **(C)** This answers the question about the topic of the meeting. Choice (A) confuses similar-sounding words *meeting* and *seating*. Choice (B) repeats the words *talk* and *meeting*.

26. **(B)** *Mr. Brown* answers the question *Who?* Choice (A) associates *photocopies* with *copy machine*. Choice (C) repeats the word *photocopies*.

27. **(A)** *A garage across the street* answers the question *Where?* Choice (B) confuses the meaning of the word *park*. Choice (C) repeats the word *car* and confuses similar-sounding words *park* and *dark*.

28. **(C)** This answers the question about a preferred place to sit. Choice (A) confuses similar-sounding words *seat* and *meat*. Choice (B) confuses similar-sounding words *prefer* and *deferred*.

29. **(B)** This is a logical response to the remark about the size of the office. Choice (A) confuses similar-sounding words *small* and *tall*. Choice (C) confuses similar-sounding words *small* and *call* and repeats the word *office*.

30. **(A)** This answers the question about *Which hotel?* Choice (B) confuses similar-sounding words *hotel* and *tell*. Choice (C) associates *hotel* with *reservation* and answers a past tense question with the future tense.

31. **(B)** This answers the question about the weather. Choice (A) would answer the question *Where?* Choice (C) would answer the question *How long?*

32. **(C)** *In your office* answers the question *Where?* Choice (A) associates *newspaper* with *news*. Choice (B) associates *newspaper* with *read*.

33. **(B)** *A few old friends* answers the question *Who?* Choice (A) confuses similar-sounding words *party* and *parts*. Choice (C) associates *party* with *food* and *dancing*.

34. **(B)** *This afternoon* answers the question *When?* Choice (A) repeats the word *report*. Choice (C) confuses similar-sounding words *ready* and *reading*.

35. **(A)** This answers the question about what was served for lunch. Choice (B) repeats the word *serve* and associates *cafeteria* with *lunch*. Choice (C) confuses similar-sounding words *lunch* and *bunch*.

36. **(C)** This is a logical response to a complaint about the dark. Choice (A) uses the word *dark* out of context. Choice (B) confuses similar-sounding words *dark* and *park*.

37. **(B)** *In my office* answers the question *Where?* Choice (A) confuses similar-sounding words *afternoon* and *soon*. Choice (C) repeats the word *afternoon*.

38. **(A)** This is a logical response to the question about the sweater. Choice (B) confuses similar-sounding words *sweater* and *better*. Choice (C) associates *sweater* with *wool*.

39. **(B)** *After midnight* answers the question *What time?* Choice (A) confuses similar-sounding words *home* and *phone*. Choice (C) repeats the word *home*.

40. **(C)** This answers the question about the time. Choice (A) associates *time* with *watch*. Choice (B) confuses similar-sounding words *time* and *mine*.

## PART 3: CONVERSATIONS

41. **(B)** The woman says there is a good movie at the theater and asks the man to go with her. Choice (A) repeats the word *show*. Choice (C) confuses similar-sounding words *work* and *walk*. Choice (D) confuses similar-sounding words *look* and *book*.

42. **(D)** The man says he has to work late. Choice (A) confuses similar-sounding words *plan* and *plane*. Choice (B) confuses similar-sounding words *ahead* and *bed*. Choice (C) is incorrect because the woman will buy the tickets.

43. **(C)** The man says, *I'll look for you by the front entrance at 9:00.* Choice (A) confuses similar-sounding words *hours* and *flowers*. Choice (B) is incorrect because the man wants to work late. Choice (D) is what the man suggests the woman do.

44. **(B)** The man says that they need to go over a report. Choice (A) is what the man suggests doing while they work but is not the reason for their meeting. Choice (C) associates *health* with *doctor's appointment*, which is where the woman will go in the afternoon. Choice (D) repeats the word *problem* and confuses similar-sounding words *appointment* and *point*.

45. **(A)** The man suggests meeting in his office. Choice (B) repeats the word *conference*. Choice (C) associates *lunch* with *restaurant*. Choice (D) is where the woman's doctor's appointment is.

46. **(A)** The woman says that she has a doctor's appointment. Choices (B) and (C) confuse *out of town* and *gown* with the similar-sounding word *downtown*. Choice (D) is what the man has to do in the morning.

47. **(C)** The woman asks *Are you going up?* and asks the man to push the button for the tenth floor, so it is an elevator. Choice (A) repeats the word *store*. Choice (B) associates *work* with *office*. Choice (D) repeats the word *apartment*.

48. **(B)** The woman says that she is visiting a colleague from work. Choice (A) confuses similar-sounding words *colleague* and *college*. Choice (C) confuses similar-sounding words *another* and *brother*. Choice (D) is incorrect because she hadn't ever met the man before this conversation.

49. **(A)** The man says that the building isn't a bad place to live and then mentions several positive things about it. Choice (B) repeats the phrase *bad building*. Choice (C) is something he mentions as a positive thing. Choice (D) confuses similar-sounding words *bad* and *sad*.

50. **(A)** The man says he wants to *book*, or reserve, a room for a meeting on Friday. Choice (B) is confused with the man's mention of the meeting schedule. Choice (C) is confused with the event that will be taking place later that morning. Choice (D) confuses the meaning of the word *book*.

51. **(B)** The man says the meeting will finish at 10:00. Choice (A) is the time the meeting will start. Choices (C) and (D) are the start and end times for the luncheon.

52. **(D)** The woman tells the man to use the chairs and then put them back in place before he leaves. Choice (A) is confused with *the chairs will be set up for the luncheon*, that is, by somebody else. Choice (B) confuses the meaning of the word *work*. Choice (C) repeats the word *place*.

53. **(B)** The man says that the hallways will be cleaned today. Choice (A) repeats the word *conference*. Choice (C) repeats the word *office*. Choice (D) repeats the word *front*.

54. **(C)** The woman says, *It's about time*, an expression used when someone has been waiting for something for a long time. Choice (A) is not mentioned. Choice (B) repeats the word *schedule*. Choice (D) repeats the word *time*.

55. **(A)** The woman says she will give a workshop on Friday of next week. Choice (B) confuses *workshop* with *shop*. Choice (C) associates *cafeteria* with *lunch*. Choice (D) repeats the word *schedule*.

56. **(A)** The woman says that she is visiting relatives in Chicago next week. Choice (B) repeats the word *vacation*. Choice (C) repeats the word *business*. Choice (D) repeats the word *visit*.

57. **(D)** The man says that the train trip takes 16 hours. Choice (A) is how long the plane trip takes. Choice (B) confuses similar-sounding words *before* and *four*. Choice (C) confuses similar-sounding words *time* and *nine*.

58. **(B)** The woman says she thinks the train will be more interesting. Choice (A) repeats the word *afraid* out of context. Choice (C) repeats the word *time*. Choice (D) is what the man says.

59. **(C)** This is the reason the woman gives. Choice (A) is not mentioned. Choice (B) confuses similar-sounding words *wait* and *late*. Choice (D) is true but not the reason that the post office is closed.

60. **(D)** The woman says that the post office is *over a mile from here*. Choice (A) is the distance to the local post office. Choice (B) confuses similar-sounding words *far* and *four*. Choice (C) repeats the word *mile*.

61. **(C)** The woman will find a taxi for the man to take. Choice (A) is what the man decided not to do. Choice (B) is what the man considers doing. Choice (D) confuses similar-sounding words *try* and *drive*.

62. **(A)** The man says that he spends his lunch break alone. Choice (B) is incorrect because the woman says she eats lunch with other friends. Choice (C) is incorrect because the assistant eats in the cafeteria and the man does not. Choice (D) is incorrect because the officemates eat at a restaurant and the man does not.

63. **(B)** The man says that he eats at his desk. Choice (A) is where the woman eats. Choice (C) is where the woman takes a walk. Choice (D) is where the man's assistant eats.

64. **(C)** The woman says that she meets friends for lunch at a café then walks in the park. Choice (A) confuses similar-sounding words *department* and *apartment*. Choice (B) is incorrect because she meets her friends rather than telephones them. Choice (D) confuses similar-sounding words *café* and *coffee*.

65. **(C)** The woman says she has a reservation for three nights but now needs to stay four nights. Choices (A) and (D) are offered by the man, but the woman doesn't request them. Choice (B) repeats the word *room*.

66. **(D)** The woman says she wants to take a walk in the park now, before dinner. Choice (A) confuses the meaning of the word *park*. Choice (B) repeats the word *dinner*. Choice (C) repeats the word *bank*.

67. **(A)** The woman says that the weather is warm. Choice (B) confuses similar-sounding words *know* and *snow*. Choice (C) confuses similar-sounding words *main* and *rain*. Choice (D) is not mentioned.

68. **(B)** The woman is getting ready to board the train to Vancouver, so the conversation takes place in a train station. Choice (A) associates *travel agency* with the context of travel and with the word *agent*. Choice (C) associates *suitcase* with *hotel*. Choice (D) associates *bank* with *check* by confusing the meaning of the word *check* (*to check a suitcase* versus *a check for money*).

69. **(C)** The woman says, *I have to find the gate quickly.* Choice (A) is incorrect because she already knows the schedule; she says that her train leaves at 10:30. Choice (B) is incorrect because she already knows the time; she says, *it's 10:15 now.* Choice (D) is incorrect because she has already made a reservation; she says, *I've booked a seat.*

70. **(D)** The woman asks for someone to carry her suitcase. Choice (A) confuses the meaning of the word *book*. Choice (B) repeats the word *ticket*. Choice (C) confuses the meaning of the word *check*.

## PART 4: TALKS

71. **(A)** The office is open from 7:00 A.M. until 9:00 P.M. Choice (B) is confused with the time the office closes. Choice (C) sounds similar to the correct answer. Choice (D) confuses similar-sounding words *through* and *two*.

72. **(D)** The instructions are to press 3 to open a new account. Choice (A) repeats the words *office hours*. Choice (B) is how to leave a message. Choice (C) is how to speak with a customer service representative.

73. **(B)** The instructions are to press 2 for billing questions. Choice (A) is done by pressing 0. Choice (C) is done by pressing 4. Choice (D) is done by staying on the line.

74. **(A)** The talk is a traffic report and tells where there are currently traffic problems in the region. Choice (B) is related to the topic of traffic but is not the main purpose of the talk. Choice (C) is discussed by the speaker but it is not the main topic. Choice (D) is incorrect because areas are described not for their interest but to explain where there are traffic problems.

75. **(C)** The White River Bridge is closed for repairs. Choice (A) is where the bridge traffic is being rerouted. Choice (B) is where there are traffic delays. Choice (D) is confused with the name of a road—*Park Avenue*.

76. **(B)** The repairs will be completed in early September. Choice (A) confuses the meaning of the word *may*. Choices (C) and (D) sound similar to the correct answer.

77. **(A)** The Legal Training Institute trains people for a career as a legal assistant. Choices (B) and (C) are confused with the described job duties of a legal assistant. Choice (D) repeats the word *career*.

78. **(D)** The course lasts six months. Choice (A) confuses homonyms *to* and *two*. Choice (B) confuses homonyms *for* and *four*. Choice (C) is confused with the price of the course.

79. **(C)** Listeners are instructed to visit the website to get an application. Choice (A) repeats the word *career*. Choice (B) is what listeners are instructed to do if they want to find out more about the career. Choice (D) confuses similar-sounding words *better* and *letter*.

80. **(C)** The words *plane, flight*, and *fly* are mentioned, so it would be heard at an airport. Choice (A) confuses similar-sounding words *plane* and *train*. Choice (B) confuses similar-sounding words *coat* and *boat*. Choice (D) confuses similar-sounding words *us* and *bus*.

81. **(D)** The speaker says that passengers should *approach Gate 11 now*. Choice (A) confuses similar-sounding words *gate* and *wait*. Choice (B) repeats the word *coats*. Choice (C) repeats the word *check*.

82. **(B)** The speaker says that boarding will begin with passengers with small children. Choice (A) is incorrect because it describes all the passengers. Choice (C) is mentioned, but these are not the passengers who will get on first. Choice (D) is the passengers who will get on second.

83. **(A)** The event is the *annual* Summer Fun Festival, so it happens once a year. Choice (B) is confused with the free event on opening night. Choices (C) and (D) are plausible but not mentioned.

84. **(A)** The speaker says that the festival is *coming up next month*. Choices (B) and (C) are confused with *July 15*, the date the festival begins. Choice (D) is not mentioned.

85. **(D)** On Thursday night, the opening ceremonies will be held, including a special concert. Choices (A), (B), and (C) refer to things that are part of the festival, but they are not specific to Thursday night.

86. **(C)** The reason for the strike is a salary freeze, meaning salaries will not change. Choice (A) confuses the meaning of *freeze*. Choice (B) repeats the word *passengers*. Choice (D) repeats the word *contract*.

87. **(C)** The strike is planned for next week. Choice (A) is when the salary freeze goes into effect. Choice (B) is when the meeting will take place. Choice (D) sounds similar to *few months*, the amount of time that the airline has been having financial difficulties.

88. **(B)** The meeting will be at the Royal Hotel. Choice (A) is confused with the representatives from the mayor's office, who will attend the meeting. Choice (C) is confused with representatives from the National Transportation Board, who will also attend the meeting. Choice (D) repeats the word *airport*.

89. **(B)** This car is the *designated quiet car*, so passengers can work quietly there. Choice (A) repeats *cold*, which is used to describe the food. Choice (C) is not mentioned. Choice (D) confuses *designated* and *design*.

90. **(D)** Smoking is prohibited on all parts of the train. Choices (A), (B), and (C) refer to things not allowed in the quiet car.

91. **(A)** In 15 minutes, the food service car will open and food and drinks will be sold. Choice (B) is the opposite of the correct answer. Choice (C) repeats the word *cold*. Choice (D) repeats the words *rear car*.

92. **(C)** The speaker mentions a *musical show*, that is, a play featuring singing and music. Choice (A) associates *musical* and *concert*. Choice (B) repeats *dog*, which is part of the title of the musical show. Choice (D) associates *puppet* with *children*.

93. **(B)** The speaker says, *Matinee tickets are $24 each*; matinee means *afternoon or daytime show*. Choice (A) costs $30. Choice (B) is not mentioned. Choice (D) is related to the word *children*.

94. **(D)** Callers are asked to leave a message if they want to reserve tickets. Choices (A) and (B) are associated with the context of a phone at the theater, but are not mentioned. Choice (C) repeats the word *mail*, but because a street address is mentioned, it is traditional mail, not e-mail, that the recording refers to.

95. **(A)** The announcer describes the weather this morning as *sun and humidity*. Choices (B) and (C) are how the weather will be later. Choice (D) is how the weather was before.

96. **(B)** This is the number the announcer says. Choices (A) and (C) sound similar to the correct answer. Choice (D) is what the high temperature will be.

97. **(C)** Because the weather will be rainy, the announcer recommends staying inside with a book. Choice (A) is associated with *gardeners*, the people who will be happy about the rainy weather. Choice (B) is what the announcer recommends not doing. Choice (D) confuses similar-sounding words *book* and *cook*.

98. **(C)** The guest will talk about mountain climbing and has tried to climb Mount Everest, so he is a mountain climber. Choices (A) and (B) are associated with the fact that he appeared in a documentary film. Choice (D) repeats the word *equipment*, something the speaker will cover in his talk.

99. **(D)** This is the price mentioned. Choice (A) confuses similar-sounding words *for* and *four*. Choices (B) and (C) sound similar to the correct answer. How much does the book cost?

100. **(C)** Next month's program has been canceled, meaning it won't happen. Choice (A) is what will happen the month after next. Choice (B) is confused with the film the speaker appeared in. Choice (D) is happening tonight.

## Reading

### PART 5: INCOMPLETE SENTENCES

101. **(A)** *No later than May 31* means that May 31 is the last date to submit. Choices (B), (C), and (D) are not used in this context.

102. **(B)** A verb is needed to complete the future verb *will have to*. Choices (A) and (C) are nouns. Choice (D) is an adjective.

103. **(B)** *Rarely* is an adverb of frequency meaning *almost never*. Choice (A) is an adjective. Choices (C) and (D) are adverbs but not adverbs of frequency, so they don't fit the sentence.

104. **(C)** *Missing* means *lost*; the sentence is about looking for lost equipment. Choices (A), (B), and (D) have meanings that don't fit the context.

105. **(C)** *Show up* means *be present*. Choices (A), (B), and (D) can be used with *show* but create meanings that don't fit the context.

106. **(D)** This is an imperative verb, giving a command or request. Choice (A) is the infinitive form. Choice (B) is the present participle or gerund. Choice (C) is present tense.

107. **(A)** This is an adverb of manner describing the verb *think*. Choice (B) is an adjective. Choice (C) is a verb. Choice (D) is a noun.

108. **(C)** This is a comparative adjective used to compare the new office to the old one. Choice (A) is a noun. Choice (B) is an adjective, but not comparative. Choice (D) is a superlative adjective.

109. **(D)** The relative pronoun *whose* at the beginning of the adjective clause indicates possession—the book belongs to Dr. Chin. Choices (A), (B), and (C) are all relative pronouns but do not indicate possession.

110. **(B)** The preposition *on* is used when telling the name of a street where something is located, but not the exact address. Choice (A) would be used for an exact address. Choice (C) would be used with the name of the city, but not the street or address. Choice (D) cannot be used in this context.

111. **(A)** *But* is used to show a contradiction between the two clauses of the sentence. Choice (B) would be used to add similar information. Choice (C) is used for comparatives. Choice (D) indicates a choice between two things.

112. **(C)** A *flaw* is an *imperfection* or *mistake*. Choices (A), (B), and (D) have meanings that don't fit the context.

113. **(D)** *Consented* means *agreed*. Choices (A), (B), and (C) have meanings that don't fit the context.

114. **(A)** *Before* tells when the documents should be on the desk relative to the hour of 8:00. Choice (B) would refer to two points in time. Choice (C) means that the documents should be removed from the desk at 8:00, which is the opposite of the meaning intended. Choice (D) refers to an action that is ongoing; putting documents on a desk is not an ongoing action.

115. **(B)** *Ascertain* means *make certain*. Choices (A), (C), and (D) have meanings that don't fit the context.

116. **(A)** This is the noun form acting as the subject of the sentence. Choice (B) is a verb. Choice (C) is an adverb. Choice (D) is an adjective.

117. **(C)** *Propose* means *suggest*. Choices (A), (B), and (D) have meanings that don't fit the context.

118. **(A)** The singular verb form *has* agrees with the singular subject *everybody*. Choice (B) is a plural verb. Choice (C) is an infinitive so cannot be used as the main verb. Choice (D) is present continuous, a form usually not used with a stative verb such as *have*.

119. **(B)** The verb *agree* is followed by an infinitive verb. Choice (A) is base form or present tense. Choice (C) is a gerund or present participle. Choice (D) is a noun.

120. **(C)** *Locally* is an adverb of manner used to describe the verb *produced*. Choice (A) is an adjective. Choice (B) is a verb. Choice (D) is a noun.

121. **(B)** The past tense unreal conditional uses the past perfect form of the verb in the *if* clause. Choice (A) is simple past tense. Choice (C) is present perfect. Choice (D) is conditional, the form required for the main clause.

122. **(D)** The verb *let* is followed by a base form verb. Choice (A) is simple past tense. Choice (B) is an infinitive. Choice (C) is simple present tense.

123. **(D)** The singular verb *is* agrees with the singular subject *number*. Choice (A) is base form. Choices (B) and (C) are plural forms.

124. **(C)** In this sentence, *or* indicates a choice between two actions. Choice (A) would be used to add a clause with similar information. Choice (B) indicates a contradiction between the two clauses. Choice (D) is used in negative sentences.

125. **(B)** *Among* means *in the middle of*. Choices (A), (C), and (D) look similar to the correct answer but have meanings that don't fit the context.

126. **(A)** *Might* is a modal so it is followed by a base form verb. Choice (B) is simple present tense. Choice (C) is future tense. Choice (D) is an incomplete future form.

127. **(D)** *Conduct* means *lead*. Choices (A), (B), and (C) have meanings that don't fit the context.

128. **(C)** A noun is needed here as the object of the verb *listening*. Choices (A) and (B) are verbs. Choice (D) is an adjective.

129. **(A)** *Regarded* means *considered* or *seen as*. Choices (B), (C), and (D) look similar to the correct answer but have meanings that don't fit the context.

130. **(C)** *As soon as* means *immediately after*. Choices (A) and (D) mean *at the same time*. Choice (B) means *before*.

131. **(B)** *Because* indicates a cause-and-effect relationship. Choices (A), (C), and (D) indicate a contradiction.

132. **(D)** *Besides* is an adverb meaning *as well*. Choices (A), (B), and (C) are all prepositions of place.

133. **(B)** *Despite* is a preposition that introduces a contradiction. Choices (A) and (C) are adverbs so don't fit the sentence structure. Choice (D) is a preposition that refers to a period of time.

134. **(D)** The singular verb *is* agrees with the singular subject *list*. Choices (A), (B), and (C) are all plural forms.

135. **(C)** The present perfect continuous verb indicates an action that began in the past and continues into the present. Choice (A) is present continuous. Choice (B) is a past tense form. Choice (D) is future perfect.

136. **(B)** *Parties* refers to the people named in a contract; they are the ones who will sign it. Choices (A), (C), and (D) do not refer to people and therefore cannot be said to sign contracts.

137. **(D)** *Identify* is the main verb of the second clause in this sentence. Choices (A) and (B) are also verbs but have meanings that don't fit the context. Choice (C) is a noun.

138. **(C)** *Discuss* is followed by a gerund. Choice (A) is base form or present tense. Choice (B) is past tense. Choice (D) is an infinitive.

139. **(A)** *Widely* in this context means *by many people*. Choices (B), (C), and (D) have meanings that don't fit the context.

140. **(A)** *Success* is a noun and acts as the subject of this sentence. Choice (B) is an adjective. Choice (C) is a verb. Choice (D) is an adverb.

## PART 6: TEXT COMPLETION

141. **(C)** This pronoun refers to the person addressed by the notice, *you, the customer*. Choice (A) would refer to the company sending the notice. Choice (B) would refer to one man. Choice (D) would refer to a thing.

142. **(A)** *Investigating* means *studying* or *researching*. Choices (B), (C), and (D) look similar to the correct answer but have meanings that don't fit the context.

143. **(D)** *Assistance* is a noun meaning *help* and is used as the object of the preposition *for* in this sentence. Choices (A) and (B) are verbs. Choice (C) is a noun, but it refers to people, not to a service.

144. **(B)** This is a simple past tense form describing a situation that was completed in the past. Choice (A) is present tense. Choice (C) is a conditional form. Choice (D) is negative so doesn't fit the meaning of the sentence.

145. **(B)** A promotion is when an employee is given a higher-level job; since Ms. Maldonado was capable of more responsibilities, her former employer wanted to promote her. Choice (A) is the opposite of the correct answer. Choice (C) often refers to a trial period given to new employees. Choice (D) is a type of punishment.

146. **(C)** *Asset* in this context means *valuable addition*. Choices (A), (B), and (D) have meanings that don't fit the context.

147. **(A)** This is a passive verb; the form does not fill itself out but is filled out by a person. Choices (B) and (C) are constructions that don't exist, because a modal is always followed by a base form verb. Choice (D) is active voice.

148. **(B)** *Following* means *next*. Choices (A), (C), and (D) all mean *before*, which would be impossible in this context.

149. **(D)** *Cooperation* means working together. Choices (A), (B), and (C) look similar to the correct answer but have meanings that don't fit the context.

150. **(B)** *Affordable* means *reasonably priced*; the topic of this paragraph is finding ways to make alternative energy systems less expensive. Choices (A), (C), and (D) could all be used to describe alternative energy systems but don't fit the context of the sentence.

151. **(A)** The verb *help* is followed by a base form verb. Choice (B) is present tense. Choice (C) is a gerund or present participle. Choice (D) is future tense.

152. **(D)** In this sentence, the gerund *reducing* acts as the subject and is modified by the adjective *simple*. Choice (A) is a noun. Choice (B) is a verb. Choice (C) is an adverb.

## PART 7: READING COMPREHENSION

153. **(B)** The new tenant will choose the paint and carpet colors as part of the renovations that will be made before move-in. Choice (A) is incorrect because the space is *pleasant and sunny*. Choice (C) is incorrect because a new carpet will be put in later, as part of the renovations. Choice (D) is incorrect because there is ample parking in the rear of the building.

154. **(C)** The phone number provided is that of a rental agency. Choice (A) is mentioned, but not as the person to call. Choice (B) is confused with the mention of the contract. Choice (D) repeats the word *tenant*.

155. **(A)** Visitors are required to keep the visitor's badge *visible at all times*. Choice (B) is incorrect because even though a visitor must wait for an escort, continuing to remain with the escort at all times is not mentioned. Choice (C) is incorrect because the cafeteria is open to the public, so anyone can go there. Choice (D) is incorrect; a visitor can leave the lobby in the company of an escort.

156. **(D)** The security officer goes off duty at 7:00 P.M., and visitors must leave the building before then. Choices (A) and (B) are confused with the office hours of the security manager. Choice (C) is when the cafeteria and lobby close.

157. **(C)** The hotel will open in September, and Ms. Hallowell will begin her new job a month before then. Choices (A) and (B) are confused with the time she worked for the tourism board. Choice (D) is when the hotel will open.

158. **(B)** Ms. Hallowell worked as a consultant for the tourism board between January and May of this year. Choice (A) is what her new job will be. Choice (C) is confused with the mention of the Hotel and Hospitality School of Fairfield, where she was a student, not an instructor. Choice (D) is a job she had more than five years ago.

159. **(D)** Ms. Hallowell worked as a tour guide in the Fiji Islands. Choice (A) is what she did before that, while still living in Fairfield. Choice (B) is associated with her work in tourism. Choice (C) is associated with her new job as hotel manager.

160. **(A)** Town residents need to show a recycling permit. Choice (B) is the cost of recycling certain items such as refrigerators. Choice (C) is confused with the mention of cars. Choice (D) is an item that can be recycled.

161. **(C)** Paint is an example of a hazardous waste, which will not be accepted for recycling on this date. Choices (A), (B), and (D) are all items listed as acceptable for recycling.

162. **(A)** *Displayed* means *shown*. Choices (B), (C), and (D) are all words that might be used about a permit but don't fit the context of the sentence.

163. **(C)** This ad is aimed at job seekers who may want to place a "job wanted" ad in the newspaper. Choice (A) is associated with job seekers. Choice (B) repeats the word *skills*. Choice (D) is associated with the subscribers mentioned in the footnote.

164. **(B)** The ad says, *Send an e-mail with your ad copy and phone number* . . . . Choice (A) repeats the word *charge*, but is incorrect because the job-wanted ads are free. Choice (C) is associated with job seekers. Choice (D) is incorrect because the job-wanted ads are free.

165. **(C)** E-mails with ad copy should be sent by Saturday to be included in the paper the following week. Choices (A), (B), and (D) are all days a free job-wanted ad could appear in the paper.

166. **(C)** The memo explains that with the 25% discount of the normal price of $50, the bus passes will cost $37.50. Choice (A) looks similar to the correct answer. Choice (B) is confused with the size of the discount. Choice (D) is the normal price.

167. **(D)** Employees are asked to complete a form and submit it to their supervisors. Choice (A) is the agency the company made an agreement with about the bus pass discount. Choice (B) is associated with buses and bus passes. Choice (C) is where the memo about the bus passes originated.

168. **(C)** The text says, *The cost will appear as a deduction on your first April paycheck.* Choice (A) uses the related word *deducted*. Choice (B) is plausible but not mentioned. Choice (D) uses the related word *check*.

169. **(A)** The new service advertised is online banking. Choices (B), (C), and (D) all repeat words mentioned in the advertisement.

170. **(D)** The advertisement says to *stop by*, or *visit*, any branch of the bank to talk with someone about online banking. Choice (A) is what to do to find out the locations of bank branches. Choice (B) is confused with the service being offered. Choice (C) is not mentioned.

171. **(D)** The bank has been in business *for more than a century*, and a century is 100 years. Choices (A) and (B) are incorrect because the word for a period of 10 years is *decade*, not *century*. Choice (C) is incorrect because it means *less than*, not *over* 100 years.

172. **(B)** *Enhance* means *improve*. Choices (A), (C), and (D) could fit the sentence but don't have the correct meaning.

173. **(B)** David Spaulding wrote the letter to say that a light rail system would provide a better solution to traffic problems than a new bridge. Choices (A) and (C) repeat issues mentioned in the letter but are not the purpose of the letter. Choice (D) repeats the phrase *city planners*, but there was no mention of the writer meeting with them.

174. **(A)** David Spaulding read an article about traffic problems and the new bridge in yesterday's paper. Choice (B) is incorrect because even though the bridge is discussed, there is no mention of visiting it. Choice (C) is incorrect because the light rail system has not been built yet. Choice (D) repeats the phrase *transportation experts*, but there was no mention of the writer meeting with them.

175. **(C)** The bridge is scheduled to be completed in two years. Choice (A) is when bridge construction will begin. Choice (B) is confused with the expression *over the coming months*, which is when traffic problems caused by bridge construction are expected to increase. Choice (D) is the amount of time a group of people has been working on a plan for a light rail system.

176. **(A)** David Spaulding's opinion is that a light rail system is a better solution to traffic problems than a new bridge. Choice (B) is incorrect because he says that the bridge *will add beauty to our city landscape.* Choice (C) is incorrect because even though David Spaulding mentions that the new bridge will be bigger, he doesn't express any opinion about this. Choice (D) is the opposite of his opinion.

177. **(B)** This article is for businesspeople who travel frequently by plane. Choices (A) and (C) are associated with plane travel. Choice (D) is associated with the discussion of health risks.

178. **(A)** The article discusses the problem of airplane passengers being exposed to disease. Choice (B) is confused with the advice to eat right. Choice (C) is a hazard of flying but is not mentioned. Choice (D) is confused with the mention of *being forced to sit for a long time.*

179. **(D)** Readers are advised to take Vitamin C to protect themselves from disease. Choices (A) and (B) are the opposite of pieces of advice given in the article. Choice (C) repeats the word *frequently.*

180. **(B)** *Obligations* means *duties.* Choices (A), (C), and (D) all could follow the word *business* but don't have the correct meaning.

181. **(B)** Monica needs to arrive before noon. She doesn't want to leave too early, so she probably won't take the 5:30 train, and the 7:45 is the only other train that will get her to Winston on time. Choice (A) is too early. Choice (C) arrives after noon. Choice (D) is the time she will arrive in Winston.

182. **(C)** Monica is traveling to Winston in order to attend a paper-producer's conference at the High Tower Hotel. Choice (A) is confused with the topic of the conference. Choices (B) and (D) are things she will do during her trip but are not the purpose of it.

183. **(B)** Monica asks Henry to book a room for her at the Inn at Winston. Choice (A) is where she doesn't want to stay. Choice (C) is where she will stay on Friday night. Choice (D) is incorrect because she won't be home until Saturday.

184. **(D)** Monica wants to leave Winston on Saturday afternoon. The 1:45 runs on weekdays only, so her only choice is the 3:30, which arrives in Pikesville at 6:45. Choices (A) and (B) are trains that leave in the morning. Choice (C) is the arrival time for the train that runs only on weekdays.

185. **(C)** Monica will leave on Wednesday, a weekday ($55) and return on Saturday, a weekend day ($43), so her total cost is $98. Choice (A) is the one-way weekend fare. Choice (B) is the one-way weekday fare. Choice (D) is the round-trip weekday fare.

186. **(A)** Ms. Kim wrote to tell Mr. Peters about her problems with a sullen waitress and an impatient golf instructor. Choice (B) is mentioned but is not the reason for the letter. Choice (C) repeats the word *menu.* Choice (D) is associated with the context of a vacation resort.

187. **(C)** Ms. Kim spends her annual, or yearly, vacation at Whispering Pines. Choices (A) and (B) are not mentioned. Choice (D) is confused with the number of years she has been visiting the resort.

188. **(D)** Mr. Peters says he will contact the manager of the inn. Choice (A) repeats the word *menu.* Choice (B) is mentioned but not as a response to Ms. Kim's letter. Choice (C) is a reasonable response to Ms. Kim's complaint but is not what Mr. Peters will do.

189. **(A)** Mr. Peters says that Ms. Kim can enjoy the same special meal she enjoyed on her last day at the resort, which was high tea. Choices (B), (C), and (D) are all things Ms. Kim had at the resort but are not what the coupon is for.

190. **(C)** Ms. Kim has spent every summer vacation at Whispering Pines for several years and she says that she plans to return there again, so that is probably what she will do on her next vacation. Choice (A) is an activity available at the resort, but Ms. Kim never mentions it. Choices (B) and (D) are things she says she won't do.

191. **(D)** Sweaters are available in burgundy red, charcoal gray, midnight black. Choices (A), (B), and (C) are all available in four colors or color combinations.

192. **(D)** He confused the price. He ordered striped shirts, which cost $65 each or $130 for two. Choice (A) is incorrect because he specified size L. Choice (B) is incorrect because the color he ordered is listed in the catalog. Choice (C) is incorrect because he wrote the item number for striped shirts.

193. **(C)** Mr. Simpson ordered three ties for a total cost of $90. Choices (A), (B), and (D) are not the number of ties he ordered.

194. **(C)** After Mr. Simpson corrects the price mistake on his short order, his subtotal will be $370. That price is still between $200 and $400, so he should pay $20 for shipping. Choice (A) is what he would pay if his order came to more than $400. Choice (B) is what he would pay if his order were less than $200. Choice (D) is confused with Choices (B) and (D).

195. **(B)** On the order form, Mr. Simpson indicated that he will pay by check. Choices (A) and (D) are not accepted by the company. Choice (C) is an option, but Mr. Simpson didn't choose it.

196. **(A)** The notice says that this information is available from the Human Resources Office. Choice (B) is the person who has to authorize the reimbursement form. Choice (C) is the place to find the reimbursement form. Choice (D) is related to the topic of professional development but is not mentioned.

197. **(B)** Muriel Hicks took a French class at the City Language Academy. Choices (A), (C), and (D) are all places where professional development opportunities are available but are not where she took a class.

198. **(C)** Ms. Hicks will be reimbursed for her tuition ($350) plus fees ($20). Choice (A) is the cost of the bus fare. Choice (B) is the cost of tuition only. Choice (D) is the cost of tuition, fees, and bus fare, but the bus fare is not reimbursable.

199. **(D)** The notice says that the form must be authorized by the employee's supervisor, and Eleanor Lee is the one who authorized the form. Choice (A) is related to the topic of professional development but is not mentioned. Choice (B) is the person who will receive the form. Choice (C) is the person who gave the class.

200. **(D)** The form must be submitted within one month of the last day of the class, August 10, and one month from that date is September 10. Choice (A) is the day the class began. Choice (B) is the last day of class. Choice (C) is one month from the first day of class.

# ANSWER SHEET
## TOEIC Practice Exam 4

## LISTENING COMPREHENSION

### Part 1: Photographs

1. Ⓐ Ⓑ Ⓒ Ⓓ
2. Ⓐ Ⓑ Ⓒ Ⓓ
3. Ⓐ Ⓑ Ⓒ Ⓓ
4. Ⓐ Ⓑ Ⓒ Ⓓ
5. Ⓐ Ⓑ Ⓒ Ⓓ
6. Ⓐ Ⓑ Ⓒ Ⓓ
7. Ⓐ Ⓑ Ⓒ Ⓓ
8. Ⓐ Ⓑ Ⓒ Ⓓ
9. Ⓐ Ⓑ Ⓒ Ⓓ
10. Ⓐ Ⓑ Ⓒ Ⓓ

### Part 2: Question-Response

11. Ⓐ Ⓑ Ⓒ
12. Ⓐ Ⓑ Ⓒ
13. Ⓐ Ⓑ Ⓒ
14. Ⓐ Ⓑ Ⓒ
15. Ⓐ Ⓑ Ⓒ
16. Ⓐ Ⓑ Ⓒ
17. Ⓐ Ⓑ Ⓒ
18. Ⓐ Ⓑ Ⓒ
19. Ⓐ Ⓑ Ⓒ
20. Ⓐ Ⓑ Ⓒ
21. Ⓐ Ⓑ Ⓒ
22. Ⓐ Ⓑ Ⓒ
23. Ⓐ Ⓑ Ⓒ
24. Ⓐ Ⓑ Ⓒ
25. Ⓐ Ⓑ Ⓒ
26. Ⓐ Ⓑ Ⓒ
27. Ⓐ Ⓑ Ⓒ
28. Ⓐ Ⓑ Ⓒ
29. Ⓐ Ⓑ Ⓒ
30. Ⓐ Ⓑ Ⓒ
31. Ⓐ Ⓑ Ⓒ
32. Ⓐ Ⓑ Ⓒ
33. Ⓐ Ⓑ Ⓒ
34. Ⓐ Ⓑ Ⓒ
35. Ⓐ Ⓑ Ⓒ
36. Ⓐ Ⓑ Ⓒ
37. Ⓐ Ⓑ Ⓒ
38. Ⓐ Ⓑ Ⓒ
39. Ⓐ Ⓑ Ⓒ
40. Ⓐ Ⓑ Ⓒ

### Part 3: Conversations

41. Ⓐ Ⓑ Ⓒ Ⓓ
42. Ⓐ Ⓑ Ⓒ Ⓓ
43. Ⓐ Ⓑ Ⓒ Ⓓ
44. Ⓐ Ⓑ Ⓒ Ⓓ
45. Ⓐ Ⓑ Ⓒ Ⓓ
46. Ⓐ Ⓑ Ⓒ Ⓓ
47. Ⓐ Ⓑ Ⓒ Ⓓ
48. Ⓐ Ⓑ Ⓒ Ⓓ
49. Ⓐ Ⓑ Ⓒ Ⓓ
50. Ⓐ Ⓑ Ⓒ Ⓓ
51. Ⓐ Ⓑ Ⓒ Ⓓ
52. Ⓐ Ⓑ Ⓒ Ⓓ
53. Ⓐ Ⓑ Ⓒ Ⓓ
54. Ⓐ Ⓑ Ⓒ Ⓓ
55. Ⓐ Ⓑ Ⓒ Ⓓ
56. Ⓐ Ⓑ Ⓒ Ⓓ
57. Ⓐ Ⓑ Ⓒ Ⓓ
58. Ⓐ Ⓑ Ⓒ Ⓓ
59. Ⓐ Ⓑ Ⓒ Ⓓ
60. Ⓐ Ⓑ Ⓒ Ⓓ
61. Ⓐ Ⓑ Ⓒ Ⓓ
62. Ⓐ Ⓑ Ⓒ Ⓓ
63. Ⓐ Ⓑ Ⓒ Ⓓ
64. Ⓐ Ⓑ Ⓒ Ⓓ
65. Ⓐ Ⓑ Ⓒ Ⓓ
66. Ⓐ Ⓑ Ⓒ Ⓓ
67. Ⓐ Ⓑ Ⓒ Ⓓ
68. Ⓐ Ⓑ Ⓒ Ⓓ
69. Ⓐ Ⓑ Ⓒ Ⓓ
70. Ⓐ Ⓑ Ⓒ Ⓓ

### Part 4: Talks

71. Ⓐ Ⓑ Ⓒ Ⓓ
72. Ⓐ Ⓑ Ⓒ Ⓓ
73. Ⓐ Ⓑ Ⓒ Ⓓ
74. Ⓐ Ⓑ Ⓒ Ⓓ
75. Ⓐ Ⓑ Ⓒ Ⓓ
76. Ⓐ Ⓑ Ⓒ Ⓓ
77. Ⓐ Ⓑ Ⓒ Ⓓ
78. Ⓐ Ⓑ Ⓒ Ⓓ
79. Ⓐ Ⓑ Ⓒ Ⓓ
80. Ⓐ Ⓑ Ⓒ Ⓓ
81. Ⓐ Ⓑ Ⓒ Ⓓ
82. Ⓐ Ⓑ Ⓒ Ⓓ
83. Ⓐ Ⓑ Ⓒ Ⓓ
84. Ⓐ Ⓑ Ⓒ Ⓓ
85. Ⓐ Ⓑ Ⓒ Ⓓ
86. Ⓐ Ⓑ Ⓒ Ⓓ
87. Ⓐ Ⓑ Ⓒ Ⓓ
88. Ⓐ Ⓑ Ⓒ Ⓓ
89. Ⓐ Ⓑ Ⓒ Ⓓ
90. Ⓐ Ⓑ Ⓒ Ⓓ
91. Ⓐ Ⓑ Ⓒ Ⓓ
92. Ⓐ Ⓑ Ⓒ Ⓓ
93. Ⓐ Ⓑ Ⓒ Ⓓ
94. Ⓐ Ⓑ Ⓒ Ⓓ
95. Ⓐ Ⓑ Ⓒ Ⓓ
96. Ⓐ Ⓑ Ⓒ Ⓓ
97. Ⓐ Ⓑ Ⓒ Ⓓ
98. Ⓐ Ⓑ Ⓒ Ⓓ
99. Ⓐ Ⓑ Ⓒ Ⓓ
100. Ⓐ Ⓑ Ⓒ Ⓓ

## READING

### Part 5: Incomplete Sentences

101. Ⓐ Ⓑ Ⓒ Ⓓ
102. Ⓐ Ⓑ Ⓒ Ⓓ
103. Ⓐ Ⓑ Ⓒ Ⓓ
104. Ⓐ Ⓑ Ⓒ Ⓓ
105. Ⓐ Ⓑ Ⓒ Ⓓ
106. Ⓐ Ⓑ Ⓒ Ⓓ
107. Ⓐ Ⓑ Ⓒ Ⓓ
108. Ⓐ Ⓑ Ⓒ Ⓓ
109. Ⓐ Ⓑ Ⓒ Ⓓ
110. Ⓐ Ⓑ Ⓒ Ⓓ

111. Ⓐ Ⓑ Ⓒ Ⓓ
112. Ⓐ Ⓑ Ⓒ Ⓓ
113. Ⓐ Ⓑ Ⓒ Ⓓ
114. Ⓐ Ⓑ Ⓒ Ⓓ
115. Ⓐ Ⓑ Ⓒ Ⓓ
116. Ⓐ Ⓑ Ⓒ Ⓓ
117. Ⓐ Ⓑ Ⓒ Ⓓ
118. Ⓐ Ⓑ Ⓒ Ⓓ
119. Ⓐ Ⓑ Ⓒ Ⓓ
120. Ⓐ Ⓑ Ⓒ Ⓓ

121. Ⓐ Ⓑ Ⓒ Ⓓ
122. Ⓐ Ⓑ Ⓒ Ⓓ
123. Ⓐ Ⓑ Ⓒ Ⓓ
124. Ⓐ Ⓑ Ⓒ Ⓓ
125. Ⓐ Ⓑ Ⓒ Ⓓ
126. Ⓐ Ⓑ Ⓒ Ⓓ
127. Ⓐ Ⓑ Ⓒ Ⓓ
128. Ⓐ Ⓑ Ⓒ Ⓓ
129. Ⓐ Ⓑ Ⓒ Ⓓ
130. Ⓐ Ⓑ Ⓒ Ⓓ

131. Ⓐ Ⓑ Ⓒ Ⓓ
132. Ⓐ Ⓑ Ⓒ Ⓓ
133. Ⓐ Ⓑ Ⓒ Ⓓ
134. Ⓐ Ⓑ Ⓒ Ⓓ
135. Ⓐ Ⓑ Ⓒ Ⓓ
136. Ⓐ Ⓑ Ⓒ Ⓓ
137. Ⓐ Ⓑ Ⓒ Ⓓ
138. Ⓐ Ⓑ Ⓒ Ⓓ
139. Ⓐ Ⓑ Ⓒ Ⓓ
140. Ⓐ Ⓑ Ⓒ Ⓓ

### Part 6: Text Completion

141. Ⓐ Ⓑ Ⓒ Ⓓ
142. Ⓐ Ⓑ Ⓒ Ⓓ
143. Ⓐ Ⓑ Ⓒ Ⓓ

144. Ⓐ Ⓑ Ⓒ Ⓓ
145. Ⓐ Ⓑ Ⓒ Ⓓ
146. Ⓐ Ⓑ Ⓒ Ⓓ

147. Ⓐ Ⓑ Ⓒ Ⓓ
148. Ⓐ Ⓑ Ⓒ Ⓓ
149. Ⓐ Ⓑ Ⓒ Ⓓ

150. Ⓐ Ⓑ Ⓒ Ⓓ
151. Ⓐ Ⓑ Ⓒ Ⓓ
152. Ⓐ Ⓑ Ⓒ Ⓓ

### Part 7: Reading Comprehension

153. Ⓐ Ⓑ Ⓒ Ⓓ
154. Ⓐ Ⓑ Ⓒ Ⓓ
155. Ⓐ Ⓑ Ⓒ Ⓓ
156. Ⓐ Ⓑ Ⓒ Ⓓ
157. Ⓐ Ⓑ Ⓒ Ⓓ
158. Ⓐ Ⓑ Ⓒ Ⓓ
159. Ⓐ Ⓑ Ⓒ Ⓓ
160. Ⓐ Ⓑ Ⓒ Ⓓ
161. Ⓐ Ⓑ Ⓒ Ⓓ
162. Ⓐ Ⓑ Ⓒ Ⓓ
163. Ⓐ Ⓑ Ⓒ Ⓓ
164. Ⓐ Ⓑ Ⓒ Ⓓ

165. Ⓐ Ⓑ Ⓒ Ⓓ
166. Ⓐ Ⓑ Ⓒ Ⓓ
167. Ⓐ Ⓑ Ⓒ Ⓓ
168. Ⓐ Ⓑ Ⓒ Ⓓ
169. Ⓐ Ⓑ Ⓒ Ⓓ
170. Ⓐ Ⓑ Ⓒ Ⓓ
171. Ⓐ Ⓑ Ⓒ Ⓓ
172. Ⓐ Ⓑ Ⓒ Ⓓ
173. Ⓐ Ⓑ Ⓒ Ⓓ
174. Ⓐ Ⓑ Ⓒ Ⓓ
175. Ⓐ Ⓑ Ⓒ Ⓓ
176. Ⓐ Ⓑ Ⓒ Ⓓ

177. Ⓐ Ⓑ Ⓒ Ⓓ
178. Ⓐ Ⓑ Ⓒ Ⓓ
179. Ⓐ Ⓑ Ⓒ Ⓓ
180. Ⓐ Ⓑ Ⓒ Ⓓ
181. Ⓐ Ⓑ Ⓒ Ⓓ
182. Ⓐ Ⓑ Ⓒ Ⓓ
183. Ⓐ Ⓑ Ⓒ Ⓓ
184. Ⓐ Ⓑ Ⓒ Ⓓ
185. Ⓐ Ⓑ Ⓒ Ⓓ
186. Ⓐ Ⓑ Ⓒ Ⓓ
187. Ⓐ Ⓑ Ⓒ Ⓓ
188. Ⓐ Ⓑ Ⓒ Ⓓ

189. Ⓐ Ⓑ Ⓒ Ⓓ
190. Ⓐ Ⓑ Ⓒ Ⓓ
191. Ⓐ Ⓑ Ⓒ Ⓓ
192. Ⓐ Ⓑ Ⓒ Ⓓ
193. Ⓐ Ⓑ Ⓒ Ⓓ
194. Ⓐ Ⓑ Ⓒ Ⓓ
195. Ⓐ Ⓑ Ⓒ Ⓓ
196. Ⓐ Ⓑ Ⓒ Ⓓ
197. Ⓐ Ⓑ Ⓒ Ⓓ
198. Ⓐ Ⓑ Ⓒ Ⓓ
199. Ⓐ Ⓑ Ⓒ Ⓓ
200. Ⓐ Ⓑ Ⓒ Ⓓ

# TOEIC Practice Exam 4

---

## LISTENING COMPREHENSION

In this section of the test, you will have the chance to show how well you understand spoken English. There are four parts to this section, with special directions for each part. You will find the Answer Sheet for Practice Exam 4 on pages 173–174. Detach it from the book and use it to record your answers. Check your answers using the Answer Key on pages 210–211 and see the Answers Explained beginning on page 213.

## Part 1: Photographs

**Track 14**

**Directions:** You will see a photograph. You will hear four statements about the photograph. Choose the statement that most closely matches the photograph and fill in the corresponding oval on your answer sheet.

**Example**

Now listen to the four statements.

Sample Answer
Ⓐ Ⓑ Ⓒ Ⓓ

Statement (B), "She's reading a magazine," best describes what you see in the picture. Therefore, you should choose answer (B).

**TIP**

If you do not have access to the MP3 files, please use the audioscripts beginning on page 384. You can also download the MP3 files and audioscripts from *http://barronsbooks.com/tp/toeic/audio/*

TOEIC PRACTICE EXAM 4

1.

3.

2.

4.

5.

6.

7.

8.

9.

10.

## Part 2: Question-Response

Track 15

**Directions:** You will hear a question and three possible responses. Choose the response that most closely answers the question and fill in the corresponding oval on your answer sheet.

**Example**

Now listen to the sample question.

You will hear:

How is the weather?

You will also hear:

(A)  It's raining.
(B)  He's fine, thanks.
(C)  He's my boss.

The best response to the question *How is the weather?* is choice (A), *It's raining.* Therefore, you should choose answer (A).

11.  Mark your answer on your answer sheet.

12.  Mark your answer on your answer sheet.

13.  Mark your answer on your answer sheet.

14.  Mark your answer on your answer sheet.

15.  Mark your answer on your answer sheet.

16.  Mark your answer on your answer sheet.

17.  Mark your answer on your answer sheet.

18.  Mark your answer on your answer sheet.

19.  Mark your answer on your answer sheet.

20.  Mark your answer on your answer sheet.

21.  Mark your answer on your answer sheet.

22.  Mark your answer on your answer sheet.

23.  Mark your answer on your answer sheet.

24.  Mark your answer on your answer sheet.

25.  Mark your answer on your answer sheet.

26.  Mark your answer on your answer sheet.

27.  Mark your answer on your answer sheet.

28.  Mark your answer on your answer sheet.

29.  Mark your answer on your answer sheet.

30.  Mark your answer on your answer sheet.

31.  Mark your answer on your answer sheet.

32.  Mark your answer on your answer sheet.

33.  Mark your answer on your answer sheet.

34.  Mark your answer on your answer sheet.

35.  Mark your answer on your answer sheet.

36.  Mark your answer on your answer sheet.

37.  Mark your answer on your answer sheet.

38.  Mark your answer on your answer sheet.

39.  Mark your answer on your answer sheet.

40.  Mark your answer on your answer sheet.

## Part 3: Conversations

**Directions:** You will hear a conversation between two people. You will see three questions on each conversation and four possible answers. Choose the best answer to each question and fill in the corresponding oval on your answer sheet.

Track 16

41. When was the phone call made?
    (A) Two minutes ago
    (B) A few minutes ago
    (C) At 4:00
    (D) Before noon

42. Who called?
    (A) The man's boss
    (B) The woman's assistant
    (C) The accountant
    (D) The budget director

43. Why did this person call?
    (A) To discuss the budget
    (B) To announce a salary raise
    (C) To ask the man to go to work early
    (D) To go over the accounts

44. Where does this conversation take place?
    (A) At a country club
    (B) At a restaurant
    (C) At a gym
    (D) At a hotel

45. How much will the woman pay?
    (A) $65
    (B) $155
    (C) $165
    (D) $220

46. What will the woman do now?
    (A) Read a book
    (B) Look at the room
    (C) Play tennis
    (D) Eat something

47. Where is Mr. Wing now?
    (A) On vacation
    (B) At a meeting
    (C) On a business trip
    (D) At the train station

48. When will he return to the office?
    (A) Tomorrow
    (B) On Friday
    (C) Next week
    (D) In three weeks

49. Who will help the woman with her project?
    (A) The man
    (B) Her boss
    (C) Mr. Wing
    (D) Mr. Wing's assistant

50. What is the man's complaint?
    (A) He didn't see any art.
    (B) The tickets were expensive.
    (C) The hotel is far away.
    (D) The museum is closed at night.

51. What does the woman suggest about the museum?
    (A) It has a good art collection.
    (B) Its paintings are not worth much.
    (C) It needs to be repainted.
    (D) It is not very big.

52. What will they do now?
    (A) Work
    (B) Go to the hotel
    (C) Park the car
    (D) Eat something

53. How is the weather today?
   (A) Cloudy
   (B) Rainy
   (C) Sunny
   (D) Icy

54. What are the speakers doing?
   (A) Working
   (B) Walking
   (C) Taking the train
   (D) Going to the store

55. When will the weather change?
   (A) Tomorrow
   (B) In two days
   (C) On the weekend
   (D) In a week

56. Why is the woman late?
   (A) She didn't have the bus fare.
   (B) She had to walk to the bus stop.
   (C) She missed the bus.
   (D) The bus was delayed.

57. How does the man get to work?
   (A) Bus
   (B) Car
   (C) Subway
   (D) Walking

58. What does the man say about the subway?
   (A) It is often delayed.
   (B) It's closer to the office.
   (C) It costs more than the bus.
   (D) It's more comfortable than the bus.

59. What does the man want to do?
   (A) Have lunch
   (B) Buy stamps
   (C) Cash a check
   (D) Open an account

60. Why does the woman tell the man to hurry?
   (A) The place is far.
   (B) It's getting late.
   (C) It's going to rain.
   (D) He'll have to wait in line.

61. What time is it now?
   (A) 1:00
   (B) Just before 1:30
   (C) Just after 1:30
   (D) 2:00

62. Why did the man leave his old job?
   (A) He didn't get enough vacation time.
   (B) It wasn't close to home.
   (C) The work was too slow.
   (D) The pay was too low.

63. How does he feel about his new job?
   (A) He's glad to have it.
   (B) He doesn't like it.
   (C) He's unsure about it.
   (D) He thinks it's too hard.

64. What does the woman indicate about her vacation time?
   (A) She uses it just once a year.
   (B) She plans to ask for more.
   (C) She's glad she has so much.
   (D) She doesn't usually use it all.

65. Where are the speakers going?
   (A) A park
   (B) A garage
   (C) The office
   (D) The theater

66. Why does the man want to leave early to get there?
   (A) He doesn't like to rush.
   (B) He thinks traffic will be heavy.
   (C) He's afraid it will be hard to find the place.
   (D) He wants to arrive before the place closes.

67. Where will they go later?

(A) A restaurant

(B) A party

(C) A game

(D) Home

68. What does the man want to drink?

(A) Coffee

(B) Hot tea

(C) Iced tea

(D) Water

69. How does the man feel?

(A) Thirsty

(B) Tired

(C) Hungry

(D) Angry

70. What does the woman offer the man?

(A) A book

(B) Some cake

(C) Some magazines

(D) A ride

## Part 4: Talks

**Directions:** You will hear a talk given by a single speaker. You will see three questions on each talk, each with four possible answers. Choose the best answer to each question and fill in the corresponding oval on your answer sheet.

Track 17

71. What is said about the flight to Caracas?
    (A) It has been overbooked.
    (B) It provides meal service.
    (C) It still has available seats.
    (D) It will leave 2 hours late.

72. What is offered to the passengers?
    (A) A free meal
    (B) A book
    (C) A suitcase
    (D) A refund check

73. How can passengers take advantage of the offer?
    (A) Board the plane
    (B) Talk to the gate agent
    (C) Wait in the lounge
    (D) Go to the baggage claim area

74. What place is opening?
    (A) A garden
    (B) An office
    (C) A store
    (D) An apartment

75. When will the opening take place?
    (A) Sunday
    (B) Monday
    (C) Friday
    (D) Saturday

76. Where is this place?
    (A) Next to the train station
    (B) Downtown
    (C) Beside a park
    (D) Across from a mall

77. What is the weather like?
    (A) Rainy
    (B) Snowy
    (C) Sunny
    (D) Warm

78. What happened this morning?
    (A) A train was delayed.
    (B) Some roads were closed.
    (C) There was a traffic accident.
    (D) Seven cars were ticketed.

79. What will happen tomorrow morning?
    (A) Snow will fall.
    (B) Schools will close.
    (C) Temperatures will become chilly.
    (D) The sky will clear up.

80. What are the tickets for?
    (A) A play
    (B) A circus
    (C) A movie
    (D) A TV show

81. How much do the tickets cost?
    (A) $15
    (B) $16
    (C) $37
    (D) $50

82. How can you get a free ticket?
    (A) Go to the theater
    (B) Send a postcard
    (C) Make a phone call
    (D) Visit a website

83. What was destroyed by a fire?
   (A) A tool shed
   (B) A park
   (C) A school
   (D) A bookstore

84. Who was hurt in the fire?
   (A) Ethel Rogers
   (B) A firefighter
   (C) Some children
   (D) No one

85. What is said about the fire?
   (A) It spread rapidly.
   (B) It was put out quickly.
   (C) It started in a storeroom.
   (D) Its cause is still unknown.

86. Why is the speaker making the call?
   (A) To tell her arrival time
   (B) To make a room reservation
   (C) To request a change of room
   (D) To ask when check-in time is

87. What does she imply about the inn?
   (A) It's her favorite place to stay.
   (B) It doesn't have enough rooms.
   (C) This will be her first visit there.
   (D) She read reviews about it online.

88. What does she mean when she says, "I can't wait?"
   (A) She's going to leave earlier than planned.
   (B) She's looking forward to her stay at the inn.
   (C) She probably won't give it a recommendation.
   (D) She doesn't have time to change her reservation.

89. What is the main purpose of this talk?
   (A) To explain the daily radio schedule
   (B) To introduce a radio program
   (C) To give contact information
   (D) To advertise a book

90. What will Dr. Silva talk about?
   (A) Office workers' health and fitness problems
   (B) The importance of business clothes that fit
   (C) How to give business talks
   (D) Writing books

91. What will Dr. Silva do after his talk?
   (A) Answer questions
   (B) Ask questions
   (C) Read the news
   (D) Go to the bank

92. What did the president do this afternoon?
   (A) Flew in a plane
   (B) Watched TV
   (C) Gave a speech
   (D) Had a meeting

93. Where will the president go tomorrow?
   (A) The capital city
   (B) Tokyo
   (C) Australia
   (D) Home

94. How long will his trip last?
   (A) 2 weeks
   (B) 3 weeks
   (C) 1 month
   (D) 4 months

95. At which one of the following times is the bank open?
   (A) Monday at 8:30 A.M.
   (B) Tuesday at 9:30 A.M.
   (C) Friday at 5:30 P.M.
   (D) Saturday at 4:30 P.M.

96. How can a customer find out the balance of his savings account?
    (A) Press 1
    (B) Press 2
    (C) Press 3
    (D) Press 4

97. What happens when a customer presses 0?
    (A) She can open a new account.
    (B) She can apply for a loan.
    (C) She can get a credit card.
    (D) She can hear the message again.

98. According to the speaker, what is the best place to look for a job?
    (A) Career counseling offices
    (B) Employment agencies
    (C) The Internet
    (D) Newspapers

99. What kinds of jobs can be found in this place?
    (A) Educational jobs only
    (B) Medical jobs only
    (C) Engineering jobs only
    (D) Any kind of job

100. According to the speaker, what is a job seeker's most important tool?
    (A) A résumé
    (B) A degree
    (C) Interview skills
    (D) Work experience

# READING

In this section of the test, you will have the chance to show how well you understand written English. There are three parts to this section, with special directions for each part.

**YOU WILL HAVE ONE HOUR AND FIFTEEN MINUTES
TO COMPLETE PARTS 5, 6, AND 7 OF THE TEST.**

## Part 5: Incomplete Sentences

> **Directions:** You will see a sentence with a missing word. Four possible answers follow the sentence. Choose the best answer to the question and fill in the corresponding oval on your answer sheet.

101. Rita put _____ some of the handouts for people who were unable to attend the staff meeting.
     (A) nearly
     (B) aside
     (C) along
     (D) beside

102. Check to make sure you have answered all the questions and signed the form _____ you submit it.
     (A) while
     (B) after
     (C) as soon as
     (D) before

103. The final report should be sent _____ the company's main office before the end of the month.
     (A) in
     (B) to
     (C) on
     (D) for

104. Since our goal is to use less electricity, we have decided to replace our refrigerator with a more _____ model.
     (A) abbreviated
     (B) thorough
     (C) efficient
     (D) limited

105. We _____ each staff member to do his or her part to get this project completed on time.
     (A) expect
     (B) predict
     (C) foresee
     (D) accomplish

106. You _____ answer all questions on the form or your request will not be considered.
     (A) must
     (B) can
     (C) might
     (D) could

107. Mr. Lutz is _____ to take on such a big responsibility because he doesn't feel prepared for it at this time.
     (A) relieved
     (B) reluctant
     (C) reliable
     (D) relocated

108. The current _____ of this office plans to leave before the end of the month.
     (A) occupancy
     (B) occupying
     (C) occupy
     (D) occupant

109. We are looking for ways to reduce expenses
     _____ our financial situation is not good.
     (A) although
     (B) but
     (C) because
     (D) or

110. The best way to _____ people to buy our
     product is to offer it at a lower price.
     (A) convince
     (B) observe
     (C) desire
     (D) discover

111. The director says that she _____ to hire
     several new staff members next year.
     (A) plan
     (B) plans
     (C) planning
     (D) planned

112. Mr. Chan _____ in charge of
     operations since the beginning of last
     year.
     (A) is
     (B) was
     (C) has been
     (D) will be

113. We never run out of ink for the printer
     because we keep a supply of _____
     cartridges in the closet.
     (A) replacement
     (B) sufficient
     (C) anticipating
     (D) adequate

114. If you wish to attend the annual conference,
     you have to sign _____ in advance.
     (A) it
     (B) out
     (C) off
     (D) up

115. Requests for extra time off should _____
     to your department head at least two weeks
     ahead of time.
     (A) submit
     (B) be submitted
     (C) be submitting
     (D) submission

116. Following a lengthy discussion, the board
     of directors finally agreed _____
     Ms. Silva's contract for another year.
     (A) renew
     (B) to renew
     (C) renewing
     (D) will renew

117. It is important to make a good first
     impression, so dress _____ when
     going on a job interview.
     (A) profess
     (B) profession
     (C) professional
     (D) professionally

118. Ms. Toth slipped and fell _____ she was
     walking on the icy sidewalk in front
     of the building.
     (A) while
     (B) during
     (C) although
     (D) but

119. Smoking is _____ in all areas of the
     building except for the designated smoking
     lounge.
     (A) rejected
     (B) disdained
     (C) prohibited
     (D) endorsed

120. All packages, bags, and bundles will
     be_____ by a security officer before
     leaving the building.
     (A) probed
     (B) inspected
     (C) analyzed
     (D) reviewed

121. The Harbor View Mall is a popular
destination, conveniently located in the
_____ of the downtown shopping
district.
(A) stern
(B) heart
(C) brink
(D) position

122. We are concerned _____ the high rate of
absenteeism among our employees.
(A) on
(B) for
(C) about
(D) of

123. The painters can't say exactly when the
work will be finished, but it should be
sometime _____ the end of June.
(A) around
(B) next to
(C) over
(D) in

124. The rent on this office is _____ than
the rent we have been paying at our old
place.
(A) high
(B) higher
(C) highly
(D) highest

125. _____ we were careful with expenses,
we still went over our budget this year.
(A) If
(B) Since
(C) Because
(D) Even though

126. She delayed _____ the contract
until she had a chance to speak with
her attorney.
(A) sign
(B) signing
(C) to sign
(D) signature

127. The woman _____ rents this office uses
it only a few days a month.
(A) who's
(B) whose
(C) who
(D) whom

128. If your passport is no longer _____,
then you should use some other form
of identification.
(A) valid
(B) validate
(C) validating
(D) validation

129. If you would like a more thorough
understanding of the issue, you can read
the article John _____ about it in last
month's newsletter.
(A) writes
(B) wrote
(C) is writing
(D) written

130. _____ your supervisor if you plan to be
away from the office for any length of time
during the day.
(A) Notify
(B) Notifying
(C) Should notify
(D) Will notify

131. Mr. Carlo was very upset when he learned
that he had been passed _____ for
the promotion.
(A) in
(B) out
(C) over
(D) through

132. We have spent too much money and
will have to _____ for the rest of
the year.
(A) economy
(B) economize
(C) economist
(D) economically

133. Time is short and we will have to work very hard to _____ our goals by the end of the year.
(A) perceive
(B) receive
(C) conceive
(D) achieve

134. You can have your paycheck mailed to you, _____ you can have your salary deposited directly into your bank account.
(A) or
(B) if
(C) but
(D) so

135. This building, _____ was built more than 100 years ago, is scheduled for demolition next month.
(A) it
(B) that
(C) was
(D) which

136. If we _____ your application by tomorrow, you will still be eligible for the job.
(A) will receive
(B) received
(C) receive
(D) receives

137. We _____ in the elevator when the electricity went out, and we were stuck there for almost an hour.
(A) rode
(B) were riding
(C) ridden
(D) had ridden

138. You must _____ every item on the form or your application will not be considered.
(A) complete
(B) to complete
(C) completing
(D) will complete

139. We feel _____ about coming to an agreement on this issue soon.
(A) hoping
(B) hopeful
(C) hopefully
(D) to hope

140. _____ in today's business world is difficult, and many new businesses fail.
(A) Compete
(B) To compete
(C) Competing
(D) Have competed

## Part 6: Text Completion

> **Directions:** You will see four passages, each with three blanks. Under each blank are four answer options. Choose the word or phrase that best completes the statement.

Questions 141–143 refer to the following memo.

---

**MEMO**

To: All staff
From: D. Rivera
Re: Office Dress Code

It has come to our attention that a number of staff members have been coming to work in inappropriate _____. Please be reminded that this is a place of

        141. (A) attire
            (B) transportation
            (C) schedules
            (D) attitudes

business and that staff members are expected to dress accordingly. This means that casual clothing such as shorts, T-shirts, sandals, and sneakers should not _____ in the office. This is of particular importance when

    142. (A) wear
        (B) worn
        (C) be wearing
        (D) be worn

meeting with clients. Remember that each one of you represents the company and needs to keep in mind the impression that you give to clients and potential clients.

If you have any questions or concerns about this policy, please let _____ know.

                143. (A) I
                     (B) him
                     (C) you
                     (D) me

I will be happy to clarify any issues for you and listen to your concerns.
Thank you for your cooperation.

---

Questions 144–146 refer to the following article.

As we age, it becomes more and more important to get regular exercise. At the same time, our work lives may become more and more _____.

144. (A) vacant
(B) relaxed
(C) hectic
(D) dull

How can a busy professional find time for exercise in an already overscheduled life? The answer is to exercise a little bit at a time over the course of the day. It all adds up, and you may find that by the end of the day you have gotten thirty minutes of exercise or more just by finding small opportunities here and there. The possibilities are endless. For example, _____ you park your car farther away from

145. (A) so
(B) if
(C) because
(D) although

your office than you normally do, you can get several minutes of walking time in, both on the way to and from the office. If you work in a tall building, _____

146. (A) consider
(B) select
(C) skip
(D) jump

the elevator and take the stairs, at least for part of the way. Climbing stairs provides good aerobic exercise. There are many more possibilities. How many can you think of?

Questions 147–149 refer to the following notice.

---

### JOB OPPORTUNITIES AT THE SHINDLIN COMPANY

Are you looking for a position that makes full use of your talents and at the same time allows you to grow in your profession? The Shindlin Company, a leading publisher of reference and educational books, provides a dynamic and creative workplace with a full package of benefits and opportunities for _____.

147. (A) advice
(B) adversity
(C) advertising
(D) advancement

We are looking for talented professionals with a wide variety of skills. We are also looking for college students and recent college graduates to fill a number of internship positions. We welcome your _____. Please review the list of

148. (A) applicant
(B) application
(C) to apply
(D) apply

job openings below, or submit your résumé along with a letter of interest to hr@shindlinco.com. We will contact you when we _____ an opening

149. (A) have
(B) will have
(C) had
(D) have had

that matches your skills and background.

---

To:       Mi Ja Kim
From:     Eun Hee Cho
Sent:     16 June 20--, 14:45
Subject:  Help with workshop

Hello, Ms. Kim,

I am working on the logistics for next week's workshop, and I need some help with planning the lunch. I've looked over the budget, and it appears that we don't have a great deal of money to spend for this. I am having a hard time finding a good _____ service that doesn't charge too

150. (A) accounting
     (B) banking
     (C) catering
     (D) organizing

much. Can you suggest one that can serve a decent meal at a decent price? I also need your suggestions for a place to serve the lunch. Mr. Song suggested one of the conference rooms, but _____ all seem too small to me. Do you think

151. (A) them
     (B) they
     (C) he
     (D) it

we could use the cafeteria? I would really _____ your

152. (A) appreciate
     (B) appreciative
     (C) appreciation
     (D) appreciated

ideas and suggestions.

Thank you very much.
Eun Hee Cho

## Part 7: Reading Comprehension

> **Directions:** You will see single and double reading passages followed by several questions. Each question has four answer choices. Choose the best answer to the question and fill in the corresponding oval on your answer sheet.

Questions 153–154 refer to the following advertisement.

---

### Does your business need more business?

Advertise in the *Daily Herald*'s Business Directory

Your ad will reach over 75,000 readers who need your services. Carpenters, plumbers, landscapers, bookkeepers, cleaners, and organizers are just some of the service providers who have found advertising in the *Daily Herald* newspaper to be a worthwhile investment.

Call 482-9872 to place your ad.
Ads are just $.50 per line per day.

---

153. Who would be interested in this ad?
  (A) Business owners
  (B) Investment advisers
  (C) Homeowners
  (D) Newspaper reporters

154. What would be the cost to run a 10-line ad for five days?
  (A) $.50
  (B) $2.50
  (C) $5.00
  (D) $25.00

Questions 155–156 refer to the following letter.

**Ming & Associates**
1800 Pacific Boulevard
Sydney

April 10, 20--

Harold Ungemach
Box 86449
Sydney

Dear Mr. Ungemach,

Thank you for sending us your résumé. Your qualifications are impressive. Unfortunately, we are rarely in the position of hiring full-time employees. We do, however, frequently have a need for consultants to work on temporary assignments. We are often looking for professionals with your background and skills to work on certain projects. If you would be interested in a temporary consulting position, please let me know. I will then keep your résumé on file and notify you when a suitable assignment becomes available. Again, thank you for thinking of us. I will look forward to hearing from you.

Sincerely,

*Mara Knightly*

Mara Knightly
Human Resources Coordinator

155. Why did Mr. Ungemach write to the Ming & Associates company?
(A) To order a product
(B) To apply for a full-time job
(C) To offer to help with a project
(D) To develop his skills

156. What does Ms. Knightly ask Mr. Ungemach to do?
(A) Send her his résumé
(B) Select a professional assignment
(C) Notify her when he is available
(D) Indicate his interest in a consulting position

Questions 157–158 refer to the following advertisement.

**HELP WANTED**

We are seeking an experienced financial professional to manage the accounting office at a rapidly growing financial services company. Responsibilities of the position include coordinating the work of a six-person accounting department, managing business accounts, and reviewing client financial information. This position reports to the chief financial officer (CFO). Requirements: university degree in accounting, a minimum of three years' management experience, up-to-date knowledge of accounting software, strong organizational and interpersonal skills. Benefits include health and dental insurance, vacation and sick leave, and a retirement plan. Interested candidates should send a cover letter and résumé to Simona Santarelli at HR@magus.com.
No phone calls please.

157. Who should apply for this job?
(A) A dentist
(B) An accountant
(C) A software engineer
(D) A health care manager

158. How can someone apply for this job?
(A) Call the HR coordinator
(B) E-mail the CFO
(C) Send a résumé to Ms. Santarelli
(D) Visit the Magus Finance, Inc. office

Questions 159–161 refer to the following article.

The Business and Industry Association will host a meeting to discuss business policy with local government officials next week. This event, which takes place each November, gives business and political leaders the opportunity to discuss business and economic concerns that will have an impact over the coming year, and to set the agenda for the next year's business regulation policy. A summary of the discussion will be provided to all members of the Business and Industry Association as well as to political representatives, and will be reported in this newsletter as well.

The meeting will take place at the Tinmouth Hotel on November 15 from 9:00 A.M. until noon. After the meeting, a luncheon will be served to all participants. Afterward Dr. Myrtle Pleasance of the Business Research Institute will address the audience on the topic of Analyzing Client Behavior. All members of the Business and Industry Association are encouraged to attend and can register by calling 583-9261 or visiting www.busind.org.

159. How often does the meeting take place?
(A) Once a week
(B) Once a month
(C) Once a year
(D) Twice a year

160. Who will participate in the discussion?
(A) Researchers
(B) Business leaders
(C) The governor
(D) Hotel administrators

161. What will happen right after the luncheon?
(A) The discussion will continue.
(B) There will be a speaker.
(C) Participants will go home.
(D) Members will call the Business and Industry Association.

Questions 162–164 refer to the following ad.

# Sale!     Sale!     Sale!

Pinkerton's announces its biggest sale of the year.
We have slashed prices on select items throughout the store.

- Printer ink cartridges—Buy one at $30, get the second one at 50% off
- Photocopier paper—Buy one pack of 500 sheets, get the second one free
- Jumbo pack notebooks—25% each pack of 10
- Desk organizers—Assorted colors, 15% off
- Office desks and computer stands—35% off
- Super-Comfort brand desk chairs—Assorted colors, 50% off

Hurry on down to Pinkerton's.
With deals like these, items will fly right off the shelves!

**Sale ends Saturday.**

162. What kind of business is Pinkerton's?
(A) Office supply store
(B) Printing company
(C) Furniture store
(D) Photocopy service

163. How much would a customer spend for two ink cartridges?
(A) $15
(B) $30
(C) $45
(D) $50

164. What does Pinkerton assume about the sale?
(A) Customers can get to their store in a hurry.
(B) On sale items will sell quickly.
(C) Desk chairs will sell faster than desk organizers.
(D) Most customers will buy just one 10-pack of notebooks.

**Chester Corp. Credit Card**
**Disputed Item Claim Form**

Please complete all items on this form and sign it before mailing. Do not include your credit card payment. This claim form must be sent in a separate envelope.

Name    *Helga Larsen*

Date    *March 25, 20--*

Amount Disputed    *$115*

Merchant    *Online Office Supplies, Inc.*

I have examined my statement and am disputing a charge made to my account for the following reason:

_____ This purchase was not made by me or by any other person authorized to use my card.

__X__ The amount shown on my statement is different from the amount I was charged at the time of purchase. Amount charged at time of purchase was __*$75*__ . (Enclose a copy of the sales receipt.)

_____ The item was to be shipped to me by mail. Expected delivery date _____. (This claim cannot be made until 30 days after the expected delivery date.)

_____ The merchandise I purchased was defective and returned by me to the merchant.

Return date _____. (Enclose copy of return receipt or postal receipt.)

Signature    *Helga Larsen*

165. What is this form for?
(A) To apply for a credit card
(B) To make a purchase
(C) To report a billing error
(D) To ask for a refund

166. What should Ms. Larsen enclose with the form?
(A) Payment
(B) A sales receipt
(C) An extra envelope
(D) Defective merchandise

167. The word *examined* in line 9 is closest in meaning to _____.
(A) paid
(B) sent in
(C) copied
(D) looked at

168. According to Ms. Larsen, how much should she pay?
(A) $15
(B) $75
(C) $115
(D) $175

Questions 169–172 refer to the following notice.

**Central Power Company**
**Account #4885 9965 0066 43**
**Notification of Discontinuation of Service**

Payment on your electric bill is now more than 30 days overdue. In compliance with National Regulation #50504, if we do not receive payment within 10 business days, we will discontinue your service. We must receive payment of $85 due on your bill plus a $15 late fee before August 31 to avoid interruption of service. Once disconnection has occurred, all outstanding charges must be paid in addition to a $50 reconnection fee before we can resume your service. You may be eligible for a monthly installment plan. Please contact our Customer Service office to discuss financing options.

See the reverse side of this notice for a complete explanation
of our rights and obligations under National Regulation #50504.

169. What is the purpose of this notice?
(A) To request an overdue payment
(B) To explain charges on an electric bill
(C) To clarify a national regulation
(D) To offer a financial service

170. If the customer pays before August 31, how much will he owe?
(A) $15
(B) $85
(C) $100
(D) $150

171. How can the customer find out about financing?
(A) Read the other side of the notice
(B) Call the Customer Service office
(C) Study National Regulation #50504
(D) Write to the power company

172. The word *resume* in line 8 is closest in meaning to _____.
(A) add to
(B) improve
(C) restart
(D) cut off

Local officials have finally reached an agreement with the Smithson Development Company regarding the construction of a new shopping mall in the Billings Bay neighborhood. A contract was signed last night, and construction is slated to begin in six months. The Smithson Development Company originally purchased the land for the mall four years ago from a horse farmer. The road to approval has been a long one. Plans for the mall have been protested by environmental groups and local residents. However, after modifying plans several times and including many environmentally friendly features as part of the construction, Smithson was finally able to win the approval of the city council.

The Billings Bay Mall will be the largest by far in our area. Space is planned for 250 retail shops as well as two large department stores, 20 restaurants, cafés, and snack shops, a 10-screen movie theater, an indoor play area, classroom space for the local community college, and a small walk-in health clinic. There will also be a 750-car underground parking garage, as well as space for at least twice as many cars in outdoor parking areas. Smithson estimates that once work on the new mall begins, according to the aforementioned schedule, construction will take no more than one year to complete. Plans for a grand opening are already under way.

173. Who is not in favor of the new shopping mall?
    (A) Local residents
    (B) The city council
    (C) A horse farmer
    (D) Mr. Smithson

174. Which one of the following things will customers NOT be able to do at the mall?
    (A) Take a class
    (B) Buy a car
    (C) Watch a movie
    (D) See a doctor

175. How many cars will be able to park in the outdoor parking lot?
    (A) 250
    (B) 500
    (C) 750
    (D) 1,500

176. When will construction of the mall probably be completed?
    (A) 6 months from now
    (B) 1 year from now
    (C) 1½ years from now
    (D) 4 years from now

Questions 177–180 refer to the following letter.

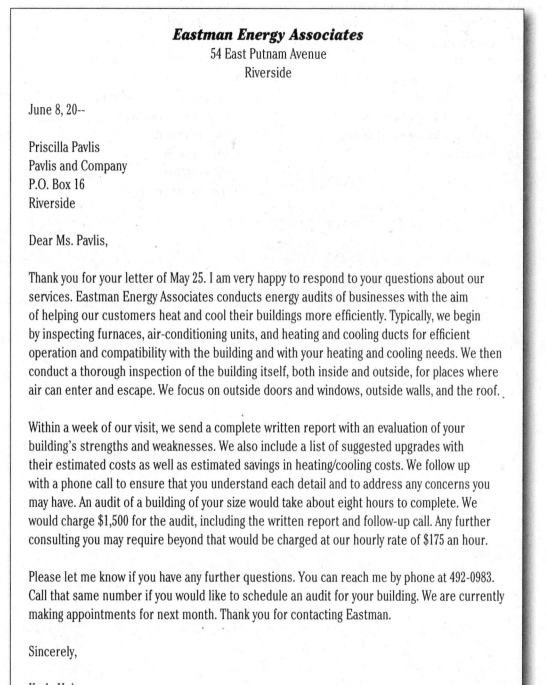

**Eastman Energy Associates**
54 East Putnam Avenue
Riverside

June 8, 20--

Priscilla Pavlis
Pavlis and Company
P.O. Box 16
Riverside

Dear Ms. Pavlis,

Thank you for your letter of May 25. I am very happy to respond to your questions about our services. Eastman Energy Associates conducts energy audits of businesses with the aim of helping our customers heat and cool their buildings more efficiently. Typically, we begin by inspecting furnaces, air-conditioning units, and heating and cooling ducts for efficient operation and compatibility with the building and with your heating and cooling needs. We then conduct a thorough inspection of the building itself, both inside and outside, for places where air can enter and escape. We focus on outside doors and windows, outside walls, and the roof.

Within a week of our visit, we send a complete written report with an evaluation of your building's strengths and weaknesses. We also include a list of suggested upgrades with their estimated costs as well as estimated savings in heating/cooling costs. We follow up with a phone call to ensure that you understand each detail and to address any concerns you may have. An audit of a building of your size would take about eight hours to complete. We would charge $1,500 for the audit, including the written report and follow-up call. Any further consulting you may require beyond that would be charged at our hourly rate of $175 an hour.

Please let me know if you have any further questions. You can reach me by phone at 492-0983. Call that same number if you would like to schedule an audit for your building. We are currently making appointments for next month. Thank you for contacting Eastman.

Sincerely,

Karla Heinz
Energy Consultant

177. Why did Ms. Heinz write this letter?
(A) To advertise her business
(B) To follow up on a consultation
(C) To reply to Ms. Pavlis's letter
(D) To explain charges on a bill

178. What does Ms. Pavlis want to do?
(A) Save money on heating and cooling
(B) Construct a new building
(C) Get new windows and doors
(D) Repair her roof

179. How much will Ms. Pavlis pay if she gets the service as outlined in the letter?
(A) $175
(B) $1,500
(C) $1,575
(D) $1,675

180. The word *upgrades* in paragraph 2, line 2 is closest in meaning to _____.
(A) materials
(B) systems
(C) builders
(D) improvements

# CRISP COMPANY

New charges for: Byron & Farrar Law Offices, account #2095687
From 03/01 to 03/31 20--

**Previous**
Balance from last bill: ...................................................$125
Payments received: ...........................................................$0
Previous balance due:....................................................$125

**Current**
Local phone service:........................................................$50
Long distance phone charges:.......................................$39
Internet services:.............................................................$35
Tax: ....................................................................................$8
Current charges:.............................................................$132

**Total due: Please pay this amount: $257**

Payments received after March 25 are not applied to this statement.
To dispute a charge, contact our customer service office in writing:

Crisp Company
Customer Service Office
45 Mountain View Road
Wilmington, KY 40205

April 18, 20--

Crisp Company
Customer Service Office
45 Mountain View Road
Wilmington, KY 40205

Dear Customer Service,

I am writing in regard to the recent bill from your company sent to us at Byron and Farrar Law Offices, account #2095687. In this bill we were charged for two months of service. This is incorrect since we owe only for this month's service. I personally paid last month's bill. According to my records, I wrote a check to your company for $125 and mailed it on March 26. I have contacted my bank and have been informed that that check has been processed and your company has received the funds. They will be providing me with a copy of the check before the end of the week, which I will then forward to you. Tomorrow I will be sending you a check for the amount owed for this month's charges only. Please correct your records to show the payment already made on last month's bill. Thank you for your attention. I expect the next bill will show the correct charges.

Sincerely,

*Robert Krumholz*

Robert Krumholz
Office Manager

181. What kind of services does Crisp Company offer?
(A) Law
(B) Delivery
(C) Phone and Internet
(D) Accounting

182. Why did Mr. Krumholz write the letter?
(A) He disagrees with a charge.
(B) He forgot his account number.
(C) He needs a copy of a check.
(D) He requires more services.

183. What mistake did Mr. Krumholz make?
(A) He wrote the wrong amount on the check.
(B) He didn't have enough money in the bank.
(C) He added the figures incorrectly.
(D) He sent in last month's payment late.

184. According to Mr. Krumholz, how much does he owe the company now?
(A) $50
(B) $125
(C) $132
(D) $257

185. What will Mr. Krumholz do tomorrow?
(A) Contact his bank
(B) Mail a check
(C) Get a copy of a check
(D) Write a letter to Crisp Company

| WORKSHOP SCHEDULE—DRAFT | | | |
|---|---|---|---|
| **Time** | **Location** | **Presentation** | **Presenter** |
| 9:30 | Room B | Changing World Markets | L. Chang |
| 11:00 | Room C | Cross-Cultural Considerations in Marketing | J. H. Lee |
| 12:15 | Room C | Lunch | |
| 1:30 | Room D | Analyzing Demographics | I. A. Kim |
| 3:00 | Room A | Internet Marketing | D. Wang |
| 4:00 | Room A | Open Discussion | All |

To:        F. Bao
From:      J. S. Park
Subject:   Workshop logistics
Date:      Monday, June 10
attch:     Workshop schedule

Ms. Bao,
I have attached a draft of the schedule for the upcoming workshop. I wish we had scheduled it for a week from today instead of for the day after tomorrow. There is still so much to do to get ready; however, we can't change the date now. I really appreciate your support in getting things ready.

Here are some things I need you to take care of. Tea and snacks should be served immediately after Mr. Chang's presentation. He plans to talk for just an hour, so there will be time for this before the next presentation begins. Also, the room that we have scheduled for lunch is one of the smaller rooms, and serving a meal there would be difficult. In addition, we have a workshop scheduled in the same place right before lunch, so there would be no time to set up. See if you can exchange places with the Demographics workshop. The room we have scheduled for that seems more convenient and comfortable for eating.

Please make sure there are enough chairs in each room for everyone. So far, 45 people have registered for the workshop, but a few more registrations could come in today or tomorrow. You should have 15 extra chairs in each room just to be safe. There is one last schedule change. Mr. Wang will have to leave right after lunch, so please give him Ms. Lee's time slot, and she can take Mr. Wang's afternoon time slot. Send me the revised schedule this afternoon. Thank you.

Jae Sun Park

186. When will there be a break for refreshments?
    (A) At 9:30
    (B) Right after the World Markets presentation
    (C) Immediately after I. A. Kim speaks
    (D) During the Open Discussion

187. Where does Mr. Park want the lunch served?
    (A) Room A
    (B) Room B
    (C) Room C
    (D) Room D

188. What does Mr. Park say about chairs for the workshop?
    (A) He isn't sure if enough chairs are available.
    (B) There should be 45 chairs in each room.
    (C) The rooms already have sufficient chairs.
    (D) Ms. Bao should place spare chairs in the rooms.

189. Who will present at 3:00?
    (A) L. Chang
    (B) J. H. Lee
    (C) I. A. Kim
    (D) D. Wang

190. What does Mr. Park want Mr. Bao to do before he goes home today?
    (A) Check the lunch menu
    (B) Change the workshop date
    (C) Create a new version of the workshop schedule
    (D) Help Mr. Wang prepare his presentation

Questions 191–195 refer to the following employee manual page and form.

**Annual Leave**

All employees of the Howland Corporation are entitled to annual leave, or vacation days, according to their length of service at Howland, as follows:

| Years Employed at Howland | Number of Annual Leave Days |
|---|---|
| 0–2 | 10 |
| 3–5 | 15 |
| 6–10 | 20 |
| 11 or more | 25 |

Annual leave days must be used up by the end of the calendar year or they will be forfeited. The actual dates when leave days may be taken are dependent on permission from the employee's supervisor. To apply to use annual leave days, the employee must complete form number 465, obtain the supervisor's permission and signature, and submit the form to the human resources director no later than 21 calendar days before the date when the requested leave will begin. Incomplete or late requests will not be reviewed and leave will not be granted.

Form No. 465

**The Howland Corporation**
Annual Leave Request Form

Name: *Daniel Ortiz*

Department: *Research and Development*

Number of annual leave days allowed: *15*

Number of leave days requested: *5*

Dates: *July 21 – July 25*     Name of Supervisor: *Nestor Perez*

Authorizing signature: _____

Please submit this form to Daisy Ortega, Room 14.

191. What is the maximum number of annual leave days a Howland employee can take?
    (A) 10
    (B) 15
    (C) 20
    (D) 25

192. How long has Daniel Ortiz probably worked at the Howland Corporation?
    (A) No more than 2 years
    (B) At least 3 years
    (C) At least 6 years
    (D) More than 11 years

193. What is the latest date Daniel Ortiz can submit this form?
    (A) July 1
    (B) July 15
    (C) July 21
    (D) July 26

194. Who has to sign the form?
    (A) Daniel Ortiz
    (B) Daisy Ortega
    (C) Nestor Perez
    (D) Mr. Howland

195. Who is Daisy Ortega?
    (A) President of the Howland Corporation
    (B) Head of the Research and Development Department
    (C) Human Resources Director
    (D) Daniel Ortiz's assistant

Questions 196–200 refer to the following advertisement and e-mail.

**FOR RENT**

Large, sunny office in convenient downtown location, near two bus routes, ample parking in rear. 900 sq. feet divided into two private offices and comfortable reception area, small kitchen, one bathroom. Modern 10-story building with two elevators. $1,750/month. First month's rent and security deposit equal to one month's rent required to move in. To see, call City Office Rentals at 382-0838 between 8:30 and 4:30, Tues.–Sat.

To:       Marilyn Sawyer
From:    Paul Lebowski
Sent:     Tuesday, October 3
Subject: Office rental

Marilyn,
Here's a link to an office rental ad I found online: www.offices.com/10-01. I think it's worth looking at even though the rent is a bit high. I know it is a good deal more than we are paying now, but look at the size. It's twice as big as our current office, and I'm sure we can use the space. And it has a kitchen and bathroom and a reception area just like we have now. Unfortunately it is nowhere near a subway station. That is a convenience I would miss having, but it does have parking, unlike our current office. I'm sure our clients would appreciate that. It would also be good to be in a building with an elevator. I'm really tired of using the stairs. I'd like to see the space as soon as possible. Could you call and make an appointment? Try and get one for tomorrow if you can, because after that I'll be away until next Monday, as you know. Thanks.
Paul

196. How big is Marilyn and Paul's current office?
(A) 450 square feet
(B) 750 square feet
(C) 900 square feet
(D) 1,750 square feet

197. What is true of Marilyn and Paul's current office?
(A) It costs more than the advertised office.
(B) It is near the subway.
(C) It is in a building with an elevator.
(D) It is in a 10-story building.

198. When does Paul want to see the office?
(A) Monday
(B) Tuesday
(C) Wednesday
(D) Thursday

199. What does the advertised office have that the current office doesn't?
(A) A kitchen
(B) A bathroom
(C) A parking area
(D) A reception area

200. How much would Marilyn and Paul have to pay before moving into the advertised office?
(A) $900
(B) $1,750
(C) $1,800
(D) $3,500

# ANSWER KEY
# Practice Exam 4

## LISTENING COMPREHENSION

### Part 1: Photographs

1. **D**
2. **B**
3. **A**
4. **C**
5. **C**
6. **A**
7. **D**
8. **B**
9. **C**
10. **A**

### Part 2: Question-Response

11. **B**
12. **A**
13. **C**
14. **C**
15. **A**
16. **B**
17. **A**
18. **C**
19. **B**
20. **B**
21. **C**
22. **A**
23. **A**
24. **C**
25. **B**
26. **A**
27. **A**
28. **C**
29. **A**
30. **C**
31. **B**
32. **A**
33. **C**
34. **C**
35. **B**
36. **A**
37. **A**
38. **C**
39. **A**
40. **C**

### Part 3: Conversations

41. **B**
42. **A**
43. **C**
44. **D**
45. **C**
46. **B**
47. **A**
48. **C**
49. **D**
50. **B**
51. **A**
52. **D**
53. **C**
54. **B**
55. **A**
56. **D**
57. **C**
58. **C**
59. **A**
60. **B**
61. **B**
62. **D**
63. **A**
64. **C**
65. **D**
66. **B**
67. **D**
68. **D**
69. **A**
70. **B**

### Part 4: Talks

71. **D**
72. **A**
73. **B**
74. **C**
75. **D**
76. **D**
77. **B**
78. **C**
79. **D**
80. **B**
81. **A**
82. **B**
83. **C**
84. **D**
85. **D**
86. **A**
87. **C**
88. **B**
89. **B**
90. **A**
91. **A**
92. **D**
93. **B**
94. **B**
95. **B**
96. **A**
97. **D**
98. **C**
99. **D**
100. **A**

# ANSWER KEY
## Practice Exam 4

## READING

### Part 5: Incomplete Sentences

| | | | |
|---|---|---|---|
| 101. **B** | 111. **B** | 121. **B** | 131. **C** |
| 102. **D** | 112. **C** | 122. **C** | 132. **B** |
| 103. **B** | 113. **A** | 123. **A** | 133. **D** |
| 104. **C** | 114. **D** | 124. **B** | 134. **A** |
| 105. **A** | 115. **B** | 125. **D** | 135. **D** |
| 106. **A** | 116. **B** | 126. **B** | 136. **C** |
| 107. **B** | 117. **D** | 127. **C** | 137. **B** |
| 108. **D** | 118. **A** | 128. **A** | 138. **A** |
| 109. **C** | 119. **C** | 129. **B** | 139. **B** |
| 110. **A** | 120. **B** | 130. **A** | 140. **C** |

### Part 6: Text Completion

| | | | |
|---|---|---|---|
| 141. **A** | 144. **C** | 147. **D** | 150. **C** |
| 142. **D** | 145. **B** | 148. **B** | 151. **B** |
| 143. **D** | 146. **C** | 149. **A** | 152. **A** |

### Part 7: Reading Comprehension

| | | | |
|---|---|---|---|
| 153. **A** | 165. **C** | 177. **C** | 189. **B** |
| 154. **D** | 166. **B** | 178. **A** | 190. **C** |
| 155. **B** | 167. **D** | 179. **B** | 191. **D** |
| 156. **D** | 168. **B** | 180. **D** | 192. **B** |
| 157. **B** | 169. **A** | 181. **C** | 193. **A** |
| 158. **C** | 170. **C** | 182. **A** | 194. **C** |
| 159. **C** | 171. **B** | 183. **D** | 195. **C** |
| 160. **B** | 172. **C** | 184. **C** | 196. **A** |
| 161. **B** | 173. **A** | 185. **B** | 197. **B** |
| 162. **A** | 174. **B** | 186. **B** | 198. **C** |
| 163. **C** | 175. **D** | 187. **D** | 199. **C** |
| 164. **B** | 176. **C** | 188. **D** | 200. **D** |

# TEST SCORE CONVERSION TABLE

Count your correct responses. Match the number of correct responses with the corresponding score from the Test Score Conversion Table (below). Add the two scores together. This is your Total Estimated Test Score. As you practice taking the TOEIC model tests, your scores should improve. Keep track of your Total Estimated Test Scores.

| # Correct | Listening Score | Reading Score | # Correct | Listening Score | Reading Score | # Correct | Listening Score | Reading Score | # Correct | Listening Score | Reading Score |
|---|---|---|---|---|---|---|---|---|---|---|---|
| 0 | 5 | 5 | 26 | 110 | 65 | 51 | 255 | 220 | 76 | 410 | 370 |
| 1 | 5 | 5 | 27 | 115 | 70 | 52 | 260 | 225 | 77 | 420 | 380 |
| 2 | 5 | 5 | 28 | 120 | 80 | 53 | 270 | 230 | 78 | 425 | 385 |
| 3 | 5 | 5 | 29 | 125 | 85 | 54 | 275 | 235 | 79 | 430 | 390 |
| 4 | 5 | 5 | 30 | 130 | 90 | 55 | 280 | 240 | 80 | 440 | 395 |
| 5 | 5 | 5 | 31 | 135 | 95 | 56 | 290 | 250 | 81 | 445 | 400 |
| 6 | 5 | 5 | 32 | 140 | 100 | 57 | 295 | 255 | 82 | 450 | 405 |
| 7 | 10 | 5 | 33 | 145 | 110 | 58 | 300 | 260 | 83 | 460 | 410 |
| 8 | 15 | 5 | 34 | 150 | 115 | 59 | 310 | 265 | 84 | 465 | 415 |
| 9 | 20 | 5 | 35 | 160 | 120 | 60 | 315 | 270 | 85 | 470 | 420 |
| 10 | 25 | 5 | 36 | 165 | 125 | 61 | 320 | 280 | 86 | 475 | 425 |
| 11 | 30 | 5 | 37 | 170 | 130 | 62 | 325 | 285 | 87 | 480 | 430 |
| 12 | 35 | 5 | 38 | 175 | 140 | 63 | 330 | 290 | 88 | 485 | 435 |
| 13 | 40 | 5 | 39 | 180 | 145 | 64 | 340 | 300 | 89 | 490 | 445 |
| 14 | 45 | 5 | 40 | 185 | 150 | 65 | 345 | 305 | 90 | 495 | 450 |
| 15 | 50 | 5 | 41 | 190 | 160 | 66 | 350 | 310 | 91 | 495 | 455 |
| 16 | 55 | 10 | 42 | 195 | 165 | 67 | 360 | 320 | 92 | 495 | 465 |
| 17 | 60 | 15 | 43 | 200 | 170 | 68 | 365 | 325 | 93 | 495 | 470 |
| 18 | 65 | 20 | 44 | 210 | 175 | 69 | 370 | 330 | 94 | 495 | 480 |
| 19 | 70 | 25 | 45 | 215 | 180 | 70 | 380 | 335 | 95 | 495 | 485 |
| 20 | 75 | 30 | 46 | 220 | 190 | 71 | 385 | 340 | 96 | 495 | 490 |
| 21 | 80 | 35 | 47 | 230 | 195 | 72 | 390 | 350 | 97 | 495 | 495 |
| 22 | 85 | 40 | 48 | 240 | 200 | 73 | 395 | 355 | 98 | 495 | 495 |
| 23 | 90 | 45 | 49 | 245 | 210 | 74 | 400 | 360 | 99 | 495 | 495 |
| 24 | 95 | 50 | 50 | 250 | 215 | 75 | 405 | 365 | 100 | 495 | 495 |
| 25 | 100 | 60 | | | | | | | | | |

Number of Correct Listening Responses _____ = Listening Score _____

Number of Correct Reading Responses _____ = Reading Score _____

Total Estimated Test Score _____

# ANSWERS EXPLAINED

## Listening Comprehension

### PART 1: PHOTOGRAPHS

1. **(D)** A group of businesspeople is riding down an escalator. Choice (A) confuses the papers they are holding with newspapers. Choice (B) confuses similar-sounding words *escalator* and *elevator*. Choice (C) refers to the documents they are holding, but no one is signing them.

2. **(B)** A ferry with cars on deck is crossing the water. Choice (A) is incorrect because the photo shows a ferry, not a bridge, crossing the water. Choice (C) is incorrect because the ferry is nowhere near a dock. Choice (D) is incorrect because the cars are on a ferry, not a highway.

3. **(A)** People are crossing the street on the painted lines, or the pedestrian crosswalk. Choice (B) confuses similar-sounding words *walking* and *talking*. Choice (C) identifies the correct location but not the action. Choice (D) confuses *crosswalk* with *sidewalk*.

4. **(C)** Two men in chef's hats are cooking food in a restaurant kitchen. Choice (A) associates *restaurant* with *kitchen*. Choice (B) confuses similar-sounding words *kitchen* and *chicken*. Choice (D) associates *kitchen* with *food*.

5. **(C)** A man holding several shopping bags is looking in a store window. Choice (A) mentions the window and confuses similar-sounding words *bags* and *rags*. Choice (B) mentions the door, but the man is not walking through it. Choice (D) is incorrect because the man is outside the store, not inside it.

6. **(A)** A pitcher with flowers in it sits on a table next to a bowl of fruit. Choices (B) and (D) are incorrect because the fruit is in a bowl on the table, not on a tree or in a bag. Choice (C) associates *garden* with *flowers*, but the photo is an indoor scene, not an outdoor garden.

7. **(D)** A man is walking through a place that has signs directing people to boarding areas and gates, so he must be in an airport. Choice (A) associates *round-trip ticket* with *airport*. Choice (B) confuses similar-sounding words *airport* and *court*. Choice (C) is incorrect because the man's suitcase is already packed.

8. **(B)** Two men are at a construction site and one is pointing something out to the other. Choice (A) is incorrect because their hats are on their heads, not in their hands. Choice (C) mentions the other man's phone, but no desk is visible in this outdoor scene. Choice (D) confuses similar-sounding words *pointing* and *painting*.

9. **(C)** A businessman is talking on the phone and looking at some papers. Choice (A) confuses similar-sounding words *talking* and *walking* and *phone* and *home*. Choice (B) associates *dialing* with *phone*. Choice (D) confuses similar-sounding words *looking* and *cooking*.

10. **(A)** A group of businesspeople is having a discussion around a table that has three computers, some drinking glasses, and some papers on it. Choice (B) confuses the drinking glasses with eyeglasses. Choice (C) is incorrect because it is a conference table, not a dinner table. Choice (D) mentions the papers, but no one is reading them.

11. **(B)** *My boss* answers the question *Who?* Choice (A) would answer *Whose?* Choice (C) would answer *Where?*

12. **(A)** The second speaker is *starving*, or very hungry, so agrees to the first speaker's suggestion of having lunch now. Choice (B) repeats the words *hour* and *lunch*. Choice (C) associates *lunch* with *restaurant*.

13. **(C)** *At the end of the week* answers the question *When?* Choice (A) confuses similar-sounding words *report* and *import*. Choice (B) uses the wrong pronoun, *he* instead of *it*, to refer to *the report*.

14. **(C)** *Across the street* answers the question *Where?* Choice (A) associates *cash that check* with *bank*. Choice (B) confuses similar-sounding words *bank* and *thank*.

15. **(A)** *The small blue one* answers the question *Which?* Choice (B) confuses similar-sounding words *car* and *far*. Choice (C) confuses similar-sounding words *yours* and *tour*.

16. **(B)** This explains why John left early. Choice (A) repeats the word *leave*. Choice (C) repeats the word *early*.

17. **(A)** *Boring* answers the question *How?* Choice (B) associates *movie* with *tickets*. Choice (C) confuses similar-sounding words *movie* and *move*.

18. **(C)** This is a reason why the second speaker cannot respond to the first speaker's request for help. Choice (A) confuses similar-sounding words *copy* and *shopping*. Choice (B) repeats the word *documents*.

19. **(B)** This answers the question about possession. Choice (A) associates *coat* with *closet*. Choice (C) repeats the word *coat*.

20. **(B)** The first speaker offers coffee, but the second speaker prefers tea. Choice (A) confuses similar-sounding words *coffee* and *coughing*. Choice (C) associates *coffee* with *cups*.

21. **(C)** *This one* answers the question *Which?* Choice (A) confuses similar-sounding words *seat* and *meat*. Choice (B) associates *seat* with *chair*.

22. **(A)** *An hour or so* answers the question *How long?* Choice (B) incorrectly answers a present tense question with the past tense. Choice (C) confuses similar-sounding words *take* and *cake* and repeats the word *there*.

23. **(A)** This explains what the second speaker did with the package. Choice (B) repeats the word *package*. Choice (C) confuses similar-sounding words *package* and *packing*.

24. **(C)** This answers the yes-no question about the meeting. Choice (A) confuses similar-sounding words *meeting* and *eating*. Choice (B) repeats the word *meeting*.

25. **(B)** This answers the question *Where?* Choice (A) confuses similar-sounding words *ink* and *think*. Choice (C) repeats the word *printer*.

26. **(A)** This is a logical response to the complaint about the rainy weather. Choice (B) confuses similar-sounding words *rain* and *train* and related words *tired* and *tiring*. Choice (C) confuses similar-sounding words *weather* and *leather*.

27. **(A)** *I* answers the question *Who?* Choice (B) confuses *papers* with *newspaper*. Choice (C) confuses the meaning of the word *sign*.

28. **(C)** This is a logical response to the question about the broken photocopy machine. Choice (A) associates *photocopy machine* with *copies*. Choice (B) confuses similar-sounding words *broken* and *spoken*.

29. **(A)** The first speaker needs a ride and the second speaker offers one. Choice (B) associates *airport* with *plane*. Choice (C) repeats the word *airport*.

30. **(C)** This answers the question about the time. Choice (A) repeats the word *time*. Choice (B) confuses similar-sounding words *time* and *fine*.

31. **(B)** *This one* answers the question *Which?* Choice (A) confuses similar-sounding words *suit* and *fruit*. Choice (C) confuses homonyms *wear* and *where*.

32. **(A)** *John's* answers the question *Whose?* Choice (B) repeats the word *car*. Choice (C) confuses the meaning of the word *park* and also confuses similar-sounding words *car* and *far*.

33. **(C)** *Next September* answers the question *When?* Choice (A) confuses similar-sounding words *conference* and *preference*. Choice (B) would answer the question *Where?*

34. **(C)** This explains the reason for going to the office. Choice (A) repeats the word *office*. Choice (B) repeats the word *Saturday*.

35. **(B)** This answers the tag question about possession. Choices (A) and (C) repeat the word *desk*.

36. **(A)** This explains what can be seen from the window. Choice (B) confuses *window* with the similar-sounding word *windy*. Choice (C) repeats the word *window*.

37. **(A)** *A cafeteria on the first floor* answers the question *Where?* Choice (B) confuses similar-sounding words *quick* and *pick*. Choice (C) confuses similar-sounding words *lunch* and *crunch*.

38. **(C)** *Three or four days* answers the question *How long?* Choice (A) confuses similar-sounding words *plan* and *plane*. Choice (B) repeats the word *stay*.

39. **(A)** This is a logical response to the question about finishing work. Choice (B) confuses similar-sounding words *budget* and *budge*. Choice (C) repeats the word *report*.

40. **(C)** This is a logical response to a remark about chilly weather. Choice (A) repeats the word *outside*. Choice (B) confuses similar-sounding words *chilly* and *hilly*.

## PART 3: CONVERSATIONS

41. **(B)** The woman heard the phone ringing a few minutes ago. Choice (A) confuses similar-sounding words *few* and *two*. Choice (C) confuses similar-sounding words *before* and *four*. Choice (D) is when the report for the accountant needs to be finished.

42. **(A)** The man says it was his boss on the phone. Choice (B) is the person the woman is expecting to call. Choice (C) is the person the man has to prepare a report for. Choice (D) repeats the word *budget*, which is what the woman's assistant is supposed to call about.

43. **(C)** The man's boss called to ask him to go to work early tomorrow to help with the report for the accountant. Choice (A) repeats the word *budget*. Choice (B) is what the woman would like the man's boss to do. Choice (D) associates *accounts* with *accountant*.

44. **(D)** The woman has a suitcase and is getting a room for the night, so she is at a hotel. Choice (A) associates the *pool, exercise room,* and *tennis courts* with a *country club*. Choice (B) associates *eat* with *restaurant*. Choice (C) associates *exercise room* with *gym*.

45. **(C)** The man says that the room costs $165. Choices (A) and (B) sound similar to the correct answer. Choice (D) is the room number.

46. **(B)** The woman says she will take her suitcase up and look at the room. Choice (A) confuses similar-sounding words *look* and *book*. Choice (C) is impossible because the tennis courts are closed. Choice (D) is what she will do after looking at the room.

47. **(A)** The man says that Mr. Wing is on vacation. Choice (B) is where the woman expected to see him. Choice (C) repeats the word *trip*. Choice (D) confuses similar-sounding words *vacation* and *station*.

48. **(C)** The man says Mr. Wing will be away until next week. Choice (A) is when Mr. Wing's assistant will be in the office. Choice (B) is when the woman's project is due. Choice (D) confuses similar-sounding words *see* and *three*.

49. **(D)** The man says that Mr. Wing's assistant will help the woman. Choice (A), one of the speakers, does not offer to help. Choice (B) is the person the work will be submitted to. Choice (C) is the person the woman wanted to ask for help.

50. **(B)** The man is complaining about how much the tickets cost. Choice (A) is incorrect because the man and woman agree that they enjoyed seeing the paintings. Choice (C) repeats the words *hotel* and *far*. Choice (D) confuses *right* with the similar-sounding word *night*.

51. **(A)** The woman says, *The paintings we saw were fantastic.* Choice (B) repeats the words *painting* and *worth*. Choice (C) relates *paintings* and *repainted*. Choice (D) is not mentioned.

52. **(D)** The woman says, *Let's get a snack*, that is, something to eat. Choice (A) confuses the meaning of the word *work*. Choice (B) repeats the word *hotel*. Choice (C) confuses the meaning of the word *park* as well as the similar-sounding words *far* and *car*.

53. **(C)** The man mentions the sunny day. Choice (A) is incorrect because the woman says that there is not a cloud in the sky. Choice (B) is how the weather was last week. Choice (D) confuses similar-sounding words *nice* and *ice*.

54. **(B)** The speakers are discussing the walk they are enjoying in the nice weather. Choice (A) confuses similar-sounding words *walk* and *work*. Choice (C) confuses similar-sounding words *rain* and *train*. Choice (D) confuses similar-sounding words *more* and *store*.

55. **(A)** The woman says that it will rain tomorrow. Choice (B) confuses similar-sounding words *today* and *two days*. Choice (C) confuses similar-sounding words *end* and *week-end*. Choice (D) repeats the word *week*.

56. **(D)** This is the explanation the woman gives. Choice (A) repeats the phrase *bus fare*. Choice (B) is incorrect because it takes the woman only two minutes to walk to the bus stop. Choice (C) is not mentioned.

57. **(C)** The man says that he takes the subway to work. Choice (A) is how the woman gets to work. Choice (B) confuses similar-sounding words *far* and *car*. Choice (D) is related to the word *walk*, the way the woman gets to the bus stop.

58. **(C)** The man says, *The bus fare is cheaper,* and then explains the difference in price. Choice (A) is what the man implies about the bus. Choices (B) and (D) are plausible but not mentioned.

59. **(A)** The man asks, *Is there a good place to eat around here?,* and the woman gives him directions to a restaurant. Choice (B) associates *post office* and *stamps*. Choices (C) and (D) associate *bank* with *check* and *account*.

60. **(B)** The woman warns the man they will stop serving lunch soon and mentions the time. Choice (A) is incorrect because the woman says that the restaurant is *just two blocks away*. Choices (C) and (D) are plausible but not mentioned.

61. **(B)** The woman says that it is *almost 1:30*. Choices (A) and (C) sound similar to the correct answer. Choice (D) is when the restaurant stops serving lunch.

62. **(D)** The man says he had to leave his job because of the low pay. Choice (A) is his complaint about the new job. Choice (B) is the opposite of what he says. Choice (C) confuses similar-sounding words *low* and *slow*.

63. **(A)** The woman says that the man is happy with his new job, and he agrees. Choice (B) is incorrect because it's the vacation he says he doesn't like, not the job itself. Choice (C) confuses similar-sounding words *sure* and *unsure*. Choice (D) is plausible but not mentioned.

64. **(C)** The woman is sorry the man only gets three weeks of vacation and says of her six weeks of vacation, *I need every one*. Choice (A) relates *one* and *once*. Choice (B) is not mentioned. Choice (D) is contradicted by the correct answer.

65. **(D)** They are going to the theater to see a play. Choice (A) confuses the meaning of the word *park*. Choice (B) repeats the word *garage*. Choice (C) is where they are now.

66. **(B)** The man says, *It'll be rush hour,* which is the time of day when traffic is heaviest. Choice (A) uses the word *rush* out of context. Choice (C) is confused with finding a place to park. Choice (D) confuses *closes* with *closed* (the parking garage is closed).

67. **(D)** The man says that they will go home when the play is over. Choice (A) confuses similar-sounding words *rest* and *restaurant*. Choice (B) confuses similar-sounding words *part* and *party*. Choice (C) confuses the meaning of the word *play* by associating it with *game*.

68. **(D)** This is what the man says he wants. Choices (A) and (B) are what the woman offers. Choice (C) repeats the words *ice* and *tea*.

69. **(A)** The man says that he is thirsty. Choice (B) confuses similar-sounding words *tried* and *tired*. Choice (C) is how the man says he does not feel. Choice (D) sounds similar to *hungry*.

70. **(B)** The woman offers the man a slice of cake. Choice (A) confuses similar-sounding words *look* and *book*. Choice (C) is where the woman found the cake recipe. Choice (D) confuses similar-sounding words *tried* and *ride*.

## PART 4: TALKS

71. **(D)** The speaker says that the flight will *depart two hours later than originally scheduled*. Choice (A) confuses similar-sounding words *rebooked* and *overbooked*. Choice (B) repeats the word *meal*. Choice (C) associates *tickets* with available seats.

72. **(A)** Passengers are invited to enjoy a complimentary, or free, meal at a restaurant in the airport. Choice (B) confuses the meaning of the word *book*. Choice (C) is what the passengers will have to pick up if they choose to rebook on another flight. Choice (D) confuses the meaning of the work *check*.

73. **(B)** Passengers have to show their boarding passes to the gate agent to get a meal ticket. Choice (A) is associated with *boarding pass*. Choice (C) repeats the word *lounge*, which is used to describe the location of the ticket office. Choice (D) is what passengers who rebook on a different flight will have to do.

74. **(C)** The place is the Mayflower and Company Department Store. Choice (A) is confused with the store's *garden supplies* department and is associated with the name of the store. Choice (B) is confused with the store's *office supplies* department. Choice (D) confuses similar-sounding words *department* and *apartment*.

75. **(D)** The grand opening is being celebrated *next Saturday*. Choices (A) and (B) sound similar to the phrase *one day*, the length of the opening event. Choice (C) is not mentioned.

76. **(D)** The store is *across the road from City Mall*. Choice (A) confuses similar-sounding words *rain* and *train*. Choice (B) is ten minutes away. Choice (C) confuses the meaning of the word *park*.

77. **(B)** Snow is falling, which has led to dangerous road conditions. Choice (A) confuses similar-sounding words *train* and *rain*. Choices (C) and (D) describe how the weather will be tomorrow.

78. **(C)** The speaker says that there was *a seven-car accident near the train station*. Choice (A) repeats the word *train*. Choice (B) is incorrect because it is schools, not roads, that are closed. Choice (D) repeats *seven car*.

79. **(D)** The speaker says, *Skies should start clearing toward morning* . . . . Choices (A), (B), and (C) are happening now.

80. **(B)** The announcement is about a circus that will be performing at the City Center Theater. Choices (A) and (C) are associated with the theater. Choice (D) repeats the word *show*.

81. **(A)** The announcer says that the tickets cost $15. Choices (B) and (D) sound similar to the correct answer. Choice (C) is confused with the show times: 3 P.M. and 7 P.M.

82. **(B)** People who want a free ticket should send a postcard to the circus owners in care of the theater. Choice (A) repeats the word *theater*. Choice (C) is how to order paid tickets. Choice (D) is not mentioned.

83. **(C)** The Riverside Park Elementary School was destroyed. Choice (A) confuses similar-sounding words *school* and *tool*. Choice (B) is confused with the name of the school. Choice (D) is mentioned as a place near the school.

84. **(D)** According to the report, there were no injuries. Choice (A) is the person who reported the fire. Choice (B) is who put out the fire. Choice (C) is confused with the schoolchildren who safely left the building hours before the fire.

85. **(D)** The speaker says, *The cause of the fire is under investigation*, meaning they are still trying to find out the cause. Choice (A) is not mentioned. Choice (B) is incorrect because it took five hours to put out the fire. Choice (C) confuses *bookstore* and *storeroom*.

86. **(A)** The speaker is calling to say that she will arrive later than the inn's check-in time, and she would like the staff to hold her reservation for her. Choice (B) is incorrect because she says she already has a reservation. Choice (C) repeats the word *room*. Choice (D) is incorrect because she already knows the check-in time.

87. **(C)** The speaker says, *I've heard so many good things about your place*, meaning that she has only heard about the place but not seen it. Choice (A) is contradicted by the correct answer. Choice (B) is not mentioned. Choice (D) associates *recommendations* (from her friends) with *reviews*.

88. **(B)** The phrase, *I can't wait* is used to express eagerness about doing something; the speaker feels this way because her friends have told her so many good things about the inn. Choices (A), (C), and (D) don't fit the meaning of this phrase or the context.

89. **(B)** The speaker welcomes listeners to the program and describes what the program will be that day. Choices (A), (C), and (D) are all confused with details of the talk but are not the main purpose.

90. **(A)** Dr. Silva will talk about *health and fitness issues facing office workers*. Choice (B) repeats the word *business* and confuses the meaning of the word *fit*. Choice (C) is confused with the name of the program, *Business Talks*. Choice (D) is associated with the fact that Dr. Silva has written a book, but his talk is about the contents of the book, not about writing it.

91. **(A)** Dr. Silva will answer phone calls from listeners who have questions. Choice (B) repeats the word *questions*. Choice (C) is confused with the contents of following programs. Choice (D) is confused with the topic of tomorrow's program.

92. **(D)** The president met with world leaders. Choice (A) is what he will do tomorrow. Choices (B) and (C) are confused with the speech he will give on TV tonight.

93. **(B)** The president will fly to Tokyo tomorrow. Choice (A) is where he is today. Choice (C) is another place he will visit on his trip. Choice (D) is where he will go when the trip is over.

94. **(B)** He will do a three-week tour of Asia and Australia. Choice (A) confuses similar-sounding words *to* and *two*. Choice (C) repeats the word *month*. Choice (D) confuses similar-sounding words *for* and *four*.

95. **(B)** The bank is open from 9:00 A.M. until 4:30 P.M. Monday through Friday; therefore, it is already open by 9:30 A.M. on Tuesday. Choices (A), (C), and (D) are all times that the bank is not open.

96. **(A)** Customers are told to press 1 to get *information on an existing checking or savings account.* Choice (B) is what to do to open a new account. Choice (C) is what to do to apply for a credit card. Choice (D) is what to do for information on loans.

97. **(D)** The recording says to press 0 *to repeat this menu.* Choice (A) is what happens by pressing 2. Choice (B) is what happens by pressing 4. Choice (C) is what happens by pressing 3.

98. **(C)** The speaker says that the Internet is the best place to look for a job. Choices (A), (B), and (D) are other places to look for a job, but they aren't the best places.

99. **(D)** According to the speaker, there is *something for everyone* on the Internet. Choices (A), (B), and (C) are all examples of some of the types of jobs that can be found on the Internet.

100. **(A)** This is what the speaker says is the most important job-seeking tool. Choices (B), (C), and (D) are other examples of tools for job seekers.

## Reading

### PART 5: INCOMPLETE SENTENCES

101. **(B)** To *put something aside* means to *put it in reserve.* Choices (A), (C), and (D) have meanings that don't fit the context.

102. **(D)** *Before* in this position means that first the form will be signed, and then it will be submitted. Choice (A) means *at the same time as.* Choices (B) and (C) would indicate the opposite order of events—submit the form first, then sign it—which isn't logical.

103. **(B)** *To* is the correct preposition to use after *send.* Choices (A), (C), and (D) cannot logically be used in this sentence.

104. **(C)** *Efficient* means *to do something without waste of effort or materials;* in this case, it refers to a refrigerator that runs with less electricity. Choice (A), (B), and (D) have meanings that don't fit the context.

105. **(A)** *Expect* in this context means *require.* Choices (B), (C), and (D) have meanings that don't fit the context of the sentence.

106. **(A)** *Must* refers to necessity or obligation. This sentence means that it is a necessity to answer all the questions on the form. Choice (B) refers to ability. Choices (C) and (D) refer to possibility.

107. **(B)** *Reluctant* means *unwilling.* Mr. Lutz is unwilling to take on a responsibility for which he is unprepared. Choices (A), (C), and (D) look similar to the correct answer but have meanings that don't fit the context of the sentence.

108. **(D)** *Occupant* is a noun referring to a person who occupies a place. Choice (A) is a noun referring to a situation. Choice (B) is a gerund. Choice (C) is a base form verb.

109. **(C)** *Because* indicates a cause-and-effect relationship. Choices (A) and (B) indicate a contradiction. Choice (D) indicates a choice.

110. **(A)** *Convince* means *persuade* or make someone want to do something. A lower price will make people want to buy the product. Choices (B), (C), and (D) have meanings that don't fit the context.

111. **(B)** This simple present verb agrees with the third person singular subject, *she*. Choice (A) does not agree with the subject. Choice (C) is a gerund and cannot be used as the main verb of the clause. Choice (D) is simple past tense.

112. **(C)** This is a present perfect verb indicating an action that began in the past and continues to the present. Choice (A) is simple present. Choice (B) is simple past. Choice (D) is future.

113. **(A)** *Replacement* cartridges are *extra* cartridges. Choices (B), (C), and (D) have meanings that don't fit the context.

114. **(D)** The phrasal verb *sign up* means *register*. Choice (A) is a pronoun without an antecedent. Choices (B) and (C) can be combined with *sign* to create phrasal verbs, but with meanings that don't fit the context.

115. **(B)** This is a passive idea. The subject, *requests*, receives the action, *submit*. Choices (A) and (C) are active-voice forms. Choice (D) is a noun.

116. **(B)** The main verb *agree* is followed by an infinitive. Choice (A) is base form or simple present tense. Choice (C) is a gerund. Choice (D) is future tense.

117. **(D)** This is an adverb of manner modifying the verb *dress*. Choice (A) is a verb. Choice (B) is a noun. Choice (C) is an adjective.

118. **(A)** *While* means *at the same time as*. Choice (B) cannot be used to introduce a clause. Choices (C) and (D) indicate a contradiction.

119. **(C)** *Prohibited* means *not allowed*. Choices (A), (B), and (D) have meanings that don't fit the context.

120. **(B)** *Inspected* means *examined*. It is the correct word to use in the context of a security officer looking at the contents of a bag. Choices (A), (C), and (D) have similar meanings but are not used in this context. They also imply a more thorough examination and possibly an evaluation, as well.

121. **(B)** *Heart* in this context means *center*. Choices (A), (C), and (D) have meanings that don't fit the context.

122. **(C)** The adjective *concerned* is used with the preposition *about*. Choices (A), (B), and (D) are not usually used with *concerned*.

123. **(A)** *Around* in this context means *close to*. Choices (B), (C), and (D) can't be used in this context.

124. **(B)** This is a comparative adjective used to compare the rent of the two offices. Choice (A) is a simple adjective form. Choice (C) is an adverb. Choice (D) is a superlative adjective.

125. **(D)** *Even though* is used to indicate a contradiction. Choice (A) indicates a condition. Choices (B) and (C) indicate cause and effect.

126. **(B)** The verb *delay* is followed by a gerund. Choice (A) is base form or simple present tense. Choice (C) is an infinitive. Choice (D) is a noun.

127. **(C)** *Who* is a relative pronoun used to refer to the noun *the woman* and acts as the subject of the adjective clause. Choice (A) is a contraction of *who* and *is*. Choice (B) is possessive. Choice (D) is an object pronoun.

128. **(A)** This is an adjective used to describe the word *passport*. Choice (B) is a verb. Choice (C) is a gerund. Choice (D) is a noun.

129. **(B)** This is a simple past tense verb that describes an action that happened last month. Choice (A) is simple present. Choice (C) is present continuous. Choice (D) is a past participle.

130. **(A)** This is an imperative verb form that is used to give a command and does not require the mention of the subject. Choice (B) is a gerund. Choices (C) and (D) require the mention of the subject.

131. **(C)** *Pass over* means *ignore* or *not choose*. Choice (A) would form *pass in*, meaning *submit*. Choice (B) would form *pass out*, meaning *distribute* or *lose consciousness*. Choice (D) would form *pass through*, meaning *go through*.

132. **(B)** The verb form is required here. Choices (A) and (C) are nouns. Choice (D) is an adverb.

133. **(D)** *Achieve* means *reach*. Choices (A), (B), and (C) look similar to the correct answer but have meanings that don't fit the context.

134. **(A)** *Or* indicates a choice. Choice (B) indicates a condition. Choice (C) indicates a contradiction. Choice (D) indicates a result.

135. **(D)** *Which* is a relative pronoun referring to the noun *building* and acts as the subject of the nonrestrictive adjective clause. Choice (A) is a pronoun, but not a relative pronoun. Choice (B) is a relative pronoun used in restrictive clauses. Choice (C) is a verb.

136. **(C)** This sentence is a future real conditional idea and requires a present tense verb in the *if* clause. Choice (A) is future tense. Choice (B) is past tense. Choice (D) is present tense but doesn't agree with the subject.

137. **(B)** The past continuous form indicates an action that was in progress when another action (*the electricity went out*) occurred. Choice (A) is simple past tense. Choice (C) is past participle. Choice (D) is past perfect.

138. **(A)** *Must* is a modal so it is followed by the base form of the verb. Choice (B) is an infinitive. Choice (C) is a gerund. Choice (D) is future tense.

139. **(B)** *Hopeful* is an adjective describing how we feel. Choice (A) is a gerund. Choice (C) is an adverb. Choice (D) is an infinitive.

140. **(C)** This is a gerund used as the subject of the sentence. Choice (A) is a base form verb. Choice (B) is an infinitive. Choice (D) is present perfect tense.

## PART 6: TEXT COMPLETION

141. **(A)** *Attire* means *clothes*, and this memo is about the right clothes to wear to work. Choices (B), (C), and (D) could fit the sentence but don't fit the context of the memo.

142. **(D)** This is a passive-voice sentence—the clothes mentioned do not wear themselves; they are worn by people. Choices (A), (B), and (C) are all active-voice forms.

143. **(D)** This is a first person object pronoun referring to the writer of the memo, who is the one who will discuss problems and concerns about the dress policy. Choice (A) is a subject pronoun. Choice (B) is third person. Choice (C) is second person.

144. **(C)** *Hectic* means *very busy*. Choices (A), (B), and (D) could fit the sentence but don't fit the context of the article.

145. **(B)** This is a present tense real conditional and *if* introduces the condition. Choice (A) introduces a result. Choice (C) introduces a reason. Choice (D) introduces a contradiction.

146. **(C)** *Skip* in this context means *avoid*. Choices (A), (B), and (D) have meanings that don't fit the context.

147. **(D)** *Opportunities for advancement* is something a company is likely to offer potential employees. Choices (A), (B), and (C) are not things a company would normally offer to job applicants.

148. **(B)** This is a noun referring to the process of asking for a job. In this sentence it acts as the object of the verb *welcome*. Choice (A) is a noun referring to the person who asks for a job. Choices (C) and (D) are verbs.

149. **(A)** A future time clause requires a present tense verb. Choice (B) is future tense. Choice (C) is past tense. Choice (D) is present perfect.

150. **(C)** Ms. Cho is looking for a service to prepare and serve lunch, that is, a catering service. Choices (A), (B), and (D) could fit the sentence but don't fit the context of the e-mail message.

151. **(B)** This is a subject pronoun acting as the subject of the clause and referring to the plural noun *rooms*. Choice (A) is an object pronoun. Choices (C) and (D) are singular pronouns.

152. **(A)** This is a base form verb following the modal *would*. Choice (B) is an adjective. Choice (C) is a noun. Choice (D) is a past tense verb.

## PART 7: READING COMPREHENSION

153. **(A)** The ad is asking business owners to advertise their businesses in the *Daily Herald* newspaper. Choice (B) repeats the word *investment*. Choice (C) is some of the people who might want to use the services business owners would advertise. Choice (D) repeats the word *newspaper*.

154. **(D)** Ten lines cost $5.00 a day, so the cost would be $25 for five days. Choice (A) is the cost of one line for one day. Choice (B) is the cost of one line for five days. Choice (C) is the cost of ten lines for one day.

155. **(B)** Ms. Knightly writes, *Unfortunately, we are rarely in the position of hiring full-time employees,* so we can assume that this is what Mr. Ungemach asked for. Choice (A) is a logical reason why someone might write to a company but is not the correct answer. Choice (C) repeats the word *product.* Choice (D) repeats the word *skills.*

156. **(D)** Ms. Knightly asks Mr. Ungemach to let her know if he would be interested in a temporary assignment as a consultant. Choice (A) is incorrect because Mr. Ungemach has already done this. Choice (B) repeats the words *professional* and *assignment.* Choice (C) is confused with Ms. Knightly's offer to notify Mr. Ungemach when a position becomes available.

157. **(B)** The job is for someone with an accounting degree to manage an accounting office. Choice (A) is associated with dental insurance, one of the job benefits. Choices (C) and (D) repeat words used on the advertisement.

158. **(C)** Interested candidates should send a letter and résumé to Simona Santarelli. Choice (A) is incorrect because the ad asks for no phone calls. Choice (B) mentions the person who will supervise whoever is hired for the position, but this is not the person who is accepting résumés. Choice (D) repeats the name of the company, but visiting the office is not mentioned.

159. **(C)** The meeting takes place every November, or once a year. Choice (A) repeats the word *week.* Choice (B) associates *November* with the word *month.* Choice (D) is incorrect because the meeting takes place only once each November.

160. **(B)** According to the article, business and political leaders will discuss business and economic concerns. Choice (A) is confused with the after-lunch speaker. Choice (C) is confused with *government officials.* Choice (D) is confused with the location of the meeting.

161. **(B)** Dr. Myrtle Pleasance of the Business Research Institute will speak. Choices (A) and (C) are logical possibilities but are not correct. Choice (D) is what should be done to register for the meeting before it takes place.

162. **(A)** All the items listed for sale are used in offices. Choice (B) is associated with the printer ink cartridges. Choice (C) is incorrect because even though Pinkerton's sells some furniture, it sells other kinds of things as well. Choice (D) is associated with the photocopier paper.

163. **(C)** The first ink cartridge costs $30, and the second is 50% of that, or $15. Choice (A) is the cost of the second cartridge only. Choice (B) is the cost of the first cartridge only. Choice (D) is confused with the size of the discount.

164. **(B)** The ad encourages customers to hurry to the store and states that sale items (*deals*) will fly right off the shelves, meaning *they will leave the shelves quickly.* Choices (A), (C), and (D) use words mentioned in the ad, but none of them are conclusions that can be drawn based on the information given.

165. **(C)** The form is to dispute an item, that is, disagree about a charge, on a credit card bill. Choices (A), (B), and (D) are all actions related to credit cards but are not the purpose of the form.

166. **(B)** Ms. Larsen is claiming that she was charged the wrong amount, and the form asks for a sales receipt in that situation. Choice (A) is incorrect because the form says to send payments separately. Choices (C) and (D) repeat words used on the form.

167. **(D)** *Examined* means *looked at.* Choices (A), (B), and (C) are all things one might do with a credit card statement but are not the correct answer.

168. **(B)** This is the amount Ms. Larsen says she was charged at the time she made the purchase. Choice (A) looks similar to the amount she was charged on the credit card statement. Choice (C) is the amount she was charged on the credit card statement. Choice (D) looks similar to the amount she was charged at the time of purchase.

169. **(A)** The notice asks for payment on an electric bill that is more than 30 days overdue. Choice (B) is incorrect because although the notice explains some charges, that is not the main purpose. Choice (C) is on the back of the notice, but not its main purpose. Choice (D) is confused with the financing options that can be discussed with Customer Service.

170. **(C)** The customer will owe the $85 already owed for electric service and a $15 late fee. Choice (A) is the late fee only. Choice (B) is the electric service charge only. Choice (D) includes the reconnection charge and is what would be owed after August 31.

171. **(B)** The customer is invited to call the Customer Service office to find out about financing options. Choice (A) is how to find out more about National Regulation #50504. Choice (C) is on the reverse of the notice but is not about financing. Choice (D) is not mentioned.

172. **(C)** *Resume* means *restart.* The other words could fit the sentence but do not have the correct meaning.

173. **(A)** Local residents, together with environmental groups, protested the mall. Choice (B) gave official approval for the mall. Choice (C) is the person who sold the land to the development company to build the mall. Choice (D) is probably the owner of the development company that will build the mall.

174. **(B)** Customers will be able to park cars but there is no mention of any business selling cars. Choice (A) is possible because there will be classroom space for the local community college. Choice (C) is possible because there will be a movie theater. Choice (D) is possible because there will be a clinic.

175. **(D)** Twice as many cars will fit outdoors as in the garage (where 750 will fit). Choice (A) is the number of stores. Choice (B) is twice the number of stores. Choice (C) is the number of cars that will fit in the garage.

176. **(C)** Construction will begin in six months and take about a year. Choice (A) is when construction will begin. Choice (B) is confused with the length of time construction will take. Choice (D) is confused with how long ago Smithson bought the land for the mall.

177. **(C)** She wrote the letter to respond to questions Ms. Pavlis had sent in a letter on May 25. Choice (A) is incorrect because Ms. Pavlis wrote to ask for information so this is not really an advertisement. Choice (B) will happen after the audit takes place. Choice (D)

is confused with the mention of costs that may have to be made to save on heating and cooling.

178. **(A)** The service offered by Eastman Energy Associates is an audit to show businesses how they can save money on heating and cooling costs. Choice (B) is confused with the discussion of different parts of the building. Choices (C) and (D) repeat words mentioned in the letter.

179. **(B)** Ms. Heinz says the audit costs $1,500, including everything. Choice (A) is the cost of one hour of consulting. Choice (C) looks similar to the costs mentioned. Choice (D) is the cost of the audit plus one hour of consulting.

180. **(D)** *Upgrades* means *improvements*. Choices (A), (B), and (C) could fit the sentence but don't have the right meaning.

181. **(C)** The bill shows charges for phone and Internet services. Choice (A) is the kind of business Mr. Krumholz works for. Choice (B) is not mentioned. Choice (D) is associated with *tax*.

182. **(A)** Mr. Krumholz believes that he owes for only one month's service when he was charged for two. Choice (B) is incorrect because he included the account number in his letter. Choice (C) is what he will get from his bank, not from Crisp Company. Choice (D) is a logical reason to write a letter to a company but is not the correct answer.

183. **(D)** Mr. Krumholz sent the payment on March 26 and the bill says that it shows only charges made until March 25. Choice (A) is incorrect because even though the check was sent late, it did have the correct amount ($125). Choice (B) repeats the word *bank*. Choice (C) is a mistake someone might make with a bill but is not the correct answer.

184. **(C)** He believes he owes the current charges only, which are $132 according to the bill. Choice (A) is what he owes for local phone service only. Choice (B) is what he owed last month. Choice (D) is what he owes according to the bill.

185. **(B)** Tomorrow he will mail a check to cover the current charges. Choice (A) is something he has already done. Choice (C) will happen before the end of the week. Choice (D) is what he is doing today.

186. **(B)** Mr. Park asks for tea and snacks to be served *immediately after Mr. Chang's presentation*, and Mr. Chang will present on *Changing World Markets*. Choice (A) is when Mr. Chang's presentation begins. Choices (C) and (D) are other points on the schedule but are not mentioned as times for refreshments.

187. **(D)** Mr. Park wants lunch served in the room that is currently scheduled for the Analyzing Demographics presentation. Choices (A), (B), and (C) are rooms where other workshop activities will take place.

188. **(D)** Mr. Park writes to Ms. Bao, *You should have 15 extra chairs in each room just to be safe.* Choice (A) is incorrect because Mr. Park asks Ms. Bao to make sure to put enough chairs in each room, so they must be available. Choice (B) is confused with the attendance numbers Mr. Park expects, but he asks for more chairs than that to be sure there are enough. Choice (C) is incorrect because Mr. Park wants more chairs placed in the rooms.

189. **(B)** Mr. Wang has to leave early, so Mr. Park wants to give him Ms. Lee's scheduled presentation time, and Ms. Lee will take Mr. Wang's time. Choices (A), (C), and (D) are people who will present at other times.

190. **(C)** Mr. Park asks for a *revised schedule this afternoon*. Choice (A) is confused with the discussion of the place for the lunch. Choice (B) is what Mr. Park wishes could be done, but he writes, *we can't change the date now*. Choice (D) is confused with the mention of changing the time of Mr. Wang's presentation.

191. **(D)** Employees who have worked at Howland for 11 or more years can take 25 annual leave days. Choices (A), (B), and (C) are the amounts of leave allowed for employees who have worked at the company for less time.

192. **(B)** According to the form, Daniel Ortiz is allowed 15 days of annual leave, which is the amount allowed for employees who have worked at Howland for three to five years. Choice (A) describes employees who get 10 days of annual leave. Choices (C) and (D) describe employees who get more than 15 days of annual leave.

193. **(A)** Daniel Ortiz wants to begin his vacation on July 21, and he must submit the form 21 days ahead of time. Choice (B) is confused with the number of leave days he is allowed. Choices (C) and (D) are confused with the dates of his vacation.

194. **(C)** The form has to be signed by Daniel Ortiz's supervisor, who, according to the form, is Nestor Perez. Choice (A) is the person requesting leave. Choice (B) is the person to whom the form should be submitted. Choice (D) is confused with the name of the company.

195. **(C)** The manual says that the form should be submitted to the human resources director, and the form says that it should be submitted to Daisy Ortega. Choices (A), (B), and (D) repeat words found on the form but are not the correct answer.

196. **(A)** The advertised office at 900 square feet is twice the size of the current office. Choices (B) and (D) are confused with the cost of the rent. Choice (C) is the size of the advertised office.

197. **(B)** The advertised office is not near the subway, and Paul says that is a convenience he would miss, so we can assume that the current office is near the subway. Choice (A) is incorrect because Paul says that the advertised office is the more expensive one. Choices (C) and (D) are true of the advertised office.

198. **(C)** Paul wants to see the office *tomorrow*, and today is Tuesday, so he wants to see it on Wednesday. Choice (A) is when Paul will return after being away. Choice (B) is today. Choice (D) is not mentioned.

199. **(C)** Paul points out that the advertised office has parking, *unlike our current office*. Choices (A), (B), and (D) are all things that can be found in both offices.

200. **(D)** The monthly rent is $1,750, and they would have to pay twice that—once for the first month's rent, and again for the security deposit. Choice (A) is confused with the size of the office. Choice (B) is one month's rent. Choice (C) is not mentioned.

# ANSWER SHEET
## New TOEIC Practice Exam A

## LISTENING COMPREHENSION

### Part 1: Photographs

1. Ⓐ Ⓑ Ⓒ Ⓓ
2. Ⓐ Ⓑ Ⓒ Ⓓ
3. Ⓐ Ⓑ Ⓒ Ⓓ
4. Ⓐ Ⓑ Ⓒ Ⓓ
5. Ⓐ Ⓑ Ⓒ Ⓓ
6. Ⓐ Ⓑ Ⓒ Ⓓ

### Part 2: Question-Response

7. Ⓐ Ⓑ Ⓒ
8. Ⓐ Ⓑ Ⓒ
9. Ⓐ Ⓑ Ⓒ
10. Ⓐ Ⓑ Ⓒ
11. Ⓐ Ⓑ Ⓒ
12. Ⓐ Ⓑ Ⓒ
13. Ⓐ Ⓑ Ⓒ
14. Ⓐ Ⓑ Ⓒ
15. Ⓐ Ⓑ Ⓒ
16. Ⓐ Ⓑ Ⓒ
17. Ⓐ Ⓑ Ⓒ
18. Ⓐ Ⓑ Ⓒ
19. Ⓐ Ⓑ Ⓒ
20. Ⓐ Ⓑ Ⓒ
21. Ⓐ Ⓑ Ⓒ
22. Ⓐ Ⓑ Ⓒ
23. Ⓐ Ⓑ Ⓒ
24. Ⓐ Ⓑ Ⓒ
25. Ⓐ Ⓑ Ⓒ
26. Ⓐ Ⓑ Ⓒ
27. Ⓐ Ⓑ Ⓒ
28. Ⓐ Ⓑ Ⓒ
29. Ⓐ Ⓑ Ⓒ
30. Ⓐ Ⓑ Ⓒ
31. Ⓐ Ⓑ Ⓒ

### Part 3: Conversations

32. Ⓐ Ⓑ Ⓒ Ⓓ
33. Ⓐ Ⓑ Ⓒ Ⓓ
34. Ⓐ Ⓑ Ⓒ Ⓓ
35. Ⓐ Ⓑ Ⓒ Ⓓ
36. Ⓐ Ⓑ Ⓒ Ⓓ
37. Ⓐ Ⓑ Ⓒ Ⓓ
38. Ⓐ Ⓑ Ⓒ Ⓓ
39. Ⓐ Ⓑ Ⓒ Ⓓ
40. Ⓐ Ⓑ Ⓒ Ⓓ
41. Ⓐ Ⓑ Ⓒ Ⓓ
42. Ⓐ Ⓑ Ⓒ Ⓓ
43. Ⓐ Ⓑ Ⓒ Ⓓ
44. Ⓐ Ⓑ Ⓒ Ⓓ
45. Ⓐ Ⓑ Ⓒ Ⓓ
46. Ⓐ Ⓑ Ⓒ Ⓓ
47. Ⓐ Ⓑ Ⓒ Ⓓ
48. Ⓐ Ⓑ Ⓒ Ⓓ
49. Ⓐ Ⓑ Ⓒ Ⓓ
50. Ⓐ Ⓑ Ⓒ Ⓓ
51. Ⓐ Ⓑ Ⓒ Ⓓ
52. Ⓐ Ⓑ Ⓒ Ⓓ
53. Ⓐ Ⓑ Ⓒ Ⓓ
54. Ⓐ Ⓑ Ⓒ Ⓓ
55. Ⓐ Ⓑ Ⓒ Ⓓ
56. Ⓐ Ⓑ Ⓒ Ⓓ
57. Ⓐ Ⓑ Ⓒ Ⓓ
58. Ⓐ Ⓑ Ⓒ Ⓓ
59. Ⓐ Ⓑ Ⓒ Ⓓ
60. Ⓐ Ⓑ Ⓒ Ⓓ
61. Ⓐ Ⓑ Ⓒ Ⓓ
62. Ⓐ Ⓑ Ⓒ Ⓓ
63. Ⓐ Ⓑ Ⓒ Ⓓ
64. Ⓐ Ⓑ Ⓒ Ⓓ
65. Ⓐ Ⓑ Ⓒ Ⓓ
66. Ⓐ Ⓑ Ⓒ Ⓓ
67. Ⓐ Ⓑ Ⓒ Ⓓ
68. Ⓐ Ⓑ Ⓒ Ⓓ
69. Ⓐ Ⓑ Ⓒ Ⓓ
70. Ⓐ Ⓑ Ⓒ Ⓓ

### Part 4: Talks

71. Ⓐ Ⓑ Ⓒ Ⓓ
72. Ⓐ Ⓑ Ⓒ Ⓓ
73. Ⓐ Ⓑ Ⓒ Ⓓ
74. Ⓐ Ⓑ Ⓒ Ⓓ
75. Ⓐ Ⓑ Ⓒ Ⓓ
76. Ⓐ Ⓑ Ⓒ Ⓓ
77. Ⓐ Ⓑ Ⓒ Ⓓ
78. Ⓐ Ⓑ Ⓒ Ⓓ
79. Ⓐ Ⓑ Ⓒ Ⓓ
80. Ⓐ Ⓑ Ⓒ Ⓓ
81. Ⓐ Ⓑ Ⓒ Ⓓ
82. Ⓐ Ⓑ Ⓒ Ⓓ
83. Ⓐ Ⓑ Ⓒ Ⓓ
84. Ⓐ Ⓑ Ⓒ Ⓓ
85. Ⓐ Ⓑ Ⓒ Ⓓ
86. Ⓐ Ⓑ Ⓒ Ⓓ
87. Ⓐ Ⓑ Ⓒ Ⓓ
88. Ⓐ Ⓑ Ⓒ Ⓓ
89. Ⓐ Ⓑ Ⓒ Ⓓ
90. Ⓐ Ⓑ Ⓒ Ⓓ
91. Ⓐ Ⓑ Ⓒ Ⓓ
92. Ⓐ Ⓑ Ⓒ Ⓓ
93. Ⓐ Ⓑ Ⓒ Ⓓ
94. Ⓐ Ⓑ Ⓒ Ⓓ
95. Ⓐ Ⓑ Ⓒ Ⓓ
96. Ⓐ Ⓑ Ⓒ Ⓓ
97. Ⓐ Ⓑ Ⓒ Ⓓ
98. Ⓐ Ⓑ Ⓒ Ⓓ
99. Ⓐ Ⓑ Ⓒ Ⓓ
100. Ⓐ Ⓑ Ⓒ Ⓓ

# ANSWER SHEET
## New TOEIC Practice Exam A

## READING

### Part 5: Incomplete Sentences

| | | | |
|---|---|---|---|
| 101. Ⓐ Ⓑ Ⓒ Ⓓ | 109. Ⓐ Ⓑ Ⓒ Ⓓ | 117. Ⓐ Ⓑ Ⓒ Ⓓ | 125. Ⓐ Ⓑ Ⓒ Ⓓ |
| 102. Ⓐ Ⓑ Ⓒ Ⓓ | 110. Ⓐ Ⓑ Ⓒ Ⓓ | 118. Ⓐ Ⓑ Ⓒ Ⓓ | 126. Ⓐ Ⓑ Ⓒ Ⓓ |
| 103. Ⓐ Ⓑ Ⓒ Ⓓ | 111. Ⓐ Ⓑ Ⓒ Ⓓ | 119. Ⓐ Ⓑ Ⓒ Ⓓ | 127. Ⓐ Ⓑ Ⓒ Ⓓ |
| 104. Ⓐ Ⓑ Ⓒ Ⓓ | 112. Ⓐ Ⓑ Ⓒ Ⓓ | 120. Ⓐ Ⓑ Ⓒ Ⓓ | 128. Ⓐ Ⓑ Ⓒ Ⓓ |
| 105. Ⓐ Ⓑ Ⓒ Ⓓ | 113. Ⓐ Ⓑ Ⓒ Ⓓ | 121. Ⓐ Ⓑ Ⓒ Ⓓ | 129. Ⓐ Ⓑ Ⓒ Ⓓ |
| 106. Ⓐ Ⓑ Ⓒ Ⓓ | 114. Ⓐ Ⓑ Ⓒ Ⓓ | 122. Ⓐ Ⓑ Ⓒ Ⓓ | 130. Ⓐ Ⓑ Ⓒ Ⓓ |
| 107. Ⓐ Ⓑ Ⓒ Ⓓ | 115. Ⓐ Ⓑ Ⓒ Ⓓ | 123. Ⓐ Ⓑ Ⓒ Ⓓ | |
| 108. Ⓐ Ⓑ Ⓒ Ⓓ | 116. Ⓐ Ⓑ Ⓒ Ⓓ | 124. Ⓐ Ⓑ Ⓒ Ⓓ | |

### Part 6: Text Completion

| | | | |
|---|---|---|---|
| 131. Ⓐ Ⓑ Ⓒ Ⓓ | 135. Ⓐ Ⓑ Ⓒ Ⓓ | 139. Ⓐ Ⓑ Ⓒ Ⓓ | 143. Ⓐ Ⓑ Ⓒ Ⓓ |
| 132. Ⓐ Ⓑ Ⓒ Ⓓ | 136. Ⓐ Ⓑ Ⓒ Ⓓ | 140. Ⓐ Ⓑ Ⓒ Ⓓ | 144. Ⓐ Ⓑ Ⓒ Ⓓ |
| 133. Ⓐ Ⓑ Ⓒ Ⓓ | 137. Ⓐ Ⓑ Ⓒ Ⓓ | 141. Ⓐ Ⓑ Ⓒ Ⓓ | 145. Ⓐ Ⓑ Ⓒ Ⓓ |
| 134. Ⓐ Ⓑ Ⓒ Ⓓ | 138. Ⓐ Ⓑ Ⓒ Ⓓ | 142. Ⓐ Ⓑ Ⓒ Ⓓ | 146. Ⓐ Ⓑ Ⓒ Ⓓ |

### Part 7: Reading Comprehension

| | | | |
|---|---|---|---|
| 147. Ⓐ Ⓑ Ⓒ Ⓓ | 161. Ⓐ Ⓑ Ⓒ Ⓓ | 175. Ⓐ Ⓑ Ⓒ Ⓓ | 189. Ⓐ Ⓑ Ⓒ Ⓓ |
| 148. Ⓐ Ⓑ Ⓒ Ⓓ | 162. Ⓐ Ⓑ Ⓒ Ⓓ | 176. Ⓐ Ⓑ Ⓒ Ⓓ | 190. Ⓐ Ⓑ Ⓒ Ⓓ |
| 149. Ⓐ Ⓑ Ⓒ Ⓓ | 163. Ⓐ Ⓑ Ⓒ Ⓓ | 177. Ⓐ Ⓑ Ⓒ Ⓓ | 191. Ⓐ Ⓑ Ⓒ Ⓓ |
| 150. Ⓐ Ⓑ Ⓒ Ⓓ | 164. Ⓐ Ⓑ Ⓒ Ⓓ | 178. Ⓐ Ⓑ Ⓒ Ⓓ | 192. Ⓐ Ⓑ Ⓒ Ⓓ |
| 151. Ⓐ Ⓑ Ⓒ Ⓓ | 165. Ⓐ Ⓑ Ⓒ Ⓓ | 179. Ⓐ Ⓑ Ⓒ Ⓓ | 193. Ⓐ Ⓑ Ⓒ Ⓓ |
| 152. Ⓐ Ⓑ Ⓒ Ⓓ | 166. Ⓐ Ⓑ Ⓒ Ⓓ | 180. Ⓐ Ⓑ Ⓒ Ⓓ | 194. Ⓐ Ⓑ Ⓒ Ⓓ |
| 153. Ⓐ Ⓑ Ⓒ Ⓓ | 167. Ⓐ Ⓑ Ⓒ Ⓓ | 181. Ⓐ Ⓑ Ⓒ Ⓓ | 195. Ⓐ Ⓑ Ⓒ Ⓓ |
| 154. Ⓐ Ⓑ Ⓒ Ⓓ | 168. Ⓐ Ⓑ Ⓒ Ⓓ | 182. Ⓐ Ⓑ Ⓒ Ⓓ | 196. Ⓐ Ⓑ Ⓒ Ⓓ |
| 155. Ⓐ Ⓑ Ⓒ Ⓓ | 169. Ⓐ Ⓑ Ⓒ Ⓓ | 183. Ⓐ Ⓑ Ⓒ Ⓓ | 197. Ⓐ Ⓑ Ⓒ Ⓓ |
| 156. Ⓐ Ⓑ Ⓒ Ⓓ | 170. Ⓐ Ⓑ Ⓒ Ⓓ | 184. Ⓐ Ⓑ Ⓒ Ⓓ | 198. Ⓐ Ⓑ Ⓒ Ⓓ |
| 157. Ⓐ Ⓑ Ⓒ Ⓓ | 171. Ⓐ Ⓑ Ⓒ Ⓓ | 185. Ⓐ Ⓑ Ⓒ Ⓓ | 199. Ⓐ Ⓑ Ⓒ Ⓓ |
| 158. Ⓐ Ⓑ Ⓒ Ⓓ | 172. Ⓐ Ⓑ Ⓒ Ⓓ | 186. Ⓐ Ⓑ Ⓒ Ⓓ | 200. Ⓐ Ⓑ Ⓒ Ⓓ |
| 159. Ⓐ Ⓑ Ⓒ Ⓓ | 173. Ⓐ Ⓑ Ⓒ Ⓓ | 187. Ⓐ Ⓑ Ⓒ Ⓓ | |
| 160. Ⓐ Ⓑ Ⓒ Ⓓ | 174. Ⓐ Ⓑ Ⓒ Ⓓ | 188. Ⓐ Ⓑ Ⓒ Ⓓ | |

# New TOEIC
# Practice Exam A

## LISTENING COMPREHENSION

In this section of the test, you will have the chance to show how well you understand spoken English. There are four parts to this section, with special directions for each part. You will find the Answer Sheet for New TOEIC Practice Exam A on pages 229–230. Detach it from the book and use it to record your answers. Check your answers using the Answer Key on pages 268–269 and see the Answers Explained beginning on page 271.

## Part 1: Photographs

 **Track 18**

**Directions:** You will see a photograph. You will hear four statements about the photograph. Choose the statement that most closely matches the photograph and fill in the corresponding oval on your answer sheet.

**Example**

Now listen to the four statements.

**Sample Answer**
Ⓐ Ⓑ Ⓒ Ⓓ

Statement (B), "She's reading a magazine," best describes what you see in the picture. Therefore, you should choose answer (B).

**TIP**

If you do not have access to the MP3 files, please use the audioscripts beginning on page 397. You can also download the MP3 files and audioscripts from *http:// barronsbooks. com/tp/toeic/ audio/*

1.

2.

3.

4.

5.

6.

## Part 2: Question-Response

7.  Mark your answer on your answer sheet.

8.  Mark your answer on your answer sheet.

9.  Mark your answer on your answer sheet.

10.  Mark your answer on your answer sheet.

11.  Mark your answer on your answer sheet.

12.  Mark your answer on your answer sheet.

13.  Mark your answer on your answer sheet.

14.  Mark your answer on your answer sheet.

15.  Mark your answer on your answer sheet.

16.  Mark your answer on your answer sheet.

17.  Mark your answer on your answer sheet.

18.  Mark your answer on your answer sheet.

19.  Mark your answer on your answer sheet.

20.  Mark your answer on your answer sheet.

21.  Mark your answer on your answer sheet.

22.  Mark your answer on your answer sheet.

23.  Mark your answer on your answer sheet.

24.  Mark your answer on your answer sheet.

25.  Mark your answer on your answer sheet.

26.  Mark your answer on your answer sheet.

27.  Mark your answer on your answer sheet.

28.  Mark your answer on your answer sheet.

29.  Mark your answer on your answer sheet.

30.  Mark your answer on your answer sheet.

31.  Mark your answer on your answer sheet.

## Part 3: Conversations

**Directions:** You will hear a conversation between two or more people. You will see three questions on each conversation and four possible answers. Choose the best answer to each question and fill in the corresponding oval on your answer sheet.

Track 20

32. Where is the man going?
    (A) A doctor's appointment
    (B) A job interview
    (C) His apartment
    (D) Out of town

33. How will he get there?
    (A) Bus
    (B) Car
    (C) Train
    (D) Walking

34. What does the woman give the man?
    (A) Money
    (B) Directions
    (C) Her umbrella
    (D) A cup of coffee

35. Why is the man going to Washington?
    (A) For a family event
    (B) For a conference
    (C) For vacation
    (D) For business

36. When is he leaving?
    (A) Tonight
    (B) Sunday
    (C) Monday
    (D) Tuesday

37. What does the woman mean when she says, "I wouldn't stay there?"
    (A) She doesn't recommend the hotel.
    (B) The man should visit several places.
    (C) She wishes she could take a trip, too.
    (D) It's hard to get a reservation at the hotel.

38. Where does this conversation take place?
    (A) A shopping mall
    (B) A lawyer's office
    (C) A café
    (D) A bus

39. What time is the man's appointment?
    (A) 1:00
    (B) 1:15
    (C) 8:00
    (D) 9:00

40. What will the man do next?
    (A) Walk with the woman
    (B) Call his lawyer
    (C) Go shopping
    (D) Have lunch

41. Why did the man make the call?
    (A) To reserve a room
    (B) To negotiate prices
    (C) To request information
    (D) To make an appointment

42. Who most likely is the woman?
    (A) A hotel events manager
    (B) A landlord
    (C) A travel agent
    (D) A party planner

43. What will the woman do on Monday?
    (A) Prepare the menus
    (B) Meet with the man
    (C) Leave on a trip
    (D) Hire an assistant

44. Where is the art gallery located?
   (A) Houston
   (B) New York
   (C) Paris
   (D) Portland

45. What kind of art is the woman looking at?
   (A) Painting
   (B) Drawing
   (C) Sculpture
   (D) Collage

46. What does the man say the woman CANNOT do with the art?
   (A) Touch it
   (B) Sit on it
   (C) Carry it
   (D) Buy it

_____

47. What did the first man do this morning?
   (A) Read a book
   (B) Paid the rent
   (C) Bought furniture
   (D) Cleaned the office

48. What do the speakers imply about their current office?
   (A) It is too small.
   (B) It needs painting.
   (C) It costs too much.
   (D) It is disorganized.

49. What will the woman do this afternoon?
   (A) Have a snack
   (B) Pack her things
   (C) Help her colleague
   (D) Visit the new office

50. Where does this conversation take place?
   (A) A restaurant
   (B) A kitchen
   (C) A store
   (D) A bank

51. What is suggested about the place?
   (A) The service is slow.
   (B) The quality is low.
   (C) It's inexpensive.
   (D) It's crowded.

52. What does the man offer to do?
   (A) Pay for everything
   (B) Ask for immediate service
   (C) Lend the woman some money
   (D) Take the woman somewhere else

_____

53. Why did the woman make the call?
   (A) To ask what time the business closes
   (B) To find out the cost of an order
   (C) To see if her order is ready
   (D) To place an order

54. What most likely is the man's profession?
   (A) Photographer
   (B) Printer
   (C) Editor
   (D) Designer

55. What is the problem with the order?
   (A) The man made too many copies.
   (B) It won't be ready on time.
   (C) The man will charge too much.
   (D) It has only two colors.

56. How often is the company picnic held?
    (A) Every month
    (B) Once a year
    (C) Twice a year
    (D) Every other year

57. Where does the woman want to hold the picnic?
    (A) At a park
    (B) At a lake
    (C) At a club
    (D) At the office

58. What does the man mean when he says, "I don't know if that will go over with the staff?"
    (A) The place is too far away for the staff to get to.
    (B) Most of the staff won't show up at the picnic.
    (C) The staff is not familiar with the place.
    (D) The staff won't like the idea.

59. What does the man imply about his former job?
    (A) It was boring.
    (B) The pay was low.
    (C) It kept him very busy.
    (D) He learned a lot from it.

60. How do the man and the woman know each other?
    (A) They met at a social event.
    (B) They are former work colleagues.
    (C) They were university classmates.
    (D) They live in the same neighborhood.

61. What does the man invite the woman to do?
    (A) Meet his work colleagues
    (B) Take a tour of his new office
    (C) Apply for a job at his new company
    (D) Have dinner with him and some friends

62. What is this conversation mainly about?
    (A) Rising prices
    (B) Lunch plans
    (C) A meeting agenda
    (D) Neighborhood restaurants

63. What does the man suggest about the cafeteria?
    (A) It's an inexpensive place to eat.
    (B) Its food has gotten better.
    (C) It's far from the office.
    (D) It's not very popular.

64. What will the speakers do next?
    (A) Attend a meeting
    (B) Go to the lobby
    (C) Visit Kerry's office
    (D) Order their lunch

65. What does the man indicate about his apartment?
    (A) It's uncomfortable.
    (B) It's expensive.
    (C) It's small.
    (D) It's noisy.

66. What will the man do on Thursday?
    (A) Go on a trip
    (B) Arrive home
    (C) See the woman
    (D) Clean his apartment

67. Look at the graphic. How much will the woman pay to use the garage?
    (A) $0
    (B) $5
    (C) $10
    (D) $15

---

**City Garage**
**PARKING**
**Monday–Friday: $5/day**
**Saturday and Sunday: Free**

68. Who most likely is Marvin?
    (A) An office assistant
    (B) The woman's friend
    (C) A workshop participant
    (D) The workshop presenter

69. What is the woman worried about?
    (A) There are too few participants.
    (B) The room won't be ready on time.
    (C) The man is spending too much money.
    (D) There aren't enough pens for everyone.

70. Look at the graphic. Which pack of pens will the man buy?
    (A) Small
    (B) Medium
    (C) Large
    (D) Jumbo

## PEN PACKS

| Size | Quantity | Price |
| --- | --- | --- |
| Small | 1 dozen | $15 |
| Medium | 2 dozen | $28 |
| Large | 4 dozen | $52 |
| Jumbo | 10 dozen | $120 |

## Part 4: Talks

**Directions:** You will hear a talk given by a single speaker. You will see three questions on each talk, each with four possible answers. Choose the best answer to each question and fill in the corresponding oval on your answer sheet.

Track 21

71. What is this talk mostly about?
 (A) The weather
 (B) Road repaving
 (C) Traffic conditions
 (D) Summer travel plans

72. What does the speaker suggest listeners do?
 (A) Drive slowly
 (B) Avoid Main Street
 (C) Walk over the bridge
 (D) Travel this afternoon

73. What will happen tomorrow?
 (A) A bridge will be closed.
 (B) Street repaving will begin.
 (C) Maple Avenue will reopen.
 (D) The weather will clear up.

74. Who is the conference for?
 (A) Landscape designers
 (B) Resort owners
 (C) Botanists
 (D) Chefs

75. Where is the conference taking place?
 (A) In a city
 (B) By a lake
 (C) At a restaurant
 (D) In the mountains

76. What will listeners do next?
 (A) Have lunch
 (B) Hear a talk
 (C) Tour the grounds
 (D) Attend workshops

77. What does the speaker imply about the weather?
 (A) People have been enjoying the weather.
 (B) Conditions will remain unchanged.
 (C) It's been raining for a long time.
 (D) The dry spell will end soon.

78. What does the speaker advise listeners to do?
 (A) Go outside
 (B) Wear a sweater
 (C) Carry an umbrella
 (D) Stay out of the sun

79. What will the weather be like on the weekend?
 (A) Rainy
 (B) Cloudy
 (C) Sunny
 (D) Warm

80. Why did the speaker make the call?
 (A) To give a reminder about an appointment
 (B) To discuss a missed appointment
 (C) To reschedule an appointment
 (D) To cancel an appointment

81. Who is Dr. Rogers?
 (A) A dentist
 (B) A foot doctor
 (C) An eye doctor
 (D) A psychiatrist

82. What does the speaker ask the listener to do?
(A) Pay a missed appointment fee
(B) Bring a completed form
(C) Call back next Monday
(D) Arrive early

83. Where will the park be built?
(A) Near some condominiums
(B) Next to a farmer's market
(C) On the site of a stadium
(D) Behind an office building

84. What does the speaker mean when he says, "I can't wait for opening day?"
(A) He's looking forward to using the park.
(B) He will be too busy to attend the opening ceremony.
(C) He plans to visit the construction site soon.
(D) He is generally an impatient person.

85. When will construction begin?
(A) Early this month
(B) The beginning of next month
(C) By the end of the year
(D) Some time next year

86. Why did the speaker make the call?
(A) To ask for a favor
(B) To express thanks
(C) To report good news
(D) To tell about an opportunity

87. What does the speaker mean when she says, "There's just one little thing?"
(A) She's not sure she will like her job.
(B) She thinks her job will be easy.
(C) She has a gift for her friend.
(D) She has a small problem.

88. What will the speaker do on Monday?
(A) Pick up her car
(B) Start her new job
(C) Call the mechanic
(D) Help her friend

89. What kind of business is Mr. Green's?
(A) Farm
(B) Restaurant
(C) Grocery store
(D) Gardening store

90. What happens on Sundays?
(A) The store is closed.
(B) Prices are lowered.
(C) Inventory is counted.
(D) The shelves are cleaned.

91. What are listeners asked to do?
(A) Pay by check
(B) Shop weekly
(C) Look at the newspaper
(D) Register on the website

92. Where does the talk take place?
(A) On a bus
(B) In a museum
(C) In a theater
(D) On a boat

93. What will they do next?
(A) Swim in the river
(B) Have a meeting
(C) Visit buildings
(D) Eat lunch

94. What does the speaker imply about the café?
(A) It's small.
(B) It's very popular.
(C) The food is not great.
(D) The view is uninteresting.

95. What kind of business does the speaker work in?
(A) Newspaper
(B) Fitness club
(C) Sports store
(D) Ticket sales

96. Look at the graphic. Which sport does the speaker want to focus on?
(A) Tennis
(B) Swimming
(C) Aerobics
(D) Strength training

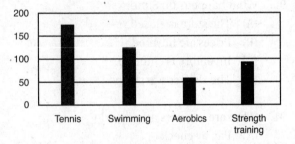

97. What does the speaker ask listeners to do?
(A) Fill out a survey
(B) State their goals
(C) Sign up for lessons
(D) Speak with their clients

_____

98. Who most likely is the speaker?
(A) A hotel manager
(B) A translator
(C) A student
(D) A teacher

99. Look at the graphic. Where is the speaker's office?
(A) Room 1
(B) Room 2
(C) Room 3
(D) Room 4

**The Oaks—Ground Floor**

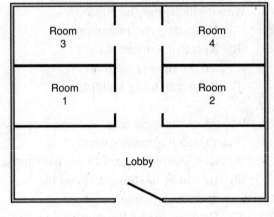

100. What does the speaker ask the listener to bring?
(A) A notebook
(B) A textbook
(C) A check
(D) Nothing

# READING

In this section of the test, you will have the chance to show how well you understand written English. There are three parts to this section, with special directions for each part.

**YOU WILL HAVE ONE HOUR AND FIFTEEN MINUTES
TO COMPLETE PARTS 5, 6, AND 7 OF THE TEST.**

## Part 5: Incomplete Sentences

**Directions:** You will see a sentence with a missing word. Four possible answers follow the sentence. Choose the best answer to the question and fill in the corresponding oval on your answer sheet.

101. The price of all cruises _____ airfare and all transfers.
    (A) have included
    (B) includes
    (C) are including
    (D) include

102. Many customers have requested that we _____ them advance notice of our sales by e-mail.
    (A) send
    (B) sends
    (C) sent
    (D) sending

103. The workers were loading the truck when the boxes _____.
    (A) have fallen
    (B) fall
    (C) fell
    (D) are falling

104. The new manager, _____ was just hired, will start tomorrow.
    (A) she
    (B) he
    (C) which
    (D) who

105. We _____ our business if we hadn't been able to get that loan from the bank.
    (A) have been losing
    (B) would have lost
    (C) will be losing
    (D) have lost

106. We expect this workshop to be well attended, so we should hold it in the _____ room available.
    (A) more bigger
    (B) big
    (C) bigger
    (D) biggest

107. The purser got his assistant _____ the passenger orientation.
    (A) conducting
    (B) to conduct
    (C) conducted
    (D) conducts

108. _____ his enthusiasm, Mr. Mosley is having a hard time keeping up with the rest of the team.
    (A) Because of
    (B) Although
    (C) Due to
    (D) Despite

109. We may have to consider _____ some of our stores unless sales improve very soon.
(A) close
(B) to close
(C) will close
(D) closing

110. I suggest leaving earlier in the afternoon because _____ 5:00, the subways and buses become very crowded.
(A) until
(B) after
(C) while
(D) when

111. The best chefs _____ recipes to suit their own cooking styles as well as the tastes of their customers.
(A) adapt
(B) adoption
(C) adept
(D) adjourn

112. My boss asked me to write a _____ report of our trip without omitting any details.
(A) tough
(B) though
(C) thorough
(D) through

113. Ms. Nyen was very embarrassed because the microphone _____ while she was giving her speech.
(A) is failing
(B) fails
(C) had failed
(D) failed

114. The clerk _____ the manual from the secretary to see if she could figure out how to fix the problem herself.
(A) lent
(B) loaned
(C) offered
(D) borrowed

115. No matter how good its business plan, a firm will not _____ if its employees are unhappy.
(A) prosper
(B) prosperous
(C) prosperity
(D) prospering

116. The director wanted me to let her know how many people showed _____ for the workshop.
(A) in
(B) up
(C) to
(D) off

117. If there _____ some restaurants near the hotel, we would not have to spend time and money on taxis.
(A) were
(B) was
(C) are
(D) would be

118. Every morning, a member of the kitchen staff turns on the ovens and _____ the coffee.
(A) brewing
(B) has brewed
(C) brews
(D) brewed

119. People in the audience began to fidget around and feel restless because the speech was so _____.
(A) boring
(B) bored
(C) bores
(D) bore

120. If the traffic report sounds bad this afternoon, then _____ the subway instead of a cab.
(A) take
(B) takes
(C) taking
(D) will take

121. There is not much agriculture in this area because the _____ yearly rainfall is so low.
 (A) available
 (B) avenging
 (C) avaricious
 (D) average

122. The year-end office party is for the enjoyment of the entire staff, and no one will be _____ from the invitation.
 (A) excused
 (B) excluded
 (C) extracted
 (D) excised

123. We _____ any problems with building maintenance until they hired the new building manager.
 (A) wouldn't have
 (B) haven't had
 (C) don't have
 (D) didn't have

124. Ms. Kim is a knowledgeable and _____ engineer and she has contributed a great deal to the work of this company.
 (A) industrious
 (B) industry
 (C) industrial
 (D) industries

125. Mr. Ross promised to prepare the earnings and expenses charts _____ tomorrow's staff meeting.
 (A) before
 (B) due to
 (C) so that
 (D) because

126. Customers who receive free samples are _____ no obligation to purchase any of our products.
 (A) on
 (B) in
 (C) with
 (D) under

127. _____ the agreement, Grayson Auto Mart will order 500 units each month over the next 14 months.
 (A) To
 (B) Per
 (C) Due
 (D) For

128. Although she hesitated at first, Ms. Paulson finally _____ to take on the role of committee chair.
 (A) consented
 (B) appealed
 (C) influenced
 (D) persuaded

129. The office next door has been _____ for months, but it appears that a new tenant has recently been found.
 (A) evicted
 (B) mislaid
 (C) scarce
 (D) vacant

130. The auditorium _____ to give every audience member an unobstructed view of the stage.
 (A) design
 (B) designs
 (C) is designed
 (D) is designing

## Part 6: Text Completion

> **Directions:** You will see four passages, each with four blanks. Under each blank are four answer options. Choose the word or phrase that best completes the sentence.

Questions 131–134 refer to the following ad.

**Part-Time Store Help Needed**

Small gift shop needs a part-time _____. Hours are Wednesday through Sunday,

131. (A) Managing
    (B) Management
    (C) Managerial
    (D) Manager

3:30 P.M. _____ 11:00 P.M. closing. Responsibilities include overseeing other employees,

132. (A) on
    (B) before
    (C) until
    (D) for

attending to customers, keeping track of sales and inventory, and locking up the store.

_____.

133. (A) Experience in a similar position is desirable but not required.
    (B) Apply only if you are familiar with the gift shop industry.
    (C) We sell handcrafted items from around the world.
    (D) You must show proof of previous employment.

We can train you if you are responsible, organized, and a quick learner. Send resume and two work and two personal _____ to Dan at P.O. Box 7, Winchester.

134. (A) uniforms
    (B) references
    (C) applications
    (D) instructions

Questions 135–138 refer to the following information.

Thank you for your purchase of the Office Wonder Super Paper Shredder.

_____. Your shredder can shred

135. (A) The shredder will fit neatly under your desk.
    (B) We know you'll love its efficiency and speed.
    (C) It is designed to match your office décor.
    (D) We also sell other popular office products.

up to 15 sheets of paper at one time, faster than any similar shredder on the market.
You can feel secure knowing that your confidential documents will be shred into tiny,

_____ pieces. Your shredder will also slice through credit cards and other

136. (A) colorful
    (B) multiple
    (C) irregular
    (D) unreadable

objects without _____ the machine.

    137. (A) damage
        (B) to damage
        (C) damaging
        (D) will damage

Please follow these safety tips when using your Office Wonder Super Paper Shredder:

• Keep loose clothing, long hair, and jewelry away from the shredder.
• To avoid jams, feed no more than 15 pieces of paper into the machine at a time.
• Do not allow children to have access to the shredder.
• Unplug the shredder when not _____.

    138. (A) in use
        (B) useful
        (C) useable
        (D) for use

## Green Thumb
## Custom Plant Care

May 6

Dear Office Manager,

Green Thumb Custom Plant Care is bringing its services to your area. Many offices such as _____ use potted plants to create a pleasant atmosphere for

139. (A) yours
     (B) ours
     (C) mine
     (D) its

staff and clients. But plants require care, and busy office staff cannot easily make the time to do this _____. That's why smart business owners

140. (A) regular
     (B) regulate
     (C) regularly
     (D) regulation

use Green Thumb's plant care services. Shouldn't you be one of them?

_____.

141. (A) Green Thumb has clients throughout the city.
     (B) Green Thumb can manage all your plants' needs.
     (C) Green Thumb has been in business for over five years.
     (D) Green Thumb provides pots, soil, and other plant supplies.

Few or many, large or small, we keep your plants healthy and happy. We water, fertilize, and prune your plants and move them around so that they are always in _____ conditions. Green Thumb takes away the worry of plant care and

142. (A) environmental
     (B) considerate
     (C) determined
     (D) optimal

ensures that your potted plants provide your workspace with a healthy, green, and flourishing environment. Please call us today to find out how we can help you.

Sincerely,

*Jonas Billings*

Jonas Billings

Questions 143–146 refer to the following notice.

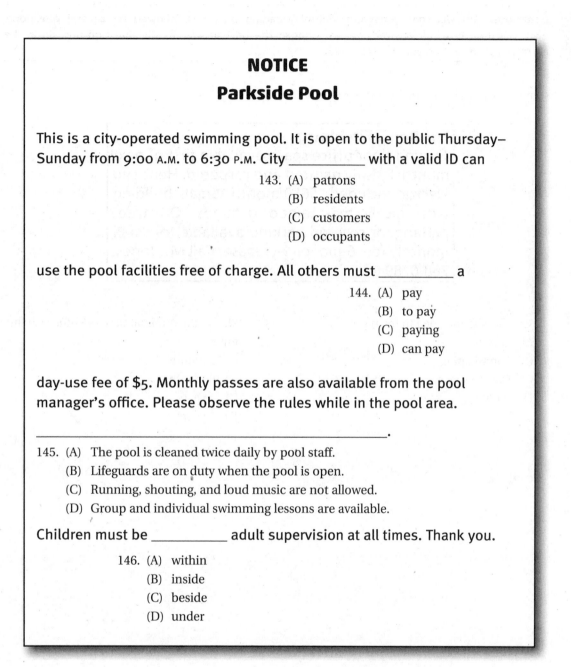

## NOTICE
## Parkside Pool

This is a city-operated swimming pool. It is open to the public Thursday–Sunday from 9:00 A.M. to 6:30 P.M. City _____ with a valid ID can

143. (A) patrons
     (B) residents
     (C) customers
     (D) occupants

use the pool facilities free of charge. All others must _____ a

144. (A) pay
     (B) to pay
     (C) paying
     (D) can pay

day-use fee of $5. Monthly passes are also available from the pool manager's office. Please observe the rules while in the pool area.

_____.

145. (A) The pool is cleaned twice daily by pool staff.
     (B) Lifeguards are on duty when the pool is open.
     (C) Running, shouting, and loud music are not allowed.
     (D) Group and individual swimming lessons are available.

Children must be _____ adult supervision at all times. Thank you.

146. (A) within
     (B) inside
     (C) beside
     (D) under

## Part 7: Reading Comprehension

**Directions:** You will see single and multiple reading passages followed by several questions. Each question has four answer choices. Choose the best answer to the question and fill in the corresponding oval on your answer sheet.

Questions 147–148 refer to the following rental ad.

**For Rent: Fitchburg**

Ground floor office space available first of next month. Freshly painted and carpeted. Heat and electric included. S650/month. Small building with nicely maintained grounds. On-street parking, or covered parking available for small monthly fee. 6-mo. or 1-yr lease. Call Ms. Jones. 768-6789.

147. What is NOT included in the rent?

(A) Utilities

(B) Landscaping

(C) Garage space

(D) Painting

148. What is the minimal time the office can be rented?

(A) 1 month

(B) 6 months

(C) 1 year

(D) 2 years

Questions 149–150 refer to the following text message chain.

Sally Fox, 12:45
The train is delayed again. Sorry. Scheduled arrival time is now 2:15.

Luisa Silva, 12:46
No problem. I'll be there.

Sally Fox, 12:47
Great. Will I still make the meeting?

Luisa Silva, 12:48
Sure. We'll take a cab. Traffic is still light that time of afternoon.

Sally Fox, 12:50
Good. Will we go straight to the office? I'd like to swing by the hotel if possible.

Luisa Silva, 12:50
We can do that. The hotel is just a couple of blocks from the office.

Sally Fox, 12:52
I'm going to need a short rest if I'm going to make it through the day. There's that meeting and then a long evening.

Luisa Silva, 12:53
Right. First there's the reception at 5:00, then the dinner at the East Side Restaurant, and I think there's something after that, too.

Sally Fox, 12:54
Full Schedule.

149. What does Luis imply about the traffic?
(A) It might delay his arrival at the train station.
(B) It will probably get worse later in the day.
(C) It is usually light near the train station.
(D) It never causes problems.

150. Where will Luis take Sally first?
(A) Hotel
(B) Office
(C) Reception
(D) Restaurant

## BUSINESS TRENDS

*"The region's most widely read business magazine"*

**Business Trends** features articles by business leaders and business journalists from around the country, with in-depth coverage of regional and national trends, profiles of local entrepreneurs, and more.

Your business advertised in **Business Trends** will be seen by thousands of readers, including business leaders, aspiring business leaders, consumers, and everybody else who is interested in the region's economic and business climate.

**Business Trends** has been awarded the Business Publication of the Year award for five years in a row.

**Business Trends** appears on the first Sunday of every month.

Advertising space deadline is one week prior.

Contact **Business Trends** pr@businesstrends.com

151. Who is the ad for?
    (A) Subscribers
    (B) Advertisers
    (C) Journalists
    (D) Business Leaders

152. How often is the magazine published?
    (A) Daily
    (B) Weekly
    (C) Monthly
    (D) Yearly

Questions 153–154 refer to the following form.

---

**Technical Writing Workshop**
**Lunch Options**

Wednesday's Technical Writing Workshop is scheduled for 9:30–4:30 with a lunch break at noon. There will be no coffee break, but snacks and a small selection of hot and cold beverages will be set out on the table at the back of the room. Please help yourself whenever you like. Please select your lunch preference from the list below.

☐ Ham and Turkey on Rye with ☐ Cheddar / ☐ American / ☐ No Cheese

☐ Tuna Fish Salad on Wheat Bread

☐ Grilled Chicken and Vegetable Wrap

☐ Large Garden Salad with ☐ Ranch / ☐ Balsamic / ☐ Carrot Ginger

---

153. What is said about drinks?
  (A) They must be selected ahead of time.
  (B) Participants must bring their own.
  (C) Only coffee and tea will be served.
  (D) They will be available all day.

154. What most likely is "Carrot Ginger"?
  (A) Salad
  (B) Salad dressing
  (C) Sandwich
  (D) Drink

Questions 155–157 refer to the following web page.

www.adventureplace.com

File   Edit   View   Favorites   Tools   Help

Home      Adventures      Family Fun      Travel Tips      About Us      Contact Us

# Adventure Place
*Excitement for the whole family*

Need to get away? Check out this week's **Adventure Place** specials!

**1.  $145**
Suite in Historic Bangkok Hotel for two with breakfast at 30% off usual price. **Learn more**. **Book now**.

**2.  $2,055**
Week-long stay at exclusive Alaskan resort. Private cabin, sleeps 4. Enjoy winter activities. Meals included. **Learn more**. **Book now**.

**3.  $325** p/p
Weekend at Serenity Hot Springs Hotel in Andes Mountains with spa privileges and more. **Learn more**. **Book now**.

**4.  $225**
Relax in Renovated Paris Hotel by Champs-Élysées. Room for 2. Includes vouchers to museums. **Learn more**. **Book now**.

**5.  $1,345** p/p
7 Days 6 Nights cruising the Caribbean. **Learn more**. **Book now**.

For exclusive discounts, daily updates, and many more benefits, join the **Adventure Place Traveler's Club** today. **Learn more. Join now.**

155. How can a customer get something for the prices listed on this web page?
(A) Reserve a trip this week
(B) Book 2 or more trips
(C) Book a family trip
(D) Join a club

156. What is the cost of the Alaskan vacation?
(A) $2,055 per person
(B) $2,055 per night
(C) $2,055 for four people
(D) $2,055 for four nights

157. Which trip would be attractive to someone who likes the sea?
(A) # 1
(B) # 3
(C) # 4
(D) # 5

Questions 158–160 refer to the following chart.

## National Economy
Economic indicators for the second half of the year are mostly encouraging overall.

| Economic Indicator | Positive | Neutral | Negative | Comments |
|---|---|---|---|---|
| Growth | x | | | The economy is predicted to pick up steam in the next few months, aided by job creation and capital investment. |
| Consumer Spending | x | | | Wages will remain steady, but new job creation should have a positive effect on overall income and spending ability. |
| Business Investment | x | | | Capital spending is set to improve over the next few months, with demand among domestic consumers expected to strengthen. |
| Housing | | x | | Slow growth in average income has affected the housing market, and this will likely continue for the rest of the year. However, housing prices have stabilized, and this could boost housing sales. |
| Global Economy | | x | | Global economic growth will slow overall, but this is not likely to have too big an impact on the national economy, which will be helped by low inflation and low interest rates. |

158. What is the purpose of this chart?
    (A) To analyze the economy of the past half year
    (B) To explain which factors affect a nation's economy
    (C) To explain how income and spending affect the economy
    (D) To predict the state of the economy over the next six months

159. What is said about the national economy?
    (A) It will strengthen due to more employment.
    (B) It has been hurt by lack of consumer spending.
    (C) It would be improved by greater investment.
    (D) It is largely affected by the global economy.

160. What is indicated about the housing market?
    (A) Housing prices are likely to go up quickly.
    (B) More houses will be built during the rest of the year.
    (C) People haven't bought houses because incomes aren't rising much.
    (D) The more housing sales there are, the higher the prices will rise.

Questions 161–163 refer to the following article.

Overwhelmed by clutter? You don't have to be. By following a simple system, you can keep clutter from taking over your life. First, take a few minutes at the end of every day to pick up your home or office. Invest in a set of decorative baskets, buckets, or boxes, choosing colors and styles that match the décor. Assign a category to each one, such as "mail," "books and magazines," "current projects," etc. Then, it is a simple job to place items in their proper baskets or boxes. Now things are out of the way but easy to access when you need them. Next, *tackle* the big jobs seasonally. People tend to wait for "spring cleaning" time to organize their closets, but it's actually easier if you work on this a bit each season. Sort through your clothes and get rid of the ones you haven't worn during the past year. Go through your boxes and decide which items you need to keep and which you can give away.

161. What is recommended as a way to manage clutter?
(A) Repaint your rooms
(B) Store baskets in closets
(C) Use containers to organize things
(D) Get rid of old books and magazines

162. The word "tackle" in line 8 is closest in meaning to _____.
(A) deal with
(B) throw down
(C) attach
(D) grab

163. How often should you organize your closets?
(A) When they are cluttered
(B) Several times a year
(C) In the spring only
(D) Every day

Questions 164–167 refer to the following online chat.

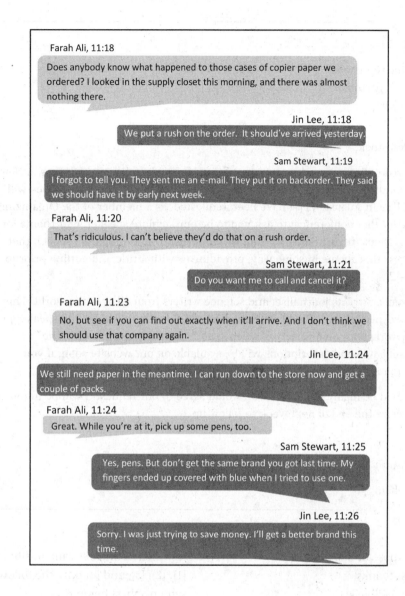

**Farah Ali, 11:18**
Does anybody know what happened to those cases of copier paper we ordered? I looked in the supply closet this morning, and there was almost nothing there.

**Jin Lee, 11:18**
We put a rush on the order. It should've arrived yesterday.

**Sam Stewart, 11:19**
I forgot to tell you. They sent me an e-mail. They put it on backorder. They said we should have it by early next week.

**Farah Ali, 11:20**
That's ridiculous. I can't believe they'd do that on a rush order.

**Sam Stewart, 11:21**
Do you want me to call and cancel it?

**Farah Ali, 11:23**
No, but see if you can find out exactly when it'll arrive. And I don't think we should use that company again.

**Jin Lee, 11:24**
We still need paper in the meantime. I can run down to the store now and get a couple of packs.

**Farah Ali, 11:24**
Great. While you're at it, pick up some pens, too.

**Sam Stewart, 11:25**
Yes, pens. But don't get the same brand you got last time. My fingers ended up covered with blue when I tried to use one.

**Jin Lee, 11:26**
Sorry. I was just trying to save money. I'll get a better brand this time.

164. How much paper is probably in the supply closet now?
(A) None
(B) Several cases
(C) A few sheets
(D) A couple of packs

165. Why didn't the company send the paper right away?
(A) They don't have it available right now.
(B) They didn't receive the order on time.
(C) They don't sell the brand ordered.
(D) They don't do rush orders.

166. What does Farah ask Sam to do?
(A) Go to the store
(B) Cancel the order
(C) Order more paper
(D) Ask for a delivery date

167. What was the problem with the pens bought last time?
(A) They were the wrong color.
(B) They were hard to hold.
(C) They cost too much.
(D) They leaked.

Questions 168–171 refer to the following letter.

---

February 2, 20—

Dr. Geraldine Comstock
Journalism Department
Bigelow College
Eastfield, VT

Dear Dr. Comstock,

I was honored to hear you present at the Modern Journalism Society seminar in New York last month. You may be aware that the annual Science Writers conference will be taking place in August.–[1]–I have been requested, as a member of the Organizing Committee for that conference, to ask you to be our keynote speaker. Our theme for this year is "Demystifying Science," and we would ask you to prepare a speech that would address that theme in some way, providing us with a title and outline prior to the event.–[2]–

The conference attracts journalists and science writers from all over the world. This year we are expecting over 2,000 attendees. In addition, there will be 125 speakers facilitating workshops on a variety of science and journalism topics.–[3]–The workshop schedule and descriptions will be available on our website soon, if you would like to refer to them.

–[4]–We would be highly honored if you would agree to our request. I will be in touch with you before the end of next week to follow up.

Sincerely,

*Robert Duchamp*

Robert Duchamp

---

168. What is the purpose of this letter?
    (A) To express thanks
    (B) To ask for feedback
    (C) To provide information
    (D) To extend an invitation

169. What happened in January?
    (A) The workshop schedule was created.
    (B) There was a journalism seminar.
    (C) The Organizing Committee met.
    (D) Conference registration opened.

170. In which of the following positions marked [1], [2], [3], and [4] does the following sentence best belong?

"The presenters include some of the country's best-known professionals in these fields."

    (A) [1]
    (B) [2]
    (C) [3]
    (D) [4]

171. What does Mr. Duchamp plan to do?
    (A) Contact Dr. Comstock again
    (B) Forward workshop information
    (C) Wait for Dr. Comstock's reply
    (D) Prepare a speech about science

Questions 172–175 refer to the following article.

The shellfish industry in the north coast region is booming, due in large part to the current popularity of seafood dishes that incorporate various kinds of shellfish. This is in sharp contrast to the state of the industry a decade ago. At that time, the catch had dwindled to less than 300,000 kilos a year. Since then, that figure has been steadily rising, and this year's catch is predicted to reach 1.5 million kilos.

The growth of the shellfish industry is attributed to a variety of factors. New regulations that manage fishing areas better and keep certain areas from being overfished have been very effective, according to fishing industry experts. "But the biggest reason," says Louise Hipper, a government fisheries manager, "is the focus on shellfish dishes in culinary circles." More and more restaurants across the nation have started featuring shellfish on their menus, prepared in a variety of ways. Shellfish from the north coast is especially desirable because of its larger size and sweeter flavor. "So many people want north coast shellfish," says restaurant owner Bill Jones, "that some days I simply can't get it, and then I have to disappoint my customers." Shellfish prices have risen along with the demand. The average price this year is $20 a kilo at the dock.

172. What is this article mostly about?
(A) Management of shellfish fishing
(B) The increasing demand for shellfish
(C) Improvements in fishing techniques
(D) The growth of the restaurant industry

173. What happened 10 years ago?
(A) Fishermen began to catch more shellfish.
(B) A new fisheries manager was hired.
(C) People stopped buying shellfish.
(D) The price of shellfish dropped.

174. The word "circles" in paragraph 2, line 5, is closest in meaning to _____.
(A) areas
(B) routes
(C) groups
(D) shapes

175. What is implied about shellfish?
(A) Its price will remain steady.
(B) It can only be bought at a dock.
(C) It has been overfished in the north coast.
(D) It costs over $20/kilo at a store or restaurant.

Questions 176–180 refer to the following receipt and e-mail.

NEW TOEIC PRACTICE EXAM A

## LIGHTHOUSE LIGHTING DESIGNS

### RECEIPT

Customer Name: Flashy Events & Catering

Customer No: 340294

Date: April 24

| QTY | DESC | PRICE/EACH | TOTAL |
|-----|------|------------|-------|
| 20 | String of LED lights/purple/10ft/Edison style | $6.50 | $130.00 |
| 10 | Table lanterns, style 30-2 | $9.25 | $92.50 |
| | | | |
| | | | |
| | | SUBTOTAL | $222.50 |
| | | DELIVERY | n/a |
| | | SALES TAX | $20.03 |
| | | TOTAL | $242.53 |

To: Emily@flashyevents.com
From: Kathleen@flashyevents.com
Sent on: April 25
Subject: Lights for tonight

Emily,

I picked up the lights last night for this evening's event. Purple this time. I'm glad we unpacked the original order ahead of time. Can you imagine what the bride would say if we showed up today with plain white lights? I also got a few extra strings, just in case. They're the same brand we used at that anniversary bash in the winter, you know, the ones we liked so much.

There was one small problem. The card was declined. Twice actually, so I had to use my own. I'll call the company this morning, but I'm thinking maybe our payment for last month's charges hasn't cleared yet. Remember everything we had to order for the Garvin graduation party?

I'll see you around noon to start setting up. Call me if you need anything.

Kathleen

176. What is the cost of one table lantern?
- (A) $6.50
- (B) $9.25
- (C) $92.50
- (D) $130.00

177. Why is there no delivery charge on the invoice?
- (A) The order was over $200.
- (B) The vendor forgot to include it.
- (C) The customer picked up the order.
- (D) The company never charges for delivery.

178. How was the order paid for?
- (A) Check
- (B) Gift card
- (C) Personal credit card
- (D) Corporate credit card

179. What was the problem with the original order?
- (A) The company charged too much.
- (B) The light strings were too short.
- (C) There weren't enough lights.
- (D) The color was wrong.

180. What kind of event will take place this evening?
- (A) Wedding
- (B) Light sale
- (C) Graduation party
- (D) Anniversary party

Questions 181–185 refer to the following course description and syllabus.

**Strategies for Branded Marketing (BUS2065)**
**Online**

This course introduces the principles of developing a brand's identity. It is ideal for small business owners, recent graduates, new project managers, and others interested in marketing concepts.

The course is offered online. New lessons are posted every Monday, with assignments due the following Friday. Each assignment is practical, similar to what a brand manager would be expected to do on the job. Lesson topics follow the provided syllabus, with the exception that the discussion of new media marketing could continue into the following week (replacing that week's topic), depending on student interest. The course also provides an instructor-monitored discussion area for participants to post and discuss current events and lesson materials. The final grade is based on assignments, participation in discussions, and two exams. Participants who achieve a final grade of 85% receive a certificate of completion.

BUS2065 Syllabus
Instructor: Michelle Crosby, MBA
Fall Quarter

A. Schedule

　　1. Introductions, Planning a Brand's Goals and Vision
　　2. The Development of Branding over the Past Century
　　3. Packaging Your Brand
　　4. Mid-term Exam
　　5. Traditional vs. New Media Marketing
　　6. Using Marketing to Drive Sales
　　7. Timelines, Milestones, and Measuring Success
　　8. Final Exam

B. Final exam must be taken by Friday of the final week. In rare cases, makeup exams may be given. Please contact the instructor to discuss.

181. What happens on Fridays?
- (A) Assignments are posted online.
- (B) Assignments are due to the instructor.
- (C) Assignments are discussed with classmates.
- (D) Assignments are reviewed by the instructor.

182. What is offered to students who pass the course?
- (A) A job
- (B) A degree
- (C) A diploma
- (D) A certificate

183. How long does the course last?
- (A) 8 days
- (B) 1 month
- (C) 8 weeks
- (D) 1 year

184. In which lesson will history be discussed?
- (A) 2
- (B) 3
- (C) 4
- (D) 5

185. Which topic might not be covered?
- (A) Planning a Brand's Goals and Vision
- (B) Traditional vs. New Media Marketing
- (C) Using Marketing to Drive Sales
- (D) Timelines, Milestones, and Measuring Success

Questions 186–190 refer to the following notice, flyer, and e-mail.

---

## Woodbury Public Library

### Hours
Monday–Friday, 10:00 A.M.–8 P.M.
Saturday, 9 A.M.–1 P.M.
Sundays and Holidays, closed

### Directory
Basement ............ Children's Room

Main Floor .......... Front Desk, Reference, Periodicals

Second Floor ..... Adult Fiction

Third Floor ......... Adult Nonfiction, Meeting Rooms

- All Woodbury residents are eligible for library cards. Apply at the front desk.
- Books can be checked out for 3 weeks at a time and can be renewed once for an additional 3 weeks.
- Overdue fine: 25 cents/day

---

workshop    workshop    workshop    workshop    workshop    workshop

### Using the Internet for Research

Whether you use the Internet for personal interest, school, or work, this workshop will provide you with the tools and knowledge you need to get the most out of your research.

Open to the public. Minimum age: 14

Free for Woodbury Public Library cardholders. All others: $15.

Saturday, May 21, 9:30 A.M.–12:00 noon, Woodbury Public Library, Meeting Room 2

*Brought to you by the Friends of the Woodbury Public Library*

---

```
From:         eleanorbrowne@pqr.com
To:           billforbes@rumpus.com
Subject:      Saturday
Date:         May 17

Hi Bill,
I am going to have to be a bit late for our lunch
date this week. I forgot that I'm giving a workshop
on Internet research at the library, and it goes till
noon. So I won't be able to meet you till around
12:30 or so. Also, it will be an early morning for me
because I'm planning to be at the library right when
it opens. That will give me half an hour to set up
and make sure all the equipment is in order. At least
I can take advantage to return my library book that's
just about due now. I haven't finished it but don't
think I'll renew. It's kind of boring. Anyhow, see you
in a few days.

Eleanor
```

186. Who can attend the workshop?

(A) Anyone
(B) Adults only
(C) Teens and adults
(D) Library card holders only

187. Where will the workshop be held?

(A) Basement
(B) Main floor
(C) Second floor
(D) Third floor

188. What time will Eleanor probably arrive at the library?

(A) 8:30
(B) 9:00
(C) 9:30
(D) 10:00

189. In the e-mail, the phrase "in order" in line 9 is closest in meaning to _____.

(A) working correctly
(B) arranged in sequence
(C) following the rules
(D) up to date

190. When did Eleanor probably check out her library book?

(A) Last week
(B) About 3 weeks ago
(C) About 6 weeks ago
(D) It is impossible to know.

Questions 191–195 refer to the following webpage, review, and flyer.

www.geraniuminn.com

File   Edit   View   Favorites   Tools   Help

Page · Safety · Tools ·

| Home | Rooms & Rates | Reservations | About Us | Contact Us |

## Geranium Inn

The Geranium Inn is conveniently located right on the green in historic Fitzburgh. Enjoy the charm of village life while relaxing on our front porch or strolling the nearby streets and window shopping in Fitzburgh's quaint shops.

At the Geranium Inn guests enjoy

* Beautiful views from each room
* Luxuriously comfortable beds
* Delicious homemade breakfasts
* Superior service

### Apple Festival Special

Reserve your room by August 15 to get our special Apple Festival price:

$325 - 2 nights (breakfast included), double occupancy
($25 each additional person).

We chose the Geranium Inn for its location and reasonable rates. Everything they promise is true—comfortable rooms, great breakfast, and good service. But the one thing they don't mention is the noise. The inn is just across the street from the green, which means it is right in the center of the action. We were there during the first weekend of the Apple Festival, and there was a lot of activity on the green, even into the late hours of the night. So we didn't get much sleep. Too bad, because the inn is a lovely place otherwise, but I don't think we'll be staying there again.

Don't miss Fitzburgh's world-famous

# APPLE FESTIVAL

September 25–27, October 2–5
On the green in Fitzburgh

❖ Enjoy home-baked apple pies and other tasty treats
❖ Purchase crafts from around the region
❖ Enjoy performances by local guitar and fiddle players
❖ See apple cider-making demonstrations

Fun for the whole family

Admission: Free
Parking is available behind Fitzburgh High School.
Please leave your pets at home.

Vendors: Applications for selling space must be submitted by July 31.

191. What does $325 pay for at the Geranium Inn?
(A) One room for one person
(B) One room for two people
(C) Two rooms for one night
(D) Two rooms for two nights

192. What did the reviewer NOT like about the Geranium Inn?
(A) Beds
(B) Food
(C) Service
(D) Location

193. In the review, the word "reasonable" in line 1 is closest in meaning to _____.
(A) inexpensive
(B) sensible
(C) logical
(D) valid

194. When did the reviewer stay at the inn?
(A) July
(B) August
(C) September
(D) October

195. What is one thing visitors can't do at the Apple Festival?
(A) Eat pies
(B) Hear music
(C) Buy crafts
(D) Bring their dogs

Questions 196–200 refer to the following e-mail, table, and notice.

From:       membership@pinevalleyhc.com
To:         sjones@ficus.com
Subject:    renew membership now
Date:       November 7


Dear Sam Jones,

Your Pine Valley Health Club membership is about to expire. Please sign into your account at www.pinevalleyhc.com/members to renew your membership.

**Membership Upgrade Special**
You have been a valued Pine Valley Health Club member for over five years. As a thank you, we are offering you an exclusive upgrade special.

Upgrade your membership to GOLD, and you will receive $100 off the usual membership price. You must renew before November 30 to take advantage of this offer.

Stay fit!
Amanda Perkins
Membership Specialist

## PINE VALLEY HEALTH CLUB
### MEMBERSHIP LEVELS

| Level | Benefits | |
|-------|----------|---|
| Day User | Includes use of all facilities for one day | $20/day |
| Silver | Includes use of all facilities, fee for group classes and private lessons | $500/yr |
| Gold | Includes use of all facilities, reduced fee for group classes and private lessons | $675/yr |
| Platinum | Includes use of all facilities, no fee for group classes, 1 hr/week private fitness instruction | $800/yr |

Welcome to the

**PINE VALLEY HEALTH CLUB**

Open 7 days a week
6:30 P.M.–8:30 P.M.

Pool hours
6:30 A.M.–8:30 A.M.   swim classes only
8:30 A.M.–9:00 A.M.   closed for cleaning
9:00 A.M.–3:00 P.M.   general swim
3:00 P.M.–6:00 P.M.   swim classes only
6:00 P.M.–8:30 P.M.   general swim

Tennis, squash, yoga, aerobics, and fitness training classes are also available. Please sign up at the front desk.

Reminder: Guests are always welcome, but they must pay the regular day user fee.

196. What level membership does Sam Jones probably have now?
(A) Day user
(B) Silver
(C) Gold
(D) Platinum

197. If Sam renews his membership at the Gold level within the month, how much will he pay?
(A) $500
(B) $550
(C) $575
(D) $675

198. In the table, the word "benefits" in the heading is closest in meaning to _____.
(A) services
(B) assistance
(C) profits
(D) advantages

199. If Sam wants to swim on his own on Saturday morning, what is the earliest time he can use the pool?
(A) 6:30 A.M.
(B) 8:30 A.M.
(C) 9:00 A.M.
(D) 3:00 P.M.

200. How much would a guest of Sam's pay to use the club for a day?
(A) $0
(B) $20
(C) It depends on Sam's membership level.
(D) Only members can use the club.

# ANSWER KEY
## New TOEIC Practice Exam A

## LISTENING COMPREHENSION

### Part 1: Photographs

| | | | |
|---|---|---|---|
| 1. **B** | 3. **C** | 5. **C** | |
| 2. **A** | 4. **D** | 6. **A** | |

### Part 2: Question-Response

| | | | |
|---|---|---|---|
| 7. **A** | 14. **A** | 21. **A** | 28. **A** |
| 8. **C** | 15. **B** | 22. **B** | 29. **A** |
| 9. **A** | 16. **C** | 23. **C** | 30. **C** |
| 10. **B** | 17. **B** | 24. **B** | 31. **B** |
| 11. **C** | 18. **C** | 25. **C** | |
| 12. **B** | 19. **C** | 26. **C** | |
| 13. **A** | 20. **B** | 27. **A** | |

### Part 3: Conversations

| | | | |
|---|---|---|---|
| 32. **B** | 42. **A** | 52. **A** | 62. **B** |
| 33. **A** | 43. **C** | 53. **C** | 63. **A** |
| 34. **C** | 44. **D** | 54. **B** | 64. **B** |
| 35. **D** | 45. **C** | 55. **A** | 65. **C** |
| 36. **B** | 46. **A** | 56. **B** | 66. **A** |
| 37. **A** | 47. **B** | 57. **C** | 67. **B** |
| 38. **D** | 48. **A** | 58. **D** | 68. **D** |
| 39. **B** | 49. **C** | 59. **A** | 69. **C** |
| 40. **A** | 50. **A** | 60. **C** | 70. **B** |
| 41. **D** | 51. **D** | 61. **D** | |

### Part 4: Talks

| | | | |
|---|---|---|---|
| 71. **C** | 79. **B** | 87. **D** | 95. **B** |
| 72. **B** | 80. **A** | 88. **B** | 96. **C** |
| 73. **A** | 81. **C** | 89. **C** | 97. **D** |
| 74. **A** | 82. **D** | 90. **B** | 98. **D** |
| 75. **D** | 83. **C** | 91. **C** | 99. **C** |
| 76. **B** | 84. **A** | 92. **A** | 100. **A** |
| 77. **C** | 85. **B** | 93. **D** | |
| 78. **A** | 86. **A** | 94. **A** | |

# ANSWER KEY
## New TOEIC Practice Exam A

### READING

### Part 5: Incomplete Sentences

| | | | |
|---|---|---|---|
| 101. **B** | 109. **D** | 117. **A** | 125. **A** |
| 102. **A** | 110. **B** | 118. **C** | 126. **D** |
| 103. **C** | 111. **A** | 119. **A** | 127. **B** |
| 104. **D** | 112. **C** | 120. **A** | 128. **A** |
| 105. **B** | 113. **D** | 121. **D** | 129. **D** |
| 106. **D** | 114. **D** | 122. **B** | 130. **C** |
| 107. **B** | 115. **A** | 123. **D** | |
| 108. **D** | 116. **B** | 124. **A** | |

### Part 6: Text Completion

| | | | |
|---|---|---|---|
| 131. **D** | 135. **B** | 139. **A** | 143. **B** |
| 132. **C** | 136. **D** | 140. **C** | 144. **A** |
| 133. **A** | 137. **C** | 141. **B** | 145. **C** |
| 134. **B** | 138. **A** | 142. **D** | 146. **D** |

### Part 7: Reading Comprehension

| | | | |
|---|---|---|---|
| 147. **C** | 161. **C** | 175. **D** | 189. **A** |
| 148. **B** | 162. **A** | 176. **B** | 190. **B** |
| 149. **B** | 163. **B** | 177. **C** | 191. **B** |
| 150. **A** | 164. **C** | 178. **C** | 192. **D** |
| 151. **B** | 165. **A** | 179. **D** | 193. **A** |
| 152. **C** | 166. **D** | 180. **A** | 194. **C** |
| 153. **D** | 167. **D** | 181. **B** | 195. **D** |
| 154. **B** | 168. **D** | 182. **D** | 196. **B** |
| 155. **A** | 169. **B** | 183. **C** | 197. **C** |
| 156. **C** | 170. **C** | 184. **A** | 198. **A** |
| 157. **D** | 171. **A** | 185. **C** | 199. **C** |
| 158. **D** | 172. **B** | 186. **C** | 200. **B** |
| 159. **A** | 173. **A** | 187. **D** | |
| 160. **C** | 174. **C** | 188. **B** | |

# TEST SCORE CONVERSION TABLE

Count your correct responses. Match the number of correct responses with the corresponding score from the Test Score Conversion Table (below). Add the two scores together. This is your Total Estimated Test Score. As you practice taking the TOEIC model tests, your scores should improve. Keep track of your Total Estimated Test Scores.

| # Correct | Listening Score | Reading Score | # Correct | Listening Score | Reading Score | # Correct | Listening Score | Reading Score | # Correct | Listening Score | Reading Score |
|---|---|---|---|---|---|---|---|---|---|---|---|
| 0 | 5 | 5 | 26 | 110 | 65 | 51 | 255 | 220 | 76 | 410 | 370 |
| 1 | 5 | 5 | 27 | 115 | 70 | 52 | 260 | 225 | 77 | 420 | 380 |
| 2 | 5 | 5 | 28 | 120 | 80 | 53 | 270 | 230 | 78 | 425 | 385 |
| 3 | 5 | 5 | 29 | 125 | 85 | 54 | 275 | 235 | 79 | 430 | 390 |
| 4 | 5 | 5 | 30 | 130 | 90 | 55 | 280 | 240 | 80 | 440 | 395 |
| 5 | 5 | 5 | 31 | 135 | 95 | 56 | 290 | 250 | 81 | 445 | 400 |
| 6 | 5 | 5 | 32 | 140 | 100 | 57 | 295 | 255 | 82 | 450 | 405 |
| 7 | 10 | 5 | 33 | 145 | 110 | 58 | 300 | 260 | 83 | 460 | 410 |
| 8 | 15 | 5 | 34 | 150 | 115 | 59 | 310 | 265 | 84 | 465 | 415 |
| 9 | 20 | 5 | 35 | 160 | 120 | 60 | 315 | 270 | 85 | 470 | 420 |
| 10 | 25 | 5 | 36 | 165 | 125 | 61 | 320 | 280 | 86 | 475 | 425 |
| 11 | 30 | 5 | 37 | 170 | 130 | 62 | 325 | 285 | 87 | 480 | 430 |
| 12 | 35 | 5 | 38 | 175 | 140 | 63 | 330 | 290 | 88 | 485 | 435 |
| 13 | 40 | 5 | 39 | 180 | 145 | 64 | 340 | 300 | 89 | 490 | 445 |
| 14 | 45 | 5 | 40 | 185 | 150 | 65 | 345 | 305 | 90 | 495 | 450 |
| 15 | 50 | 5 | 41 | 190 | 160 | 66 | 350 | 310 | 91 | 495 | 455 |
| 16 | 55 | 10 | 42 | 195 | 165 | 67 | 360 | 320 | 92 | 495 | 465 |
| 17 | 60 | 15 | 43 | 200 | 170 | 68 | 365 | 325 | 93 | 495 | 470 |
| 18 | 65 | 20 | 44 | 210 | 175 | 69 | 370 | 330 | 94 | 495 | 480 |
| 19 | 70 | 25 | 45 | 215 | 180 | 70 | 380 | 335 | 95 | 495 | 485 |
| 20 | 75 | 30 | 46 | 220 | 190 | 71 | 385 | 340 | 96 | 495 | 490 |
| 21 | 80 | 35 | 47 | 230 | 195 | 72 | 390 | 350 | 97 | 495 | 495 |
| 22 | 85 | 40 | 48 | 240 | 200 | 73 | 395 | 355 | 98 | 495 | 495 |
| 23 | 90 | 45 | 49 | 245 | 210 | 74 | 400 | 360 | 99 | 495 | 495 |
| 24 | 95 | 50 | 50 | 250 | 215 | 75 | 405 | 365 | 100 | 495 | 495 |
| 25 | 100 | 60 | | | | | | | | | |

Number of Correct Listening Responses _____ = Listening Score _____

Number of Correct Reading Responses _____ = Reading Score _____

Total Estimated Test Score _____

# ANSWERS EXPLAINED

## Listening Comprehension

### PART 1: PHOTOGRAPHS

1. **(B)** People are eating at an outdoor café. Choice (A) mentions the chairs, but no one is putting them inside. Choice (C) mentions the tables, but no one is moving them around. Choice (D) confuses *outdoors* with *doors*.

2. **(A)** A cargo ship is in the middle of the ocean. Choice (B) confuses similar-sounding words *boat* and *coat* and associates the *water* with *wet*. Choice (C) associates *ship* with *captain* and *deck*, but no captain is visible. Choice (D) is incorrect because the ocean surface is smooth and calm.

3. **(C)** A young woman is reading a book in a library. Choice (A) confuses similar-sounding words *book* and *cook*. Choice (B) confuses similar-sounding words *reading* and *meeting*. Choice (D) confuses similar-sounding words *pages* and *cages*.

4. **(D)** A group of people is walking down the street carrying different kinds of bags. Choice (A) refers to the buildings in the background, but no one is entering them. Choice (B) confuses similar-sounding words *walking* and *working*. Choice (C) confuses similar-sounding words *walking* and *talking*.

5. **(C)** A man is painting a picture of an outdoor scene. Choice (A) uses the word *brush* out of context. Choice (B) uses the word *picture* out of context. Choice (D) repeats the word *painter*, but this painter is an artist, not a house painter preparing a wall to be painted.

6. **(A)** Some people are listening to a presentation in a hotel conference room. Choice (B) correctly identifies the screen but not the action and confuses similar-sounding words *sitting* and *setting*. Choice (C) correctly identifies the location but not the action. Choice (D) correctly identifies the action but not the object.

### PART 2: QUESTION-RESPONSE

7. **(A)** The second speaker is starving, so is happy to hear that dinner will be ready soon. Choice (B) confuses *read* with the similar-sounding word *ready*, and *afternoon* with the similar-sounding word *soon*. Choice (C) confuses *thinner* with the similar-sounding word *dinner*.

8. **(C)** *Wilson Boulevard* answers the question about an address. Choice (A) confuses similar-sounding words *address* and *dress*. Choice (B) confuses similar-sounding words *address* and *adding*.

9. **(A)** *A cleaning company* answers the question *Who?* Choice (B) repeats the word *office*. Choice (C) confuses *office* with the similar-sounding phrase *his voice*.

10. **(B)** *On the bus* answers the question *Where?* Choice (A) associates *umbrella* with *raining*. Choice (C) confuses *leave* with *leisure*.

11. **(C)** Because the printer ran out of paper, the second speaker says that there is more paper in the closet. Choice (A) repeats the word *printer*. Choice (B) confuses *newspaper* with *paper*.

12. **(B)** This is a logical response to the suggestion made by the first speaker. Choices (A) and (C) repeat the word *newspaper*.

13. **(A)** *Once* answers the question *How many times?* Choice (B) confuses the meaning of the word *China* by associating it with *dishes*. Choice (C) confuses the meaning of the word *time*.

14. **(A)** This is a logical response to a question about a past action. Choice (B) confuses similar-sounding words *fax* and *facts*. Choice (C) confuses similar-sounding words *sent* and *rent*.

15. **(B)** *Sales staff* answers the question *Who?* Choice (A) confuses *marketing* with *market*. Choice (C) confuses the meaning of the word *develop*.

16. **(C)** This is a time clause used to answer the question *When?* Choice (A) confuses *purpose* with *purchase*. Choice (B) confuses similar-sounding words *computer* and *commuter*.

17. **(B)** *Summer* answers the question about a season. Choice (A) confuses similar-sounding words *season* and *reason*. Choice (C) confuses the meaning of the word *fall*, using it as a verb, not as the name of a season.

18. **(C)** This explains the reason for being late. Choice (A) confuses similar-sounding words *late* and *ate*. Choice (B) confuses similar-sounding words *late* and *date*.

19. **(C)** This describes the more comfortable chair. Choice (A) confuses similar-sounding words *chair* and *there* and repeats the word *more*. Choice (B) confuses similar-sounding words *comfortable* and *table*.

20. **(B)** The first speaker wants an appointment with Ms. Park, and the second speaker suggests a convenient time. Choice (A) confuses *pointed* with the similar-sounding word *appointment*. Choice (C) confuses *dark* with the similar-sounding word *Park*.

21. **(A)** This answers the question *Where?* Choice (B) associates *post office* with *letter* and repeats the word *office*. Choice (C) associates *post office* with *postal workers*.

22. **(B)** This is a polite response to the request. Choice (A) repeats the word *pass*. Choice (C) confuses similar-sounding words *salt* and *insulted*.

23. **(C)** This explains the purpose of the visit. Choice (A) uses the related word *visitors*. Choice (B) confuses similar-sounding words *purpose* and *porpoise*.

24. **(B)** This is a logical response to the suggestion to take a break. Choice (A) confuses the noun *break* with the verb *break* by relating it to *broken*. Choice (C) repeats the word *take*.

25. **(C)** This explains the reason for postponing the meeting. Choice (A) confuses similar-sounding words *postponed* and *phone*. Choice (B) confuses similar-sounding words *meeting* and *meat*.

26. **(C)** This answers the question *When?* Choice (A) confuses similar-sounding words *memo* and *menu*. Choice (B) associates *computer* with *written*.

27. **(A)** *In the hall closet* answers the question *Where?* Choice (B) confuses *suitcase* with the similar-sounding phrase *in case*. Choice (C) confuses *suitcases* with *suits*.

28. **(A)** The second speaker offers to pick Susan up at her 4:30 train. Choice (B) associates *tickets* with *train*. Choice (C) confuses *stain* with the similar-sounding word *train*.

29. **(A)** This answers the question about languages. Choice (B) associates *languages* with *linguist*. Choice (C) repeats the word *speak*.

30. **(C)** This is a logical response to the question about retirement plans. Choice (A) confuses the use of the verb *retire*, making it mean *go to bed* rather than *stop working*. Choice (B) confuses similar-sounding words *retire* and *tire*.

31. **(B)** *Another two weeks* answers the question *When?* Choice (A) uses the related word *exhibit*. Choice (C) confuses homonyms *close* and *clothes*.

## PART 3: CONVERSATIONS

32. **(B)** The man says, *I'm on my way downtown right now for an interview.* Choice (A) is where the woman is going. Choice (C) confuses similar-sounding words *appointment* and *apartment*. Choice (D) confuses *downtown* and *out of town*.

33. **(A)** The man says that he is taking the bus. Choice (B) is incorrect because the woman says she can't drive him. Choice (C) confuses similar-sounding words *rain* and *train*. Choice (D) is plausible but not mentioned.

34. **(C)** The woman says, *Here, you'd better take my umbrella.* Choice (A) is plausible but not mentioned. Choice (B) confuses the usage of the word *direction*—the woman says she is going *in the opposite direction.* Choice (D) confuses similar-sounding words *offer* and *coffee*.

35. **(D)** The man says he has *client meetings* and *presentations*, so it is a business trip. Choices (A) and (C) aren't mentioned. Choice (B) is associated with *presentations* but not with *client meetings*.

36. **(B)** The woman says, *You're flying out on Monday, right*, and the man replies *No, Sunday*. Choice (A) confuses similar-sounding words *right* and *tonight*. Choice (C) repeats *Monday*. Choice (D) confuses *two days* and *Tuesday*.

37. **(A)** When a person says he *wouldn't do something* it means he doesn't recommend it; the woman doesn't recommend the hotel because *the beds are lumpy and it's not very clean*. Choices (B), (C), and (D) don't fit the meaning of the expression or the context of the conversation.

38. **(D)** The speakers talk about where they are going and then the woman says, *Oh, here's my stop*, so they are on a bus. Choice (A) is where the woman is going. Choice (B) is where the man is going. Choice (C) is associated with the woman's mention of *lunch hour*.

39. **(B)** The man says, *I'm not due at the lawyer's till one fifteen.* Choice (A) sounds similar to the correct answer. Choice (C) confuses similar-sounding words *late* and *eight*. Choice (D) confuses similar-sounding words *time* and *nine*.

40. **(A)** The man says, *I'll get off and walk with you.* Choice (B) repeats the word *lawyer*. Choice (C) is what the woman will do. Choice (D) repeats the word *lunch*.

41. **(D)** The man wants to have the woman show him the available rooms next week. Choice (A) is something he might do in the future. Choice (B) is unlikely since the man says the prices look great. Choice (C) is presumably what he did when he spoke with the woman last week.

42. **(A)** The man is speaking with the woman about renting a room at her hotel for a banquet, so she is probably the hotel events manager. Choice (B) is associated with *rent*. Choice (C) is associated with *hotel*. Choice (D) is associated with the topic of the banquet.

43. **(C)** The woman says, *I'm leaving for Paris on Monday*. Choice (A) repeats *menu*, previously mentioned by the man. Choice (B) is what the man wants her to do. Choice (D) repeats *assistant*, who, the woman says, is available to meet with the man.

44. **(D)** The man says that the artist lives in Portland and then adds, *He lives around the corner*, meaning that he lives nearby, so the conversation must be taking place in Portland, too. Choices (A), (B), and (C) are other cities mentioned as places where the artist has lived.

45. **(C)** The woman refers to the art as a *statue*, which is a type of sculpture. Choices (A), (B), and (C) are other types of art but are not mentioned.

46. **(A)** The man says, *I have to ask you to take your hands off the art*, meaning he doesn't want the woman to touch it. Choice (B) repeats *sit*, the position that the statue is in. Choice (C) is not mentioned. Choice (D) repeats *buy*, which the man implies that the woman can do.

47. **(B)** The man says he went to the new office *to leave a check with the landlord*. Choice (A) confuses similar-sounding words *look* and *book*. Choice (C) repeats *furniture*, which the man says they can move to the new office soon. Choice (D) repeats *clean*, which the man says the new office needs.

48. **(A)** The woman says, *I'm tired of being so cramped here*, and the second man says, *It'll be great to have more space*. Choice (B) is what is happening at the new office. Choice (C) is related to the rent check for the new office. Choice (D) is confused with the woman's saying, *I'm good at organizing*, but she is referring to packing.

49. **(C)** The second man says that he is not good at packing, and the woman offers to help him pack later in the afternoon. Choice (A) confuses similar-sounding words *pack* and *snack*. Choice (B) is incorrect because it is her colleague's things she will pack, not her own. Choice (D) is what the first man did this morning.

50. **(A)** The speakers are waiting for a table, looking at a menu, and the man says, *Everything here is cooked fresh*, so they are at a restaurant. Choice (B) is associated with *cooked*. Choices (C) and (D) are associated with the mention of *prices* and *money*.

51. **(D)** The speakers think they might have to wait for a while to get a table, which implies that the place is crowded. Choice (A) repeats the word *service*, but there is no implication that it is slow. Choices (B) and (C) are the opposite of what is implied.

52. **(A)** The woman expresses concern about the high prices, and the man says, *It's on me*, meaning he will pay for their meal. Choice (B) repeats the word *service*. Choice (C) is what the woman asks for. Choice (D) is plausible but not mentioned.

53. **(C)** The woman asks if she can pick up the order today. Choice (A) is mentioned but is not the purpose of the call. Choice (B) is not mentioned. Choice (D) was done before this conversation.

54. **(B)** The woman ordered brochures with two colors and photographs, and the man made 2,500 copies, so he is a printer. Choice (A) relates *photographer* and *photographs*. Choices (C) and (D) are associated with *brochure*.

55. **(A)** The man made 2,500 copies but the woman ordered 2,000. Choice (B) is incorrect because the man says that the brochures are ready. Choice (C) is confused with the man's mention that he won't charge for the extra copies. Choice (D) is true but not a problem because it is what the woman ordered.

56. **(B)** The woman mentions the picnic of *last year*, and the man mentions the picnic of *this year*, so it happens once every year. Choice (A) repeats the word *month*—the picnic will be next month. Choice (C) repeats the word *year*. Choice (D) is confused with *the other years*.

57. **(C)** The woman doesn't like the park by the lake where the picnic is usually held and says she is considering the country club. Choices (A) and (B) are where the picnic was held last year. Choice (D) isn't mentioned.

58. **(D)** If something *goes over* with someone, it means it is accepted, so the man thinks that the woman's idea about the country club won't be accepted by the staff. Choices (A), (B), and (C) don't fit the meaning of the expression or the context.

59. **(A)** The man says that his work now is interesting, unlike his old job, and that he used to fall asleep in the office every day, all of which imply that the job was boring. Choice (B) is incorrect because he says I was already earning well before. Choices (C) and (D) are what he says about his new job.

60. **(C)** The woman reminds the man of how he fell asleep in class at university, so they knew each other then. Choices (A) and (D) are not mentioned. Choice (B) is related to the discussion of the man's former job.

61. **(D)** The man says, *I'm getting together with some of our old mates tonight*, and then asks the woman to meet them for *a bite to eat*. Choices (A), (B), and (C) are related to the discussion of the man's job but are not mentioned.

62. **(B)** The speakers are talking about their plans to have lunch in the cafeteria with their colleague, Kerry. Choice (A) refers to the mention of the cafeteria prices. Choices (C) and (D) refer to things that are mentioned but are not the main topic of the conversation.

63. **(A)** The man says, *you can't beat the prices*, meaning the prices are very good, and goes on to explain that neighborhood restaurants are much more expensive. Choice (B) is confused with the woman's saying, *I wish the food there were better*, meaning she doesn't like the food. Choice (C) is incorrect because the man says, *we don't really have time to go anywhere else*, meaning the cafeteria is close. Choice (D) is not mentioned.

64. **(B)** The woman reminds the man that they are supposed to meet Kerry in the lobby, and the man says, *We'd better get going*, meaning that they have to hurry to do that. Choices (A) and (D) are things they will do later. Choice (C) repeats the name *Kerry*.

65. **(C)** The man says about his apartment, *It's not large.* Choices (A) and (D) are incorrect because the man describes the apartment as *peaceful and comfortable.* Choice (B) is not mentioned.

66. **(A)** The man says, *I'm taking off for the lake on Thursday morning.* Choice (B) repeats *arrive*—the woman says she will arrive Friday morning. Choice (C) is incorrect because the woman won't arrive until Friday. Choice (D) is plausible but not mentioned.

67. **(B)** The woman will use the garage from Friday through Sunday, so she will pay $5 for Friday and nothing more for Saturday and Sunday. Choices (A), (C), and (D) are contradicted by the correct answer.

68. **(D)** Marvin has given directions about materials for the workshop and the room setup, so it is likely he is the workshop presenter. Choice (A) is likely what the two speakers are. Choice (B) doesn't make sense as this isn't a social situation. Choice (C) is related to the situation but is not a likely person to be involved in planning the event.

69. **(C)** The woman says, *But we're already over budget. You can't spend any more.* Choice (A) is incorrect because the woman is happy about the number of participants. Choice (B) refers to the woman's mention of setting up the room, but she doesn't express worry about getting it done on time. Choice (D) refers to the pens the man will buy, but the woman isn't worried about getting enough.

70. **(B)** The man says that he will only get as many pens as needed and that there will be 24, that is, two dozen, participants in the workshop. Choice (A) doesn't have enough pens. Choices (C) and (D) have too many pens.

## PART 4: TALKS

71. **(C)** The speaker is describing traffic conditions in the area, including traffic problems caused by road repair work. Choice (A) repeats the word *weather*—road repair has begun because of the warm weather. Choice (B) is mentioned but is not the focus of the talk. Choice (D) repeats the word *travel.*

72. **(B)** After mentioning the repaving work on Main Street, the speaker says, *stay away from that part of town.* Choice (A) confuses *slowdown* and *slowly.* Choice (C) repeats the word *bridge.* Choice (D) repeats the words *travel* and *afternoon.*

73. **(A)** The speaker says that the Mid Town Bridge will be closed for repairs starting tomorrow. Choice (B) is incorrect because the repaving has already begun. Choice (C) repeats *Maple Avenue*, but no mention is made of either closing or opening it. Choice (D) repeats the words *weather* and *clear.*

74. **(A)** The conference attendees will see plants they may want to use in their designs, attend workshops on landscaping topics, and listen to an expert on designing outdoor spaces, so they are probably landscape designers. Choice (B) refers to the location of the conference. Choice (C) is associated with the mention of plants. Choice (D) repeats the word *chefs*, mentioned in relation to breakfast.

75. **(D)** The speaker says that they are in a *beautiful mountain setting.* Choice (A) is where the conference is usually held. Choice (C) is associated with the mention of *breakfast, chefs,* and *lunch.* Choice (B) confuses similar-sounding words *take* and *lake.*

76. **(B)** After describing the day's activities, the speaker says, *We'll begin the day with a talk*, and then welcomes the speaker. Choices (A), (C), and (D) are all activities that will occur later.

77. **(C)** The speaker says that the rain will finally stop and that *it seemed like we'd never see the sun again*. Choices (A), (B), and (D) are contradicted by the correct answer.

78. **(A)** The speaker says, *get out there and enjoy the warmth and sunshine while you can*. Choices (B) and (C) are things he says aren't needed. Choice (D) is the opposite of what he advises.

79. **(B)** The speaker says, *Clouds will move back in over the weekend*. Choice (A) won't happen again until next week. Choices (C) and (D) describe the weather tomorrow.

80. **(A)** The speaker is reminding the listener about the appointment for next week. Choice (B) is confused with the mention of the missed appointment fee. Choice (C) is related to the topic but is not mentioned. Choice (D) is confused with the mention of how to cancel an appointment.

81. **(C)** The speaker reminds the listener to bring eyeglasses and mentions the possibility of the doctor's prescribing new glasses. Choices (A), (B), and (D) are other types of doctors.

82. **(D)** The speaker says, *We ask all our patients to arrive ten minutes before the scheduled time*. Choice (A) is confused with the mention of the missed appointment fee for patients who don't cancel their appointments. Choice (B) is incorrect because the listener will complete the form in the doctor's office. Choice (C) repeats *Monday*, the day of the appointment.

83. **(C)** The speaker says that the park will *be built in the place where the former football stadium stood*. Choices (A), (B), and (D) are other ideas that were proposed for the stadium site.

84. **(A)** The expression *I can't wait* is used to mean that the speaker is looking forward to something, and the speaker says that the park will offer many great recreational opportunities. Choices (B), (C), and (D) don't fit the meaning of the expression or the context of the talk.

85. **(B)** The speaker says, *Work on the park will begin early next month*. Choice (A) is confused with the correct answer. Choice (C) is when the work will be completed. Choice (D) sounds similar to the completion date.

86. **(A)** The speaker called to ask her friend to pick up her car for her. Choice (B) is presumably what she will do after the friend does the favor. Choice (C) is mentioned (the new job) but is not the purpose of the call. Choice (D) is not mentioned.

87. **(D)** After saying this, the speaker goes on to describe her problem—she can't pick up her car herself. Choices (A), (B), and (C) don't fit the meaning of the phrase or the context.

88. **(B)** The speaker says that Monday will be her first day of work. Choice (A) is what she wants her friend to do. Choice (C) repeats the word *mechanic*. Choice (D) is something she might do at another time in return for the favor, but it is not mentioned.

89. **(C)** Mr. Green's sells produce, dairy products, canned goods, and other food items, so it is a grocery store. Choice (A) is associated with the mention of fruits and vegetables. Choice (B) is associated with the mention of the different food items. Choice (D) is associated with the mention of fruits and vegetables and organic produce.

90. **(B)** The speaker says that Sunday is sale day and that there are *huge discounts* then. Choice (A) is contradicted by the correct answer. Choice (C) confuses similar-sounding words *discount* and *counted*. Choice (D) repeats the word *shelves*.

91. **(C)** The speaker says, *Check your local newspaper for our weekly coupon specials*. Choice (A) confuses the meaning of the word *check*. Choice (B) repeats the word *weekly*. Choice (D) repeats the word *website*.

92. **(A)** The speaker says, *we're going to get moving in a minute* and *There can be no standing in the aisle*, and she is conducting a city tour, so she is probably on a bus. Choice (B) is the place she has just left. Choice (C) is associated with *seats* and *aisle*. Choice (D) is associated with *river*.

93. **(D)** The speaker says, *next on the agenda is food* and then goes on to talk about the café. Choice (A) repeats *river*, but swimming in it is not mentioned. Choice (B) associates *agenda* with *meeting*. Choice (C) is what they will do later.

94. **(A)** The speaker says that the café *lacks in size*, meaning that it's small. Choice (B) is not mentioned. Choice (C) is incorrect because the speaker mentions the *amazing menu*. Choice (D) is incorrect because she mentions the *fantastic view*.

95. **(B)** The speaker works at a place that gives lessons in tennis, swimming, and other sports, and he also mentions *members*, so it is a fitness club. Choices (A), (C), and (D) are all types of businesses that could have some relationship to sports, but they are not the correct answer.

96. **(C)** The graph shows how many members signed up for lessons in each type of sport. The speaker wants to talk about the *least popular sport*, that is, the one where the fewest members signed up for lessons. According to the graph, that sport is aerobics. Choices (A), (B), and (D) are sports that were more popular.

97. **(D)** The speaker asks the listeners to use a survey to ask clients about their interests and goals. Choices (A), (B), and (C) are things that the clients should do.

98. **(D)** The speaker is welcoming the listener to a Spanish class, has received a check from her, and has a textbook for her, so she is probably a teacher. Choice (A) is associated with *lobby*. Choice (B) is associated with the mention of a language (Spanish). Choice (C) repeats the word *student*.

99. **(C)** The speaker says her office is *down the hall, second door on your left*, after going through the lobby, so that makes it Room 3. Choices (A), (B), and (D) don't fit this description.

100. **(A)** The speaker says, *I don't think you need to bring anything else except a notebook*. Choice (B) is what the speaker will give to the listener. Choice (C) is what the listener has already given to the speaker. Choice (D) is confused with the fragment *I don't think you need to bring anything . . . .*

# Reading

## PART 5: INCOMPLETE SENTENCES

101. **(B)** This agrees with the singular subject *price*. Choices (A), (C), and (D) are all plural.

102. **(A)** The causative verb *request* is followed by a base form verb. Choice (B) is present tense. Choice (C) is past tense. Choice (D) is a gerund.

103. **(C)** The simple past tense is used here to indicate an action that interrupted another action in progress in the past. Choice (A) is present perfect. Choice (B) is present tense. Choice (D) is present continuous.

104. **(D)** The relative pronoun *who* introduces the adjective clause and refers to a person, the new manager. Choices (A) and (B) are not relative pronouns. Choice (C) is used to refer to a thing.

105. **(B)** This is a past unreal conditional, so it uses *would + have + a past participle verb* in the main clause. Choices (A), (C), and (D) are verb forms not used for a past unreal conditional.

106. **(D)** Superlative adjectives use *most* or *–est*. Choice (A) is an incorrect comparative form. Choice (B) is a simple adjective form. Choice (C) is the comparative form.

107. **(B)** The causative *get* is followed by an infinitive verb. Choice (A) is a gerund. Choice (C) is past tense. Choice (D) is present tense.

108. **(D)** *Despite* introduces a contradiction. We would expect Mr. Mosley's enthusiasm to help him keep up with the team, but apparently it doesn't. Choices (A) and (C) introduce a cause. Choice (B) introduces a contradiction but at the beginning of a clause, not a phrase.

109. **(D)** The verb *consider* is followed by a gerund. Choice (A) is base form. Choice (B) is infinitive. Choice (C) is future.

110. **(B)** *After* establishes a logical time reference. Choices (A), (C), and (D) are not logical.

111. **(A)** *Adapt* means *modify*. Choices (B), (C), and (D) look similar to the correct answer but do not fit the context of the sentence.

112. **(C)** *Thorough* means *complete*. Choices (A), (B), and (D) look similar to the correct answer but have meanings that don't fit the context.

113. **(D)** The simple past tense is used here to indicate an action that interrupted another action in progress in the past. Choice (A) is present continuous. Choice (B) is present tense. Choice (C) is past perfect.

114. **(D)** *Borrow* is used with *from*. This sentence means that the manual belonged to the secretary and the clerk used it. Choices (A), (B), and (C) would use *to* instead of *from* and would indicate that the manual belonged to the clerk and the secretary used it.

115. **(A)** The verb form is needed here to complete the future tense with *will*. Choice (B) is an adjective. Choice (C) is a noun. Choice (D) is a gerund.

116. **(B)** The phrasal verb *show up* means *appear* or *arrive*. Choices (A), (C), and (D) can be used with *show* but have meanings that don't fit the context.

117. **(A)** In an unreal present conditional, *were* is the correct form of the verb *be* in the *if* clause. Choices (B), (C), and (D) are the wrong form to use in the *if* clause.

118. **(C)** Use the simple present form to match the first verb, *turns on*, and indicate a habitual action in the present. Choice (A) is a gerund. Choice (B) is present perfect. Choice (D) is past tense.

119. **(A)** The speech causes the audience to feel restless; it is active so uses the present participle. Choice (B) is the past participle. Choice (C) is present tense. Choice (D) is base form or present tense.

120. **(A)** Commands require the base form of the verb. Choice (B) is present tense. Choice (C) is present participle. Choice (D) is future.

121. **(D)** *Average* means *typical amount.* Choices (A), (B), and (C) look similar to the correct answer but do not fit the context of the sentence.

122. **(B)** *Excluded* means *left out* or *omitted.* Choices (A), (C), and (D) look similar to the correct answer but have meanings that don't fit the context of the sentence.

123. **(D)** The entire sentence is about the past, so a simple past verb is needed. Choice (A) is conditional. Choice (B) is present perfect. Choice (C) is simple present.

124. **(A)** The adjective *industrious* describes the noun *engineer.* Choices (B) and (D) are nouns. Choice (C) is an adjective but is not used to describe people.

125. **(A)** This tells us when Mr. Ross will prepare the charts. Choices (B) and (D) introduce a reason. Choice (C) introduces a result.

126. **(D)** To be *under obligation* means to be *obligated* or to *have to do something.* Choices (A), (B), and (C) are words that are not used in this expression.

127. **(B)** *Per* in this sentence means *according to.* Choices (A), (C), and (D) cannot be used in this context.

128. **(A)** *Consented* means *agreed.* Choices (B), (C), and (D) have meanings that don't fit the context.

129. **(D)** *Vacant* means *empty* and is often used to describe living and work spaces. Choices (A), (B), and (C) have meanings that don't fit the context.

130. **(C)** This is a passive verb form; the subject, *auditorium*, does not design itself but *is designed* by a person. Choices (A), (B), and (D) are all active verb forms.

**PART 6: TEXT COMPLETION**

131. **(D)** *Manager* is a noun referring to a person. Choice (A) is a gerund. Choice (B) is a noun, but it refers to a situation, not a person. Choice (C) is an adjective.

132. **(C)** *Until* means *up to the time; until 11:00 P.M.* means that the job day continues up to 11:00. Choices (A), (B), and (D) don't fit the context.

133. **(A)** This sentence about experience being unnecessary logically precedes the following sentence, *We can train you.* Choices (B) and (D) imply that experience is important. Choice (C) doesn't fit the context.

134. **(B)** Job applicants are usually asked to supply references, which may be personal (from friends) or work-related. Choices (A), (C), and (D) don't fit the context.

135. **(B)** This sentence introduces the information in the following sentences, which describe the efficiency and speed of the shredder. Choices (A), (C), and (D) could describe a paper shredder but don't fit logically in this place.

136. **(D)** People use paper shredders to make their confidential documents unreadable. Choices (A), (B), and (C) could describe the paper pieces that come out of a shredder, but they don't fit the context of *confidential documents*.

137. **(C)** The gerund form follows the preposition *without*. Choice (A) is base form or present tense. Choice (B) is infinitive. Choice (D) is future tense.

138. **(A)** *In use* means *being used*. Choices (B), (C), and (D) are related forms but don't have this meaning.

139. **(A)** This is a second person possessive pronoun meaning *your office*, that is, the office of the person that the letter is addressed to. Choices (B) and (C) are first person. Choice (D) is third person.

140. **(C)** This is an adverb of manner modifying the verb *do*. Choice (A) is an adjective. Choice (B) is a verb. Choice (D) is a noun.

141. **(B)** This sentence introduces the topic of the paragraph—how Green Thumb takes care of plants. Choices (A), (C), and (D) don't introduce the topic of the paragraph.

142. **(D)** *Optimal* means *ideal* or the *best*. Choices (A), (B), and (C) have meanings that don't fit the context.

143. **(B)** *Residents* are people who live in a place. Choices (A) and (C) have meanings that don't fit the context. Choice (D) has a similar meaning to the correct answer but generally is used when referring to the specific building where a person lives.

144. **(A)** The modal *must* is followed by a base form verb. Choice (B) is infinitive. Choice (C) is a gerund. Choice (D) includes another modal.

145. **(C)** The previous sentence mentions rules, and then this sentence tells what the rules are. Choices (A), (B), and (D) don't fit the context.

146. **(D)** To be *under supervision* means to be *managed by*. Choices (A), (B), and (C) are words that are not used with *supervision*.

## PART 7: READING COMPREHENSION

147. **(C)** The ad mentions a *small monthly fee* for covered parking. Choice (A) is incorrect because the ad states *heat and electric included*. Choice (B) is incorrect because the ad mentions that the building has *nicely maintained grounds*. Choice (D) is incorrect because the office has been *freshly painted*.

148. **(B)** The ad mentions a *6-mo. or 1-yr lease*. Choices (A), (C), and (D) are contradicted by the correct answer.

149. **(B)** Luis writes, *Traffic is still light*, implying that later it will stop being light; that is, it will get worse. Choice (A) is not mentioned. Choice (C) repeats the word *light*. Choice (D) is contradicted by the correct answer.

150. **(A)** Sally wants to go by the hotel first, and Luis replies, *We can do that*. Choices (B), (C), and (D) are places they will go later.

151. **(B)** The ad mentions the benefits of advertising a business in the magazine and also mentions the deadline for advertising space. Choice (A) is confused with the description of the magazine's readers. Choices (C) and (D) repeat words used in the ad.

152. **(C)** The magazine is published *on the first Sunday of every month*. Choices (A), (B), and (D) aren't mentioned.

153. **(D)** The information says that beverages will be on a table and *Please help yourself whenever you like*. Choice (A) is confused with the request to select a lunch preference. Choice (B) is contradicted by the correct answer. Choice (C) is not likely because there will be both *hot and cold beverages*.

154. **(B)** *Carrot Ginger* is one of the choices to go with the garden salad, so it is probably salad dressing. Choice (A) is what *carrot ginger* will be served with. Choices (C) and (D) are other things that will be available at the workshop.

155. **(A)** The web page shows this week's specials, so we can assume that the prices shown are valid this week only. Choice (B) is not mentioned. Choice (C) refers to the tagline, *Excitement for the whole family*, but no family discounts are mentioned. Choice (D) is mentioned as a way to get *exclusive discounts* but is not connected with the discounts on this page.

156. **(C)** This price buys a week in a cabin that *sleeps four*, that is, that has room for four people to sleep. Choices (A), (B), and (D) confuse the meaning of this phrase.

157. **(D)** Trip #5 involves a cruise, or boat trip, in the Caribbean Sea. Choices (A), (B), and (C) don't mention anything related to the sea and are in places that are not near the sea.

158. **(D)** The chart shows economic indicators and predicts the state of each one over the next half year. Choice (A) is incorrect because the language in the chart comments is clearly about the future, not the past. Choice (B) refers to the economic indicators shown, but explaining how they effect the economy in general is not the purpose of the chart. Choice (C) repeats words used in the chart to describe the predictions.

159. **(A)** The first comment predicts that the economy will *pick up steam, aided by job creation*, meaning it will start moving ahead, that is strengthen or grow, because there will be more jobs. Choices (B), (C), and (D) use words and phrases from the chart but are not what the comments indicate.

160. **(C)** The comment about housing states, *Slow growth in average income has affected the housing market*, implying that since incomes aren't growing, people aren't buying houses. Choices (A), (B), and (D) use words and phrases from the comments but are not correct interpretations of the comments.

161. **(C)** The article recommends sorting items into baskets, buckets, or boxes, that is, containers. Choice (A) is confused with the suggestion to choose containers in colors that match the room décor. Choice (B) repeats the words *baskets* and *closets*. Choice (D) repeats *books and magazines*, but the suggestion is to put them into containers, not get rid of them.

162. **(A)** To *tackle* a job means to *deal with* it or to *do* it. Choices (B), (C), and (D) are other meanings that *tackle* can have, but they don't fit the context.

163. **(B)** The article suggests organizing closets *each season*, which would be several times a year. Choice (A) repeats *clutter*. Choice (C) is what is specifically not recommended. Choice (D) is how often you should pick up your rooms.

164. **(C)** Farah writes that when she looked for paper *there was almost nothing* in the closet. Choice (A) is confused with nothing. Choice (B) is what they have ordered. Choice (D) is what Jin will get at the store.

165. **(A)** The paper has been put on *backorder*, meaning that the company doesn't have it in stock and is waiting to receive it from the paper supplier. Choice (B) is not mentioned. Choice (C) is confused with the discussion of the pens. Choice (D) is incorrect because a rush was put on the order.

166. **(D)** Farah asks Sam to *find out exactly when it'll arrive*. Choice (A) is what Jin offers to do. Choice (B) is what Sam asks about. Choice (C) is related to the discussion but is not mentioned.

167. **(D)** Sam says about the pens, *My fingers ended up covered with blue*, which we can assume means that blue ink leaked out of the pen he used. Choice (A) is associated with the mention of the blue ink. Choice (B) is associated with fingers. Choice (C) is incorrect because Jin says, *I was just trying to save money*, implying that the pens were inexpensive.

168. **(D)** Mr. Duchamp is inviting Dr. Comstock to be a speaker at a conference. Choices (A) and (C) are included in the letter but are not the main purpose. Choice (B) is not mentioned.

169. **(B)** Mr. Duchamp mentions that he saw Dr. Comstock at a journalism seminar *last month*; the letter is dated *February*, so the seminar was in January. Choices (A), (C), and (D) are all things that have happened or will happen, but there is no indication of when.

170. **(C)** The sentence previous to this position mentions *speakers*, that is, *presenters*, and the inserted sentence then gives further information about them. Choices (A), (B), and (D) are not the right context for this sentence.

171. **(A)** Mr. Duchamp ends the letter with, *I will be in touch with you before the end of next week*, meaning he will contact Dr. Comstock again soon. Choice (B) is incorrect because he directs Dr. Comstock to a website for this information. Choice (C) is contradicted by the correct answer. Choice (D) is what he is asking Dr. Comstock to do.

172. **(B)** The article explains that more shellfish is being caught, mostly because it has become a popular food. Choice (A) is mentioned but is not the main focus of the article. Choices (C) and (D) are not mentioned.

173. **(A)** The article explains that the catch was very low a decade ago but has been rising ever since. Choices (B), (C), and (D) use words from the article but are not mentioned.

174. **(C)** The phrase *culinary circles* in this article refers to groups of people who are interested in cooking, probably restaurant owners. Choices (A), (B), and (D) are other uses of the word *circles* but don't fit the context.

175. **(D)** Shellfish costs $20 a kilo *at the dock,* that is, directly from the fisherman, so we can assume that it costs more once it reaches a store or restaurant. Choice (A) is not mentioned. Choice (B) repeats the phrase *at the dock.* Choice (C) is not likely since the article says shellfish is being managed to avoid overfishing.

176. **(B)** The receipt shows this as the price for each table lantern. Choice (A) is the price of one string of LED lights. Choice (C) is the price paid for ten table lanterns. Choice (D) is the price paid for twenty strings of LED lights.

177. **(C)** In the e-mail, Kathleen writes that she picked up the lights last night. Choice (A) is true but not the reason for no charge. Choices (B) and (C) are plausible but not mentioned.

178. **(C)** In the e-mail, Kathleen writes that the card was declined *so I had to use my own.* Since the purchase was for the business, we can assume she tried to pay with the company credit card first, but then she had to use her personal card. Choice (A) is not mentioned. Choice (B) repeats the word *card,* but we know it is a credit card, not a gift card, that is meant because gift cards are not declined since they are almost the same as cash. Choice (D) is how she originally tried to pay.

179. **(D)** Kathleen points out that she got purple lights this time, implying that last time (the original order) they got a different color. Choices (A) and (B) are not mentioned. Choice (C) is confused with the fact that she mentions getting a few extra strings, but there is no indication that this was because there were too few in the original order.

180. **(A)** Kathleen mentions *the bride,* so the event is a wedding. Choice (B) is confused with the items Kathleen purchased. Choices (C) and (D) are other events that Kathleen's company has worked at.

181. **(B)** The information states that assignments are due on Friday. Choice (A) happens on Monday. Choice (C) can happen any time. Choice (D) is not mentioned.

182. **(D)** The information states that certificates are given to students *who achieve a final grade of 85%.* Choices (A), (B), and (C) are not mentioned.

183. **(C)** The syllabus shows 8 lessons, and the course description mentions that new lessons are posted every Monday. Choices (A), (B), and (D) are contradicted by the correct answer.

184. **(A)** The topic of lesson 2 involves a discussion of branding *over the past century,* that is, in history. Choices (B), (C), and (D) are lessons that have other topics.

185. **(C)** The course description says the discussion of new media marketing *could continue into the following week,* replacing the topic of that week; which is *Using Marketing to Drive Sales.* Choices (A) and (D) don't immediately follow the discussion of new media marketing. Choice (B) is the topic that might continue to another week.

186. **(C)** Even though the flyer states *Open to the public,* it then adds the detail *Minimum age: 14.* Choice (A) is confused with the *Open to the public* statement. Choice (B) is incorrect because teenagers can attend. Choice (D) is incorrect because a fee is mentioned for non-cardholders.

187. **(D)** According to the flyer, the workshop will be in Meeting Room 2 and, according to the directory, the meeting rooms are on the third floor. Choices (A), (B), and (C) are other floors mentioned in the directory.

188. **(B)** In her e-mail, Eleanor writes that she plans to arrive when the library opens so she'll have half an hour to set up, and according to the notice, the library opens at 9:00 on Saturday. Choice (A) is half an hour before the library opens. Choice (C) is when the workshop begins. Choice (D) is when the library opens on weekdays.

189. **(A)** Eleanor wants to arrive early to make sure that the equipment she will be using for her workshop is working correctly. Choices (B), (C), and (D) are other possible meanings for the phrase, but they don't fit the context.

190. **(B)** In her e-mail, Eleanor writes that her library book is *just about due now,* and according to the library notice, books can be checked out for 3 weeks. We know that it probably hasn't been renewed for an additional 3 weeks because Eleanor writes that she doesn't plan to do that, and it can only be done once. Choice (A) is not mentioned. Choice (C) would mean that she has renewed the book. Choice (D) is incorrect because we do have the information.

191. **(B)** The special festival price of $325 is for two nights in one *double occupancy* room, that is, a room for two people. Choices (A), (C), and (D) don't fit this description.

192. **(D)** The reviewer didn't like the inn's location because of the noisy activity on the green. Choices (A), (B), and (C) are all things the reviewer liked.

193. **(A)** *Reasonable rates* means *inexpensive prices.* Choices (B), (C), and (D) are other meanings that reasonable can have, but they don't fit the context.

194. **(C)** The reviewer stayed at the inn during the first weekend of the Apple Festival, which, according to the flyer, was in September. Choice (A) is mentioned on the flyer as the time to submit vendor applications. Choice (B) is mentioned on the web page as the time to reserve a room at the inn. Choice (D) is the month of the second weekend of the festival.

195. **(D)** The flyer says, *Please leave your pets at home.* Choices (A), (B), and (C) are all mentioned on the flyer as festival activities.

196. **(B)** Sam's current level must be lower than Gold since the e-mail suggests that he *upgrade* to Gold, that is, move to a higher level. Silver is the only level lower than Gold, since Day User isn't really a membership.

197. **(C)** According to the e-mail, he will get $100 off the usual price, that is, $100 less than $675. Choice (A) is the price for the Silver level. Choice (B) isn't mentioned. Choice (D) is the usual Gold price.

198. **(A)** The items listed in the *Benefits* column are club services that a member receives in return for the membership fee. Choices (B), (C), and (D) are other meanings that *benefits* can have, but they don't fit the context.

199. **(C)** This is the earliest time the pool is open for general swim. Choices (A) and (D) are when the pool first opens for classes. Choice (B) is when the pool closes for cleaning.

200. **(B)** The notice states that guests must pay the day user fee, which is, according to the table, $20. Choices (A), (C), and (D) are contradicted by the correct answer.

# ANSWER SHEET
## New TOEIC Practice Exam B

**LISTENING COMPREHENSION**

### Part 1: Photographs

1. Ⓐ Ⓑ Ⓒ Ⓓ      3. Ⓐ Ⓑ Ⓒ Ⓓ      5. Ⓐ Ⓑ Ⓒ Ⓓ
2. Ⓐ Ⓑ Ⓒ Ⓓ      4. Ⓐ Ⓑ Ⓒ Ⓓ      6. Ⓐ Ⓑ Ⓒ Ⓓ

### Part 2: Question-Response

7. Ⓐ Ⓑ Ⓒ      14. Ⓐ Ⓑ Ⓒ      21. Ⓐ Ⓑ Ⓒ      28. Ⓐ Ⓑ Ⓒ
8. Ⓐ Ⓑ Ⓒ      15. Ⓐ Ⓑ Ⓒ      22. Ⓐ Ⓑ Ⓒ      29. Ⓐ Ⓑ Ⓒ
9. Ⓐ Ⓑ Ⓒ      16. Ⓐ Ⓑ Ⓒ      23. Ⓐ Ⓑ Ⓒ      30. Ⓐ Ⓑ Ⓒ
10. Ⓐ Ⓑ Ⓒ      17. Ⓐ Ⓑ Ⓒ      24. Ⓐ Ⓑ Ⓒ      31. Ⓐ Ⓑ Ⓒ
11. Ⓐ Ⓑ Ⓒ      18. Ⓐ Ⓑ Ⓒ      25. Ⓐ Ⓑ Ⓒ
12. Ⓐ Ⓑ Ⓒ      19. Ⓐ Ⓑ Ⓒ      26. Ⓐ Ⓑ Ⓒ
13. Ⓐ Ⓑ Ⓒ      20. Ⓐ Ⓑ Ⓒ      27. Ⓐ Ⓑ Ⓒ

### Part 3: Conversations

32. Ⓐ Ⓑ Ⓒ Ⓓ      42. Ⓐ Ⓑ Ⓒ Ⓓ      52. Ⓐ Ⓑ Ⓒ Ⓓ      62. Ⓐ Ⓑ Ⓒ Ⓓ
33. Ⓐ Ⓑ Ⓒ Ⓓ      43. Ⓐ Ⓑ Ⓒ Ⓓ      53. Ⓐ Ⓑ Ⓒ Ⓓ      63. Ⓐ Ⓑ Ⓒ Ⓓ
34. Ⓐ Ⓑ Ⓒ Ⓓ      44. Ⓐ Ⓑ Ⓒ Ⓓ      54. Ⓐ Ⓑ Ⓒ Ⓓ      64. Ⓐ Ⓑ Ⓒ Ⓓ
35. Ⓐ Ⓑ Ⓒ Ⓓ      45. Ⓐ Ⓑ Ⓒ Ⓓ      55. Ⓐ Ⓑ Ⓒ Ⓓ      65. Ⓐ Ⓑ Ⓒ Ⓓ
36. Ⓐ Ⓑ Ⓒ Ⓓ      46. Ⓐ Ⓑ Ⓒ Ⓓ      56. Ⓐ Ⓑ Ⓒ Ⓓ      66. Ⓐ Ⓑ Ⓒ Ⓓ
37. Ⓐ Ⓑ Ⓒ Ⓓ      47. Ⓐ Ⓑ Ⓒ Ⓓ      57. Ⓐ Ⓑ Ⓒ Ⓓ      67. Ⓐ Ⓑ Ⓒ Ⓓ
38. Ⓐ Ⓑ Ⓒ Ⓓ      48. Ⓐ Ⓑ Ⓒ Ⓓ      58. Ⓐ Ⓑ Ⓒ Ⓓ      68. Ⓐ Ⓑ Ⓒ Ⓓ
39. Ⓐ Ⓑ Ⓒ Ⓓ      49. Ⓐ Ⓑ Ⓒ Ⓓ      59. Ⓐ Ⓑ Ⓒ Ⓓ      69. Ⓐ Ⓑ Ⓒ Ⓓ
40. Ⓐ Ⓑ Ⓒ Ⓓ      50. Ⓐ Ⓑ Ⓒ Ⓓ      60. Ⓐ Ⓑ Ⓒ Ⓓ      70. Ⓐ Ⓑ Ⓒ Ⓓ
41. Ⓐ Ⓑ Ⓒ Ⓓ      51. Ⓐ Ⓑ Ⓒ Ⓓ      61. Ⓐ Ⓑ Ⓒ Ⓓ

### Part 4: Talks

71. Ⓐ Ⓑ Ⓒ Ⓓ      79. Ⓐ Ⓑ Ⓒ Ⓓ      87. Ⓐ Ⓑ Ⓒ Ⓓ      95. Ⓐ Ⓑ Ⓒ Ⓓ
72. Ⓐ Ⓑ Ⓒ Ⓓ      80. Ⓐ Ⓑ Ⓒ Ⓓ      88. Ⓐ Ⓑ Ⓒ Ⓓ      96. Ⓐ Ⓑ Ⓒ Ⓓ
73. Ⓐ Ⓑ Ⓒ Ⓓ      81. Ⓐ Ⓑ Ⓒ Ⓓ      89. Ⓐ Ⓑ Ⓒ Ⓓ      97. Ⓐ Ⓑ Ⓒ Ⓓ
74. Ⓐ Ⓑ Ⓒ Ⓓ      82. Ⓐ Ⓑ Ⓒ Ⓓ      90. Ⓐ Ⓑ Ⓒ Ⓓ      98. Ⓐ Ⓑ Ⓒ Ⓓ
75. Ⓐ Ⓑ Ⓒ Ⓓ      83. Ⓐ Ⓑ Ⓒ Ⓓ      91. Ⓐ Ⓑ Ⓒ Ⓓ      99. Ⓐ Ⓑ Ⓒ Ⓓ
76. Ⓐ Ⓑ Ⓒ Ⓓ      84. Ⓐ Ⓑ Ⓒ Ⓓ      92. Ⓐ Ⓑ Ⓒ Ⓓ      100. Ⓐ Ⓑ Ⓒ Ⓓ
77. Ⓐ Ⓑ Ⓒ Ⓓ      85. Ⓐ Ⓑ Ⓒ Ⓓ      93. Ⓐ Ⓑ Ⓒ Ⓓ
78. Ⓐ Ⓑ Ⓒ Ⓓ      86. Ⓐ Ⓑ Ⓒ Ⓓ      94. Ⓐ Ⓑ Ⓒ Ⓓ

# ANSWER SHEET
## New TOEIC Practice Exam B

**READING**

### Part 5: Incomplete Sentences

101. Ⓐ Ⓑ Ⓒ Ⓓ    109. Ⓐ Ⓑ Ⓒ Ⓓ    117. Ⓐ Ⓑ Ⓒ Ⓓ    125. Ⓐ Ⓑ Ⓒ Ⓓ
102. Ⓐ Ⓑ Ⓒ Ⓓ    110. Ⓐ Ⓑ Ⓒ Ⓓ    118. Ⓐ Ⓑ Ⓒ Ⓓ    126. Ⓐ Ⓑ Ⓒ Ⓓ
103. Ⓐ Ⓑ Ⓒ Ⓓ    111. Ⓐ Ⓑ Ⓒ Ⓓ    119. Ⓐ Ⓑ Ⓒ Ⓓ    127. Ⓐ Ⓑ Ⓒ Ⓓ
104. Ⓐ Ⓑ Ⓒ Ⓓ    112. Ⓐ Ⓑ Ⓒ Ⓓ    120. Ⓐ Ⓑ Ⓒ Ⓓ    128. Ⓐ Ⓑ Ⓒ Ⓓ
105. Ⓐ Ⓑ Ⓒ Ⓓ    113. Ⓐ Ⓑ Ⓒ Ⓓ    121. Ⓐ Ⓑ Ⓒ Ⓓ    129. Ⓐ Ⓑ Ⓒ Ⓓ
106. Ⓐ Ⓑ Ⓒ Ⓓ    114. Ⓐ Ⓑ Ⓒ Ⓓ    122. Ⓐ Ⓑ Ⓒ Ⓓ    130. Ⓐ Ⓑ Ⓒ Ⓓ
107. Ⓐ Ⓑ Ⓒ Ⓓ    115. Ⓐ Ⓑ Ⓒ Ⓓ    123. Ⓐ Ⓑ Ⓒ Ⓓ
108. Ⓐ Ⓑ Ⓒ Ⓓ    116. Ⓐ Ⓑ Ⓒ Ⓓ    124. Ⓐ Ⓑ Ⓒ Ⓓ

### Part 6: Text Completion

131. Ⓐ Ⓑ Ⓒ Ⓓ    135. Ⓐ Ⓑ Ⓒ Ⓓ    139. Ⓐ Ⓑ Ⓒ Ⓓ    143. Ⓐ Ⓑ Ⓒ Ⓓ
132. Ⓐ Ⓑ Ⓒ Ⓓ    136. Ⓐ Ⓑ Ⓒ Ⓓ    140. Ⓐ Ⓑ Ⓒ Ⓓ    144. Ⓐ Ⓑ Ⓒ Ⓓ
133. Ⓐ Ⓑ Ⓒ Ⓓ    137. Ⓐ Ⓑ Ⓒ Ⓓ    141. Ⓐ Ⓑ Ⓒ Ⓓ    145. Ⓐ Ⓑ Ⓒ Ⓓ
134. Ⓐ Ⓑ Ⓒ Ⓓ    138. Ⓐ Ⓑ Ⓒ Ⓓ    142. Ⓐ Ⓑ Ⓒ Ⓓ    146. Ⓐ Ⓑ Ⓒ Ⓓ

### Part 7: Reading Comprehension

147. Ⓐ Ⓑ Ⓒ Ⓓ    161. Ⓐ Ⓑ Ⓒ Ⓓ    175. Ⓐ Ⓑ Ⓒ Ⓓ    189. Ⓐ Ⓑ Ⓒ Ⓓ
148. Ⓐ Ⓑ Ⓒ Ⓓ    162. Ⓐ Ⓑ Ⓒ Ⓓ    176. Ⓐ Ⓑ Ⓒ Ⓓ    190. Ⓐ Ⓑ Ⓒ Ⓓ
149. Ⓐ Ⓑ Ⓒ Ⓓ    163. Ⓐ Ⓑ Ⓒ Ⓓ    177. Ⓐ Ⓑ Ⓒ Ⓓ    191. Ⓐ Ⓑ Ⓒ Ⓓ
150. Ⓐ Ⓑ Ⓒ Ⓓ    164. Ⓐ Ⓑ Ⓒ Ⓓ    178. Ⓐ Ⓑ Ⓒ Ⓓ    192. Ⓐ Ⓑ Ⓒ Ⓓ
151. Ⓐ Ⓑ Ⓒ Ⓓ    165. Ⓐ Ⓑ Ⓒ Ⓓ    179. Ⓐ Ⓑ Ⓒ Ⓓ    193. Ⓐ Ⓑ Ⓒ Ⓓ
152. Ⓐ Ⓑ Ⓒ Ⓓ    166. Ⓐ Ⓑ Ⓒ Ⓓ    180. Ⓐ Ⓑ Ⓒ Ⓓ    194. Ⓐ Ⓑ Ⓒ Ⓓ
153. Ⓐ Ⓑ Ⓒ Ⓓ    167. Ⓐ Ⓑ Ⓒ Ⓓ    181. Ⓐ Ⓑ Ⓒ Ⓓ    195. Ⓐ Ⓑ Ⓒ Ⓓ
154. Ⓐ Ⓑ Ⓒ Ⓓ    168. Ⓐ Ⓑ Ⓒ Ⓓ    182. Ⓐ Ⓑ Ⓒ Ⓓ    196. Ⓐ Ⓑ Ⓒ Ⓓ
155. Ⓐ Ⓑ Ⓒ Ⓓ    169. Ⓐ Ⓑ Ⓒ Ⓓ    183. Ⓐ Ⓑ Ⓒ Ⓓ    197. Ⓐ Ⓑ Ⓒ Ⓓ
156. Ⓐ Ⓑ Ⓒ Ⓓ    170. Ⓐ Ⓑ Ⓒ Ⓓ    184. Ⓐ Ⓑ Ⓒ Ⓓ    198. Ⓐ Ⓑ Ⓒ Ⓓ
157. Ⓐ Ⓑ Ⓒ Ⓓ    171. Ⓐ Ⓑ Ⓒ Ⓓ    185. Ⓐ Ⓑ Ⓒ Ⓓ    199. Ⓐ Ⓑ Ⓒ Ⓓ
158. Ⓐ Ⓑ Ⓒ Ⓓ    172. Ⓐ Ⓑ Ⓒ Ⓓ    186. Ⓐ Ⓑ Ⓒ Ⓓ    200. Ⓐ Ⓑ Ⓒ Ⓓ
159. Ⓐ Ⓑ Ⓒ Ⓓ    173. Ⓐ Ⓑ Ⓒ Ⓓ    187. Ⓐ Ⓑ Ⓒ Ⓓ
160. Ⓐ Ⓑ Ⓒ Ⓓ    174. Ⓐ Ⓑ Ⓒ Ⓓ    188. Ⓐ Ⓑ Ⓒ Ⓓ

# New TOEIC Practice Exam B

## LISTENING COMPREHENSION

In this section of the test, you will have the chance to show how well you understand spoken English. There are four parts to this section, with special directions for each part. You will find the Answer Sheet for New TOEIC Practice Exam B on pages 287–288. Detach it from the book and use it to record your answers. Check your answers using the Answer Key on pages 325–326 and see the Answers Explained beginning on page 328.

## Part 1: Photographs

 **Track 22**

**Directions:** You will see a photograph. You will hear four statements about the photograph. Choose the statement that most closely matches the photograph and fill in the corresponding oval on your answer sheet.

**Example**

Now listen to the four statements.

Sample Answer
Ⓐ Ⓑ Ⓒ Ⓓ

Statement (B), "She's reading a magazine," best describes what you see in the picture. Therefore, you should choose answer (B).

**TIP**

If you do not have access to the MP3 files, please use the audioscripts beginning on page 412. You can also download the MP3 files and audioscripts from *http://barronsbooks.com/tp/toeic/audio/*

1.

2.

3.

4.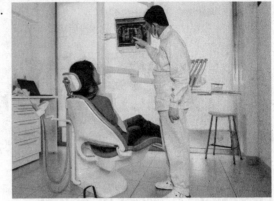

5.

6.

## Part 2: Question-Response

**Track 23**

**Directions:** You will hear a question and three possible responses. Choose the response that most closely answers the question and fill in the corresponding oval on your answer sheet.

**Example**

Now listen to the sample question.

You will hear:

How is the weather?

You will also hear:

(A)  It's raining.
(B)  He's fine, thanks.
(C)  He's my boss.

The best response to the question *How is the weather?* is choice (A), *It's raining*. Therefore, you should choose answer (A).

---

7.  Mark your answer on your answer sheet.

8.  Mark your answer on your answer sheet.

9.  Mark your answer on your answer sheet.

10.  Mark your answer on your answer sheet.

11.  Mark your answer on your answer sheet.

12.  Mark your answer on your answer sheet.

13.  Mark your answer on your answer sheet.

14.  Mark your answer on your answer sheet.

15.  Mark your answer on your answer sheet.

16.  Mark your answer on your answer sheet.

17.  Mark your answer on your answer sheet.

18.  Mark your answer on your answer sheet.

19.  Mark your answer on your answer sheet.

20.  Mark your answer on your answer sheet.

21.  Mark your answer on your answer sheet.

22.  Mark your answer on your answer sheet.

23.  Mark your answer on your answer sheet.

24.  Mark your answer on your answer sheet.

25.  Mark your answer on your answer sheet.

26.  Mark your answer on your answer sheet.

27.  Mark your answer on your answer sheet.

28.  Mark your answer on your answer sheet.

29.  Mark your answer on your answer sheet.

30.  Mark your answer on your answer sheet.

31.  Mark your answer on your answer sheet.

## Part 3: Conversations

**Track 24**

**Directions:** You will hear a conversation between two or more people. You will see three questions on each conversation and four possible answers. Choose the best answer to each question and fill in the corresponding oval on your answer sheet.

32. What will take place at the hotel this weekend?
    (A) A book fair
    (B) A crafts market
    (C) A conference
    (D) A wedding

33. What will happen on Saturday night?
    (A) A cooking class
    (B) A banquet
    (C) A dance
    (D) A party

34. What event will the woman participate in on Sunday morning?
    (A) A planning session
    (B) A work meeting
    (C) A shopping trip
    (D) A workshop

---

35. Why did the woman make the call?
    (A) To find out the status of an order
    (B) To ask about buying a camera
    (C) To invite the man to an event
    (D) To sell the man a service

36. What will the man do tomorrow?
    (A) Go to a banquet
    (B) Send photographs
    (C) Attend a meeting
    (D) E-mail some files

37. What project is the woman working on now?
    (A) Arranging for staff photos
    (B) Learning to be a photographer
    (C) Organizing the annual meeting
    (D) Producing the company newsletter

38. What is the woman going to rent?
    (A) A car
    (B) A house
    (C) An office
    (D) An apartment

39. What does the woman mean when she says, "No problem?"
    (A) She will read the lease before signing.
    (B) She can pay what the man asks.
    (C) She thinks the rental cost is fair.
    (D) She agrees with the terms of the lease.

40. What will the woman do next?
    (A) Go home
    (B) Park her car
    (C) Sign the lease
    (D) Ask a question

---

41. What does the woman want to do?
    (A) Drive the man to the airport
    (B) Share a ride to the airport
    (C) Meet the man at the airport
    (D) Look for a friend at the airport

42. What time does the man's flight leave?
    (A) 7:00
    (B) 9:00
    (C) 11:00
    (D) 12:00

43. Why is the woman going to Toronto?
    (A) For a vacation
    (B) For a conference
    (C) For a job interview
    (D) For a client meeting

44. Where does this conversation take place?
    (A) At an employment office
    (B) At a grocery store
    (C) At a fitness club
    (D) At a bank

45. How much does membership cost?
    (A) $0
    (B) $10
    (C) $25
    (D) $75

46. What will the man probably do next?
    (A) Show his card
    (B) Check his bill
    (C) Look at a sign
    (D) Fill out a form

47. When will the meeting take place?
    (A) Today
    (B) Tomorrow afternoon
    (C) In two days
    (D) Next week

48. What will the woman report on at the meeting?
    (A) Sales
    (B) New clients
    (C) The budget
    (D) The hiring fair

49. What do the speakers imply about the meeting?
    (A) It takes place every week.
    (B) It has been well planned.
    (C) It will start late.
    (D) It will be long.

50. How did the man send the proposal?
    (A) By personal messenger
    (B) By delivery service
    (C) By postal mail
    (D) By e-mail

51. What does the woman mean when she says, "I'm sorry?"
    (A) She made a mistake.
    (B) She forgot to read the proposal.
    (C) She doesn't recognize the caller.
    (D) She wasn't in the office yesterday.

52. What will the woman do this morning?
    (A) Send the proposal back
    (B) Review the proposal
    (C) Check her in-box
    (D) Plan the budget

53. What is Mr. Kim's job?
    (A) Department supervisor
    (B) Marketing assistant
    (C) Assistant director
    (D) Office manager

54. How long has Mr. Kim worked at the company?
    (A) One week
    (B) Two weeks
    (C) One year
    (D) Four years

55. What do the speakers imply about Mr. Kim?
    (A) He's a hard worker.
    (B) He's a slow learner.
    (C) He's friendly.
    (D) He's shy.

56. Where does the conversation take place?
    (A) At a conference center
    (B) At a restaurant
    (C) At an office
    (D) At a hotel

57. What is suggested about the place?
    (A) It's not well known.
    (B) It's not very big.
    (C) It's popular.
    (D) It's quiet.

58. What are the speakers mostly talking about?
    (A) An office party
    (B) A client meeting
    (C) Grocery shopping
    (D) Their appointments

59. Where will the man be next week?
    (A) In a sales meeting
    (B) Visiting a client
    (C) At a seminar
    (D) On vacation

60. How will he get there?
    (A) By bicycle
    (B) By plane
    (C) By train
    (D) By car

61. What does the woman suggest about this mode of transportation?
    (A) It is too slow.
    (B) It is unreliable.
    (C) It is easy to use.
    (D) It is uncomfortable.

62. What does the woman want?
    (A) Another sweater
    (B) A lower price
    (C) A credit card
    (D) A refund

63. What is the matter with the sweater?
    (A) It's the wrong color.
    (B) It's the wrong size.
    (C) It's damaged.
    (D) It's too heavy.

64. What does the man say about the sweater style?
    (A) There are no more blue ones.
    (B) The store has run out of it.
    (C) The price has increased.
    (D) It doesn't come in large sizes.

65. Why did the man make the call?
    (A) To buy a ticket
    (B) To find out the schedule
    (C) To change his reservation
    (D) To find out the cost of a ticket

66. What will the man do in Washington?
    (A) Have a business meeting
    (B) Attend a conference
    (C) Go sightseeing
    (D) Look for a job

67. Look at the graphic. Which train will the man take?
    (A) 11
    (B) 21
    (C) 32
    (D) 43

**Train Schedule–to Washington**

| Train No. | Leave | Arrive |
|-----------|-------|--------|
| 11 | 6:10 | 9:35 |
| 21 | 7:20 | 10:45 |
| 32 | 8:30 | 11:55 |
| 43 | 10:20 | 1:45 |

68. What does the man imply about the prices?
    (A) They are lower at other restaurants.
    (B) They have gone up recently.
    (C) They are a good deal.
    (D) They never change.

69. Look at the graphic. What does the man order?
    (A) Spaghetti plate
    (B) Roast beef sandwich
    (C) Turkey and vegetables
    (D) Cheese sandwich

70. What will the woman do next?
    (A) Add up the bill
    (B) Clean the table
    (C) Bring the man a drink
    (D) Show the man the menu

```
Garden Restaurant
Lunch Specials

1. Spaghetti plate with
   soup and salad.....................................$17

2. Roast beef sandwich
   with salad and pie ...............................$15

3. Turkey and vegetables
   with soup.............................................$19

4. Cheese sandwich
   with salad and cake............................$14
```

## Part 4: Talks

**Directions:** You will hear a talk given by a single speaker. You will see three questions on each talk, each with four possible answers. Choose the best answer to each question and fill in the corresponding oval on your answer sheet.

Track 25

71. Who is the speaker?
    (A) A professional organizer
    (B) A college professor
    (C) A real estate agent
    (D) A housekeeper

72. How long has she worked in this business?
    (A) A little less than ten years
    (B) Ten years exactly
    (C) More than ten years
    (D) Fourteen years

73. What does the speaker mean when she says, "Don't be shy?"
    (A) She wants people to be sociable.
    (B) She wants people to ask questions.
    (C) She is inviting people to listen to her talk.
    (D) She is helping people improve their manners.

74. Where does this talk take place?
    (A) In a museum
    (B) In a theater
    (C) In a school
    (D) In a hotel

75. What will happen at 2:30?
    (A) Tea will be served.
    (B) A movie will be shown.
    (C) The garden will be watered.
    (D) The gift shop will be opened.

76. What are listeners asked to do?
    (A) Sit on the ground
    (B) Go out the door
    (C) Form a line
    (D) Buy tickets

77. What is true about the event?
    (A) It is for hospital patients only.
    (B) The speakers are doctors.
    (C) It happens monthly.
    (D) Tickets cost $5.

78. What can listeners sign up for?
    (A) A doctor's appointment
    (B) Nutrition counseling
    (C) A health class
    (D) A newsletter

79. What will Ms. Holmes talk about?
    (A) Losing weight
    (B) How to stay fit
    (C) Food as medicine
    (D) Hospital research

80. Why did the speaker make the call?
    (A) To offer employment
    (B) To respond to a message
    (C) To ask for information
    (D) To advertise his business

81. Where does the speaker work?
    (A) At a bank
    (B) At a rental agency
    (C) At an accountant's office
    (D) An employment agency

82. What does the speaker ask the listener to do?
    (A) Pay the rent
    (B) Call him back
    (C) Do some research
    (D) Make an appointment

83. What does the speaker mean when she says, "I couldn't have said it better myself?"
    (A) She is a professional speaker.
    (B) She agrees that there has been too much rain.
    (C) She has better information than her audience does.
    (D) She thinks her listeners are good weather reporters.

84. When will the weather change?
    (A) Today
    (B) In the evening
    (C) In two days
    (D) In a week

85. What will the weather be like on Saturday?
    (A) Rainy
    (B) Cloudy
    (C) Snowy
    (D) Windy

86. What is the purpose of the talk?
    (A) To promote a book
    (B) To introduce a speaker
    (C) To sign up new members
    (D) To explain the evening program

87. What does the speaker imply about the meeting?
    (A) The discussions are always interesting.
    (B) Refreshments are always served.
    (C) It takes place once a year.
    (D) Films are rarely shown.

88. What will happen next?
    (A) Dues will be collected.
    (B) Cookies will be served.
    (C) The film will be shown.
    (D) Books will be sold.

89. What should passengers for City Hall do?
    (A) Go downstairs
    (B) Take the express train
    (C) Wait for the next train
    (D) Get off at University Park

90. What will happen in two minutes?
    (A) The train will arrive at the airport.
    (B) Passengers will begin boarding.
    (C) The train will leave the station.
    (D) Tickets will be sold.

91. What is true abut the express train?
    (A) It only stops at the airport.
    (B) It leaves after the local train.
    (C) The seats are not comfortable.
    (D) A blue ticket is required to ride it.

92. What will the Windward Company use the building for?
    (A) Company headquarters
    (B) A new branch office
    (C) Retail sales
    (D) A factory

93. Who can use the fitness club?
    (A) Members only
    (B) Company staff
    (C) Customers
    (D) The public

94. When will the renovations be finished?
    (A) This month
    (B) Next month
    (C) Before the end of this year
    (D) Near the beginning of next year

95. Look at the graphic. Why was the caller's car towed?
(A) She parked all day.
(B) She parked before 6:00 P.M.
(C) She parked on the weekend.
(D) She parked without paying a fee.

**Resident Parking Only**
Monday–Friday  6 P.M.–7 A.M.
Saturday and Sunday all day
Cars will be towed at owner's expense

96. Why did the caller use the parking lot last Saturday?
(A) She was working at her office.
(B) She was shopping at a nearby store.
(C) She was playing tennis in the neighborhood.
(D) She was visiting a friend in the apartment building.

97. What does the caller want the listener to do?
(A) Issue her a parking sticker
(B) Give her money back
(C) Return her car
(D) Pay for damages

98. How often does the staff meeting take place?
(A) Once a month
(B) Twice a month
(C) Once a year
(D) Twice a year

99. Look at the graphic. Which topic will be discussed first?
(A) Professional development opportunity
(B) New scheduling system
(C) New staff
(D) Annual staff evaluations

**Romo, Inc.**
Staff Meeting
April 18

1. Professional development opportunity
2. New scheduling system
3. New staff
4. Annual staff evaluations

100. What problem does the speaker mention?
(A) A presenter is late.
(B) Attendance is low.
(C) The projector is not working.
(D) The agenda is hard to understand.

# READING

In this section of the test, you will have the chance to show how well you understand written English. There are three parts to this section, with special directions for each part.

**YOU WILL HAVE ONE HOUR AND FIFTEEN MINUTES
TO COMPLETE PARTS 5, 6, AND 7 OF THE TEST.**

## Part 5: Incomplete Sentences

> **Directions:** You will see a sentence with a missing word. Four possible answers follow the sentence. Choose the best answer to the question and fill in the corresponding oval on your answer sheet.

101. A full report on the company's financial investments and profits over the past year will be _____ next week.
    (A) released
    (B) observed
    (C) investigated
    (D) acknowledged

102. The instructions recommend _____ any unused portion of the product after one year.
    (A) discard
    (B) discarded
    (C) discarding
    (D) will discard

103. The car _____ to the company, and employees may use it for company-related business only.
    (A) belongs
    (B) possesses
    (C) borrows
    (D) holds

104. Committee members met last night _____ finalize the plans for the new project.
    (A) about
    (B) for
    (C) by
    (D) to

105. The job requirements include five or more years of experience in a _____ position.
    (A) supervise
    (B) supervisor
    (C) supervisory
    (D) superintendent

106. The company normally charges for shipping but will _____ this fee for first-time customers.
    (A) continue
    (B) waive
    (C) impose
    (D) relieve

107. We will have to move our offices to a less expensive part of town _____ rents continue to rise in this neighborhood.
    (A) then
    (B) but
    (C) so
    (D) if

108. The company decided to hire Ms. Silva because of _____ experience with international clients.
    (A) she
    (B) her
    (C) its
    (D) their

109. Stephen couldn't get a ticket on tonight's train so he will have to travel tomorrow _____.
   (A) instead
   (B) despite
   (C) although
   (D) nevertheless

110. Although many people expressed interest in attending the workshop, _____ anybody actually showed up.
   (A) hard
   (B) hardly
   (C) hardy
   (D) hardiness

111. We will continue working under the terms of the old contract _____ a new agreement has been reached.
   (A) whenever
   (B) since
   (C) once
   (D) until

112. The machine is very complicated and should not be used by anyone except a certified _____.
   (A) operate
   (B) operator
   (C) operative
   (D) operation

113. The company has a tradition of _____ an annual picnic for clients and their families.
   (A) inviting
   (B) offering
   (C) hosting
   (D) expecting

114. The new brochure will look much better once the art department has completed the _____.
   (A) illustrates
   (B) illustrator
   (C) illustrated
   (D) illustrations

115. Oronco delayed _____ its latest product until concerns about the safety of some of its features could be addressed.
   (A) launching
   (B) to launch
   (C) launched
   (D) launch

116. Every company has its own culture, and new employees will need some time to _____ to the customs of their new workplace.
   (A) expect
   (B) change
   (C) adapt
   (D) modify

117. George's outgoing personality and ability to gain the trust of his clients helped him _____ in his business.
   (A) excel
   (B) excellent
   (C) excellence
   (D) excellently

118. _____ it does little advertising, the store has been able to attract many new customers.
   (A) Because
   (B) Although
   (C) When
   (D) Unless

119. Now that the bridge has been completed, the island is _____ accessible by car.
   (A) eventually
   (B) barely
   (C) unusually
   (D) readily

120. Before you agree to the terms of the new contract, you should find out if the salary is _____.
   (A) negotiate
   (B) negotiator
   (C) negotiable
   (D) negotiation

121. In the case of cancellation due to unforeseen circumstances, workshop participants will _____ by e-mail.
(A) notify
(B) notifying
(C) to notify
(D) be notified

122. Our budget is _____, but we think we can complete the project with the funds we have on hand.
(A) tight
(B) narrow
(C) compact
(D) thin

123. We decided that a _____ darker color would be better for the walls in this office.
(A) slight
(B) slighted
(C) slightly
(D) slightness

124. _____ the increase in price, this product is still selling in large numbers.
(A) In spite
(B) Despite
(C) Because of
(D) Further

125. The manager reminded us that we don't have a large budget, and we should _____ all unnecessary expenses.
(A) avoid
(B) avoiding
(C) avoidance
(D) avoidable

126. Because of the steady _____ in the number of subscribers, the company decided to stop publishing that magazine.
(A) scarcity
(B) suspension
(C) recession
(D) decline

127. _____ I was waiting for comments on the first report, I started work on the second one.
(A) During
(B) While
(C) Therefore
(D) Moreover

128. Many of my colleagues found this book _____ interesting, but a few of us thought it was boring.
(A) minimally
(B) overly
(C) highly
(D) rarely

129. All team members _____ ideas were used in writing up the proposal should have their names on the front cover.
(A) who's
(B) whose
(C) that
(D) which

130. I usually don't order things from that website _____ their shipping charges are so high.
(A) since
(B) due to
(C) so
(D) though

## Part 6: Text Completion

> **Directions:** You will see four passages each with four blanks. Under each blank are four answer options. Choose the word or phrase that best completes the sentence.

Questions 131–134 refer to the following information.

Thank you for buying the Hillard ZX 3-in-1 printer. _____ printer uses the latest

        131. (A) They're

            (B) Their

            (C) Your

            (D) You're

technology to print, scan, and copy documents and photos of the highest quality. Included
in the box is a packet of free samples of photographic paper in _____ sizes.

        132. (A) vary

            (B) various

            (C) variety

            (D) variously

Use the _____ coupon to order more paper at a 25% discount.

    133. (A) enclosed

        (B) available

        (C) incorporated

        (D) added

134. (A) Hillard has many other fine products useful for your home or
      home office.

   (B) Professional photographers often turn to Hillard for their
      photographic supplies.

   (C) Visit the Hillard website for tutorials on choosing the best printers,
      computers, and other electronics for your needs.

   (D) We know you will be pleased with the professional quality of the
      photographs printed by the Hillard ZX.

Questions 135–138 refer to the following letter.

Cynthia Blau
PO Box 459
Wilmington, MO

Dear Ms. Blau,

I very much enjoyed meeting with you last week. At this time, I am pleased to offer you the _____ of Office Manager here at Sligo, Inc.

135. (A) information
    (B) opportunity
    (C) address
    (D) position

_____. If you choose to accept this offer, please sign the second copy of this letter

136. (A) Sligo offers accounting service to businesses throughout the city.
    (B) As we discussed, your starting date will be February 15.
    (C) I am in my office most mornings during the week.
    (D) We have a number of job openings at this time.

and return it to me as soon as possible. As soon as we _____ your acceptance,

137. (A) are receiving
    (B) will receive
    (C) to receive
    (D) receive

we will send you information on employee benefits as well as enrollment forms. We look forward to _____ with you at Sligo. Please let me know if you have any questions

138. (A) working
    (B) worked
    (C) works
    (D) work

or need any additional information.

Sincerely,

*Jose Marquez*

Jose Marquez

Questions 139–142 refer to the following letter.

---

## Notice to Recreation Center Users

The Recreation Center building will be closed next week _____ painting

139. (A) to
(B) for
(C) when
(D) because

and repairs. _____.

140. (A) During this time no one will be permitted to enter the building for any reason.
(B) Use of the Recreation Center facilities is free for all residents of this city.
(C) Please call our office to request information about any of our programs.
(D) This work is being funded in part by a grant from the Mayor's Office.

Use of all outdoor facilities, however, including the basketball and tennis courts and the pool, will continue as usual. Please use the form on our website to reserve court time. The pool will be open as usual from 8:00 A.M. to 8:00 P.M. All club meetings that are _____ held in the building will be canceled for next

141. (A) normally
(B) frequently
(C) appropriately
(D) reasonably

week. The regular schedule will _____ on Monday, July 10. We apologize

142. (A) adjust
(B) remain
(C) resume
(D) modify

for any inconvenience this may cause.

Questions 143–146 refer to the following notice.

Dear Neighbor,

The High Towers Tenants Association cordially invites you to the annual building holiday party. Festivities _____ in the second floor party room next

143. (A) hold
(B) will hold
(C) to be held
(D) will be held

Saturday from 5:00 P.M. to 8:00 P.M. There will be refreshments, dancing and, most of all, the chance to _____ with your neighbors.

144. (A) consult
(B) socialize
(C) introduce
(D) toil

Please contact the Tenants Association president, Amy Smith, if you would like to help out with the arrangements for this event.

_____ .

145. (A) We can always use assistance with decorations, food preparation, and other tasks.
(B) In addition, we plan to have a building-wide barbecue in the summer.
(C) Furthermore, you are welcome to bring guests, if you would like to.
(D) This is a popular event and most building residents attend it.

We _____ to see you next Saturday!

146. (A) wish
(B) want
(C) hope
(D) expect

## Part 7: Reading Comprehension

> **Directions:** You will see single and multiple reading passages followed by several questions. Each question has four answer choices. Choose the best answer to the question and fill in the corresponding oval on your answer sheet.

Questions 147–148 refer to the following employment ad.

---

**We're looking for self-motivated, enthusiastic team players** to join our team.

Job responsibilities include:

- Marketing products and services to current customers
- Contacting potential customers and establishing new accounts
- Submitting orders
- Recommending changes in products and services

Minimum 3 years experience in a similar position and proficiency with office software required. Apply to Mr. Rogers at samrogers@zrx.com. Include a resume and names of three references. No phone calls, please.

---

147. What kind of job is advertised?
    (A) Customer service provider
    (B) Sales representative
    (C) Software developer
    (D) Market analyst

148. How can someone apply for the job?
    (A) Visit the office
    (B) Mail a resume
    (C) Send an email
    (D) Call Mr. Rogers

Questions 149–150 refer to the following text message chain.

> **Phil Takubo, 10:45**
> I'm at the store now. What kind of paper did you want me to get? Large?
>
> **Marie Ochs, 10:46**
> Not paper. Envelopes, large manila envelopes.
>
> **Marie Ochs, 10:47**
> Next time I'll send you with a list. Then you might remember.
>
> **Phil Takubo, 10:48**
> Sorry, they have boxes of 500. It's cheaper per envelope to buy in large quantities.
>
> **Marie Ochs, 10:50**
> We'll never use that many. Just get 250.
>
> **Phil Takubo, 10:50**
> OK. 250. See you at the café for lunch in 10 minutes.
>
> **Marie Ochs, 10:52**
> I'm on my way.
>
> **Phil Takubo, 10:53**
> On the bus?
>
> **Marie Ochs, 10:54**
> Taxi. I missed the bus and didn't want to be late. I'll be there in 5 minutes.

149. What does Marie imply about Phil?
   (A) He's often late.
   (B) He has a bad memory.
   (C) He likes to save money.
   (D) He uses a lot of envelopes.

150. Where is Marie now?
   (A) In the store
   (B) At the office
   (C) At the café
   (D) In a taxi

## Foreclosure Auction

Office Building on Binghamton Road

Two-story building with four offices, lobby, and off-street parking. All offices currently occupied. Close to two bus lines. Serviced by municipal water and sewer. Tax map 46, Lot 10. Inspections: interior and exterior, one hour prior to auction, no appointments necessary. Photos available at www.wilsonrealestate.com

151. What is the advertisement for?
    (A) Mortgages for business property
    (B) Building safety inspections
    (C) A building for sale
    (D) Offices for rent

152. What can people do online?
    (A) Check water and sewer services
    (B) View pictures of the building
    (C) Make an appointment
    (D) Look at a map

Questions 153–154 refer to the following article.

> **TelTime Telecommunications Service** plans to bring the Internet to over 20 underserved rural communities in the central district. Many of the 23 towns in the company's service area currently have no Internet service at all, while nine of the towns have service in certain areas. TelTime expects to have Internet service up and running for both residential and commercial customers in all of these towns by the end of next year. Residents of the towns in the TelTime service area are being asked to express interest in receiving TelTime Internet by going to the TelTime website and presubscribing. No deposit or fee is charged for this. TelTime will initiate its installation of Internet services in the community with the largest number of presubscribers. Work will begin at the end of next month.

153. How many towns will TelTime service altogether?
    (A)  9
    (B)  20
    (C)  23
    (D)  29

154. Which town will get Internet service first?
    (A)  The town where the most interest is expressed
    (B)  The town closest to the TelTime central offices
    (C)  The town with the largest number of customers
    (D)  The town that has both residential and commercial customers

Questions 155–157 refer to the following invoice.

## Montshire Heating Fuel

Account no. 496903-2          Statement date: January 12

| Date | Description | Total |
|------|-------------|-------|
| January 10 | 100 gallons  #2 fuel | $375 |
| | furnace repair | $120 |
| | late fee (previous statement) | $25 |
| | | |
| | amount due | $520 |
| | credit limit | $1,500 |

### Terms and Conditions

**Payment**   Amount due is payable upon receipt. Overdue accounts are subject to a late fee, and credit terms may be canceled.

**Errors and Inquiries About Your Bill**   If you believe there is an error or you require an explanation of an item on your bill, send your inquiry by certified mail within 60 days of the date on this statement. Include your name and account number and a description of the error or problem, including the amount you believe you owe. Within 90 days, we will mail you a written notice of any corrections we have made or explain why we believe the original statement is correct.

**Payment Options**   You may make your payment by mail, credit card, or electronic transfer, or you may pay in cash by visiting any of our branch offices.

Customer Service: 800-674-9483                         *www.monshirefuel.com*

155. What is the $25 charge for?
    (A) Delayed payment on an earlier bill
    (B) Late delivery of heating fuel
    (C) Repairs to the furnace
    (D) Interest on credit

156. When is the payment due?
    (A) When the bill is received
    (B) When the fuel is delivered
    (C) Within 60 days of the delivery date
    (D) Within 90 days of the statement date

157. What should the customer do if there is a disagreement about the bill?
    (A) Check the website for instructions
    (B) Call Customer Service
    (C) Visit a branch office
    (D) Write a letter

# WINDWARD
## Customer Satisfaction Survey

**Trip** ☑ Island Romp  ☐ Mountain Adventure  ☐ City Exploration

**Date of trip** _April 18-22_

Please rate the following:

| **Accommodations** | **Meals** |
|---|---|
| ☑ excellent | ☐ excellent |
| ☐ good | ☑ good |
| ☐ fair | ☐ fair |
| ☐ poor | ☐ poor |
| **Itinerary** | **Transportation** |
| ☐ excellent | ☐ excellent |
| ☑ good | ☐ good |
| ☐ fair | ☑ fair |
| ☐ poor | ☐ poor |

Comments: _Our guide was fantastic, very knowledgeable, but there were too many activities packed into each day. The bus driver was quite nice and the bus was clean enough, but the seats could have been softer and a bit more spacious._

158. What kind of business is Windward?
    (A) A vacation resort
    (B) A tour company
    (C) A travel agency
    (D) A bus service

159. What was the customer most satisfied with?
    (A) The hotel
    (B) The food
    (C) The schedule
    (D) The bus

160. What does the customer suggest about the bus?
    (A) It was not very clean.
    (B) The driver was unfriendly.
    (C) The seats were uncomfortable.
    (D) There were too many passengers.

Questions 161–163 refer to the following web page.

161. What is implied about Spotless Cleaning Services?
  (A) Its employees all have previous experience.
  (B) It cleans both homes and offices.
  (C) It cleans homes only.
  (D) It is a new business.

162. What should you do if you want to get services from Spotless?
  (A) Complete an application form on the website.
  (B) Order individual services through the website.
  (C) Call the office to get an estimate over the phone.
  (D) Make an appointment with a customer representative.

163. What happens if a customer is not satisfied with a cleaning job?
  (A) The contract is canceled.
  (B) The next cleaning job is free.
  (C) The cleaning fee will be given back.
  (D) The staff will repeat the job within 24 hours.

Questions 164–167 refer to the following online chat.

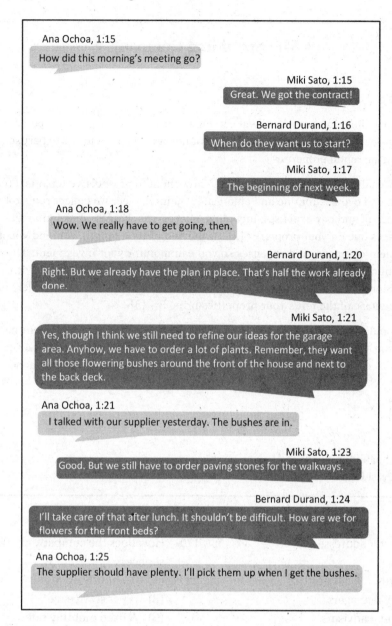

Ana Ochoa, 1:15
How did this morning's meeting go?

Miki Sato, 1:15
Great. We got the contract!

Bernard Durand, 1:16
When do they want us to start?

Miki Sato, 1:17
The beginning of next week.

Ana Ochoa, 1:18
Wow. We really have to get going, then.

Bernard Durand, 1:20
Right. But we already have the plan in place. That's half the work already done.

Miki Sato, 1:21
Yes, though I think we still need to refine our ideas for the garage area. Anyhow, we have to order a lot of plants. Remember, they want all those flowering bushes around the front of the house and next to the back deck.

Ana Ochoa, 1:21
I talked with our supplier yesterday. The bushes are in.

Miki Sato, 1:23
Good. But we still have to order paving stones for the walkways.

Bernard Durand, 1:24
I'll take care of that after lunch. It shouldn't be difficult. How are we for flowers for the front beds?

Ana Ochoa, 1:25
The supplier should have plenty. I'll pick them up when I get the bushes.

164. What kind of business are they most likely involved in?
(A) Nursery
(B) Landscaping
(C) Real estate agency
(D) Home construction

165. Who did Miki meet with this morning?
(A) A client
(B) Her lawyer
(C) The supplier
(D) Bernard and Ana

166. At 1:21, what does Ana mean when she writes, "The bushes are in?"
(A) The bushes have already been planted.
(B) The bushes should be ordered soon.
(C) The bushes are available now.
(D) The bushes are very popular.

167. What will Bernard do today?
(A) Review the contract
(B) Pick up flowers
(C) Plant the front beds
(D) Order paving stones

---

### ✦ The Spaulding Company ✦

Dear Neighbor,

The Spaulding Company has been serving the needs of Springvale property owners for over three decades and is well-known in the area for its expertise in overseeing rental properties.

–[1]–We advertise your available units, show them to prospective tenants, create leases, and oversee routine and emergency maintenance. We collect rents on your behalf and pay expenses, including any service charges, association fees, and taxes due on your property.–[2]–At the end of each month, we send you a statement of income and expenses so you can monitor your investment. The amount of time we spend and the number of services we provide varies with each month, but our fee to you is always the same because we base it solely on a percentage of the rents your properties bring in.–[3]–

We would welcome the opportunity to discuss your property management needs with you.–[4]–If you would like to learn more about how we can help you get the most out of your real estate investments, please contact us by telephone at 305-0822.

Sincerely,

*Irene Spaulding*

Irene Spaulding
Vice President

---

168. Who is the letter addressed to?
   (A) Tenants
   (B) Landlords
   (C) Property managers
   (D) Investment advisors

169. The word "prospective" in paragraph 2, line 1, is closest in meaning to
   (A) recommended
   (B) qualified
   (C) possible
   (D) new

170. How does the company charge for its services?
   (A) An hourly wage
   (B) A per service fee
   (C) A fixed monthly rate
   (D) A percentage of rents

171. In which of the following positions marked [1], [2], [3], and [4] does the following sentence best belong?

   "We take the stress out of property ownership by providing a complete range of services."

   (A) [1]
   (B) [2]
   (C) [3]
   (D) [4]

Questions 172–175 refer to the following article.

---

### Local Farmer's Market Booming

–[1]–The farmer's market at City Park has grown from just five vendors to close to 20 in just under two years. "When we started the market," says market manager Coleen Smith, "we had no idea it would become so popular." –[2]–"People shop here because they've come to realize the value of fresh fruits and vegetables, which you can only get truly fresh if they are grown right here in this region," says Malcolm Brown, a farmer and market vendor. "The prices are higher than in most grocery stores, sure," Brown explains, "but customers know they are getting their money's worth."

–[3]–When we visited the market last Saturday, the place was crowded with shoppers even though it was still early. Vendors were busy selling fresh herbs, salad greens, and especially strawberries. "These are the first of the season," explained strawberry farmer Suzanne Reed. "And customers just can't seem to get enough of them. I will probably be sold out before noon."

City Park's Saturday market seems to have started a trend.–[4]–At least two other farmer's markets have appeared in the area in the past year, one downtown and one in the city's university district.

---

172. When was the farmer's market at City Park started?
    (A) Last week
    (B) A year ago
    (C) Two years ago
    (D) 20 years ago

173. What is true about the farmer's market at City Park?
    (A) It takes place once a week.
    (B) It is the only market in the city.
    (C) Some of the products are prepackaged.
    (D) Products cost less than in grocery stores.

174. What does the farmer mean in paragraph 2, line 4, when she is quoted as saying, "Customers just can't seem to get enough of them"?
    (A) Strawberries are a popular item.
    (B) It's hard to find strawberries at the market.
    (C) There are too many strawberry vendors at the market.
    (D) Customers prefer to buy small amounts of strawberries.

175. In which of the following positions marked [1], [2], [3], and [4] does the following sentence best belong?

    "Vendors attribute the huge success of the market to a growing nationwide trend for a preference for locally produced foods."

    (A) [1]
    (B) [2]
    (C) [3]
    (D) [4]

Questions 176–180 refer to the following brochure excerpt and e-mail.

---

*Regional Train System*
*Spring Excursions*

**Hatsford River Excursion**
*April 22, 23, 29, 30 and May 6, 7*
Experience the famous Hatsford River Celebration at the Hatsford Riverfront Fairgrounds like never before. Enjoy outdoor concerts on the banks of the river, see performances by individual artists from all around the world, watch the spectacular Old Town Marching Band march through the grounds at noon, and much, much more. There will also be a food tent and hourly guided tours of historic Hatsford. The package includes round-trip rail fare, taxi from the station to the waterfront, and discounted admission to the fairgrounds. Book now at *www.regionalts.com.*

---

From:  Melinda Hayes
Subj:  Mr. Kim's visit
Date:  April 5
To:    Robert Springer

Robert,

I had a thought as I was going over the plans for Mr. Kim's visit at the beginning of next month. Since he is coming from overseas, I thought it would be nice if he could have a chance to experience some sort of local cultural event, and the Hatsford River Celebration is coming up. I think you can get some sort of package deal from the Regional Train System, so he could go up there for the day, enjoy the event, and be back at his hotel in the evening. I think it would be a relaxing time for him after a week filled with meetings, conferences, and clients. So, please contact Regional Train and see what you can arrange. Thanks.

Melinda

---

176. What kind of event is the Hatsford River Celebration?
(A) A food fair
(B) An art show
(C) A music festival
(D) A riverboat cruise

177. What is NOT included in the Hatsford River Excursion package?
(A) Train ticket
(B) Food vouchers
(C) Cab ride to the event
(D) Reduced event entrance fee

178. Who is Mr. Kim, most likely?
(A) Melinda's business associate
(B) Melinda's assistant
(C) Melinda's relative
(D) Melinda's friend

179. When will Mr. Kim probably go to the event?
(A) April 22 or 23
(B) April 29
(C) May 6 or 7
(D) May 8

180. The phrase "coming up" in line 5 of the e-mail is closest in meaning to _____.
(A) appearing
(B) occurring
(C) growing
(D) rising

## ❧ Hubert's ❧
### Party Supply Rental Company

You've chosen a date, hired a caterer, and sent out the invitations. You're all set, right?

Wrong!

Your table settings are as important as every other aspect of your carefully planned event. Whether you are planning a family wedding or a board of director's dinner, a formal affair or a relaxed and casual party, Hubert's can supply you with complete table settings that are just right for the occasion.

No more plain white linens and china from the caterer! At Hubert's, you can choose from a wide selection of colors and styles to create the atmosphere you envision for your event.

❖ Basics: We provide everything needed for a festive table, including linens, china, silverware, and glassware for individual place settings.
❖ Extras: We can also provide matching serving platters, water pitchers, and flower vases.

Call now for a free estimate.
Book before October 5 and get 15% off your entire order.
No rush jobs, sorry. All events must be booked at least three weeks in advance.

---

| From: | Roland Perry |
|---|---|
| Subj: | Annual office party |
| Date: | September 14 |
| To: | Priscilla Hubert |

Dear Ms. Hubert,

I recently saw your flyer advertising your party supply rental business. I am the office manager at the Antwerp Company. Our annual office party is coming up next week, and this year we've decided to try having a sit-down lunch for a change. We've already arranged for a very nice meal from a local catering service and, after seeing your flyer, I thought it would a nice touch to have festive table settings. The lunch is scheduled for Friday of next week at noon. There will be approximately 50 people attending, all of them members of our staff. The caterers will be arriving at our offices at around 11:00, but you can come in as early as you like to set up. Can you give me an estimate of what you would charge for an event of this size? We have a little money to spare, so I think we would probably want to include most of the extras you offer as well as the basic china and linens. I would also like to see the selection of colors and styles available.

Thank you very much.
Roland Perry

181. What is suggested about Hubert's?
    (A) It works only on large events.
    (B) It can supply flowers for weddings.
    (C) It provides party planning services.
    (D) Its clients are both businesses and individuals.

182. The word "envision" in line 10 of the flyer is closest in meaning to _____.
    (A) imagine
    (B) promise
    (C) require
    (D) estimate

183. How can a customer get a discount?
    (A) Book the event three weeks ahead of time
    (B) Choose plain white linens and china
    (C) Place the order by October 5
    (D) Include extras in the order

184. Why will Hubert's not be able to supply the Antwerp lunch?
    (A) There will be too many guests.
    (B) The event wasn't booked early enough.
    (C) They won't be allowed to set up before 11:00.
    (D) They don't offer the desired colors and styles.

185. What is suggested about the annual office party?
    (A) It doesn't usually include a sit-down lunch.
    (B) Managers and supervisors are not invited.
    (C) Most staff members attend it.
    (D) The budget for it is limited.

Questions 186–190 refer to the following webpage, e-mail, and schedule.

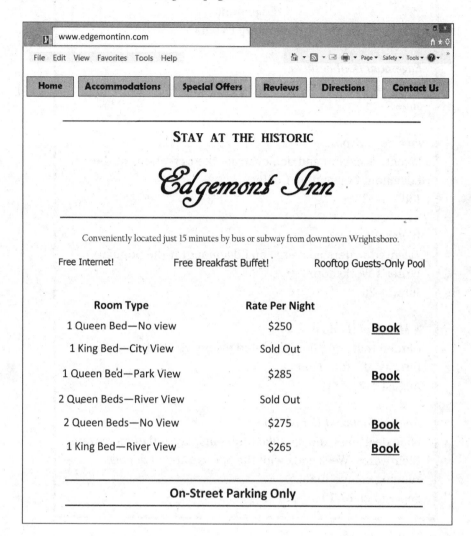

www.edgemontinn.com

File   Edit   View   Favorites   Tools   Help

| Home | Accommodations | Special Offers | Reviews | Directions | Contact Us |

## STAY AT THE HISTORIC

# Edgemont Inn

Conveniently located just 15 minutes by bus or subway from downtown Wrightsboro.

Free Internet!          Free Breakfast Buffet!          Rooftop Guests-Only Pool

| Room Type | Rate Per Night | |
| --- | --- | --- |
| 1 Queen Bed—No view | $250 | **Book** |
| 1 King Bed—City View | Sold Out | |
| 1 Queen Bed—Park View | $285 | **Book** |
| 2 Queen Beds—River View | Sold Out | |
| 2 Queen Beds—No View | $275 | **Book** |
| 1 King Bed—River View | $265 | **Book** |

**On-Street Parking Only**

---

From:   Melissa Schwartz
Subj:   room reservation
Date:   May 10
To:     Edgemont Inn

Hi,

I recently booked a room at your hotel, but I need to change the dates of my reservation. Can you do that for me? It doesn't have to be the same room. My original reservation was for the week of the Inventor's Expo, but it turns out I was able to get a spot in the Writer's Workshop, and I don't have time to do both. So if you could change my reservation to the week of the workshop, that would be great. I need a room with two queen-size beds. I'd like a river view, if possible, because I enjoy watching the boats go by, but that's not essential. What's important is the dates and the two queen beds. Thank you so much.

Melissa Schwartz

**Edgemont**
**Upcoming Events**

*Edgemont Boat Festival*
Week-long spectacle of boats on the Edgemont River.
June 7–14

*Inventor's Expo*
Inventors exhibit and demonstrate their creations at the
Edgemont Convention Center.
July 12–19

*Writer's Workshop*
Talented writers converge on Edgemont for the popular
Writer's Workshop.
July 20–26

*A Month of Gardens*
Garden tours and flower-related events go on throughout
the city all month long.
August 1–31

*Annual Footwear Convention*
Shoe designers and manufacturers display and demonstrate
their wares. Week ends with the *Sports Shoe Challenge*
running competition.
September 15–19

186. What is true about the Edgemont hotel?
(A) It is near public transportation.
(B) It has a downtown location.
(C) It is in a modern building.
(D) It has a parking garage.

187. What is NOT included with each room
at the Edgemont Inn?
(A) Breakfast
(B) A king-size bed
(C) Internet access
(D) Use of a swimming pool

188. When will Ms. Schwartz be in Wrightsboro?
(A) June 7–11
(B) July 12–19
(C) July 20–26
(D) August 1

189. Which room will Ms. Schwartz probably get?
(A) 1 king bed/river view
(B) 1 queen bed/park view
(C) 2 queen beds/no view
(D) 2 queen beds/river view

190. When can visitors to Wrightsboro see a race?
(A) June
(B) July
(C) August
(D) September

Questions 191–195 refer to the following online order form and two e-mails.

**www.officethings.com**

Place your order

| Item | Qty | Price | Total |
|---|---|---|---|
| Multipurpose paper, case | 3 | $25.00 | $75.00 |
| Felt-tip pens, 12/pk | 4 | $15.00 | $60.00 |
| Jumbo paper clips, 1,000/pk | 2 | $10.00 | $20.00 |
| | | coupon code | |
| | | shipping | $0.00 |
| | | sales tax | $0.00 |
| | | TOTAL ORDER | $155.00 |

Free shipping on orders over $100

**Our blog**      **Join our Frequent Buyer's Club**

From:     Office Things
Subject:  Your order has shipped!
Date:     April 26
To:       George Rollins

Part of your order has been shipped. You should receive your items on or before May 1. The rest of your items will be shipped soon.

Order no.: OT12345

Shipping information:
George Rollins
P.O. Box 10
Green River, VT

Shipping method: Standard shipping

Items shipped:

| Item | Qty | Price | Total |
|---|---|---|---|
| Multipurpose paper, case | 3 | $25.00 | $75.00 |
| Felt-tip pens, 12/pk | 4 | $15.00 | $60.00 |

Thank you for your order!

```
From:       Office Things
Subject:    Canceled items
Date:       May 8
To:         George Rollins

We're writing to inform you that items from your order, listed below, have
been canceled. Unfortunately, those items are out of stock indefinitely.
You will not be billed for these items. If you wish to change your order,
please contact a customer service representative at 1-800-555-1212.
We may have similar items in stock.
```

| Item | Qty | Price | Total |
|------|-----|-------|-------|
| Jumbo paper clips, 1,000/pk | 2 | $10.00 | $20.00 |

191. How many pens did the customer order?
  (A) 4 pens
  (B) 12 pens
  (C) 4 packs of 12 pens
  (D) 12 packs of 12 pens

192. Why is there no shipping charge?
  (A) The order is over $100.
  (B) The customer used a coupon.
  (C) The customer is a frequent buyer.
  (D) The company never charges for shipping.

193. When will the shopper receive the paper and pens?
  (A) On April 26
  (B) By May 1
  (C) On May 8
  (D) After May 8

194. Why was the order for paper clips canceled?
  (A) The customer doesn't need them anymore.
  (B) The paper clips are no longer available.
  (C) The company has gone out of business.
  (D) The customer didn't pay for them.

195. For what purpose does the company suggest calling customer service?
  (A) To complain about the cancellation
  (B) To reorder the same item
  (C) To cancel the bill
  (D) To order a similar item

Questions 196–200 refer to the following agenda, memo, and e-mail.

---

**THE GOLDEN CORPORATION**
MEETING AGENDA
SEPTEMBER 15, 1:30 PM
CONFERENCE ROOM C

1. New advertising campaign presentation ................Bob Meyers

2. Sales report ..........................................................Yuki O'Hara

3. Market research plans ...............................................Li Chang

4. Plans for NYC conference product exhibition.........Rose Stern

---

**THE GOLDEN CORPORATION**

**Memo**

Date:    September 12
To:      All Staff
From:    Joe Bing
Re:      Carpet cleaning

Please be aware that the carpet cleaning project will continue through this week. Every area that was not cleaned last week is on the cleaning schedule for this week, including:

• all the conference rooms
• the break room
• the second floor reception area
• the large back office

Please stay away from these areas this week. Any activities scheduled for these areas need to be rescheduled for another time or place. Please contact me to arrange this. We are sorry for the inconvenience and thank you for your cooperation. Things should be back to normal next week.

| From: | Eileen Brach |
| Subject: | This week's meeting |
| Date: | September 12 |
| To: | Department list |

Hi all,

I hope you all saw the agenda for this week's meeting that I sent out this morning. There will be a few small changes to that. It looks like the carpet cleaning is still going on, so we'll have to move to a different location. We'll be meeting at the same time, but in the front office on the first floor. It's a smaller space but should be big enough for our needs. The only drawback is that there's no projector there and really no other way for Bob to display his information, so he has agreed to put off his presentation until next month. Other than that, everything else will stay the same. Please make every effort to be on time.

Eileen

196. What department is the meeting probably for?
(A) Marketing
(B) Human resources
(C) Product development
(D) Accounting

197. What will be discussed first at the meeting?
(A) New advertising campaign presentation
(B) Sales report
(C) Market research plans
(D) Plans for NYC conference product exhibition

198. What is indicated about the carpet cleaning project?
(A) It is very expensive.
(B) It will be rescheduled.
(C) It will be completed this week.
(D) It is taking longer than expected.

199. What is implied about the front office?
(A) It doesn't have many chairs.
(B) Its carpet was cleaned last week.
(C) It isn't usually used for meetings.
(D) It is larger than the conference rooms.

200. The word "drawback" in line 6 of the e-mail is closest in meaning to _____.
(A) change
(B) quality
(C) removal
(D) problem

## LISTENING COMPREHENSION

### Part 1: Photographs

1. **B**
2. **C**
3. **A**
4. **C**
5. **D**
6. **B**

### Part 2: Question-Response

7. **A**
8. **B**
9. **B**
10. **A**
11. **A**
12. **B**
13. **C**
14. **A**
15. **B**
16. **A**
17. **A**
18. **B**
19. **C**
20. **C**
21. **A**
22. **B**
23. **A**
24. **C**
25. **C**
26. **B**
27. **A**
28. **C**
29. **A**
30. **B**
31. **C**

### Part 3: Conversations

32. **C**
33. **B**
34. **D**
35. **A**
36. **B**
37. **D**
38. **D**
39. **B**
40. **A**
41. **B**
42. **C**
43. **C**
44. **B**
45. **A**
46. **D**
47. **A**
48. **C**
49. **D**
50. **D**
51. **C**
52. **B**
53. **B**
54. **A**
55. **C**
56. **B**
57. **C**
58. **B**
59. **D**
60. **A**
61. **D**
62. **A**
63. **B**
64. **A**
65. **C**
66. **A**
67. **B**
68. **B**
69. **D**
70. **C**

### Part 4: Talks

71. **A**
72. **C**
73. **B**
74. **A**
75. **B**
76. **C**
77. **C**
78. **D**
79. **B**
80. **B**
81. **A**
82. **D**
83. **B**
84. **C**
85. **D**
86. **D**
87. **B**
88. **A**
89. **A**
90. **C**
91. **D**
92. **A**
93. **B**
94. **D**
95. **C**
96. **C**
97. **B**
98. **B**
99. **D**
100. **A**

## READING

### Part 5: Incomplete Sentences

| | | | | | | | |
|---|---|---|---|---|---|---|---|
| 101. | A | 109. | A | 117. | A | 125. | A |
| 102. | C | 110. | B | 118. | B | 126. | D |
| 103. | A | 111. | D | 119. | D | 127. | B |
| 104. | D | 112. | B | 120. | C | 128. | C |
| 105. | C | 113. | C | 121. | D | 129. | B |
| 106. | B | 114. | D | 122. | A | 130. | A |
| 107. | D | 115. | A | 123. | C | | |
| 108. | B | 116. | C | 124. | B | | |

### Part 6: Text Completion

| | | | | | | | |
|---|---|---|---|---|---|---|---|
| 131. | C | 135. | D | 139. | B | 143. | D |
| 132. | B | 136. | B | 140. | A | 144. | B |
| 133. | A | 137. | D | 141. | A | 145. | A |
| 134. | D | 138. | A | 142. | C | 146. | C |

### Part 7: Reading Comprehension

| | | | | | | | |
|---|---|---|---|---|---|---|---|
| 147. | B | 161. | C | 175. | B | 189. | C |
| 148. | C | 162. | D | 176. | C | 190. | D |
| 149. | B | 163. | B | 177. | B | 191. | C |
| 150. | D | 164. | B | 178. | A | 192. | A |
| 151. | C | 165. | A | 179. | C | 193. | B |
| 152. | B | 166. | C | 180. | B | 194. | B |
| 153. | C | 167. | D | 181. | D | 195. | D |
| 154. | A | 168. | B | 182. | A | 196. | A |
| 155. | A | 169. | C | 183. | C | 197. | B |
| 156. | A | 170. | D | 184. | B | 198. | C |
| 157. | D | 171. | A | 185. | A | 199. | B |
| 158. | B | 172. | C | 186. | A | 200. | D |
| 159. | A | 173. | A | 187. | B | | |
| 160. | C | 174. | A | 188. | C | | |

# TEST SCORE CONVERSION TABLE

Count your correct responses. Match the number of correct responses with the corresponding score from the Test Score Conversion Table (below). Add the two scores together. This is your Total Estimated Test Score. As you practice taking the TOEIC model tests, your scores should improve. Keep track of your Total Estimated Test Scores.

| # Correct | Listening Score | Reading Score | # Correct | Listening Score | Reading Score | # Correct | Listening Score | Reading Score | # Correct | Listening Score | Reading Score |
|---|---|---|---|---|---|---|---|---|---|---|---|
| 0 | 5 | 5 | 26 | 110 | 65 | 51 | 255 | 220 | 76 | 410 | 370 |
| 1 | 5 | 5 | 27 | 115 | 70 | 52 | 260 | 225 | 77 | 420 | 380 |
| 2 | 5 | 5 | 28 | 120 | 80 | 53 | 270 | 230 | 78 | 425 | 385 |
| 3 | 5 | 5 | 29 | 125 | 85 | 54 | 275 | 235 | 79 | 430 | 390 |
| 4 | 5 | 5 | 30 | 130 | 90 | 55 | 280 | 240 | 80 | 440 | 395 |
| 5 | 5 | 5 | 31 | 135 | 95 | 56 | 290 | 250 | 81 | 445 | 400 |
| 6 | 5 | 5 | 32 | 140 | 100 | 57 | 295 | 255 | 82 | 450 | 405 |
| 7 | 10 | 5 | 33 | 145 | 110 | 58 | 300 | 260 | 83 | 460 | 410 |
| 8 | 15 | 5 | 34 | 150 | 115 | 59 | 310 | 265 | 84 | 465 | 415 |
| 9 | 20 | 5 | 35 | 160 | 120 | 60 | 315 | 270 | 85 | 470 | 420 |
| 10 | 25 | 5 | 36 | 165 | 125 | 61 | 320 | 280 | 86 | 475 | 425 |
| 11 | 30 | 5 | 37 | 170 | 130 | 62 | 325 | 285 | 87 | 480 | 430 |
| 12 | 35 | 5 | 38 | 175 | 140 | 63 | 330 | 290 | 88 | 485 | 435 |
| 13 | 40 | 5 | 39 | 180 | 145 | 64 | 340 | 300 | 89 | 490 | 445 |
| 14 | 45 | 5 | 40 | 185 | 150 | 65 | 345 | 305 | 90 | 495 | 450 |
| 15 | 50 | 5 | 41 | 190 | 160 | 66 | 350 | 310 | 91 | 495 | 455 |
| 16 | 55 | 10 | 42 | 195 | 165 | 67 | 360 | 320 | 92 | 495 | 465 |
| 17 | 60 | 15 | 43 | 200 | 170 | 68 | 365 | 325 | 93 | 495 | 470 |
| 18 | 65 | 20 | 44 | 210 | 175 | 69 | 370 | 330 | 94 | 495 | 480 |
| 19 | 70 | 25 | 45 | 215 | 180 | 70 | 380 | 335 | 95 | 495 | 485 |
| 20 | 75 | 30 | 46 | 220 | 190 | 71 | 385 | 340 | 96 | 495 | 490 |
| 21 | 80 | 35 | 47 | 230 | 195 | 72 | 390 | 350 | 97 | 495 | 495 |
| 22 | 85 | 40 | 48 | 240 | 200 | 73 | 395 | 355 | 98 | 495 | 495 |
| 23 | 90 | 45 | 49 | 245 | 210 | 74 | 400 | 360 | 99 | 495 | 495 |
| 24 | 95 | 50 | 50 | 250 | 215 | 75 | 405 | 365 | 100 | 495 | 495 |
| 25 | 100 | 60 | | | | | | | | | |

Number of Correct Listening Responses _____ = Listening Score _____

Number of Correct Reading Responses _____ = Reading Score _____

Total Estimated Test Score _____

# ANSWERS EXPLAINED

## Listening Comprehension

### PART 1: PHOTOGRAPHS

1. **(B)** A man is standing at a sink rinsing a pile of plates. Choice (A) correctly identifies the action, *washing*, but the man is washing plates or dishes, not his hands. Choice (C) correctly identifies the plates but not the action. Choice (D) correctly identifies the action, cleaning , and also the sink, but the man is cleaning dishes in the sink, he is not cleaning the sink itself.

2. **(C)** A café scene shows a table in the foreground with empty chairs around it. Choice (A) correctly identifies the location, but there are no people in the photo. Choice (B) correctly identifies the cup, but there is no waiter in the photo. Choice (D) correctly identifies the location, but there are no customers.

3. **(A)** A mechanic is working on a car engine. Choice (B) correctly identifies the car, but no one is parking it. Choice (C) correctly identifies the woman's gloves, but she isn't taking them off. Choice (D) associates *car* with *passenger*.

4. **(C)** A dentist is pointing at an X-ray displayed on a screen while a patient watches. Choice (A) correctly identifies the patient but confuses the X-ray with a TV screen. Choice (B) is incorrect because it is the patient, not the doctor, who is sitting on the chair. Choice (D) confuses similar-sounding words *watching* and *washing*.

5. **(D)** A bicycle leans against a fence with a view across the water of houses on an island. Choice (A) is incorrect because the bench is in the foreground, far from the houses on the island. Choice (B) relates *bicycle* to *cyclist*, but there is no cyclist in the photo. Choice (C) confuses similar-sounding words *biker* and *hiker*.

6. **(B)** A man is standing in what appears to be a bus stop shelter looking at his watch. Choices (A) and (C) are incorrect because there is no bus in the photo. Choice (D) correctly identifies the trash can, but the man is not standing behind it.

### PART 2: QUESTION-RESPONSE

7. **(A)** This answers the *Where* question. Choice (B) repeats the word *suit*. Choice (C) uses the word *suit* with a different meaning.

8. **(B)** This answers the *How much* question. Choice (A) would answer a *What* question. Choice (C) would answer a *What time* question.

9. **(B)** *Next Monday* answers the *When* question. Choice (A) would answer a *Where* question. Choice (C) repeats the word *vacation*.

10. **(A)** *A colleague* answers the *Who* question. Choice (B) associates *phone* and *call*. Choice (C) repeats *talk*.

11. **(A)** This answers the *Which* question. Choice (B) would answer a *Whose* question. Choice (C) repeats the word *house*.

12. **(B)** This is a logical response to the yes–no question about eating lunch. Choice (A) would answer a *Where* question. Choice (C) would answer a *What* question.

13. **(C)** This answers the indirect *What time* question. Choice (A) repeats the word *know*. Choice (B) would answer a *Where* question.

14. **(A)** *It's Lisa's* answers the *Whose* question. Choice (B) repeats *phone*. Choice (C) associates *phone* with *message*.

15. **(B)** This is a polite response to the offer to hang up the coat. Choice (A) repeats *let*. Choice (C) repeats *coat*.

16. **(A)** This answers the *When* question. Choice (B) would answer a yes-no question. Choice (C) repeats the word *proposal*.

17. **(A)** This answers the *What* question about the content of the meeting. Choice (B) would answer a *Where* question. Choice (C) would answer a *What time* question.

18. **(B)** This answers the *How* question. Choice (A) would answer a *How long* question. Choice (C) would answer a yes–no question.

19. **(C)** This is a logical response to the comment about the copier not working. Choice (A) repeats *working*. Choice (B) associates *copier* and *copies*.

20. **(C)** This answers the *What time* question. Choice (A) would answer *When,* but not *What time.* Choice (B) confuses similar-sounding words *arrive* and *drive.*

21. **(A)** This answers the yes–no question about seeing a movie. Choice (B) uses related words *told* and *tell.* Choice (C) would answer a *Where* question.

22. **(B)** This is a logical response to the offer of a ride to work. Choice (A) repeats the phrase *work tomorrow.* Choice (C) repeats the word *work.*

23. **(A)** This is a logical response to the tag question about which department the person works in. Choice (B) repeats the word *sales.* Choice (C) confuses similar-sounding words *department* and *apartment.*

24. **(C)** This is a logical response to the statement that the office isn't big enough. Choice (A) repeats the word *enough.* Choice (B) confuses similar-sounding words *meeting* and *eating.*

25. **(C)** This answers the *Where* question. Choice (A) associates *snack* with *apple* and *cookie.* Choice (B) would answer a *What time* question.

26. **(B)** This is a logical response to the indirect yes–no question about the length of the workshop. Choice (A) confuses *workshop* with the words *works* and *shop.* Choice (C) confuses *workshop* with *shop.*

27. **(A)** This is a logical response to the question about preference. Choice (B) would answer a yes–no question. Choice (C) confuses similar-sounding words *walk* and *work.*

28. **(C)** This is a logical response to the invitation to play tennis. Choice (A) would answer a *Who* question. Choice (B) would answer a *Where* question.

29. **(A)** This is a logical response to the request to turn off the lights. Choice (B) repeats the phrase *leave tonight.* Choice (C) would answer a *What time* question.

30. **(B)** This answers the *How many* question. Choice (A) would answer a *Who* question. Choice (C) would answer a *Where* question.

31. **(C)** This answers the *When* question. Choice (A) would answer a *Where* question. Choice (B) would answer a *Why* question.

## PART 3: CONVERSATIONS

32. **(C)** The man says a lot of people will be attending the conference this weekend, and the implication is that is the reason the hotel is full (booked). Choice (A) confuses the meaning of the word *booked*. Choice (B) confuses the meaning of the word *marketing*. Choice (D) confuses similar-sounding words *regretting* and *wedding*.

33. **(B)** The man says that he is looking forward to the banquet on Saturday night. Choice (A) confuses similar-sounding words *looking* and *cooking*. Choice (C) confuses similar-sounding words *chance* and *dance*. Choice (D) confuses similar-sounding words *part* and *party*.

34. **(D)** The woman says that she has to plan for a workshop she'll be giving on Sunday morning. Choice (A) is related to the word *plan*. Choices (B) and (C) are both confused with the word *workshop*.

35. **(A)** The woman says she is calling to find out if the photos her company hired the man to take are ready yet. Choice (B) associates *photos* with *camera*. Choice (C) refers to the events the man took photos of; it is in the past so this choice doesn't make sense. Choice (D) is incorrect because it is the man who has sold a service (photography) to the woman.

36. **(B)** The man says that he will *send the prints on over first thing tomorrow morning* (*prints* refers to photographs on paper). Choices (A) and (C) refer to the events where the man took the photographs; he has already attended these events. Choice (D) is what he will do this afternoon.

37. **(D)** The woman says, *I'm putting together the Silco monthly bulletin now*, a *bulletin* is a newsletter. Choices (A) and (B) are confused with the discussion about photos. Choice (C) is where the man took the photos.

38. **(D)** Both the man and the woman mention an apartment. Choice (A) is confused with the woman's asking about parking for tenants. Choice (B) is associated with the word *home*. Choice (C) repeats the word *office*—the man asks the woman to drop off the signed lease at his office.

39. **(B)** The man asks for a check for the first month's rent and the security deposit, and the woman replies *No problem*, meaning she can pay this easily. Choice (A) is something the woman will do, but she doesn't mention this until later in the conversation. Choices (C) and (D) are related to the context of the conversation but don't respond to the man's request.

40. **(A)** The woman says, *I'll take the lease home with me now*. Choice (B) is confused with the woman's asking about parking for tenants. Choices (C) and (D) are what she will do later.

41. **(B)** The woman says, *I was hoping we could take a taxi to the airport together*. Choices (A), (C), and (D) are related to the context but are not the correct answer.

42. **(C)** The man tells the woman that his flight leaves at 11:00. Choice (A) sounds similar to the correct answer. Choice (B) confuses similar-sounding words *fine* and *nine*. Choice (D) is when the woman's flight leaves.

43. **(C)** The woman says, *I've applied for a position at a firm there* (meaning *in Toronto*), and that she's going there for an interview. Choices (A) and (D) are plausible but are not the correct answer. Choice (B) is the reason for the man's trip to Chicago.

44. **(B)** The woman mentions a buyer's club and discounts on purchases and the man mentions his grocery bill, so they are at a grocery store. Choice (A) associates *employment* with *benefits*. Choice (C) repeats the word *club*. Choice (D) is associated with the mention of money.

45. **(A)** The woman says, *It's a free benefit*. Choices (B) and (C) are confused with the discounts mentioned (10% and 25%). Choice (D) is the total the man owns for the purchase he is making now.

46. **(D)** The woman says the way to become a member of the buyer's club is to fill out a form, and at the end the man says, *Sure I'll sign up*, meaning he wants to become a member of the club. Choice (A) repeats the word *card*, which the man will get after he fills out the form to become a member. Choice (B) repeats the word *bill*. Choice (C) confuses the meaning of the word *sign*.

47. **(A)** The woman mentions *this afternoon's meeting*. Choice (B) repeats *afternoon*. Choice (C) is not mentioned. Choice (D) is when the hiring fair will take place.

48. **(C)** The woman says, *My budget report is done*. Choice (A) is what the first man will report on. Choices (B) and (D) are other items on the agenda.

49. **(D)** The speakers discuss different items on the agenda, implying that there are more than usual and the woman says, *It'll be five o'clock before we get out of here*, implying that she thinks the meeting will end later than usual or later than she would want it to. Choice (A) is incorrect because there is no mention of the frequency of the meeting. Choice (B) is related to the discussion of the agenda, but the quality of the planning is not mentioned or implied. Choice (C) is confused with the woman's implication that it will end late.

50. **(D)** The man asks the woman if she has seen the proposal that *we e-mailed to you yesterday*. Choices (A) and (B) are plausible but not mentioned. Choice (C) repeats the word *mail*.

51. **(C)** After she says, *I'm sorry*, the woman asks which company the man is with by saying, *Where are you calling from?* Choices (A), (B), and (D) are reasons one might say *I'm sorry* but don't fit the context.

52. **(B)** The woman says, *I'll look it over . . . before noon today*, where *it* refers to the proposal. Choice (A) confuses *send back* with *get back*. Choice (A) repeats the word *in-box*. Choice (C) repeats the word *budget*.

53. **(B)** The man says that Mr. Kim is the *new assistant in the marketing department*. Choice (A) repeats the word *department*. Choice (C) repeats the word *assistant*. Choice (D) confuses *managed* with the related word *manager*.

54. **(A)** The woman says, *He's been here only a week.* Choice (B) sounds similar to the correct answer. Choice (C) refers to *a year,* the amount of time the man was at the company before he started meeting people. Choice (D) repeats *year* and confuses similar-sounding words *before* and *four.*

55. **(C)** The speakers discuss how Mr. Kim has introduced himself to people and learned the names of everyone in the office, and the woman says, *he certainly isn't shy.* Choice (A) repeats the word *hard.* Choice (B) repeats *learn.* Choice (D) repeats *shy.*

56. **(B)** The speakers discuss food and arranging lunch with a client, so they are at a restaurant. Choice (A) repeats the word *conference.* Choice (C) repeats the word *office.* Choice (D) associates *reservation* with *hotel.*

57. **(C)** The first woman says the place looks crowded and the man agrees, saying *A lot of people like to eat here.* Choices (A) and (D) are contradicted by the woman's and man's statements. Choice (B) is not mentioned.

58. **(B)** The speakers are talking about making arrangements for having lunch with clients at the restaurant and discussing a contract with them. Choice (A) repeats the word *office.* Choice (C) associates *food* with *grocery.* Choice (D) associates *date* with *appointments.*

59. **(D)** The man says that he will be relaxing at his cabin at the lake. Choices (A) and (C) are confused with the sales seminar mentioned by the woman. Choice (B) is confused with the client reports mentioned by the woman.

60. **(A)** The man says, *I plan to bike up there.* Choices (B) and (C) confuse *rain* with the similar-sounding words *plane* and *train.* Choice (D) confuses *far* with the similar-sounding word *car.*

61. **(D)** The woman mentions riding over bumpy roads and the possibility of rain. Choice (A) associates *leisurely,* the man's description of his vacation, with *slow.* Choice (B) is plausible but not mentioned. Choice (C) repeats the word *easy.*

62. **(A)** The man offers the woman store credit and she happily accepts it, saying, *I'll just get the same sweater but larger.* Choice (B) is related to the context but is not mentioned. Choice (C) confuses *store credit* with *credit card.* Choice (D) is what the man says he cannot give.

63. **(B)** The woman says that the sweater is *too small.* Choice (A) repeats the word *color.* Choices (C) and (D) are plausible but not mentioned.

64. **(A)** After the woman says she wants the same style sweater, the man says, *we don't have any more in blue.* Choice (B) is incorrect because the man says, *We still have plenty.* Choice (C) is related to the context but is not mentioned. Choice (D) is confused with the woman saying that she wants a larger sweater.

65. **(C)** The man says that he has a reservation, but his schedule changed and he needs to arrive earlier. Choices (A), (B), and (C) are plausible in the context but are not the reason for the call.

66. **(A)** The man mentions a meeting with his client. Choices (B) and (D) are plausible but not mentioned. Choice (C) is what the man says he doesn't have time to do.

67. **(B)** The man says he has a meeting at 11:00, so he has to arrive before then, and he says, *Just put me on a train that gets me there as close to 11:00 as possible.* Choice (A) arrives too early. Choice (C) arrives too late. Choice (D) is the train he currently has a reservation for, which he wants to change.

68. **(B)** The man says about the prices, *I know I didn't pay this much last time I was here.* Choice (A) is incorrect because no other restaurants are mentioned or implied. Choices (C) and (D) are contradicted by the correct answer.

69. **(D)** The man says he is looking for something without meat, and then he orders a sandwich. Choice (D) is the only menu item that fits this description. Choice (A) is not a sandwich and may or may not have meat. Choice (B) has meat. Choice (C) has meat and is not a sandwich.

70. **(C)** The man asks for a glass of water, and the woman replies, *Right away.* Choice (A) is not likely because the man has just ordered his food. Choice (B) fits the restaurant context but is not mentioned. Choice (D) is incorrect because the man is already looking at the menu.

## PART 4: TALKS

71. **(A)** She mentions *getting organized*, helping people *keep their homes and family life organized*, and a *well-organized office*, so her profession involves helping people get their lives organized. Choice (B) associates *research* with *professor*. Choice (C) is associated with the mention of getting a home ready for sale. Choice (D) is associated with the mention of making a house look nice.

72. **(C)** The speaker says, *I've been in the business for over ten years*; *over* means *more than*. Choices (A) and (B) don't mean the same as *over ten years*. Choice (D) is not mentioned.

73. **(B)** The speaker asks, *. . . are there any questions*, and then says, *Come on, don't be shy*, as a way of encouraging people to ask their questions. Choices (A), (C), and (D) could be situations where someone would say *Don't be shy* but don't fit the context.

74. **(A)** The speaker describes the building's past and then says that now *it is our local history museum.* Choice (B) associates *film* with *theater*. Choices (C) and (D) are past uses of the building.

75. **(B)** The speaker mentions a film and then says it will begin at 2:30. Choice (A) is something that can happen after the tour is over. Choices (C) and (D) both mention places that listeners are told they can visit.

76. **(C)** The speaker says, *please line up here by the door.* Choice (A) is confused with the suggestion to *walk the grounds.* Choice (B) repeats *door.* Choice (D) is what the listeners have probably already done.

77. **(C)** The speaker says that the event takes place *every month.* Choices (A) and (B) associates *hospital*, the location of the event, with *patients* and *doctors.* Choice (D) is incorrect because the speaker says that the event is *free.*

78. **(D)** The speaker invites listeners to *sign up for our e-mail newsletter.* Choice (A) associates *hospital* with *doctor.* Choice (B) associates *dietician*, the profession of the

speaker, with *nutrition*. Choice (C) is confused with the fact that the speaker teaches at the local college.

79. **(B)** The speaker describes the topic of the talk as *how food and exercise can help us keep in shape*. Choices (A) and (C) are associated with *dietician*. Choice (D) is mentioned as a topic that is sometimes covered in the monthly talks.

80. **(B)** The speaker says, *I got your message*, and then goes on to provide information that was requested in the message. Choice (A) relates *employee wages* and *employment*. Choice (C) is what the speaker is providing, not asking for. Choice (D) is plausible but is not the correct answer.

81. **(A)** The speaker mentions *accounts for small businesses, personal account*, and *loans*, so he works at a bank. Choice (B) relates *rent* and *rental*. Choice (C) relates *account* and *accountant*. Choice (D) relates *employee wages* and *employment*.

82. **(D)** The speakers suggests that the listener call to *set up a time* to discuss things. Choice (A) repeats the word *rent*. Choice (B) is plausible in the context. Choice (C) is not mentioned.

83. **(B)** This expression is usually used to express agreement with something that has been said, in this case, that there has been enough rain. Choices (A), (C), and (D) don't fit the meaning of the expression or the context.

84. **(C)** The speaker says that the weather will be the same *for another couple of days*, and then it will change. Choice (A) sounds similar to *Tuesday*, the day the weather will change. Choice (B) repeats *evening*, the time of the weather report. Choice (D) repeats *week*.

85. **(D)** The speaker says that there will be *high winds* on Saturday. Choice (A) is how the weather is now. Choice (B) is related to *clouds*, which the speaker says will be moving out. Choice (C) is not mentioned.

86. **(D)** The speaker is describing what will happen this evening. Choice (A) refers to the books that are for sale. Choice (B) is incorrect because the speaker will not be there. Choice (C) associates *club* with *members*.

87. **(B)** The speaker says, *we'll have our usual cookies and tea*. Choice (A) repeats *discussion*, but no mention is made of whether or not it will be interesting. Choice (C) is incorrect because there is no mention of the frequency of the program. Choice (D) repeats *film*, but there is no mention of the frequency of films.

88. **(A)** The speaker mentions that it's time to pay dues and then says, *Our treasurer is coming around now to pick up your checks*. Choices (B) and (C) will happen later. Choice (D) will happen, but it is unclear when.

89. **(A)** The speaker says that passengers for City Hall *should go downstairs to the east platform and take the local train*. Choice (B) is incorrect because the speaker says that City Hall is a local stop. Choice (C) is not mentioned. Choice (D) repeats the name of another stop.

90. **(C)** The speaker says, *This train is scheduled to leave the station in two minutes*. Choice (A) is the train's final destination, but no mention is made of the arrival time. Choice (B) is happening now. Choice (D) repeats the word *tickets*.

91. **(D)** The speaker says, *You must have a blue ticket to ride this train*, referring to the express train. Choice (A) is incorrect because the speaker mentions two other stops that the train makes. Choice (B) is incorrect because the departure time of the local train is not mentioned. Choice (C) is not mentioned.

92. **(A)** The speaker says that *the company plans to use the building to house its main offices*. Choice (B) is contradicted by the correct answer. Choice (C) is not mentioned. Choice (D) is the former use of the building.

93. **(B)** The speaker says that the fitness club is *for use of company employees*. Choice (A) associates *club* and *members*. Choice (C) is not mentioned. Choice (D) is who the showroom is for.

94. **(D)** The speaker says that the renovation work will *be completed shortly after the new year*. Choice (A) repeats the word *month*. Choice (B) is when the renovation work will begin. Choice (C) repeats the word *year*.

95. **(C)** According to the sign, nonresidents of the building cannot use the lot at any time on weekends; the caller, who is a nonresident, parked there on a Saturday. Choices (A) and (B) are allowable on weekdays, which is when the caller usually parks there. Choice (D) is incorrect because there is no parking fee mentioned.

96. **(C)** The caller says she used the lot *because I had a tennis game at the nearby courts*. Choice (A) is why she usually uses the lot. Choice (B) repeats the word *nearby*. Choice (D) is plausible but not mentioned.

97. **(B)** The caller says, *I would like to be reimbursed for the towing fee*. Choice (A) repeats *parking sticker*, which the caller says she doesn't have, but she doesn't ask for one. Choice (C) is incorrect because she has already gotten her car back. Choice (D) is incorrect because the caller says the car wasn't damaged.

98. **(B)** The speaker says that the meeting is *bimonthly*. Choice (A) confuses the meaning of bimonthly. Choices (C) and (D) repeat the word *year*, mentioned later in the talk.

99. **(D)** The speaker says he wants to change the agenda to *start with the final item*, which is, according to the graphic, *Annual staff evaluations*. Choices (A), (B), and (C) are not the final item on the agenda.

100. **(A)** The speaker says that Ms. Jones, who will talk about professional development, *is running a bit behind schedule*. Choice (B) is incorrect because the speaker says, *It looks like almost everybody is here*. Choice (C) relates *projected* and *projector*. Choice (D) is confused with the mention of last year's misunderstandings about staff evaluations.

## Reading

### PART 5: INCOMPLETE SENTENCES

101. **(A)** *Released* in this context means *made public*. Choices (B), (C), and (D) have meanings that don't fit the context.

102. **(C)** *Recommend* is followed by a gerund. Choice (A) is present tense or base form. Choice (B) is past tense. Choice (D) is a gerund or future tense.

103. **(A)** *Belongs* means *is owned by*. Choice (B) refers to the owner, not the thing that is owned. Choices (C) and (D) don't fit the context.

104. **(D)** This is an infinitive of purpose; *to finalize* describes the purpose of the meeting. Choices (A), (B), and (C) don't fit the context.

105. **(C)** *Supervisory* is an adjective modifying the noun *position*. Choice (A) is a verb. Choices (B) and (D) are nouns.

106. **(B)** *Waive* means *give up* or *cancel*. Choices (A) and (C) have the opposite meaning. Choice (D) doesn't fit the context.

107. **(D)** *If* introduces a condition. Choice (A) introduces the next or resulting action. Choice (B) introduces a contradiction. Choice (C) introduces a result.

108. **(B)** *Her* in this sentence is a singular possessive adjective referring to a woman, *Ms. Silva*. Choice (A) is a subject pronoun. Choice (C) is a possessive adjective referring to a thing. Choice (D) is a plural possessive adjective.

109. **(A)** *Instead* means *as a substitute*. Choices (B) and (C) have meanings that don't fit the context and cannot be placed at the end of a clause. Choice (D) is similar in meaning to *but* or *however*, so doesn't fit the context.

110. **(B)** *Hardly* is an adverb meaning *scarcely* or *almost none*; almost nobody showed up for the workshop. Choice (A) is an adjective meaning *not soft*. Choice (C) is an adjective meaning *strong and healthy*. Choice (D) is a noun meaning *strength*.

111. **(D)** *Until* means *up to the time*. Choice (A) means *every time*. Choice (B) means *because*. Choice (C) means *when*.

112. **(B)** *Operator* is a noun referring to a person who operates something. Choice (A) is a verb. Choice (C) is an adjective. Choice (D) is a noun but doesn't refer to a person.

113. **(C)** *Host* means *to hold a social event*. Choice (A) is what the guests do. Choices (B) and (D) have meanings that don't fit the context.

114. **(D)** This is a noun, the object of the verb *completed*. Choices (A) and (C) are verbs. Choice (B) is a noun that refers to a person.

115. **(A)** The verb *delay* is followed by a gerund. Choice (B) is infinitive. Choice (C) is past tense. Choice (D) is present tense or base form.

116. **(C)** *Adapt* means to get used to something new. Choices (A), (B), and (C) have meanings that don't fit the context.

117. **(A)** This is a base form verb following the main verb *helped*. Choice (B) is an adjective. Choice (C) is a noun. Choice (D) is an adverb.

118. **(B)** *Although* introduces a contradiction. Choice (A) introduces a cause. Choice (C) introduces a time clause. Choice (D) introduces a condition.

119. **(D)** *Readily* means *easily*. Choices (A), (B), and (C) have meanings that don't fit the context.

120. **(C)** This is an adjective modifying the noun *salary*. Choice (A) is a verb. Choices (B) and (D) are nouns.

121. **(D)** A passive verb is needed because the subject, *participants*, is not active; the subjects don't notify themselves, but someone else notifies them. Choices (A), (B), and (C) are not passive forms.

122. **(A)** *Tight*, in this context, means *limited*. Choices (B), (C), and (D) have meanings that don't fit the context.

123. **(C)** This is an adverb modifying the adjective *darker*. Choice (A) is an adjective or verb. Choice (B) is a past tense verb. Choice (D) is a noun.

124. **(B)** *Despite* is similar in meaning to *although*; it introduces a noun phrase. Choice (A) has the correct meaning but must be followed by *of*. Choices (C) and (D) have meanings that don't fit the context.

125. **(A)** This is a base form verb following the modal *should*. Choice (B) is a gerund. Choice (C) is a noun. Choice (D) is an adjective.

126. **(D)** *Decline* means *drop* or *decrease*. The company stopped publishing the magazine because there weren't many subscribers. Choices (A), (B), and (C) have meanings that don't fit the context.

127. **(B)** *While* means *at the same time as*. Choice (A) has a similar meaning but is a preposition so is not used to introduce a clause. Choice (C) means *as a result*. Choice (D) means *in addition*.

128. **(C)** *Highly* means *very*. Choices (A), (B), and (C) have meanings that don't fit the context.

129. **(B)** *Whose* in this sentence is a relative pronoun; it is possessive and means *team members' ideas*. Choices (A), (C), and (D) can all be used as relative pronouns but are not possessive.

130. **(A)** *Since* introduces a reason. Choice (A) has a similar meaning but cannot be used to introduce a clause. Choice (C) introduces a result. Choice (D) introduces a contradiction.

## PART 6: TEXT COMPLETION

131. **(C)** This is a second person possessive adjective referring to the person being addressed, the buyer of the printer. Choices (A) and (D) are not possessive adjectives; they are contractions of pronouns and *are*. Choice (B) is a third person possessive adjective.

132. **(B)** *Various* is an adjective and modifies the noun *sizes*. Choice (A) is a verb. Choice (C) is a noun. Choice (D) is an adverb.

133. **(A)** *Enclosed* means *included with* and usually refers to something that is included in an envelope or package. Choices (B), (C), and (D) have meanings that don't fit the context.

134. **(D)** This sentence logically follows the information about printing photographs. Choices (A) and (C) are too general. Choice (B) doesn't fit the context because of the reference to professional photographers.

135. **(D)** The purpose of the letter is to offer employment, or, a *position*. Choices (A), (B), and (C) have meanings that don't fit the context.

136. **(B)** This sentence fits the context of offering a job; it is one of the details that needs to be agreed on. Choices (A), (C), and (D) don't fit the context.

137. **(D)** This is a future time clause, so a present tense verb is needed. Choice (A) is present continuous. Choice (B) is future tense. Choice (C) is infinitive.

138. **(A)** The expression *look forward to* is followed by a gerund. Choice (B) is past tense. Choice (C) is present tense. Choice (D) is present tense or base form.

139. **(B)** *For* in this case introduces a purpose or reason. Choice (A) is not followed by a gerund when it is used to express a purpose. Choice (C) introduces a time clause. Choice (D) introduces a clause that describes a reason.

140. **(A)** The sentence fits the context of the notice, explaining what will happen when the building is closed. Choices (B), (C), and (D) are related to the topic of the Recreation Center but not to the information about the building being closed.

141. **(A)** *Normally* means *usually*. Choices (B), (C), and (D) have meanings that don't fit the context.

142. **(C)** *Resume* means *begin again*. Choices (A), (B), and (D) have meanings that don't fit the context.

143. **(D)** This is passive voice because the subject, *festivities*, is not active; the festivities do not hold themselves, they are held by the Tenants Association. Choices (A) and (B) are active verb forms. Choice (C) is infinitive, not a correct form for the main verb.

144. **(B)** *Socialize* means *to interact with people at a social event*; it describes what people do at a party. Choices (A) and (D) would more likely describe work-related activities. Choice (C) is a possible activity in the context but is not used with the preposition *with*; in this case, the correct structure would be *introduce yourself to*.

145. **(A)** This sentence logically follows the preceding sentence; people are invited to help out with the party, and Choice (A) gives examples of ways they can help. Choices (B), (C), and (D) are all related to the party invitation context but do not logically follow the preceding sentence.

146. **(C)** *Hope* is the verb usually used to express the desire to see someone at a social event. Choices (A), (B), and (D) have similar meanings but are not normally used in this context.

## PART 7: READING COMPREHENSION

147. **(B)** The job responsibilities describe the duties of a sales representative. Choices (A), (C), and (D) repeat words used in the text but are not the correct answer.

148. **(C)** The ad provides an e-mail address for applying. Choice (A) is not mentioned. Choice (B) should be done by e-mail, not regular mail. Choice (D) is incorrect because the ad states, *No phone calls*.

149. **(B)** Phil thinks that Marie asked him to buy paper, not envelopes, and Marie replies that she should give him a list to help him remember, *for once*, implying that his forgetfulness happens often. Choice (A) is confused with Marie's mention that she doesn't want to be late to the café. Choice (C) is incorrect because it is Phil himself, not Marie, who mentions saving money per envelope by buying the larger quantity. Choice (D) is not mentioned.

150. **(D)** Marie says that she is on her way to the café in a taxi. Choice (A) is where Phil is. Choice (B) is plausible but not mentioned. Choice (C) is where Marie is going, but she hasn't arrived yet.

151. **(C)** An auction is a type of sale, and a foreclosure auction is a sale that takes place when a property owner has not been able to make mortgage payments. Choice (A) associates *foreclosure* and *auction*. Choice (B) repeats the word *inspections*, which the ad invites potential buyers to do. Choice (D) is associated with the description given of the building but is incorrect because an auction is not a rental.

152. **(B)** The ad states, *Photos available at www.wilsonrealestate.com.* Choice (A) refers to the mention of available water and sewer services. Choice (C) is stated as not necessary. Choice (D) refers to the map that is mentioned as a means of locating the property.

153. **(C)** The text states that there are 23 towns in the service area and that Internet service will be provided to *all these towns.* Choice (A) is the number of towns that currently have partial Internet service. Choice (B) is confused with the statement *over 20 towns* (meaning *more than 20 towns*). Choice (D) is not mentioned.

154. **(A)** People are asked to express interest by presubscribing, and then the text states that the company will *initiate its installation of Internet services in the community with the largest number of presubscribers.* Choices (B), (C), and (D) are plausible but not mentioned.

155. **(A)** The $25 charge is described as being for a late fee, and the Terms and Conditions section explains that *overdue accounts are subject to a late fee.* Choices (B), (C), and (D) refer to other items on the invoice.

156. **(A)** The Terms and Conditions section states, *Amount due is payable upon receipt.* Choices (B) is incorrect because the *receipt* refers to the bill, not the fuel. Choices (C) and (D) are confused with time periods mentioned in the Errors and Inquiries section.

157. **(D)** If a customer believes there is an error on the bill, that means she disagrees with it; in this case, customers are instructed to *send your inquiry by certified mail.* Choices (A), (B), and (C) are mentioned as ways to contact the company to make payments or for other reasons.

158. **(B)** Windward offers trips that include a guide, a bus, a hotel, and meals, so it is a tour company. Choice (A) is incorrect because a resort doesn't normally include a bus tour with a guide. Choice (C) is incorrect because a travel agency doesn't normally organize guided tours. Choice (D) is incorrect because a bus service provides transportation only, not the other things mentioned on the survey.

159. **(A)** The customer gave an excellent rating only to *Accommodations*, that is, to the hotel. Choices (B), (C), and (D) refer to the other items on the survey, which were all rated less than excellent.

160. **(C)** About the bus, the customer comments that *the seats could have been softer and a bit more spacious*, meaning that the seats were hard and too small. Choice (A) is incorrect because the customer comments that the bus was clean. Choice (B) is incorrect because the customer comments that the driver was nice. Choice (D) is not mentioned.

161. **(C)** The website describes Spotless as a *residential cleaning service* and mentions signing a contract *to clean your residence*. There is no mention of cleaning any kind of place other than residences. Choice (A) is incorrect because, even though employee training is mentioned, previous experience is not. Choice (B) is incorrect because only residential cleaning is mentioned. Choice (D) is incorrect because the text states that the business has been serving the community *for over a decade*.

162. **(D)** The second paragraph describes the process of getting an on-site estimate from a customer representative and says this is required of every customer before signing a contract. Choices (A) and (B) are plausible but not mentioned. Choice (C) is contradicted by the correct answer.

163. **(B)** In the third paragraph, customers who are not satisfied are instructed to call the office to arrange to have their *next cleaning done at no charge*. Choices (A) and (C) are plausible but not mentioned. Choice (D) repeats *24 hours*, which is the time period for arranging the free cleaning.

164. **(B)** They are talking about ordering flowers, bushes, and paving stones for the front of the house and the deck, so they work in a landscaping business. Choice (A) would be the business that supplies them with plants. Choices (C) and (D) are associated with the mention of *house, deck,* and *garage.*

165. **(A)** Miki met with the client, who hired them (*We got the contract*) to do landscaping work. Choice (B) associates *contract* with *lawyer*. Choice (C) is who Ana talked with yesterday. Choice (D) is incorrect because they are the ones asking Miki about what happened at the meeting.

166. **(C)** Miki mentions the need to order bushes and Ana replies, *The bushes are in,* meaning *The bushes are at the suppliers ready to be purchased.* Choice (A) could be the meaning of this sentence in a different context (The bushes are in the ground). Choices (B) and (D) don't fit the meaning of the expression or the context.

167. **(D)** Miki mentions the need to order paving stones, and Bernard replies, *I'll take care of that,* meaning *I'll do that.* Choice (A) repeats the word *contract*, but there is no mention made of reviewing it. Choice (B) is what Ana will do. Choice (C) repeats words used in the chat but is not the correct answer.

168. **(B)** The letter is addressed to *property owners* who have *tenants*. Choice (A) repeats the word *tenants*. Choice (C) is what the company that sent the letter does. Choice (D) repeats the word *investment.*

169. **(C)** *Prospective* means *possible*; the company shows rental units to people who may possibly become tenants. Choices (A), (B), and (D) don't fit the meaning of the word.

170. **(D)** The letter states near the end of the second paragraph that the fee is based *solely on a percentage of the rents*. Choices (A) and (B) are incorrect because the letter says that even though time and service vary, *our fee to you is always the same*. Choice (C) is not mentioned.

171. **(A)** This sentence introduces the paragraph, which then goes on to describe in detail the *range of services* mentioned in the sentence. Choices (B), (C), and (D) are not the right context for this sentence.

172. **(C)** At the beginning of the article, it is stated that the market has grown *in just under two years*, implying that it started two years ago. Choice (A) is when the writer visited the market. Choice (B) is not mentioned. Choice (D) is confused with the number of vendors.

173. **(A)** In the last paragraph, the market is described as a *Saturday market*, implying that it takes place only on Saturdays. Choice (B) is incorrect because the last paragraph mentions two other markets in the city. Choice (C) is not mentioned. Choice (D) is incorrect because in paragraph 1 it is stated that the prices are higher.

174. **(A)** When people *can't get enough* of something, it means they want a lot because they really like it. Choices (B), (C), and (D) don't fit the meaning of the expression or the context.

175. **(B)** This sentence follows the quote about the popularity of the market that sells local foods and is followed itself by a further explanation of the popularity of local foods. Choices (A), (C), and (D) are not the right context for this sentence.

176. **(C)** The event includes concerts, performances by artists, and a marching band, so it is a music event. Choice (A) repeats the word *food*, but that is not the focus of the event. Choice (B) is related to *artists*, but the context makes it clear that it is musical, not visual, artists. Choice (D) is associated with the location of the event.

177. **(B)** Food is mentioned as part of the event but not as part of the package. Choice (A) is included in the package description as *round-trip rail fare*. Choice (C) is included in the description as *taxi from the station*. Choice (D) is included in the description as discounted *admission to the fairgrounds*.

178. **(A)** Melinda is planning a visit for Mr. Kim, which will include *meetings, conferences, and clients*, so he must be a business associate. Choice (B) is who Robert is. Choices (C) and (D) are not mentioned and don't fit the context.

179. **(C)** Melinda writes that Mr. Kim's visit is at the beginning of next month, the e-mail is dated April 5, and May 6 and 7 are the only dates in May for the excursion. Choices (A)and (B) are other dates shown in the brochure for the excursion, but they aren't in May. Choice (D) is in May, but it is not shown in the brochure.

180. **(B)** *Occurring* is one possible meaning of *coming up*, and it makes sense in the context. Choices (A), (C), and (D) don't make sense in the context.

181. **(D)** Both *a family wedding* and *a board of director's dinner* are mentioned, so the company works with both business and individual clients. Choice (A) is incorrect because no event size is mentioned. Choice (B) is confused with the mention of *flower vases*,

but the flowers themselves are not mentioned. Choice (C) is incorrect because only supplies are mentioned, not planning services.

182. **(A)** *Envision* means *picture in one's mind,* that is, *imagine.* Choices (B), (C), and (D) could fit the context but are not the correct meaning for this word.

183. **(C)** The flyer says, *Book before October 5 and get 15% off your entire order.* Choices (A), (B), and (C) are all mentioned in the flyer but not as ways to get a discount.

184. **(B)** The flyer says, *All events must be booked at least three weeks in advance,* and the e-mail says that the event is next week. Choice (A) is incorrect because the flyer makes no mention about limiting the number of guests. Choice (C) contradicts the information in the e-mail. Choice (D) is incorrect because the writer of the e-mail hasn't even seen the selection of colors and styles yet.

185. **(A)** The writer of the e-mail states about the party *this year we've decided to try having a sit-down lunch for a change,* implying that this hasn't been done before. Choice (B) is not mentioned. Choice (C) is confused with the description of the attenders: *all of them members of our staff,* which does not have the same meaning. Choice (D) is incorrect because the e-mail states, *We have a little money to spare,* meaning they have some extra money.

186. **(A)** The information on the web page says that it is convenient to get downtown by bus or subway. Choice (B) is incorrect because the information states that it is 15 minutes away from downtown. Choice (C) is incorrect because the inn is described as *historic.* Choice (D) is incorrect because there is on-street parking only.

187. **(B)** Only two of the rooms are described as having king-size beds. Choices (A), (C), and (D) are all mentioned near the top of the web page.

188. **(C)** In her e-mail, Ms. Schwartz asks for a room for the week of the Writer's Workshop, which, according to the schedule, takes place July 20–26. Choices (A) and (D) are dates given for other activities. Choice (B) is the dates of the Inventor's Expo, which Ms. Schwartz had originally planned to attend.

189. **(C)** Ms. Schwartz needs a room with two queen-size beds, and this is the only one available. Choices (A) and (B) don't have 2 queen-size beds. Choice (C) has the beds and the view Ms. Schwartz wants, but it is sold out.

190. **(D)** The Footwear Convention in September ends with a *running competition.* The events described for the months mentioned in Choices (A), (B), and (C) do not include any kind of race.

191. **(C)** The order form shows in the first column that pens are sold in packs of 12 and in the second column that the customer ordered 4 packs. Choices (A), (B), and (D) confuse the references of *4* and *12.*

192. **(A)** At the bottom of the order form it is stated that there is *Free shipping on orders over $100,* and the order total is $155. Choice (B) is incorrect because the space for a coupon code has been left blank. Choice (C) refers to the link to join the frequent buyer's club, but there is no indication that the customer has done this. Choice (D) is contradicted by the correct answer.

193. **(B)** The first e-mail states that the customer will receive the order *on or before May 1*. Choice (A) is the date the first e-mail was sent. Choices (C) and (D) mention the date the second e-mail was sent.

194. **(B)** The second e-mail states, *those items are out of stock indefinitely*, meaning that the company doesn't have them and doesn't know when they might be available again, if ever. Choices (A), (C), and (D) are plausible but not mentioned.

195. **(D)** The second e-mail provides a phone number *If you wish to change your order* and then states, *We may have similar items in stock*. Choices (A), (B), and (C) are plausible but not mentioned.

196. **(A)** The meeting agenda items mention *advertising, sales, market research*, and a *product exhibition*, so it is likely for the marketing department. Choices (B), (C), and (D) are not departments that are likely to be discussing all these topics.

197. **(B)** The first item on the agenda, which Bob was supposed to present, has been postponed, according to the e-mail. Since the e-mail states that everything else will stay the same, we can assume that the order of agenda items doesn't change, making the sales report first. Choice (A) is the postponed item. Choices (C) and (D) are later on the agenda.

198. **(C)** The memo states, *Things should be back to normal next week*, implying that the carpet cleaning job will be finished before then. Choices (A), (B), and (D) are not mentioned.

199. **(B)** The areas being cleaned this week are the ones that were not cleaned last week; therefore, the areas that are not being cleaned this week and that are available for use were cleaned last week. Choices (A) and (C) are not mentioned. Choice (D) is the opposite of what is implied about the size.

200. **(D)** *Drawback* means *problem* or *disadvantage*. Choices (A), (B), and (C) are not the correct meaning for this word.

# Audioscripts

## TOEIC PRACTICE EXAM 1

### Listening Comprehension

#### PART 1: PHOTOGRAPHS

> **Directions:** You will see a photograph. You will hear four statements about the photograph. Choose the statement that most closely matches the photograph and fill in the corresponding oval on your answer sheet.
>
> **Track 2**
>
> **Example**
>
> Now listen to the four statements.
>
> (A) She's getting on a plane.
> (B) She's reading a magazine.
> (C) She's taking a nap.
> (D) She's holding a glass.
>
> Statement (B), "She's reading a magazine," best describes what you see in the picture. Therefore, you should choose answer (B).

1. Look at the photo marked number 1 in your test book.
   (A) They're shaking hands.
   (B) They're filling their glasses.
   (C) They're applauding the speaker.
   (D) They're waving to their friends.

   [5-second pause]

2. Look at the photo marked number 2 in your test book.
   (A) The train is moving fast.
   (B) It's a rainy day.
   (C) Their umbrellas are in the closet.
   (D) They're walking on the sidewalk.

   [5-second pause]

3. Look at the photo marked number 3 in your test book.
   (A) The carpenter is using a drill.
   (B) The patient is sitting up.
   (C) The driver is wearing gloves.
   (D) The dentist is treating the man.

   [5-second pause]

4. Look at the photo marked number 4 in your test book.
   (A) They're talking about the house.
   (B) They're closing the window.
   (C) They're printing the plans.
   (D) They're catching a mouse.

   [5-second pause]

5. Look at the photo marked number 5 in your test book.
   (A) The plane has already landed.
   (B) The passengers are ready to board.
   (C) The train has left the station.
   (D) The pilot has a uniform.

   [5-second pause]

6. Look at the photo marked number 6 in your test book.
   (A) Their hats are in their hands.
   (B) The window is broken.
   (C) Their bags are in the car.
   (D) They're looking at clothes.

[5-second pause]

7. Look at the photo marked number 7 in your test book.
   (A) He's walking down the hall.
   (B) He's wearing a bathing suit.
   (C) He's talking to his colleagues.
   (D) He's looking out the window.

[5-second pause]

8. Look at the photo marked number 8 in your test book.
   (A) The customers are sitting inside.
   (B) The chairs are on the sidewalk.
   (C) The waiter is standing by the window.
   (D) The tables are in the kitchen.

[5-second pause]

9. Look at the photo marked number 9 in your test book.
   (A) She's reading a newspaper.
   (B) She's eating a meal.
   (C) She's looking at new shoes.
   (D) She's reporting the news.

[5-second pause]

10. Look at the photo marked number 10 in your test book.
    (A) There is a big truck on the road.
    (B) The bridge crosses a river.
    (C) There isn't any traffic on the highway.
    (D) The cars are passing under the bridge.

[5-second pause]

## PART 2: QUESTION-RESPONSE

**Directions:** You will hear a question and three possible responses. Choose the response that most closely answers the question and fill in the corresponding oval on your answer sheet.

Track 3

**Example**

Now listen to the sample question.

You will hear:

How is the weather?

You will also hear:

(A) It's raining.
(B) He's fine, thanks.
(C) He's my boss.

The best response to the question *How is the weather?* is choice (A), *It's raining.* Therefore, you should choose answer (A).

11. What time did the program begin?
    (A) Just after ten o'clock.
    (B) Yes, he can program computers.
    (C) Please begin again.

[5-second pause]

12. Is this your coat?
    (A) Yes, this wall needs a new coat of paint.
    (B) Yes, it's mine.
    (C) Yes, I saw the note.

[5-second pause]

13. It looks like it's starting to rain.
    (A) I hope we'll meet again.
    (B) Yes, he looks like he's ready to start.
    (C) Here, please take my umbrella.

[5-second pause]

14. Where did you leave the newspaper?
    (A) Yes, it's brand new.
    (B) I put it on your desk.
    (C) I usually read it before breakfast.

[5-second pause]

15. How many people showed up for the meeting?
    (A) There will be a lot of people here.
    (B) I showed them to everybody.
    (C) More than 20.

    [5-second pause]

16. Who gave you this assignment?
    (A) My boss told me to do it.
    (B) I haven't signed it yet.
    (C) He gave it to me yesterday.

    [5-second pause]

17. How long did the plane ride last?
    (A) About five hours.
    (B) No, it wasn't long.
    (C) She was the last one to get there.

    [5-second pause]

18. It's very warm in here.
    (A) I think it's in here.
    (B) I warned you about it.
    (C) I'll open a window.

    [5-second pause]

19. That's your desk by the door, isn't it?
    (A) I plan to buy a new desk.
    (B) No, mine's over there.
    (C) Let's sit by the door.

    [5-second pause]

20. When will they arrive?
    (A) I expect them in an hour.
    (B) They plan to drive.
    (C) They'll arrive by train.

    [5-second pause]

21. Who was that on the phone?
    (A) Please call later.
    (B) I'll give you my phone number.
    (C) It was Mr. Kim.

    [5-second pause]

22. What color is your car?
    (A) It's silver with a black interior.
    (B) No, that's not my car.
    (C) It's fairly new.

    [5-second pause]

23. Where can I find the copy machine?
    (A) I agree. We need a new copy machine.
    (B) It's just down the hall to the left.
    (C) You'll find that it works very well.

    [5-second pause]

24. I'm really hungry.
    (A) There's no need to hurry.
    (B) Please don't be angry.
    (C) Me, too. Let's take a lunch break.

    [5-second pause]

25. Why did they get here so late?
    (A) We're going to need eight.
    (B) Their train was delayed.
    (C) They're getting in later this afternoon.

    [5-second pause]

26. Where do you want to eat?
    (A) I don't care for that kind of food.
    (B) Let's try the restaurant across the street.
    (C) No, there's no heat. You'll have to put on a warm sweater.

    [5-second pause]

27. It takes about an hour to get to the airport.
    (A) Then we should leave here by 3:00.
    (B) It's a very modern airport.
    (C) I don't really like to fly.

    [5-second pause]

28. How much did the new computer cost?
    (A) Not much. I bought it on sale.
    (B) No, we're not lost.
    (C) I rarely use a computer.

    [5-second pause]

29. What day is the meeting?
   (A) We'll be meeting many new people.
   (B) There isn't enough seating.
   (C) It's scheduled for Friday.

   [5-second pause]

30. Who did you have dinner with?
   (A) She's looking much thinner.
   (B) Just a few business colleagues.
   (C) We ate in a hurry.

   [5-second pause]

31. Do you work in this building?
   (A) Yes, on the third floor.
   (B) It's quite an old building.
   (C) I often work weekends.

   [5-second pause]

32. Whose briefcase is this?
   (A) I think it's mine.
   (B) Please be brief.
   (C) Take it, just in case.

   [5-second pause]

33. Did you mail those letters?
   (A) We can talk about it later.
   (B) There are some envelopes in my desk.
   (C) Yes, I took them to the post office
       at noon.

   [5-second pause]

34. Why weren't you at the office yesterday?
   (A) I was feeling sick.
   (B) This is your office.
   (C) Yes, today is the day.

   [5-second pause]

35. This is a very nice hotel.
   (A) Don't worry. I won't tell.
   (B) Yes, it is. I always stay here.
   (C) You'll need to make a reservation.

   [5-second pause]

36. How can I get downtown?
   (A) Just put it down here.
   (B) The subway is the fastest way.
   (C) You can get some tomorrow.

   [5-second pause]

37. When can I call you?
   (A) There's a phone on my desk.
   (B) Just call me Kim.
   (C) Call me at my office tomorrow.

   [5-second pause]

38. What's the matter with Tom?
   (A) He just lost his job.
   (B) Please stop that chatter.
   (C) Yes, that's the one that belongs to Tom.

   [5-second pause]

39. What would you like to drink?
   (A) Here's a clean glass.
   (B) I don't know what to think.
   (C) Just some hot tea, please.

   [5-second pause]

40. Where did you leave your car?
   (A) He gave me his card.
   (B) I parked it across the street.
   (C) I drive almost every day.

   [5-second pause]

## PART 3: CONVERSATIONS

**Track 4**

**Directions:** You will hear a conversation between two people. You will see three questions on each conversation and four possible answers. Choose the best answer to each question and fill in the corresponding oval on your answer sheet.

Questions 41–43 refer to the following conversation.

Woman: His plane is due to arrive at four thirty. I think we should go pick him up at the airport.

Man: Good idea. But we'll need to leave at three if we're going to be on time. It's a bit far to get there.

Woman: You're right. And I don't think we should take a taxi. The subway's much faster.

Man: Okay. That sounds like a good plan. I'll meet you at your office and we can walk to the station together.

41. What time will they leave for the airport?

[8-second pause]

42. How will they get to the airport?

[8-second pause]

43. Where will the speakers meet?

[8-second pause]

Questions 44–46 refer to the following conversation.

Man: Excuse me. Can you tell me where I can find manila envelopes?

Woman: They're on Aisle six, on the shelf below the printer paper. And you're in luck. They're on sale this week for twenty percent off.

Man: Great. I always love to save money.

Woman: If you don't see the style you want, I'd be happy to order some for you, and you'd still get the twenty percent discount if you order today.

44. Where does this conversation take place?

[8-second pause]

45. What is the man looking for?

[8-second pause]

46. What does the woman offer to do?

[8-second pause]

Questions 47–49 refer to the following conversation.

Woman:   Mr. Lee called. He'd like to set up an appointment with you at eleven tomorrow morning to go over the marketing plan.

Man:   Can't do it. I'll be in a meeting with the accountants then. Do you think he can do it later in the day?

Woman:   I'll call and find out. What time would be best for you?

Man:   See if he can meet with me at two o'clock. That'll give me time to get some lunch after I'm finished with the accountants.

47. What will the man be doing at eleven o'clock tomorrow morning?

[8-second pause]

48. What does Mr. Lee want to discuss?

[8-second pause]

49. What does the woman want to know?

[8-second pause]

Questions 50–52 refer to the following conversation.

Man:   Do you think you can have those copies ready this afternoon? They need to be mailed out as soon as possible.

Woman:   I'm sorry. I didn't get the originals until just before lunch, and you need them all collated and stapled, right? I'll have them for you tomorrow morning.

Man:   All right. That'll have to do. I asked for seventy-five copies, didn't I?

Woman:   Yes, but I'm going to make eighty-five. We'll need those ten extra for the office staff and the file. By the way, could you give me the addresses so I can get the labels ready?

50. When will the copies be ready?

[8-second pause]

51. What are the extra copies for?

[8-second pause]

52. What does the woman ask the man for?

[8-second pause]

Questions 53–55 refer to the following conversation.

Man:   I called the Grand Hotel this morning and booked you a room for Wednesday and Thursday nights.

Woman:   Would you mind calling back and asking them to add a night? I'd like to stay over Friday and get some sightseeing in.

Man:   I'll do it after lunch, if you don't mind. Right now I have to finish typing these reports.

Woman:   Fine. That's not a problem. Just please don't forget to do it.

53. Who is the man, most likely?

   [8-second pause]

54. How many nights does the woman want to stay at the hotel?

   [8-second pause]

55. What does the woman ask the man to do?

   [8-second pause]

Questions 56–58 refer to the following conversation.

| | |
|---|---|
| Woman: | What terrible weather. Have you ever seen such thick fog? I've heard it's caused a lot of problems on the highway. |
| Man: | I know. As a matter of fact, Jack just called and said he'll be at least an hour late because the traffic is so heavy. |
| Woman: | He should have taken the train. I did, and I wasn't delayed even one minute. |
| Man: | Lucky you. I hope it clears up soon because I have to get to a two o'clock meeting. |

56. What's the weather like?

   [8-second pause]

57. How does Jack probably get to work?

   [8-second pause]

58. What will the man be doing at two o'clock?

   [8-second pause]

Questions 59–61 refer to the following conversation.

| | |
|---|---|
| Man: | Can you tell me how to get to the post office, please? |
| Woman: | Certainly. Just go straight ahead for five blocks, turn left, go down two blocks and you'll see it on the corner, next to the bank. |
| Man: | Thank you. Do you know if there's any parking near there? |
| Woman: | Oh, yes. The library parking lot is just across the street. You can usually find a space there, and it's free. |

59. Where does the man want to go?

   [8-second pause]

60. Where is it?

   [8-second pause]

61. What does the woman say about the library?

   [8-second pause]

Questions 62–64 refer to the following conversation.

Man:       Listen. You won't believe this. I just found out I've been chosen employee of the
           year.
Woman:     How exciting! You deserve it. I suppose you'll have to give a speech at the annual
           banquet.
Man:       Yes, I'm a little nervous about that part of it. I guess I'll have to do some
           preparation for it.
Woman:     You'd better get started soon. It's already September and the banquet is next
           month. I could help you write your speech if you'd like.

62. Why is the man excited?

[8-second pause]

63. When is the banquet?

[8-second pause]

64. What does the woman offer to do?

[8-second pause]

Questions 65–67 refer to the following conversation.

Woman:     It looks like this restaurant is closed. What'll we do? I am so hungry!
Man:       I know a café that stays open late. I can call and check if they're still open. If you
           don't mind ordering sandwiches, that is. That's all they serve.
Woman:     I don't mind sandwiches. I guess we shouldn't have waited till so late to eat. Oh,
           and I forgot my wallet, too. Did you bring a credit card?
Man:       No, but don't worry. I'll pay. I have plenty of cash on me. It's only ten o'clock.
           We should be able to find some place that's open.

65. What does the woman want to do?

[8-second pause]

66. What is the problem?

[8-second pause]

67. How will the man pay?

[8-second pause]

Questions 68–70 refer to the following conversation.

Woman:   I'm looking for a business suit, but not for myself. I want it for a birthday present for my husband.

Man:   These summer suits just arrived. The material is very fine, and look at these colors—white, beige . . .

Woman:   This light blue is very nice, but I need another color, something more serious. It's for a conference with his boss. This black suit is just what I want.

Man:   Yes, it's a very fine suit and a real bargain, too, at only five hundred dollars. You couldn't get a suit like this for less than that.

68. Who is the woman shopping for?

[8-second pause]

69. What color suit does the woman want?

[8-second pause]

70. What does the man say about the suit?

[8-second pause]

**PART 4: TALKS**

**Track 5**

**Directions:** You will hear a talk given by a single speaker. You will see three questions on each talk, each with four possible answers. Choose the best answer to each question and fill in the corresponding oval on your answer sheet.

Questions 71–73 refer to the following announcement.

May I have your attention, please? Train number sixteen scheduled to depart for New York City at seven thirty will begin boarding in five minutes. All passengers for New York, please approach Gate eleven now. Have your ticket ready to show the gate agent. This is an all-reserved train. Please check your ticket to make sure you have a reservation on this train before approaching the gate. Carry-on luggage is permitted on this train and must be stored on the overhead racks. Let the gate agent know if you will need assistance with this.

71. What will happen in five minutes?

[8-second pause]

72. Who can ride this train?

[8-second pause]

73. What should passengers do with their luggage?

[8-second pause]

Questions 74–76 refer to the following recording.

Thank you for calling the Prescott downtown office. If you know your party's extension, you may dial it at any time. To open a new account, press one. To transfer funds between accounts, press two. For questions about an existing account or to report a lost or stolen credit card, press three. To order checks, press four. To apply for a loan, press five. To speak with a customer service representative, press six. To hear this menu again, press zero at any time.

74. What kind of a business is Prescott?

[8-second pause]

75. What should a caller press to speak to a customer service representative?

[8-second pause]

76. What can a caller do by pressing zero?

[8-second pause]

Questions 77–79 refer to the following talk.

Are there times when you find your energy lagging at work? Many people do. Most people do their best work in the morning. After lunch, however, people often find that it is hard to feel energetic enough to tackle the afternoon's work. How can you keep working productively until the workday ends? First, don't make the mistake of drinking coffee. After the caffeine has worn off, you will just feel more tired than ever. Sugary snacks have the same effect. Instead, stand up and take a brisk walk around the office. Do this for five minutes every hour to stay refreshed and energized.

77. When do people often lack energy?

[8-second pause]

78. What does the speaker recommend to maintain energy?

[8-second pause]

79. How often should this be done?

[8-second pause]

Questions 80–82 refer to the following advertisement.

Magruder's is closing its uptown branch, and everything in the store must go. Come on in to find the bargains of a lifetime. Desks, chairs, computer stands, bookshelves, filing cabinets, you name it, we've got it on sale. You won't have to look far to find bargains here. Everything is marked down sixty-five percent off its usual price. The sale begins next week and continues until the end of the month. Don't miss this sale. We promise you won't go home empty-handed.

80. What kind of business is Magruder's?

[8-second pause]

81. What is suggested about Magruder's?

[8-second pause]

82. What will happen at Magruder's this month?

[8-second pause]

Questions 83–85 refer to the following advertisement.

Are you feeling bored at your job? Do you want to be earning more money? At the Computer Training Institute, we will train you to become a sought-after, high-earning computer technician. You will learn how to repair computers and related equipment. After you finish our six-month course, our employment office will prepare you for job interviews and help you find a position as a computer technician or technical assistant. Take advantage of our special low tuition. You pay only two thousand dollars for six months of training. That's all! New courses start soon. Visit our website today to sign up.

83. What is being offered?

[8-second pause]

84. How much does it cost?

[8-second pause]

85. How can one take advantage of the offer?

[8-second pause]

Questions 86–88 refer to the following weather report.

Welcome to the midday weather update. It's time to put away those shorts and sandals. Winter has arrived. Snow is falling over much of our region and will continue to fall throughout the afternoon and evening. The weather has caused dangerous road conditions, and several accidents have been reported. Commuter trains are also experiencing numerous delays. If you don't have urgent business away from home, then don't go out. Snowfall will continue overnight and will end by early tomorrow morning. Tomorrow promises to be clear, but cold and windy.

86. How is the weather today?

[8-second pause]

87. What does the speaker suggest listeners do?

[8-second pause]

88. When will the weather change?

[8-second pause]

Questions 89–91 refer to the following announcement.

Good morning, and welcome to the third annual conference of the Business Owners Association. All conference workshops will take place in the conference rooms on the first floor of the hotel. At noon, lunch will be served in the Garden Restaurant on the ground floor. Following lunch, we will enjoy hearing our guest speaker, Dr. Lucille Snow of the Ambient Company. Afternoon workshops begin at one thirty. At two there will be a computer software demonstration in the auditorium for anyone interested. Because the weather is so nice, we will enjoy our afternoon refreshments outside on the patio between five and six o'clock.

89. What is the main purpose of this talk?

[8-second pause]

90. Who is Lucille Snow, most likely?

[8-second pause]

91. Where will refreshments be served?

[8-second pause]

Questions 92–94 refer to the following announcement.

May I have your attention, please? Because of construction work, Park Street Station is closed. All passengers for Park Street Station will have to exit the train at Center Station. Bus service is available at Center Station to carry passengers to Park Street. After exiting the station, please line up at the curb for a bus. Please avoid crowding. Buses will leave frequently, but there may be some delays because of street traffic. We are very sorry for the inconvenience. The station is scheduled to reopen in three weeks. Thank you for your cooperation.

92. What is the problem?

[8-second pause]

93. What is the cause of the problem?

[8-second pause]

94. How long will the problem last?

[8-second pause]

Questions 95–97 refer to the following news report.

The president left early Tuesday for a five-nation tour of South America. During his ten-day tour, he will meet with national leaders to discuss the current economic situation. He will also attend a banquet given by the International Science Association, where he will present awards to leading international scientists. On his return, the president plans to take a few days of rest, which he will spend with his family at their beach house.

95. How many countries will the president visit on his tour?

[8-second pause]

96. What will the president talk about with national leaders?

[8-second pause]

97. What will the president do when his trip is over?

[8-second pause]

Questions 98–100 refer to the following talk.

Before we end the meeting, I'd like to let you all know of an opportunity. A management training workshop is being offered next month, on Tuesday, December thirteenth. If any of you would like to attend, let me know and I will make the arrangements. The workshop will last all day and should be quite interesting. They will provide lunch, so all you will need to bring is a laptop computer, which we can provide from the office. I understand that they will be filming this session, so be prepared to appear on camera! Please let me know before the end of this week if you would like to attend, and I will put your name on the list.

98. What opportunity is offered?

[8-second pause]

99. When will it happen?

[8-second pause]

100. What should people bring?

[8-second pause]

# TOEIC PRACTICE EXAM 2

## Listening Comprehension

### PART 1: PHOTOGRAPHS

**Track 6**

**Directions:** You will see a photograph. You will hear four statements about the photograph. Choose the statement that most closely matches the photograph and fill in the corresponding oval on your answer sheet.

**Example**

Now listen to the four statements.

(A) She's getting on a plane.
(B) She's reading a magazine.
(C) She's taking a nap.
(D) She's holding a glass.

Statement (B), "She's reading a magazine," best describes what you see in the picture. Therefore, you should choose answer (B).

1. Look at the photo marked number 1 in your test book.
   (A) The car is parked in the garage.
   (B) The street is covered with snow.
   (C) The man is driving slowly.
   (D) The white flowers are in bloom.

   [5-second pause]

2. Look at the photo marked number 2 in your test book.
   (A) The janitor is fixing the lights.
   (B) The author is writing a book.
   (C) The professor is giving a lecture.
   (D) The student is cleaning the blackboard.

   [5-second pause]

3. Look at the photo marked number 3 in your test book.
   (A) The ship is loaded with cargo.
   (B) The passenger is standing on the deck.
   (C) The boat is in the middle of the ocean.
   (D) The captain is giving orders.

   [5-second pause]

4. Look at the photo marked number 4 in your test book.
   (A) She's drinking the liquid.
   (B) She's removing her mask.
   (C) She's washing her gloves.
   (D) She's looking at a test tube.

   [5-second pause]

5. Look at the photo marked number 5 in your test book.
   (A) The computers are on the table.
   (B) The curtains are closed.
   (C) The man has a magazine.
   (D) The woman is looking at the man.

   [5-second pause]

6. Look at the photo marked number 6 in your test book.
   (A) She's looking for a suit.
   (B) She's picking apples from the tree.
   (C) She's going to buy some fruit.
   (D) She's cleaning pears to make a pie.

   [5-second pause]

7. Look at the photo marked number 7 in your test book.
   (A) The waiters are drinking from glasses.
   (B) The two men are shaking hands.
   (C) The workers are filing the documents.
   (D) The women are climbing the stairs.

   [5-second pause]

8. Look at the photo marked number 8 in your test book.
   (A) They're waiting to enter the museum.
   (B) They're taking pictures of the room.
   (C) They're looking at paintings on the wall.
   (D) They're sitting on a bench.

   [5-second pause]

9. Look at the photo marked number 9 in your test book.
   (A) They are painting the fence.
   (B) Bushes are growing along the fence.
   (C) The fence is taller than the houses.
   (D) There is a fence between the two houses.

   [5-second pause]

10. Look at the photo marked number 10 in your test book.
    (A) He's putting on his jacket.
    (B) He's opening his briefcase.
    (C) He's trying on the trousers.
    (D) He's lying on the bed.

    [5-second pause]

## PART 2: QUESTION-RESPONSE

**Track 7**

**Directions:** You will hear a question and three possible responses. Choose the response that most closely answers the question and fill in the corresponding oval on your answer sheet.

**Example**

Now listen to the sample question.

You will hear:

How is the weather?

You will also hear:

(A) It's raining.
(B) He's fine, thanks.
(C) He's my boss.

The best response to the question *How is the weather?* is choice (A), *It's raining.* Therefore, you should choose answer (A).

11. It was nice meeting you.
    (A) It was a pleasure to meet you, as well.
    (B) No, it was a boring meeting.
    (C) He said that the meeting will be tomorrow.

    [5-second pause]

12. Does Mr. Kim work here?
    (A) Yes, he left it here.
    (B) He's a hard worker.
    (C) No, his office is down the hall.

    [5-second pause]

13. Why can't you open the door?
    (A) We don't need more.
    (B) I don't have a key.
    (C) There's a pen on the floor.

    [5-second pause]

14. Whose car is that?
    (A) He has a brand new car.
    (B) It belongs to my boss.
    (C) Let's take a drive.

    [5-second pause]

15. What time did they arrive?
    (A) She'll arrive before the movie begins.
    (B) There were five of them.
    (C) They got here at six o'clock.

    [5-second pause]

16. Did you forget something?
    (A) Yes, I left my coat at the office.
    (B) No, don't get anything.
    (C) I can get you something.

    [5-second pause]

17. Where is the bus stop?
    (A) It makes frequent stops.
    (B) It was a long ride.
    (C) It's right across the street.

    [5-second pause]

18. How often are there staff meetings?
    (A) About twice a month.
    (B) They're in the conference room.
    (C) He's reading very well.

    [5-second pause]

19. May I have your address?
    (A) We moved to a new house last month.
    (B) Thank you. It's a new dress.
    (C) I live at 16 Maple Avenue.

    [5-second pause]

20. Did anyone call while I was out?
    (A) Yes, there's a phone message on your desk.
    (B) No, it isn't cold outside.
    (C) I'll call you back tomorrow.

    [5-second pause]

21. What do you want for dinner?
    (A) I almost never cook.
    (B) How about a steak and some salad?
    (C) He used to be thinner.

    [5-second pause]

22. How many books did you sell?
    (A) I read as often as I can.
    (B) I sold only ten.
    (C) I don't think he looks well.

    [5-second pause]

23. When is your vacation?
    (A) To the beach
    (B) At the station
    (C) Next August

    [5-second pause]

24. Why didn't they come to lunch with us?
    (A) I don't usually drink punch.
    (B) They were too busy with work.
    (C) It was at a nice little restaurant.

    [5-second pause]

25. Do you need anything from the store?
    (A) Yes, I could use some paper and envelopes.
    (B) No, there were fewer than four.
    (C) I go shopping about once a week.

    [5-second pause]

26. Where do you keep pens?
    (A) They're in my desk drawer.
    (B) I prefer to use black ink.
    (C) That's my pen, I believe.

    [5-second pause]

27. It looks like it might rain soon.
    (A) Night will come soon.
    (B) The train arrives at noon.
    (C) Then don't forget to take your umbrella.

    [5-second pause]

28. Which coat is yours?
    (A) That's a very nice coat.
    (B) It's that black one in the closet.
    (C) I need it because it's very cold today.

    [5-second pause]

29. This room is very warm.
    (A) I warned you about them.
    (B) Let's open all the windows.
    (C) There's not enough room.

    [5-second pause]

30. How close is the subway station?
    (A) It's just down the street.
    (B) You can wear those clothes.
    (C) They just remodeled the station.

    [5-second pause]

31. Where can I buy a newspaper?
    (A) We could use some new paper.
    (B) I read it every day.
    (C) At the store on the corner.

    [5-second pause]

32. What's your favorite sport?
    (A) It's a very busy port.
    (B) I enjoy playing tennis.
    (C) He did me a favor.

    [5-second pause]

33. I thought the movie was very interesting.
    (A) No, he's not interested in movies.
    (B) Yes, I liked it, too.
    (C) We're moving tomorrow.

[5-second pause]

34. Where did you put the package?
    (A) I left it on your desk.
    (B) I'll mail it tomorrow.
    (C) I packed all the suitcases.

[5-second pause]

35. Weren't you at the workshop last Friday?
    (A) No, I was sick that day.
    (B) Yes, I work in that shop.
    (C) It's closed on Fridays.

[5-second pause]

36. Who was at the meeting this morning?
    (A) He's always greeting everyone.
    (B) We're meeting in the morning.
    (C) Almost the whole staff was there.

[5-second pause]

37. You look hungry.
    (A) I am. I didn't have breakfast this morning.
    (B) No, I'm not in a hurry.
    (C) Yes, I've already had a chance to look at it.

[5-second pause]

38. Where do you live?
    (A) You can leave it on my desk.
    (B) In a small apartment downtown.
    (C) You don't need to give anything.

[5-second pause]

39. When will the copies be ready?
    (A) I need fifty copies.
    (B) I'll have them for you this afternoon.
    (C) This machine makes very clear copies.

[5-second pause]

40. Will you need more paper?
    (A) This paper is thicker.
    (B) No, I think this is enough.
    (C) I write quite a lot.

[5-second pause]

## PART 3: CONVERSATIONS

**Track 8**

**Directions:** You will hear a conversation between two people. You will see three questions on each conversation and four possible answers. Choose the best answer to each question and fill in the corresponding oval on your answer sheet.

Questions 41–43 refer to the following conversation.

Woman:  I'm calling an emergency meeting for tomorrow morning at ten. Do you think you can be there?

Man:  I can be there, but not on time. I'll probably be about fifteen minutes late. Why are you calling the meeting, anyhow?

Woman:  The accounting department has been having some difficulties, and paychecks will be delayed until next week. I want to explain the situation to everyone.

Man:  You know this has happened before. It's really getting to be a bad problem. I can't pretend not to be annoyed about it.

41.  What does the man tell the woman?

[8-second pause]

42.  Why is the woman calling a meeting?

[8-second pause]

43.  How does the man feel about the situation?

[8-second pause]

Questions 44–46 refer to the following conversation.

Man:  May I see your ticket, please? Thank you. You're in Row ten, Seat A, right next to the window.

Woman:  Great. Thanks. Can you tell me how long the flight will be?

Man:  There shouldn't be any delays on a nice cloudless day like today, so I expect we'll be arriving right on schedule at two o'clock. We'll begin food service in about half an hour.

Woman:  I didn't know there would be food. That's wonderful. I'm starving. Will there be a movie, too?

44.  Where does this conversation take place?

[8-second pause]

45.  What's the weather like?

[8-second pause]

46.  What will happen in a half an hour?

[8-second pause]

Questions 47–49 refer to the following conversation.

Woman: Do you think you could help me move this desk to the other side of the room? I want to put it near the window so I can work in the daylight.

Man: I'm sorry. I hurt my back. I'm not supposed to lift heavy things. Why don't you get Samantha to help you?

Woman: She's not here. She'll be at a meeting downtown all afternoon. I guess I'll just have to wait until tomorrow and have her help me then.

Man: Yes, she'll be here tomorrow. She should be able to help you out.

47. What does the woman want to do?

[8-second pause]

48. Why can't the man help her do it?

[8-second pause]

49. What does the woman decide to do?

[8-second pause]

Questions 50–52 refer to the following conversation.

Man: I'm looking for some warm winter gloves. My wife said you had them on sale.

Woman: Yes, these gloves are on sale. They come with matching hats. We also have these scarves that would look just right with them.

Man: Yes, that's all very nice, but I really just want the gloves. That's what I came down here for. I'll take this black pair.

Woman: Very good. That comes to fifteen dollars and fifty cents with tax. Would you like me to put them in a bag for you?

50. What will the man buy?

[8-second pause]

51. What color will he take?

[8-second pause]

52. How much will he pay?

[8-second pause]

Questions 53–55 refer to the following conversation.

Man: Could you make some copies of this report for me please? I need two hundred and twenty-five. I hope that's not too many.

Woman: It's not, but I hope you don't need them soon. Things are really busy now and there are three jobs ahead of you.

Man: That's okay. I actually don't need them today at all, but can you have them ready before the conference tomorrow morning?

Woman: That shouldn't be a problem. I'll have them all copied, collated, and stapled before the conference begins.

53. When does he need them?

[8-second pause]

54. Why can't the woman make the copies now?

[8-second pause]

55. What does the woman decide to do?

[8-second pause]

Questions 56–58 refer to the following conversation.

Woman:  Good morning. I'd like to see Mr. Lee, please.
Man:    I'm sorry. He's not here. He's out of town on a business trip. Do you have an appointment?
Woman:  Well, actually, no. I thought I could just come by. I didn't realize he was away. When do you expect him back?
Man:    Not until next week. If you leave your name and phone number, I can have him call you when he returns to the office.

56. What does the woman want to do?

[8-second pause]

57. Where is Mr. Lee?

[8-second pause]

58. What does the man suggest that the woman do?

[8-second pause]

Questions 59–61 refer to the following conversation.

Man:    Oh, no! Look at the time! There's no way I can make it downtown on time for my doctor's appointment.
Woman:  Sure you can. Take my car. Just bring it back in time for me to get to my computer class tonight. Here's the key.
Man:    Great. Thanks. Is it parked in the garage?
Woman:  No, it's that old blue van across the street. Drive carefully. It looks like it might rain.

59. Where does the man have to go?

[8-second pause]

60. Where is the woman's car?

[8-second pause]

61. What does the woman warn the man about?

[8-second pause]

Questions 62–64 refer to the following conversation.

Man: I'm sorry, Ms. Jones has already left the office and gone home.

Woman: She left already? That's not possible. She knew we had a meeting this afternoon.

Man: Well, she left right around three o'clock. She wanted to avoid the traffic. You know how bad it gets when there's a heavy rain like this.

Woman: I'll have to call her at home, then. This report can't wait. We have to talk about it before tomorrow.

62. Why did Ms. Jones leave the office early?

[8-second pause]

63. What is the woman surprised about?

[8-second pause]

64. What is the weather like?

[8-second pause]

Questions 65–67 refer to the following conversation.

Woman: I mailed you those photographs the other day. Did you get them?

Man: No. I've been looking out for them, but they haven't arrived yet. When did you mail them?

Woman: Three days ago. I think I should report them as lost.

Man: Relax. You mailed them Monday and today's only Thursday. Let's just wait another day before we panic. Then if they aren't here by tomorrow, you can resend them. You have copies, don't you?

65. What did the woman send the man?

[8-second pause]

66. How long does the man suggest waiting?

[8-second pause]

67. What does the woman want to do now?

[8-second pause]

Questions 68–70 refer to the following conversation.

Woman: We're playing tennis at the park this afternoon. Would you like to join us?

Man: Thanks, but I was at the club all morning playing golf, and I'm really wiped out.

Woman: Then you'd better rest. You're planning on going to the banquet at the hotel tonight, aren't you? There will be dinner and dancing.

Man: Yes, I wouldn't miss it for anything. I've been looking forward to it. I bought my tickets weeks ago.

68. What does the woman invite the man to do?

[8-second pause]

69. Why doesn't the man want to do it?

[8-second pause]

70. Where will the man be tonight?

[8-second pause]

## PART 4: TALKS

**Directions:** You will hear a talk given by a single speaker. You will see three questions on each talk, each with four possible answers. Choose the best answer to each question and fill in the corresponding oval on your answer sheet.

Track 9

Questions 71–73 refer to the following recording.

Thank you for calling Jiffy Computer Services, your neighborhood computer sales and repair service. Is your computer giving you problems? No problem! We'll have it up and running in no time. Our technicians are available to help you twenty-four hours a day, seven days a week. To speak with Tech Support, please stay on the line. If you would like to purchase a new computer, press one to speak with the next available sales consultant. To make an appointment for a consultation in your home or office, press two. For billing questions, press three. To hear this menu again, press zero.

71. When can a customer speak with a technician?

[8-second pause]

72. How can a caller make an appointment?

[8-second pause]

73. What can a caller do by pressing three?

[8-second pause]

Questions 74–76 refer to the following talk.

Welcome to the first lecture in our series. We are fortunate to have as our speaker tonight Dr. Clothilde Swanson, who is visiting us as part of her book promotion tour. Dr. Swanson will talk with us tonight about her newest book, *Small Business Success*. She will explain the innovative business system that she has outlined in her book, a system that will result in success for any small-business man or woman. After the talk, Dr. Swanson's book will be available for sale at the back of the room near the exit sign. Books are twenty-five dollars each. Unfortunately, because of unforeseen circumstances, refreshments will not be served this evening. Don't miss next month's lecture on Thursday, March first, when Arnold Jones will speak about customer relations in the twenty-first century.

74. What will Dr. Swanson talk about?

[8-second pause]

75. What will happen after the talk?

[8-second pause]

76. When will the next lecture take place?

[8-second pause]

Questions 77–79 refer to the following advertisement.

Your comfort is important. That's why we developed the EZ Sit desk chair. Its special ergonomic construction supports your posture while you sit at your desk. Its high-class design looks great in any office. Go ahead and work at your computer all day. With the EZ Sit chair you'll feel so comfortable, you'll never want to leave your desk! But don't take our word for it. Visit your local EZ Furniture Showroom and try out our chairs in person. Or phone our customer service line at eight hundred-three-eight-seven-nine-eight-seven-six for a free catalog and order form. Mention this ad and receive a fifteen percent discount off your first in-store or catalog purchase of an EZ Sit chair. Offer ends May twentieth.

77. What product is being advertised?

[8-second pause]

78. Where would this product be used?

[8-second pause]

79. How much is the discount?

[8-second pause]

Questions 80–82 refer to the following weather report.

Good morning and welcome to the weather update. The drought continues today with clear skies and plenty of sunshine. Temperatures will reach a high of around eighty-five degrees this afternoon, with overnight lows in the high sixties. Expect more of the same tomorrow and for the rest of the week. But don't despair. Change is in the air! Over the weekend a cold front will be moving in, bringing with it cloudy skies, so we should be getting that long-awaited rain by Sunday.

80. What is the weather like today?

[8-second pause]

81. What is suggested about the weather?

[8-second pause]

82. When will the weather change?

[8-second pause]

Questions 83–85 refer to the following talk.

If you travel frequently for business, you may find it difficult to maintain a healthful diet. When you're worn out from travel or work, you might just settle for the most convenient or cheapest meal—fast food, a salty snack, or a sweet dessert. Don't give up so easily. There is a simple way to make sure you get your basic nutrition even while on the road. The solution is to make sure to eat a big breakfast every morning. Most restaurants offer healthful breakfast choices such as cereal and eggs. By eating a big breakfast, you guarantee that you get at least one nutritious meal a day. In addition, you will have the energy to work all morning.

83. Who is the talk for?

[8-second pause]

84. What does the speaker recommend eating?

[8-second pause]

85. Why is this recommended?

[8-second pause]

Questions 86–88 refer to the following recording.

Thank you for calling the dental office of Dr. Elizabeth Pekar. If this is an emergency, hang up immediately and contact the on-call dentist, Dr. Rogers, at three-two-four-nine-zero-one-four. Our normal office hours are Monday through Friday from seven thirty until four o'clock, and Saturday from nine until noon. To make an appointment for an office visit, please call back when the office is open. If you would like to speak with the doctor or any of the office staff, please leave a message after the beep and we will get back to you as soon as possible.

86. What should a caller do in an emergency?

[8-second pause]

87. What times does the office close on Saturday?

[8-second pause]

88. Why should a caller leave a message?

[8-second pause]

Questions 89–91 refer to the following announcement.

The fifth annual Center City Job Fair will take place this coming Saturday at the Royal Hotel from eleven thirty until four o'clock. Representatives from more than one hundred companies will be on hand to talk with you about career opportunities in their fields. Preliminary job application forms will be available, and attendees are advised to bring up to twenty-five copies of their résumé. Throughout the day special seminars will be offered on topics such as The Successful Job Interview, Write a Winning Résumé, and Dressing for Business Success. Admission is just ten dollars, and tickets will be available at the door.

Don't miss the event that the Center City Daily newspaper has called "the best job fair in the country."

89. Who would be most interested in the advertised event?

    [8-second pause]

90. What costs ten dollars?

    [8-second pause]

91. What should people bring to the event?

    [8-second pause]

Questions 92–94 refer to the following announcement.

Welcome aboard flight three-oh-five to Mexico City. Our travel time today will be just under six hours, putting us in Mexico City at four fifteen. The rain clouds that were threatening us earlier have cleared up and we should have smooth sailing all the way to our destination, with bright, sunny skies. If you'll look out the windows on the left side, you should be able to see Lake Pine in the distance, with a view of the mountains behind it. Enjoy your trip and thank you for flying with us.

92. Where would this announcement be heard?

    [8-second pause]

93. What does the speaker suggest about the trip?

    [8-second pause]

94. What can be seen out the window?

    [8-second pause]

Questions 95–97 refer to the following news report.

The heavy rains this month have caused flooding throughout the region. In Woodsville last night, the Green River overflowed its banks, sending water rushing through the main streets of the town. Streets are still under water this morning, and most of the downtown area has been closed off by the police. Citizens are asked to stay away from downtown until the streets have been reopened. Local flooding and mudslides have caused hazardous driving conditions throughout the area, so drive with caution. Clear skies are predicted for the next few days, and the floods should recede by the weekend.

95. What is the problem?

    [8-second pause]

96. What are citizens asked to do?

    [8-second pause]

97. When will the situation improve?

    [8-second pause]

Questions 98–100 refer to the following advertisement.

Spend your next vacation with us. The Lakeside Hotel and Resort offers a relaxing location with spectacular views and luxuriously comfortable rooms, April through January. Relax by the lake or enjoy the many activities available—lake and pool swimming, tennis, hiking, and boating. In the evenings enjoy a four-course meal at our top-rated restaurant. Our early season weekend package, including room, breakfast buffet, one dinner, and access to all resort activities costs just seven hundred dollars per couple. This special low rate is available from April fifteenth through May thirty-first. If you enjoy winter sports, call to find out about our winter vacation specials available December through January.

98. What can guests do at the Lakeside Resort?

    [8-second pause]

99. How much does the special weekend package cost?

    [8-second pause]

100. When is the resort closed?

    [8-second pause]

# TOEIC PRACTICE EXAM 3

## Listening Comprehension

### PART 1: PHOTOGRAPHS

**Track 10**

**Directions:** You will see a photograph. You will hear four statements about the photograph. Choose the statement that most closely matches the photograph and fill in the corresponding oval on your answer sheet.

**Example**

Now listen to the four statements.

(A) She's getting on a plane.
(B) She's reading a magazine.
(C) She's taking a nap.
(D) She's holding a glass.

Statement (B), "She's reading a magazine," best describes what you see in the picture. Therefore, you should choose answer (B).

1. Look at the photo marked number 1 in your test book.
   (A) The scientists are using a microscope.
   (B) The teachers are using a telescope.
   (C) The doctors are examining the patient.
   (D) The professors are hanging up their coats.

   [5-second pause]

2. Look at the photo marked number 2 in your test book.
   (A) All the bookshelves are empty.
   (B) There is a book on the sofa.
   (C) A man is sitting on the sofa.
   (D) The carpet is next to the table.

   [5-second pause]

3. Look at the photo marked number 3 in your test book.
   (A) The drivers are having an argument.
   (B) The cars are parked in the lot.
   (C) The taxman is going to his office.
   (D) The cab is moving down the street.

   [5-second pause]

4. Look at the photo marked number 4 in your test book.
   (A) They're arranging the seating.
   (B) They're having a meeting.
   (C) They're fixing the heating.
   (D) They're enjoying what they're eating.

   [5-second pause]

5. Look at the photo marked number 5 in your test book.
   (A) It's starting to rain.
   (B) They're on a plane.
   (C) The aisle is crowded.
   (D) The bookstore is open.

   [5-second pause]

6. Look at the photo marked number 6 in your test book.
   (A) They're standing on the steps.
   (B) They're waving good-bye to each other.
   (C) They're walking up the stairs.
   (D) They're holding on to the railing.

   [5-second pause]

7. Look at the photo marked number 7 in your test book.
   (A) The customer is ordering drinks.
   (B) He's pouring the tea.
   (C) The man is drinking water.
   (D) The waiter is carrying a tray.

   [5-second pause]

8. Look at the photo marked number 8 in your test book.
   - (A) The attendant is parking the van.
   - (B) The passenger is sitting in front.
   - (C) The mechanic is repairing the car.
   - (D) The driver is ready to leave.

   [5-second pause]

9. Look at the photo marked number 9 in your test book.
   - (A) The cooks are finished working.
   - (B) The shelves are filled with books.
   - (C) The library is closed now.
   - (D) The woman is writing a book.

   [5-second pause]

10. Look at the photo marked number 10 in your test book.
    - (A) He's fixing the shelf.
    - (B) He's opening the boxes.
    - (C) He's lifting a heavy load.
    - (D) He's driving through the city.

    [5-second pause]

## PART 2: QUESTION-RESPONSE

Track 11

**Directions:** You will hear a question and three possible responses. Choose the response that most closely answers the question and fill in the corresponding oval on your answer sheet.

**Example**

Now listen to the sample question.

You will hear:

How is the weather?

You will also hear:

(A) It's raining.
(B) He's fine, thanks.
(C) He's my boss.

The best response to the question *How is the weather?* is choice (A), *It's raining.* Therefore, you should choose answer (A).

11. What time will they arrive?
    - (A) Around noon, I think.
    - (B) I had a good time, too.
    - (C) It was almost midnight when they got here.

    [5-second pause]

12. Is Mr. Kim away on vacation?
    - (A) Yes, the train is at the station.
    - (B) Yes, he'll be back next week.
    - (C) Yes, she's enjoying her time off.

    [5-second pause]

13. I don't have a pen with me.
    - (A) Write your name on the line.
    - (B) It will be open tomorrow.
    - (C) Here, please use mine.

    [5-second pause]

14. Where can I put my coat?
    - (A) It was a long trip by boat.
    - (B) Hang it in this closet.
    - (C) I bought it at the mall downtown.

[5-second pause]

15. How many books did you buy?
    - (A) The time went by so fast.
    - (B) These books cost under twenty dollars.
    - (C) I bought only two.

[5-second pause]

16. Who did you have lunch with?
    - (A) An old school friend.
    - (B) At the restaurant on the corner.
    - (C) I'm not very hungry.

[5-second pause]

17. How long did the meeting last?
    - (A) He's always reading something.
    - (B) We usually meet on the last Friday of the month.
    - (C) Only about thirty minutes.

[5-second pause]

18. This store looks very crowded.
    - (A) Then let's shop someplace else.
    - (B) I think I'd like some more.
    - (C) It's a very cloudy day.

[5-second pause]

19. How long have you worked here?
    - (A) Yes, I work here.
    - (B) For close to five years.
    - (C) No, I'm sorry, he's not here.

[5-second pause]

20. The carpet looks very dirty.
    - (A) The books are in the car.
    - (B) My car is outside.
    - (C) It's time to get it cleaned.

[5-second pause]

21. How much did your train ticket cost?
    - (A) They got lost in the rain.
    - (B) About four hours or so.
    - (C) More than two hundred dollars.

[5-second pause]

22. The bank is open today, isn't it?
    - (A) Yes, it's open every day except Sunday.
    - (B) No, it's not a very fine day.
    - (C) I opened an account there yesterday.

[5-second pause]

23. Why isn't Ms. Lee here today?
    - (A) She's away on a business trip.
    - (B) I'm sorry, I didn't hear.
    - (C) I'll tell her when I see her.

[5-second pause]

24. How far is the restaurant from here?
    - (A) The food is really delicious.
    - (B) It's about a five-minute walk.
    - (C) I ate there last week.

[5-second pause]

25. What did they talk about at the meeting?
    - (A) The seating was not very comfortable.
    - (B) Almost everyone talked at the meeting.
    - (C) They discussed the budget for next year.

[5-second pause]

26. Who made these photocopies?
    - (A) Use the copy machine downstairs.
    - (B) Mr. Brown made them.
    - (C) I made ten photocopies.

[5-second pause]

27. Where can I park my car?
    - (A) There's a garage across the street.
    - (B) The park is two blocks from here.
    - (C) My car is a dark color, too.

[5-second pause]

28. Which seat would you prefer?
    (A) I don't usually eat meat.
    (B) Their appointment was deferred.
    (C) I'd like to sit by the window.

[5-second pause]

29. This office is very small.
    (A) No, she's not that tall.
    (B) Yes, I'm looking for a bigger one.
    (C) You can call me at the office.

[5-second pause]

30. Which hotel did you stay at?
    (A) We stayed at the one by the airport.
    (B) I promise not to tell.
    (C) I'll make the reservation soon.

[5-second pause]

31. How was the weather during your vacation?
    (A) We went to the beach.
    (B) It was sunny every day.
    (C) We were there for two weeks.

[5-second pause]

32. Where did you put the newspaper?
    (A) Because I like to keep up with the news.
    (B) I read it before breakfast.
    (C) I left it in your office.

[5-second pause]

33. Who did you see at the party?
    (A) Divide it into three parts.
    (B) Just a few old friends.
    (C) There was food and dancing.

[5-second pause]

34. When will the report be ready?
    (A) I usually listen to the news report.
    (B) I'll finish it this afternoon.
    (C) I like reading.

[5-second pause]

35. What did they serve for lunch?
    (A) A really delicious chicken dish.
    (B) They served it in the cafeteria.
    (C) It was just a small bunch.

[5-second pause]

36. It's very dark in here.
    (A) He always wears dark colors.
    (B) I'm sorry. You can't park here.
    (C) I'll turn on some lights.

[5-second pause]

37. Where will you be this afternoon?
    (A) We'll be there very soon.
    (B) In my office, as usual.
    (C) It's a lovely afternoon.

[5-second pause]

38. Is that a new sweater?
    (A) Yes. Do you like it?
    (B) No, he isn't any better.
    (C) It's made of pure wool.

[5-second pause]

39. What time did you get home last night?
    (A) You can use the phone on my desk.
    (B) It was after midnight by the time I
        got there.
    (C) Their home is quite modern.

[5-second pause]

40. Excuse me. Do you have the time?
    (A) That's a good-looking watch.
    (B) No, I think this one's mine.
    (C) Yes, it's half past eight.

[5-second pause]

## PART 3: CONVERSATIONS

**Track 12**

**Directions:** You will hear a conversation between two people. You will see three questions on each conversation and four possible answers. Choose the best answer to each question and fill in the corresponding oval on your answer sheet.

Questions 41–43 refer to the following conversation.

Woman:    They're showing a great movie at the theater tonight. Do you want to go with me?

Man:      I wish I could, but I have to work late. Why don't you go ahead without me?

Woman:    You're always working late. The movie doesn't start till after nine. Why don't you just work a few hours and then meet me at the theater?

Man:      That's a good plan. You go early and get the tickets. I'll look for you by the front entrance at around nine.

41. What does the woman want to do?

    [8-second pause]

42. Why does the man say he can't do this?

    [8-second pause]

43. What does the man say he will do?

    [8-second pause]

Questions 44–46 refer to the following conversation.

Man:      We really need to go over this report together. Why don't we meet in my office tomorrow at noon and look at it then. I could order some lunch to eat while we work.

Woman:    That might be a problem. I have a doctor's appointment in the early afternoon and it's all the way downtown.

Man:      Could we meet in the morning, then? I have a conference early, but I'd be free by ten thirty.

Woman:    That should be all right. I'll see you tomorrow.

44. Why does the man want to meet with the woman?

    [8-second pause]

45. Where will they meet?

    [8-second pause]

46. What does the woman have to do tomorrow afternoon?

    [8-second pause]

Questions 47–49 refer to the following conversation.

Woman: Are you going up? Great. Could you push the button for the tenth floor, please?
Man: Of course. Do you live in this building?
Woman: No, I'm just visiting a colleague from work. She recently moved here from another city. She has an apartment on the tenth floor. Do you live here?
Man: Yes, I do. It's not a bad building to live in, really. It's close to all the stores, the rooms are spacious, and there are nice views from the top floors.

47. Where does this conversation take place?

[8-second pause]

48. Who is the woman visiting?

[8-second pause]

49. What is the man's opinion of the building?

[8-second pause]

Questions 50–52 refer to the following conversation.

Man: Could I book Conference Room three for a meeting next Friday morning?
Woman: That depends. Will you be done before eleven o'clock? The room's already booked from eleven to one for a luncheon.
Man: I don't think that'll be a problem. We're scheduled to start at eight and should be finished by ten.
Woman: That should work out, then. You can use the chairs that will be set up for the luncheon. Just be sure to put them back in place before you leave.

50. What does the man want to do?

[8-second pause]

51. What time will he finish?

[8-second pause]

52. What does the woman ask him to do?

[8-second pause]

Questions 53–55 refer to the following conversation.

Man: After hours of conference, they've finally agreed on a cleaning schedule. They're starting on the hallways today.
Woman: It's about time. They're filthy! What about the front office? And the cafeteria?
Man: The front office is scheduled for cleaning on Wednesday. I don't know about the cafeteria, but I suppose they'll get to it someday soon.
Woman: Well, I hope they get to it before the end of next week. I'm giving a workshop that Friday, and I need to use the cafeteria space.

53. What will be cleaned today?

    [8-second pause]

54. What does the woman suggest about the office cleaning?

    [8-second pause]

55. What will the woman do next week?

    [8-second pause]

Questions 56–58 refer to the following conversation.

Woman:  I'm visiting relatives in Chicago next week. How long do you think it would take me to get there by train?

Man:    Oh, it's a long trip—sixteen hours at least. Why don't you take the plane? It would get you there in two hours.

Woman:  I've done that too many times before, I'm afraid. I thought it would be more interesting to try the train this time.

Man:    I think it sounds like a waste of time. I always fly, myself. If I'm going on a business trip or on vacation, I always take a plane, even if it is expensive.

56. Why is the woman going to Chicago?

    [8-second pause]

57. How long does the trip take by train?

    [8-second pause]

58. Why does the woman prefer the train to the plane?

    [8-second pause]

Questions 59–61 refer to the following conversation.

Man:    This package can't wait. I have to mail it today. Where's the local post office?

Woman:  It's just two blocks from here, but it's closed for the holiday. You could try the main post office, but it's more than a mile from here.

Man:    Maybe that's a bit far to walk. I suppose I could take the bus.

Woman:  The buses are so slow on holidays, and the weather is getting bad. Take a taxi. I'll go find one for you.

59. Why is the local post office closed?

    [8-second pause]

60. How far away is the main post office?

    [8-second pause]

61. How will the man get to the post office?

    [8-second pause]

Questions 62–64 refer to the following conversation.

Man:       I really enjoy my lunch break. It's the only time I have in the day to be alone.

Woman:   Don't you eat in the cafeteria with everyone else from your department?

Man:       No. My assistant eats there, and most of the rest of my officemates go to a restaurant together, but I prefer to eat at my desk and have forty-five minutes to myself.

Woman:   I usually meet some friends for a half-hour lunch at a café. Then I walk in the park for fifteen minutes before going back to the office.

62. Who does the man eat lunch with?

[8-second pause]

63. Where does the man eat lunch?

[8-second pause]

64. What does the woman do during her lunch break?

[8-second pause]

Questions 65–67 refer to the following conversation.

Woman:   I reserved a room for three nights, but it turns out I'm going to have to stay four.

Man:       That shouldn't be a problem. Here's your key—Room one-oh-seven. Do you have any luggage?

Woman:   Just this one suitcase. You know, it's so nice and warm out, I thought I'd go for a walk now before dinner. Is there a park near here?

Man:       Yes, very near. Just go down to the corner, where you'll see a bank. Take a left onto Main Street, and you'll see the park right in front of you.

65. What does the woman request?

[8-second pause]

66. What does the woman want to do now?

[8-second pause]

67. What is the weather like?

[8-second pause]

Questions 68–70 refer to the following conversation.

Woman:   I've booked a seat on the ten-thirty train to Vancouver, and, look, it's ten fifteen now. I have to find the gate quickly.

Man:       It's boarding now at Gate nine, right over there. May I see your ticket?

Woman:   Here it is. Is there someone who can carry my suitcase for me? It's quite heavy.

Man:       You can give it to the agent at the gate, and she'll check it for you.

68. Where does this conversation take place?

[8-second pause]

69. What does the woman want to do?

[8-second pause]

70. What does the woman need help with?

[8-second pause]

## PART 4: TALKS

Track 13

**Directions:** You will hear a talk given by a single speaker. You will see three questions on each talk, each with four possible answers. Choose the best answer to each question and fill in the corresponding oval on your answer sheet.

Questions 71–73 refer to the following recording.

Thank you for calling West Regional Electrical Utilities Company. Your call is important to us. Our regular office hours are seven A.M. until nine P.M., Monday through Friday. If you are calling outside of office hours, please press zero to leave a message. To report a power outage or other emergency, press one. For billing questions, press two. To open a new account, press three. To hear this message in Spanish, press four. To repeat this message, press five. If you wish to speak directly with a customer service representative, please stay on the line, and your call will be answered in turn.

71. What time does the office open?

[8-second pause]

72. How can a caller open an account?

[8-second pause]

73. What can a caller do by pressing two?

[8-second pause]

Questions 74–76 refer to the following report.

This is your early-morning traffic update. Traffic is moving smoothly throughout the region with the exception of Highway ten near the approach to the White River Bridge. Because of repairs, the bridge is closed and all traffic is being rerouted down Park Avenue to the City Tunnel. Expect delays in this area of up to twenty minutes during the morning rush hour. Unfortunately, this situation may continue for several more months, as repairs aren't due to be completed until early September. Tune in for the next traffic update at nine o'clock.

74. What is the main purpose of this talk?

[8-second pause]

75. What is being repaired?

[8-second pause]

76. When will the repairs be finished?

[8-second pause]

Questions 77–79 refer to the following advertisement.

Are you looking for a better career? Why not try the exciting field of law? In just six short months, you can become a legal assistant. That's right! At the Legal Training Institute, we prepare you to work in any law office, assisting with document preparation, research, computer data entry, and customer service. Our evening and weekend class schedule is designed for busy people like you who work all day, and our low, low prices, starting at just five hundred dollars for introductory-level classes, will fit any budget. Call now to find out if a career as a legal assistant is right for you. Already convinced? Visit our website to download an application and start studying as soon as next week.

77. What kind of job does this school train for?

[8-second pause]

78. How many months does the course last?

[8-second pause]

79. How can someone get an application?

[8-second pause]

Questions 80–82 refer to the following announcement.

Good afternoon. Flight five-forty-six to Honolulu is about to begin boarding at Gate eleven. All passengers for Honolulu, please approach Gate eleven now. We will board passengers with small children first, and then we will begin boarding from the back of the plane, starting with Rows thirty to thirty-five. Please remember, only one piece of carry-on luggage, excluding purses and coats, is allowed. Passengers are asked to check extra luggage with the gate attendant. Have a pleasant trip and thank you for flying with us.

80. Where would this announcement be heard?

[8-second pause]

81. What are passengers asked to do now?

[8-second pause]

82. Who will get on first?

[8-second pause]

Questions 83–85 refer to the following announcement.

Don't miss the annual Summer Fun Festival coming up next month. Games, food, dancing, and crafts will be available to all at the City Fairgrounds from Thursday, July fifteenth through Sunday, July eighteenth, all for the low, low admission price of twenty dollars. Thursday night's opening ceremonies are free and open to the public and will feature a special concert performed by local musicians. Remember, this event is free, but tickets must be reserved in advance. Call the Public Events Office to reserve your tickets now.

83. What is indicated about the event?

[8-second pause]

84. When will the event take place?

[8-second pause]

85. What will happen on Thursday night?

[8-second pause]

Questions 86–88 refer to the following report.

The National Airport Workers Union threatened a strike today following the announcement by Blue Sky Airlines that there will be a salary freeze for all airport workers effective immediately. This is because of the financial difficulties and the decrease in the number of passengers the airline has been suffering over the past few months. Airport workers had been expecting a salary increase next month. Blue Sky claims that they are acting within the terms of their contract with the airport workers. Union leaders disagree and plan to strike next week. Blue Sky officials and representatives from the mayor's office and the National Transportation Board will meet with union leaders at the Royal Hotel tomorrow afternoon to discuss ways to avert the strike.

86. Why will airport workers go on strike?

[8-second pause]

87. When will the strike begin?

[8-second pause]

88. Where will union leaders and airline officials meet?

[8-second pause]

Questions 89–91 refer to the following announcement.

Welcome aboard train number six to New York City. We should be arriving at our destination in just under three hours. Please remember, smoking is prohibited on all parts of the train. The fourth car from the rear is the designated quiet car. Cell phone use is not permitted in that car and laptops may be used only with the sound turned off. The food service car will open in fifteen minutes. Hot and cold drinks, sandwiches, and snacks will be available for sale. Enjoy your trip!

89. What is suggested about the fourth car from the rear?

[8-second pause]

90. What is not allowed anywhere on the train?

[8-second pause]

91. What will happen in fifteen minutes?

[8-second pause]

Questions 92–94 refer to the following recording.

Thank you for calling the Deluxe Downtown Theater. Tickets are now available for our new musical show, *Cats and Dogs!*, opening next week. Show times are Saturday and Sunday at two P.M. for the matinee, and Thursday through Saturday at eight P.M. for the evening show. Matinee tickets are twenty-four dollars each, and evening tickets are thirty dollars. Children under age twelve can see the show for half the price of a regular adult ticket. To reserve your tickets, wait for the beep, then leave a message. Be sure to speak slowly and clearly. Or, send your request by mail to the Deluxe Downtown Theater, fifty-six State Street, Springfield.

92. What kind of show will take place at the theater?

[8-second pause]

93. What costs twenty-four dollars?

[8-second pause]

94. How can tickets be reserved?

[8-second pause]

Questions 95–97 refer to the following weather report.

Gardeners will be happy over the next few days as heavy rains arrive in our area, putting an end to the long dry spell. The sun and humidity we are enjoying this morning will give way to increasingly cloudy skies this afternoon. Expect heavy rains overnight with partial clearing toward morning. Today's highs will reach eighty around noon, then fall steadily throughout the afternoon. Expect lows of around fifty overnight. Rain is expected to continue on and off throughout the week, so put aside those beach plans, folks, and stay home with a good book. This is not the week to be outdoors.

95. What is the weather like now?

[8-second pause]

96. What will the low temperature be tonight?

[8-second pause]

97. What does the announcer recommend doing this week?

[8-second pause]

Questions 98–100 refer to the following announcement.

Welcome to the Adventure Vacations lecture series. Our guest speaker this evening is Jonas Jones, who will talk to us about the exciting adventures of mountain climbing. Mr. Jones was featured in a recent documentary film about climbing Mount Everest, a climb he has attempted several times. Tonight he will share with us the basics of extreme mountain climbing and talk about how to prepare and what equipment to buy. He has available for sale copies of his book *How to Climb Mountains,* for a special price of thirty-two dollars. As a reminder, next month's program has been canceled because of unforeseen circumstances. The following month we will enjoy a talk on scuba diving.

98. Who is the guest speaker?

[8-second pause]

99. How much does the book cost?

[8-second pause]

100. What will happen next month?

[8-second pause]

# TOEIC PRACTICE EXAM 4

## Listening Comprehension

### PART 1: PHOTOGRAPHS

> **Track 14** 🔊
>
> **Directions:** You will see a photograph. You will hear four statements about the photograph. Choose the statement that most closely matches the photograph and fill in the corresponding oval on your answer sheet.
>
> **Example**
>
> Now listen to the four statements.
>
> (A) She's getting on a plane.
> (B) She's reading a magazine.
> (C) She's taking a nap.
> (D) She's holding a glass.
>
> Statement (B), "She's reading a magazine," best describes what you see in the picture. Therefore, you should choose answer (B).

1. Look at the photo marked number 1 in your test book.
   (A) They're delivering newspapers.
   (B) They're riding in an elevator.
   (C) They're signing the documents.
   (D) They're going down the escalator.

   [5-second pause]

2. Look at the photo marked number 2 in your test book.
   (A) The bridge crosses to the other shore.
   (B) The ferry is carrying cars over the water.
   (C) The boat is ready to tie up at the dock.
   (D) The cars are driving down a wide highway.

   [5-second pause]

3. Look at the photo marked number 3 in your test book.
   (A) They're in the pedestrian crosswalk.
   (B) They're talking with their friends.
   (C) They're driving their cars through the city.
   (D) They're strolling down the sidewalk.

   [5-second pause]

4. Look at the photo marked number 4 in your test book.
   (A) The customers are in the restaurant.
   (B) The man is feeding the chickens.
   (C) The chefs are in the kitchen.
   (D) The waiter is serving the meal.

   [5-second pause]

5. Look at the photo marked number 5 in your test book.
   (A) He's cleaning the window with rags.
   (B) He's walking through the door.
   (C) He's holding several bags.
   (D) He's shopping inside the store.

   [5-second pause]

6. Look at the photo marked number 6 in your test book.
   (A) The flowers are in the pitcher.
   (B) The fruit is growing on the tree.
   (C) There are many flowers in the garden.
   (D) The peaches are in a bag.

   [5-second pause]

7. Look at the photo marked number 7 in your test book.
   (A) He's buying a round-trip ticket.
   (B) He's on his way to court.
   (C) He's going to pack his bags.
   (D) He's walking through the airport.

   [5-second pause]

8. Look at the photo marked number 8 in your test book.
   (A) Their hats are in their hands.
   (B) One man is pointing at something.
   (C) The phone is on the desk.
   (D) They're painting one of the buildings.

[5-second pause]

9. Look at the photo marked number 9 in your test book.
   (A) He's walking home.
   (B) He's dialing a number.
   (C) He's talking on the phone.
   (D) He's cooking a meal.

[5-second pause]

10. Look at the photo marked number 10 in your test book.
   (A) They're having a conference.
   (B) They're all wearing glasses.
   (C) They're eating dinner.
   (D) They're reading the papers.

[5-second pause]

## PART 2: QUESTION-RESPONSE

**Track 15**

**Directions:** You will hear a question and three possible responses. Choose the response that most closely answers the question and fill in the corresponding oval on your answer sheet.

**Example**

Now listen to the sample question.

You will hear:

How is the weather?

You will also hear:

(A) It's raining.
(B) He's fine, thanks.
(C) He's my boss.

The best response to the question *How is the weather?* is choice (A), *It's raining.* Therefore, you should choose answer (A).

11. Who were you talking to on the phone earlier?
   (A) I think it belongs to John.
   (B) I was chatting with my boss about work.
   (C) I left it on my desk this morning.

[5-second pause]

12. Let's take our lunch hour now.
   (A) Great idea. I'm starving.
   (B) I take an hour for lunch.
   (C) I usually have it at a restaurant.

[5-second pause]

13. Do you know when the report is due?
   (A) We import most of our supplies.
   (B) He's due here later on this afternoon.
   (C) We need to hand it in at the end of the week.

[5-second pause]

14. Where's the nearest bank?
    (A) They'll cash that check for you there.
    (B) I'd like to thank them for their help.
    (C) There's one right across the street.

[5-second pause]

15. Which car did you say is yours?
    (A) It's the small blue one over there.
    (B) I believe it's rather far from here.
    (C) We took a very interesting tour.

[5-second pause]

16. Why did John leave the office early?
    (A) You can just leave them on my desk.
    (B) He had an urgent appointment.
    (C) It's still too early to have lunch.

[5-second pause]

17. How was the movie?
    (A) It was really boring.
    (B) We got the tickets online.
    (C) Just move everything over there.

[5-second pause]

18. Could you help me copy these documents?
    (A) I don't enjoy shopping.
    (B) I signed the documents.
    (C) I'm sorry. I'm too busy right now.

[5-second pause]

19. Does anyone know whose coat this is?
    (A) I believe he put it in the closet.
    (B) I'm quite sure it's Mary's.
    (C) I have a coat just like it.

[5-second pause]

20. Will you have some coffee?
    (A) I can't stop coughing.
    (B) No, thank you. I'd prefer tea.
    (C) The cups are in the kitchen.

[5-second pause]

21. Which seat would you prefer?
    (A) I rarely eat meat.
    (B) It's not a comfortable chair.
    (C) I'll take this one by the window.

[5-second pause]

22. How long does it take to get there?
    (A) Only about an hour or so.
    (B) It didn't take very long at all.
    (C) They make delicious cake there.

[5-second pause]

23. What did you do with the package?
    (A) I put it on your desk.
    (B) It wasn't a heavy package.
    (C) They were packing all night.

[5-second pause]

24. Will you be at the meeting this afternoon?
    (A) No, I don't think they've finished eating yet.
    (B) The meeting was over sooner than expected.
    (C) Yes, but I'll be a few minutes late.

[5-second pause]

25. Can you tell me where the printer ink is kept?
    (A) Yes, I think that's a really good idea.
    (B) It's on the top shelf of that closet.
    (C) We bought that printer just last month.

[5-second pause]

26. I'm really tired of this rainy weather.
    (A) It's supposed to be sunny tomorrow.
    (B) Yes, train rides can be tiring.
    (C) This jacket is genuine leather.

[5-second pause]

27. Who signed the papers on our behalf?
    (A) I did, after reading them thoroughly.
    (B) You can buy newspapers downstairs.
    (C) That exit sign needs to be replaced.

[5-second pause]

28. Is the photocopy machine still broken?
    (A) I'll make the copies later.
    (B) Yes, he's already spoken.
    (C) No, it was repaired this morning.

[5-second pause]

29. I need a ride to the airport early tomorrow morning.
    (A) I'd be happy to drive you.
    (B) The plane is due to arrive at noon.
    (C) It's located right beside the airport.

[5-second pause]

30. Excuse me. Would you mind telling me the time?
    (A) You can get there by train in a very short time.
    (B) We'll go tomorrow if the weather is fine.
    (C) Certainly. It's five minutes past ten.

[5-second pause]

31. Which suit do you think I should wear?
    (A) There's some fruit on the kitchen table.
    (B) This one looks best on you.
    (C) He didn't tell me where he bought it.

[5-second pause]

32. Whose car is that parked by the front door?
    (A) I believe it's John's.
    (B) It's a really old car.
    (C) The park isn't far.

[5-second pause]

33. When is the conference?
    (A) It's not my preference.
    (B) It's at a hotel.
    (C) It's next September.

[5-second pause]

34. Why did you go to the office on Saturday?
    (A) I go to the office by bus.
    (B) Yes, I'll see you on Saturday.
    (C) I had a lot of work to do.

[5-second pause]

35. This is your desk, isn't it?
    (A) Yes, it's a desk.
    (B) No, mine's the one by the door.
    (C) We each have our own desk.

[5-second pause]

36. What can you see from that window?
    (A) A great view of the city.
    (B) It's very windy.
    (C) The window cleaner comes tomorrow.

[5-second pause]

37. Where can I get a quick lunch near here?
    (A) There's a cafeteria on the first floor.
    (B) You can pick whichever one you want.
    (C) If you give me a minute, I'll crunch the numbers.

[5-second pause]

38. How long are they planning to stay?
    (A) It was a short plane ride.
    (B) They're staying at a hotel.
    (C) Three or four days at the most.

[5-second pause]

39. Have you finished the budget report yet?
    (A) No, I'll finish it tomorrow.
    (B) It's too heavy to budge.
    (C) I heard the news report this morning.

[5-second pause]

40. It's quite chilly outside this morning.
    (A) He left it just outside the door.
    (B) The path is long and rather hilly.
    (C) Then I'll put on a heavy jacket.

[5-second pause]

## PART 3: CONVERSATIONS

 **Track 16**

**Directions:** You will hear a conversation between two people. You will see three questions on each conversation and four possible answers. Choose the best answer to each question and fill in the corresponding oval on your answer sheet.

Questions 41–43 refer to the following conversation.

Woman:  Was there a call for me? I thought I heard the phone ringing a few minutes ago, and I'm expecting my assistant to call with figures for the budget.

Man:  You did hear the phone ring, but the call was for me. My boss wants me to go in to work early tomorrow.

Woman:  Again? He's always asking you to do that. When's he going to call to offer you a bonus? Or a raise?

Man:  He needs me to help finish the report for the accountant and wants it done before noon. If I go in early as he asks, maybe one day I will get that raise.

41.  When was the phone call made?

[8-second pause]

42.  Who called?

[8-second pause]

43.  Why did this person call?

[8-second pause]

Questions 44–46 refer to the following conversation.

Man:  Room two twenty is smaller than our other rooms, but the price is just one hundred and sixty-five dollars for the night.

Woman:  Does that include use of the pool and the exercise room?

Man:  Of course. It includes the use of all facilities except the tennis courts, which are closed for the winter.

Woman:  Okay, I'll take it. I'll just carry my suitcase up and have a quick look at the room, and then I'm going out for a bite to eat. I'm starving.

44.  Where does this conversation take place?

[8-second pause]

45.  How much will the woman pay?

[8-second pause]

46.  What will the woman do now?

[8-second pause]

Questions 47–49 refer to the following conversation.

Woman:    I was surprised to see that Mr. Wing wasn't at the meeting this morning.
Man:      No, he'll be out of the office until next week. He's on vacation.
Woman:    Oh, I didn't realize he was away on a trip. That's unfortunate, because I wanted his help with my project. My boss wants it done by Friday.
Man:      Why don't you ask Mr. Wing's assistant? She'll be in tomorrow. She'll help you with it.

47. Where is Mr. Wing now?

    [8-second pause]

48. When will he return to the office?

    [8-second pause]

49. Who will help the woman with her project?

    [8-second pause]

Questions 50–52 refer to the following conversation.

Man:      I can't believe how much those museum tickets cost. I've never paid so much before to see art.
Woman:    Yes, but don't you think it was worth it? The paintings we saw were fantastic.
Man:      I guess you're right. There was some very fine work there. So, do you want to go back to the hotel now?
Woman:    No, it's only three o'clock. Let's get a snack, then we can take a walk in the park. It's not far from here.

50. What is the man's complaint?

    [8-second pause]

51. What does the woman suggest about the museum?

    [8-second pause]

52. What will they do now?

    [8-second pause]

Questions 53–55 refer to the following conversation.

Man:      What a nice, sunny day. I'm really enjoying this walk.
Woman:    Me, too. There's not a cloud in the sky. What a treat this is after all that rain last week.
Man:      We should walk more often. We should do it every day.
Woman:    Well, not every day. The weather is nice today, but that'll end. Tomorrow it's supposed to rain again.

53. How is the weather today?

   [8-second pause]

54. What are the speakers doing?

   [8-second pause]

55. When will the weather change?

   [8-second pause]

Questions 56–58 refer to the following conversation.

Woman:   I'm so sorry I'm late. The bus was delayed by the bad weather.

Man:    You should take the subway to work like I do. It's faster and the weather doesn't affect it.

Woman:   That wouldn't work for me. The subway station is too far from my house, but the bus stop is just a two-minute walk.

Man:    The bus fare is cheaper, too, isn't it? You pay just two fifty a ride and I pay a dollar fifty more than that for the subway.

56. Why is the woman late?

   [8-second pause]

57. How does the man get to work?

   [8-second pause]

58. What does the man say about the subway?

   [8-second pause]

Questions 59–61 refer to the following conversation.

Man:    I'm starving. Is there a good place to eat around here?

Woman:   Yes, there's a restaurant just two blocks away. Go to the corner, turn right, go one more block, and you'll see it just before the post office.

Man:    Turn right at the corner. Do you mean by the bank?

Woman:   No, the other corner, by the grocery store. But hurry. They stop serving lunch at two o'clock and it's almost one thirty.

59. What does the man want to do?

   [8-second pause]

60. Why does the woman tell the man to hurry?

   [8-second pause]

61. What time is it now?

   [8-second pause]

Questions 62–64 refer to the following conversation.

Man: I'm so glad I left my old job. It was closer to home than my new job, but the pay was so low, I had to leave.

Woman: So you're happy with the new job.

Man: I am. The only thing I don't like is the vacation time. I get only three weeks a year.

Woman: That's too bad. I get six weeks a year, and you can be sure I need every one of them.

62. Why did the man leave his old job?

[8-second pause]

63. How does he feel about his new job?

[8-second pause]

64. What does the woman indicate about her vacation time?

[8-second pause]

Questions 65–67 refer to the following conversation.

Woman: If we leave the office by six fifteen, we should get to the theater in plenty of time.

Man: Oh, no. We should leave here by five forty-five at the latest. It'll be rush hour, and then it'll take time to find a place to park. The parking garage is closed, don't forget.

Woman: That's right. I forgot about that part. Say, I hope the play isn't over too late. I'm feeling a bit tired.

Man: Don't worry. As soon as it's over, we'll go straight home and you can get your rest.

65. Where are the speakers going?

[8-second pause]

66. Why does the man want to leave early to get there?

[8-second pause]

67. Where will they go later?

[8-second pause]

Questions 68–70 refer to the following conversation.

Woman: Would you like a nice cup of hot tea, or would you prefer coffee?

Man: Actually, I'd like to have a glass of water, if you don't mind. With ice. I'm really quite thirsty.

Woman: Of course. You haven't tried this cake, have you? I got the recipe out of a magazine. Let me serve you a slice.

Man: Oh, no thank you. It looks very good, but I'm not at all hungry.

68. What does the man want to drink?

[8-second pause]

69. How does the man feel?

[8-second pause]

70. What does the woman offer the man?

[8-second pause]

## PART 4: TALKS

Questions 71–73 refer to the following announcement.

May I have your attention, please. Flight forty-three for Caracas, scheduled for departure at five o'clock, has been delayed. It is now scheduled to depart two hours later than the originally scheduled time. In the meantime, all ticketed passengers for Flight forty-three to Caracas are invited to enjoy a complimentary meal at the Sky View Restaurant. To receive your meal ticket, please show your boarding pass to the gate agent. Any passengers wishing to be rebooked on a different flight are asked to approach the ticket office on the other side of the main lounge. You will be asked to pick up your suitcases from the baggage claim area and recheck them when receiving your new boarding pass.

71. What is said about the flight to Caracas?

[8-second pause]

72. What is offered to the passengers?

[8-second pause]

73. How can passengers take advantage of the offer?

[8-second pause]

Questions 74–76 refer to the following advertisement.

Mayflower and Company, the area's newest and largest department store, will be celebrating its grand opening next Saturday. Don't miss this once-in-a-lifetime event. Free food and entertainment for the whole family will be provided. Take advantage of deep discounts on items in all store departments—home furnishings, office supplies, garden supplies, clothing, and more! Discounts will be in effect for one day only. This event will be held rain or shine, from eight in the morning until eight in the evening. Free parking will be available all day. So come on down! Mayflower and Company is just ten minutes from downtown across the road from City Mall.

74. What place is opening?

[8-second pause]

75. When will the opening take place?

[8-second pause]

76. Where is this place?

[8-second pause]

Questions 77–79 refer to the following report.

Road conditions are dangerous out there folks, so stay home and don't drive anywhere unless absolutely necessary. This morning's snowfall has already led to a seven-car accident near the train station. Schools are closed and many businesses are as well. Snow is expected to continue falling throughout the afternoon and evening, and temperatures will remain chilly. The skies should start clearing toward morning, and tomorrow should be sunny and a good bit warmer.

77. What is the weather like?

[8-second pause]

78. What happened this morning?

[8-second pause]

79. What will happen tomorrow morning?

[8-second pause]

Questions 80–82 refer to the following announcement.

The City Center Theater announces that the Smith Brothers Circus is coming to town next month. The circus will be performing at the theater during the first week of August with two shows daily at three P.M. and seven P.M. Tickets are just fifteen dollars each and are available by calling eight-hundred-nine-six-four-eight-four-three-four. Smith Brothers Circus will also be giving away a limited number of free tickets. To request your free ticket, simply send a postcard to the Smith Brothers in care of the theater. Include your name and address and a brief statement explaining why you love the circus. You could be one of the twenty-five lucky winners!

80. What are the tickets for?

[8-second pause]

81. How much do the tickets cost?

[8-second pause]

82. How can you get a free ticket?

[8-second pause]

Questions 83–85 refer to the following report.

The Riverside Park Elementary School was destroyed by fire last night. The fire was first reported by Ethel Rogers, owner of the Corner Bookstore, located on the same block. As Ms. Rogers was leaving the store around nine o'clock, she noticed smoke rising out of the school building and immediately notified authorities. Firefighters arrived on the scene within minutes and worked for five hours to put out the blaze. Fortunately, there were no injuries. All the schoolchildren and school staff had left the building several hours before the fire was noticed. The cause of the fire is under investigation.

83. What was destroyed by a fire?

[8-second pause]

84. Who was hurt in the fire?

[8-second pause]

85. What is said about the fire?

[8-second pause]

Questions 86–88 refer to the following phone message.

Hi, this is Rosalie Smith calling. I have a reservation for a room at your inn next Friday night. I know your check-in time is from five till nine, but the problem is I'm coming in on a late flight, so I probably won't get there till ten o'clock or a bit later. I hope that's OK, and that you'll be able to hold my reservation for me. I've heard so many good things about your place. All my friends give it high recommendations. OK, see you Friday. I can't wait.

86. Why is the speaker making the call?

[8-second pause]

87. What does she imply about the inn?

[8-second pause]

88. What does she mean when she says, "I can't wait?"

[8-second pause]

Questions 89–91 refer to the following talk.

Good afternoon, and welcome to today's edition of *Business Talks*, the radio program that brings listeners information and ideas for the modern businessperson every afternoon from one fifteen until two o'clock. Our guest today is Dr. Jose Silva, author of the best-selling book *Keeping Fit in the Office*. Dr. Silva will talk with us about health and fitness issues facing office workers. After his talk, Dr. Silva will answer calls from you, our listeners. Call seven-five-six-nine-eight-eight-seven if you have a question for Dr. Silva. Following our program will be the *Up-to-the-Minute News* at two o'clock. And don't forget to tune in to tomorrow's *Business Talks* program, when we will discuss banks and banking.

89. What is the main purpose of this talk?

[8-second pause]

90. What will Dr. Silva talk about?

[8-second pause]

91. What will Dr. Silva do after his talk?

[8-second pause]

Questions 92–94 refer to the following news report.

The president met with world leaders in the capital city this afternoon to discuss the current economic situation. He will speak about the issues discussed at the meeting when he addresses the nation on TV tonight. Tomorrow he flies to Tokyo, where he will begin his three-week tour of Asia and Australia to promote his international economic program. After his return home, he will prepare for the International Conference on the Environment, to take place next month.

92. What did the president do this afternoon?

[8-second pause]

93. Where will the president go tomorrow?

[8-second pause]

94. How long will his trip last?

[8-second pause]

Questions 95–97 refer to the following recording.

Thank you for calling the State Street Bank. We're here to serve you. Our hours are Monday through Friday from nine A.M. until four thirty P.M., and Saturday from eight thirty A.M. until two P.M. For information on an existing checking or savings account, press one. To open a new checking or savings account, press two. To apply for a credit card, press three. To get information about loans, press four. For all other issues, press five. To repeat this menu, press zero.

95. At which one of the following times is the bank open?

[8-second pause]

96. How can a customer find out the balance of his savings account?

[8-second pause]

97. What happens when a customer presses zero?

[8-second pause]

Questions 98–100 refer to the following talk.

All job seekers need a good strategy. The first thing to consider is where to look for jobs. In the past, people relied on newspaper ads, university career counseling offices, and employment agencies for job leads. These things still exist, but the best place to look for jobs is on the Internet. It provides the most current and the widest range of job opportunities, of all sorts. Online you can find job listings in all fields, from education to medicine to engineering. There is something for everyone. When applying for a job, you need to have a good résumé prepared. It is your most important tool, more important even than interview skills, university degrees, or work experience. It is the image you present.

98. According to the speaker, what is the best place to look for a job?

[8-second pause]

99. What kinds of jobs can be found in this place?

[8-second pause]

100. According to the speaker, what is a job seeker's most important tool?

[8-second pause]

# NEW TOEIC PRACTICE EXAM A

## Listening Comprehension

### PART 1: PHOTOGRAPHS

**Directions:** You will see a photograph. You will hear four statements about the photograph. Choose the statement that most closely matches the photograph and fill in the corresponding oval on your answer sheet.

**Track 18**

**Example**

Now listen to the four statements.

(A) She's getting on a plane.
(B) She's reading a magazine.
(C) She's taking a nap.
(D) She's holding a glass.

Statement (B), "She's reading a magazine," best describes what you see in the picture. Therefore, you should choose answer (B).

1. Look at the photo marked number 1 in your test book.
   (A) They're putting the chairs inside.
   (B) They're enjoying their food outdoors.
   (C) They're moving the tables around.
   (D) They're walking through the doors.

   [5-second pause]

2. Look at the photo marked number 2 in your test book.
   (A) The ship is at sea.
   (B) The coat got wet.
   (C) The captain is on deck.
   (D) The ocean is rough.

   [5-second pause]

3. Look at the photo marked number 3 in your test book.
   (A) She's learning to cook.
   (B) She's meeting her friends.
   (C) She's reading a book.
   (D) She's cleaning the cages.

   [5-second pause]

4. Look at the photo marked number 4 in your test book.
   (A) They're entering the building.
   (B) They're working very hard.
   (C) They're talking about business.
   (D) They're all carrying bags.

   [5-second pause]

5. Look at the photo marked number 5 in your test book.
   (A) The barber is using a brush.
   (B) The photographer is taking a picture.
   (C) The artist is painting the scene.
   (D) The painter is preparing the walls.

   [5-second pause]

6. Look at the photo marked number 6 in your test book.
   (A) They're listening to a presentation.
   (B) They're setting up the screen.
   (C) They're cleaning up the room.
   (D) They're looking out the window.

   [5-second pause]

## PART 2: QUESTION-RESPONSE

**Track 19**

**Directions:** You will hear a question and three possible responses. Choose the response that most closely answers the question and fill in the corresponding oval on your answer sheet.

**Example**

Now listen to the sample question.

You will hear:

How is the weather?

You will also hear:

(A) It's raining.
(B) He's fine, thanks.
(C) He's my boss.

The best response to the question *How is the weather?* is choice (A), *It's raining.* Therefore, you should choose answer (A).

7. Dinner will be ready soon.
   (A) Great. I'm starving.
   (B) Yes, I read it this afternoon.
   (C) I think she's much thinner.

   [5-second pause]

8. What is your address?
   (A) The woman's dress is blue.
   (B) The adding machine is mine.
   (C) I live on Wilson Boulevard.

   [5-second pause]

9. Who cleans the offices?
   (A) A cleaning company comes in at night.
   (B) The office is closed.
   (C) His voice is awful.

   [5-second pause]

10. Where did you leave your umbrella?
    (A) It's raining now.
    (B) Probably on the bus.
    (C) My leisure time is spent at home.

    [5-second pause]

11. The printer's out of paper.
    (A) We just bought a new printer.
    (B) I read the newspaper this morning.
    (C) There's more in the supply closet.

    [5-second pause]

12. Why didn't you put an ad in the newspaper?
    (A) They wrapped the food in newspaper.
    (B) That would have been a good idea.
    (C) I'll put the newspaper on the table.

    [5-second pause]

13. How many times have you been to China?
    (A) Only once.
    (B) We bought several sets of dishes.
    (C) It's time to go.

    [5-second pause]

14. Has the fax been sent?
    (A) Yes, it was sent this morning.
    (B) No, the facts weren't checked.
    (C) The rent was paid on time.

    [5-second pause]

15. Who developed the marketing plan?
    (A) The market sells vegetables.
    (B) Our sales staff.
    (C) The film was developed overnight.

    [5-second pause]

16. When will you purchase a new computer?
    (A) The purpose is for education.
    (B) The commuter train leaves at 6:00 A.M.
    (C) When the prices go down.

    [5-second pause]

17. What is the best season to visit?
    (A) There's only one reason.
    (B) I think summer is best.
    (C) The stock prices may fall.

    [5-second pause]

18. Why were you late?
    (A) Yes, I already ate.
    (B) The date has not been set.
    (C) My watch was slow.

[5-second pause]

19. Which chair is more comfortable?
    (A) There are more coming.
    (B) The table by the window is wider.
    (C) I like this big, soft one.

[5-second pause]

20. I'd like to make an appointment with
Ms. Park.
    (A) She pointed it out to us.
    (B) She's free tomorrow at two o'clock.
    (C) She thinks it's too dark.

[5-second pause]

21. Where is the post office?
    (A) It is just a couple of blocks from here.
    (B) The letter was delivered to the office.
    (C) The postal workers are on duty.

[5-second pause]

22. Would you pass the salt, please?
    (A) Cars must not pass on hills.
    (B) Certainly. Here you are.
    (C) The woman was insulted.

[5-second pause]

23. What is the purpose of your visit?
    (A) The visitors are in the next room.
    (B) Porpoises are sea mammals.
    (C) I'm here on business.

[5-second pause]

24. Who would like to take a break?
    (A) All of the rules were broken.
    (B) Let's all rest for a while.
    (C) We take a walk every week.

[5-second pause]

25. Why was the meeting postponed?
    (A) Use the mail or the phone.
    (B) The meat market is across from the
        post office.
    (C) Because the participants were ill.

[5-second pause]

26. When was this memo written?
    (A) The menu was in French.
    (B) On the computer.
    (C) The same day it was sent.

[5-second pause]

27. Where are our suitcases?
    (A) In the hall closet.
    (B) I came in case you needed me.
    (C) They're very nice suits.

[5-second pause]

28. Susan's train gets in at four thirty.
    (A) I'll meet her at the station.
    (B) I'll get the tickets next week.
    (C) I don't think it'll stain.

[5-second pause]

29. Doesn't your receptionist speak other
languages?
    (A) No, only English.
    (B) The linguist's lecture was well received.
    (C) She speaks very softly.

[5-second pause]

30. What will you do when you retire?
    (A) I'll read this book before going to bed.
    (B) There are new tires on the car.
    (C) I plan to play a lot of golf.

[5-second pause]

31. When will the exhibition close?
    (A) The models are on exhibit.
    (B) It will be open for another two weeks.
    (C) I put my clothes in the closet.

[5-second pause]

## PART 3: CONVERSATIONS

 **Track 20** **Directions:** You will hear a conversation between two or more people. You will see three questions on each conversation and four possible answers. Choose the best answer to each question and fill in the corresponding oval on your answer sheet.

Questions 32–34 refer to the following conversation.

Woman: You look like you're all dressed up for the office. Have you found a job?

Man: Not yet, but maybe soon. I'm on my way downtown right now for an interview, and I should get going. The bus will be leaving soon.

Woman: Here, you'd better take my umbrella. It looks like rain. And sorry I can't offer to drive you, but I've got a doctor's appointment in the opposite direction.

32. Where is the man going?

   [8-second pause]

33. How will he get there?

   [8-second pause]

34. What does the woman give the man?

   [8-second pause]

Questions 35–37 refer to the following conversation.

Man: I think I'm all set for my trip to Washington. I've got the client meetings scheduled, my presentation's all ready . . .

Woman: You're flying out on Monday, right?

Man: No, Sunday. Just two days away. But I think I'm ready. I've booked my room at the Peacham Hotel . . .

Woman: The Peacham? I wouldn't stay there if I were you. The beds are lumpy, and it's not very clean.

35. Why is the man going to Washington?

   [8-second pause]

36. When is he leaving?

   [8-second pause]

37. What does the woman mean when she says, "I wouldn't stay there?"

   [8-second pause]

Questions 38–40 refer to the following conversation.

Woman:  Oh, hi. I didn't expect to see you here in the middle of the day. Where are you going?

Man:  I have an appointment with my lawyer. You?

Woman:  I'm on my way to the mall to get a little shopping done during my lunch hour. I'll probably get back to the office a bit late, but I don't care. Oh, here's my stop.

Man:  I'll get off and walk with you as far as the mall. I have a little extra time. I'm not due at the lawyer's till one fifteen.

38. Where does this conversation take place?

[8-second pause]

39. What time is the man's appointment?

[8-second pause]

40. What will the man do next?

[8-second pause]

Questions 41–43 refer to the following conversation.

Man:  Hi, Rita. This is Ken from the Sunstar Company. I talked to you last week about renting a room at your hotel for our annual banquet.

Woman:  Yes, I remember.

Man:  So I've looked over the materials you sent me. The menu, the prices, everything looks great. But I'd like to come take a look at the available rooms some time next week.

Woman:  Unfortunately, I'm leaving for Paris on Monday, and I'll be gone all week. But my assistant would be happy to show you around.

41. Why did the man make the call?

[8-second pause]

42. Who is the woman, most likely?

[8-second pause]

43. What will the woman do on Monday?

[8-second pause]

Questions 44–46 refer to the following conversation.

Woman: Excuse me, can you tell me a little about the artist of this work?
Man: I can. He's originally from Houston and studied in New York and Paris. He now lives in Portland. He lives around the corner, actually.
Woman: That's interesting. This statue is amazing, so lifelike.
Man: Yes. The artist works in a style called ultra-realism. It's meant to look like a real, live person.
Woman: It does. It seems like a real person is really sitting here. What's the material? It feels so smooth.
Man: I'll have to ask you to take your hands off the art, please. That's not allowed. Unless you're planning to buy it, of course.

44. Where is the art gallery located?

[8-second pause]

45. What kind of art is the woman looking at?

[8-second pause]

46. What does the man say the woman CANNOT do with the art?

[8-second pause]

Questions 47–49 refer to the following conversation.

Man 1: I went over to the new office this morning to leave a check with the landlord. So I took advantage and had a look around.
Woman: And?
Man 1: It looks great. We should be able to move in soon. They just need to finish the painting and do a little clean up, and then we can start moving our furniture over.
Woman: I can't wait. I'm tired of being so cramped here.
Man 2: I know what you mean. It'll be great to have more space. I'm not looking forward to packing, though.
Woman: I can help you pack. I'm good at organizing. How about we get started later this afternoon?
Man 2: Thanks. I would really appreciate it.

47. What did the first man do this morning?

[8-second pause]

48. What do the speakers imply about their current office?

[8-second pause]

49. What will the woman do this afternoon?

[8-second pause]

Questions 50–52 refer to the following conversation.

Woman: Look at this place. Do you think we'll ever get a table?
Man: We might have to wait a bit. Let's look at the menu while we wait. They usually have good daily specials.
Woman: Wow! These prices are a bit steep.
Man: Yes, but you get your money's worth. Everything here is cooked fresh, and the service is something special.
Woman: That may be so, but I might have to ask you to lend me a few dollars.
Man: Don't worry about it. It's on me.
Woman: Thank you. That's very generous.

50. Where does this conversation take place?

[8-second pause]

51. What is suggested about the place?

[8-second pause]

52. What does the man offer to do?

[8-second pause]

Questions 53–55 refer to the following conversation.

Woman: Hi. I'm calling from Green Associates to find out about our order. Can I pick it up today?
Man: Remind me which order that was.
Woman: The promotional brochure, two-color, with black and white photos.
Man: Right. Yes, I have it. Twenty-five hundred copies ready for pick up any time today before six.
Woman: Twenty-five hundred copies? But we only ordered two thousand.
Man: Oh, yes, I see. Well, don't worry, I won't charge you for the extra five hundred.
Woman: Thanks. I'll come by and get them before you close this evening.

53. Why did the woman make the call?

[8-second pause]

54. What most likely is the man's profession?

[8-second pause]

55. What is the problem with the order?

[8-second pause]

Questions 56–58 refer to the following conversation.

Man:     How're the plans for the company picnic coming along?
Woman: We haven't started on them yet. We still have a whole month.
Man:     Right. That's not much time.
Woman: I guess not. Well, I was thinking we could have it someplace else for a change. I
             didn't like that park by the lake where we had it last year. It's so cold there.
Man:     So, where?
Woman: Maybe at the country club. They have nice gardens.
Man:     I don't know if that'll go over with the staff. It'll look strange to have it there this
             year when we've had it at the park all the other years.
Woman: It's just an idea. I'll see what others have to say.

56. How often is the company picnic held?

    [8-second pause]

57. Where does the woman want to hold the picnic?

    [8-second pause]

58. What does the man mean when he says, "I don't know if that will go over with the
    staff?"

    [8-second pause]

Questions 59–61 refer to the following conversation.

Man:     Things at my new job couldn't be better. I'm really glad I made the move.
Woman: That's great to hear.
Man:     Yes. I'm a lot busier now, but the work is so interesting, always something new to
             learn. Nothing like my old position.
Woman: And the pay is better, too, I bet.
Man:     A little. I was already earning well before, but at least now I'm not falling asleep at
             my desk every day.
Woman: Ha ha. Like you used to back at university. Remember those early morning
             classes?
Man:     How could I forget? Say, I'm getting together with some of our old mates tonight.
             Wanna meet us for a bite to eat?
Woman: Sure. Thanks.

59. What does the man imply about his former job?

    [8-second pause]

60. How do the man and woman know each other?

    [8-second pause]

61. What does the man invite the woman to do?

    [8-second pause]

Questions 62–64 refer to the following conversation.

Woman: So, are we eating in the cafeteria today?
Man: We might as well. We have that staff meeting later, remember? So we don't really have time to go anywhere else.
Woman: True. Though I wish the food there were better.
Man: I know, but you can't beat the prices. It'd cost twice as much to eat at any of the neighborhood restaurants.
Woman: I can't deny that. Kerry wants to eat with us, too. I told her we'd wait for her in the lobby at noon.
Man: At noon? We'd better get going, then.

62. What is this conversation mainly about?

[8-second pause]

63. What does the man suggest about the cafeteria?

[8-second pause]

64. What will the speakers do next?

[8-second pause]

Questions 65–67 refer to the following conversation and sign.

Woman: Thanks for letting me use your apartment while you're away next weekend.
Man: Sure. It's not large, but I think you'll find it peaceful and comfortable.
Woman: I'm sure I will. But I wonder if there's a place to park. I'll be there three days, and I'd rather not park on the street.
Man: There's a garage just across the street. I'm not sure what they charge, though.
Woman: It doesn't matter. So, I plan to arrive Friday morning and leave Sunday evening.
Man: Then I'll just miss you. I'm taking off for the lake on Thursday morning.

65. What does the man indicate about his apartment?

[8-second pause]

66. What will the man do on Thursday?

[8-second pause]

67. Look at the graphic. How much will the woman pay to use the garage?

[8-second pause]

Questions 68–70 refer to the following conversation and price list.

Man:     Everything's just about ready for tomorrow's workshop. Marvin said he wants
         everyone to have a notepad and pen. There are notepads in the supply closet, but
         I have to buy the pens.

Woman: But we're already over budget. You can't spend any more.

Man:     Marvin wants each participant to have a pen. They're not expensive, and I'll only
         get as many as we need. There will be twenty-four participants.

Woman: Great! All the spots are taken. What time do you want me to help you set up the
         room?

Man:     Let's start at twelve. That should give us plenty of time. Marvin has already
         explained to me how he wants the room set up.

68. Who is Marvin, most likely?

   [8-second pause]

69. What is the woman worried about?

   [8-second pause]

70. Look at the graphic. Which pack of pens will the man buy?

   [8-second pause]

## PART 4: TALKS

**Directions:** You will hear a talk given by a single speaker. You will see three
questions on each talk, each with four possible answers. Choose the best
answer to each question and fill in the corresponding oval on your answer
sheet.

Track 21

Questions 71–73 refer to the following report.

Man:     The warm weather is here and you know what that means, folks—road repair
         season has arrived. Traffic has been backed up all morning on Main Street due
         to repaving work there, so stay away from that part of town if at all possible. The
         roads throughout the rest of the area look clear with no slowdowns anywhere,
         except for a small back up on Maple Avenue. Traffic should remain light for the
         rest of the afternoon, though tomorrow may be another story. Starting tomorrow
         and continuing all week, the Mid Town Bridge will be closed for repairs. So plan
         your travel accordingly, and use alternate routes over the Park Street Bridge or the
         Valley Bridge.

71. What is this talk mostly about?

[8-second pause]

72. What does the speaker suggest listeners do?

[8-second pause]

73. What will happen tomorrow?

[8-second pause]

Questions 74–76 refer to the following talk.

Woman: Good morning and welcome to our annual conference. We are very fortunate this year to be able to get out of the city and hold the conference here in the beautiful mountain setting of the View Top Resort. I hope you enjoyed your breakfast as much as I did. The chefs here are top notch. We have a full schedule this weekend. This morning, we'll get outside and take advantage of our location with tours of the grounds as we learn about native and garden plants we may want to incorporate into our design work. After lunch, we'll have workshops on various landscaping topics. We'll begin the day with a talk by Mary Jameson, internationally known for her work designing outdoor spaces. Welcome, Ms. Jameson.

74. Who is the conference for?

[8-second pause]

75. Where is the conference taking place?

[8-second pause]

76. What will listeners do next?

[8-second pause]

Questions 77–79 refer to the following report.

Man: This is Matt Dow with the morning weather update. You'll be glad to hear that the rain will be moving out today—finally! I know it seemed like we'd never see the sun again, but never fear, we will! After a rainy morning, cloudy skies this afternoon will clear up overnight, and things will be bright and sunny for the rest of the week. So put away those umbrellas and sweaters and get out there and enjoy the warmth and sunshine while you can. Clouds will move back in over the weekend; however, no significant rain is expected again until at least the middle of next week.

77. What does the speaker imply about the weather?

[8-second pause]

78. What does the speaker advise listeners to do?

[8-second pause]

79. What will the weather be like on the weekend?

[8-second pause]

Questions 80–82 refer to the following phone message.

Woman: Hi. This is Martha O'Neill calling from Dr. Rogers' office about your appointment for your annual exam. We have you down for ten o'clock next Monday morning. We ask all our patients to arrive ten minutes before the scheduled time to fill out the intake forms. Also, please don't forget to bring your eyeglasses with you, and remember, if the doctor prescribes new lenses for you, we have a wide selection of frames you can choose from. If for some reason you can't be here at the scheduled time, we require a twenty-four-hour cancellation notice, or we will have to charge you a missed appointment fee. Thank you for your understanding.

80. Why did the speaker make the call?

[8-second pause]

81. Who is Dr. Rogers?

[8-second pause]

82. What does the speaker ask the listener to do?

[8-second pause]

Questions 83–85 refer to the following news report.

Man: City officials announced today that plans have been approved for a new park to be built in the place where the former football stadium stood. Since the new stadium opened five years ago, the old stadium has remained vacant. Ideas proposed for the site have ranged from an office or condominium complex to a farmer's market. After years of discussions, agreement has finally been reached on the plans for the new park. I, for one, think this is an excellent use of the land and that the park will provide local residents with many great recreational opportunities. In fact, I can't wait for opening day. Work on the park will begin early next month and is expected to be completed before the end of the year.

83. Where will the park be built?

[8-second pause]

84. What does the speaker mean when he says, "I can't wait for opening day?"

[8-second pause]

85. When will construction begin?

[8-second pause]

Questions 86–88 refer to the following phone message.

Woman: Hi Patsy. Guess what? I got that job I applied for, you know, the one I told you about. Anyhow, they want me to start right away, which is great, but there's just one little thing. I left my car at the mechanic's, and it'll be ready to be picked up on Monday morning, but that'll be my first day at work, so of course I won't have time. So do you think you could pick up the car for me? I'd really appreciate it. It's the mechanic I always use, on the corner of Oak Street, and you can get the car any time before noon. Let me know if you can do this. I'd really appreciate it.

86. Why did the speaker make the call?

[8-second pause]

87. What does the speaker mean when she says, "There's just one little thing?"

[8-second pause]

88. What will the speaker do on Monday?

[8-second pause]

Questions 89–91 refer to the following advertisement.

Man: Are you looking for fresh, organic produce? Look no more! At Mr. Green's, we sell the finest, freshest fruits and vegetables you can buy, all guaranteed to be one hundred percent organic. We also sell organic eggs, milk, and cheese, as well as flours, cereals, canned goods, and everything else you need to stock your pantry shelves at prices you can afford. At Mr. Green's, we care about our customers. That's why every Sunday is sale day. Look for huge discounts throughout the store, and double your savings with coupons. Check your local newspaper for our weekly coupon specials, or visit the Mr. Green's website.

89. What kind of business is Mr. Green's?

[8-second pause]

90. What happens on Sundays?

[8-second pause]

91. What are listeners asked to do?

[8-second pause]

Questions 92–94 refer to the following talk.

Woman: Hi. Is everybody on board? OK, we're going to get moving in a minute, so I'd like to ask you to please take your seats now. There can be no standing in the aisle once we are moving. I hope you all enjoyed our museum visit. They really have a fantastic art collection. And, I hope you worked up an appetite because next on the agenda is food. We'll be stopping at the gorgeous Riverside Café—a great place. What it lacks in size it makes up for with an amazing menu, plus it has a fantastic view across the river. So, you'll have a chance to satisfy your appetites and rest up for the afternoon, when we'll be visiting several historic buildings.

92. Where does the talk take place?

[8-second pause]

93. What will they do next?

[8-second pause]

94. What does the speaker imply about the café?

[8-second pause]

Questions 95–97 refer to the following excerpt from a meeting and graph.

Man: Now if you would take a look at this graph, you'll see the types of lessons we offer and how many members signed up for each type during the past six months. Tennis remains popular, as always, but what I'm most concerned about is the areas where we are attracting the least interest, especially this one here. So this is what I want us to talk about today, the least popular sport and how we can increase its popularity and get more people signed up for lessons in this area. To that end, I have developed a short survey, which I'd like you to take a look at. You can share this with your clients and use it to find out about their interests and goals.

95. What kind of business does the speaker work in?

[8-second pause]

96. Look at the graphic. Which sport does the speaker want to focus on?

[8-second pause]

97. What does the speaker ask listeners to do?

[8-second pause]

Questions 98–100 refer to the following phone message and floor plan.

Woman:  Hi, Hilda. I got your message, and I'm so glad you will be joining our private Spanish class. There are just three other students, so it's a nice little group. We meet every Monday afternoon at four o'clock in my office in the Oaks building. Just come through the front door, walk straight across the lobby through the double doors, and my office is down the hall, second door on your left. Let's see. I already have your check, thanks, so I don't think you need to bring anything else except a notebook. I have a copy of the textbook for you. OK, see you Monday.

98. Who is the speaker, most likely?

[8-second pause]

99. Look at the graphic. Where is the speaker's office?

[8-second pause]

100. What does the speaker ask the listener to bring?

[8-second pause]

# NEW TOEIC PRACTICE EXAM B

## Listening Comprehension

### PART 1: PHOTOGRAPHS

> 🔊 **Track 22**
>
> **Directions:** You will see a photograph. You will hear four statements about the photograph. Choose the statement that most closely matches the photograph and fill in the corresponding oval on your answer sheet.
>
> **Example**
>
> Now listen to the four statements.
>
> (A) She's getting on a plane.
> (B) She's reading a magazine.
> (C) She's taking a nap.
> (D) She's holding a glass.
>
> Statement (B), "She's reading a magazine," best describes what you see in the picture. Therefore, you should choose answer (B).

1. Look at the photo marked number 1 in your test book.
   - (A) He's washing his hands.
   - (B) He's rinsing the dishes.
   - (C) He's putting the plates away.
   - (D) He's cleaning the sink.

   [5-second pause]

2. Look at the photo marked number 2 in your test book.
   - (A) People are drinking coffee in a café.
   - (B) The waiter is pouring coffee into the cup.
   - (C) The chairs around the table are empty.
   - (D) The café is full of customers.

   [5-second pause]

3. Look at the photo marked number 3 in your test book.
   - (A) The mechanic is checking the engine.
   - (B) The driver is parking the car.
   - (C) The woman is taking off her gloves.
   - (D) The passenger is opening the door.

   [5-second pause]

4. Look at the photo marked number 4 in your test book.
   - (A) The patient is turning on the TV.
   - (B) The doctor is sitting on the chair.
   - (C) The dentist is pointing at the screen.
   - (D) The woman is washing the walls.

   [5-second pause]

5. Look at the photo marked number 5 in your test book.
   - (A) The bench is next to the houses.
   - (B) The cyclist is ready to ride.
   - (C) The hiker is enjoying the view.
   - (D) The bicycle is leaning against the fence.

   [5-second pause]

6. Look at the photo marked number 6 in your test book.
   - (A) The bus is arriving on time.
   - (B) The man is checking the time.
   - (C) The passengers are boarding the bus.
   - (D) The man is standing behind the trash can.

## PART 2: QUESTION-RESPONSE

**Track 23**

**Directions:** You will hear a question and three possible responses. Choose the response that most closely answers the question and fill in the corresponding oval on your answer sheet.

**Example**

Now listen to the sample question.

You will hear:

How is the weather?

You will also hear:

(A) It's raining.
(B) He's fine, thanks.
(C) He's my boss.

The best response to the question *How is the weather?* is choice (A), *It's raining.* Therefore, you should choose answer (A).

7. Where did you get that suit?
   (A) At that new clothing store in the mall.
   (B) It's a business suit.
   (C) It suits you very well.

   [5-second pause]

8. How much is the lunch special?
   (A) Soup and a sandwich.
   (B) Eight dollars and fifty cents.
   (C) From eleven A.M. till one P.M.

   [5-second pause]

9. When will John be back from vacation?
   (A) He went to the beach.
   (B) Next Monday.
   (C) Yes, I could use a vacation.

   [5-second pause]

10. Who were you talking to on the phone?
    (A) Just a colleague from work.
    (B) I'll call you later today.
    (C) We talked this morning.

    [5-second pause]

11. Which house is theirs?
    (A) It's the one on the corner.
    (B) It's Mary's house.
    (C) It's not a new house.

    [5-second pause]

12. Have you eaten lunch yet?
    (A) We usually eat at the café across the street.
    (B) No, and I'm very hungry.
    (C) Just a salad and a small sandwich.

    [5-second pause]

13. Do you know what time Mr. Kim left the office?
    (A) Yes, I know him very well.
    (B) Down the hall on the left.
    (C) At about half past four.

    [5-second pause]

14. Whose turn is it to answer the phones?
    (A) It's Lisa's, I think.
    (B) There's a phone on my desk.
    (C) He left a message.

    [5-second pause]

15. Let me hang up your coat for you.
    (A) He usually lets me do it.
    (B) Thank you.
    (C) Yes, it's my coat.

    [5-second pause]

16. When will the proposal be ready?
    (A) By the end of the week.
    (B) No, it isn't ready yet.
    (C) Yes, we will submit a proposal.

[5-second pause]

17. What was discussed at the meeting?
    (A) The budget for next year.
    (B) In the main conference room.
    (C) At ten o'clock.

[5-second pause]

18. How was your trip to Paris?
    (A) Just three days.
    (B) I enjoyed it very much.
    (C) Yes, I went to Paris.

[5-second pause]

19. The copier in your office isn't working.
    (A) I'm working now.
    (B) Make ten copies, please.
    (C) Then use the one in the front office.

[5-second pause]

20. What time will Mr. Lee arrive?
    (A) Sometime next week.
    (B) Mr. Lee will drive.
    (C) His plane gets in at seven.

[5-second pause]

21. Did you see the movie I told you about?
    (A) Yes, it was very interesting.
    (B) No, you didn't tell me.
    (C) At the movie theater.

[5-second pause]

22. Would you like me to give you a ride to work tomorrow?
    (A) I'm going to work tomorrow.
    (B) Sure. Can you pick me up at eight?
    (C) I can give it to you.

[5-second pause]

23. You used to work in the sales department, didn't you?
    (A) Yes, but now I work in production.
    (B) No, there aren't any sales today.
    (C) It's quite a large apartment.

[5-second pause]

24. Your office isn't big enough for our meeting.
    (A) There is probably enough.
    (B) I still haven't finished eating.
    (C) Let's meet in the conference room instead.

[5-second pause]

25. Where can I get a snack?
    (A) An apple and a cookie would be nice.
    (B) Usually at around three o'clock.
    (C) There's a café across the street.

[5-second pause]

26. Do you think the workshop will be long?
    (A) I think he works in that shop.
    (B) It'll probably last two or three hours.
    (C) I usually shop on Saturdays.

[5-second pause]

27. Would you prefer to walk or take a cab?
    (A) A cab would be faster.
    (B) Yes, I'll take one.
    (C) It's time to get to work.

[5-second pause]

28. Do you want to play tennis after work today?
    (A) With my friend Robert, usually.
    (B) At the courts in the park.
    (C) Yes, that's a great idea.

    [5-second pause]

29. Would you mind turning off all the lights before you leave tonight?
    (A) Sure, no problem.
    (B) Yes, I plan to leave tonight.
    (C) Probably at around nine o'clock.

    [5-second pause]

30. How many boxes of paper should I order?
    (A) Mr. Kim will take your order.
    (B) I think five will be enough.
    (C) Put the boxes over there.

    [5-second pause]

31. When will the awards banquet take place?
    (A) At that big hotel downtown.
    (B) To acknowledge the company employees.
    (C) Near the end of September.

## PART 3: CONVERSATIONS

**Directions:** You will hear a conversation between two or more people. You will see three questions on each conversation and four possible answers. Choose the best answer to each question and fill in the corresponding oval on your answer sheet.

Track 24

Questions 32–34 refer to the following conversation.

Man: The hotel is completely booked this weekend. It looks like a lot of people will be attending the conference.

Woman: It's a popular event because it's such a great chance to make connections with other people in marketing and sales.

Man: This will be my first year attending. I'm especially looking forward to the banquet Saturday night. In fact, that's a large part of the reason I'm going at all.

Woman: Yeah, the banquet's a lot of fun, and I'm really regretting that I'll have to miss it. But I'll need that time to plan for the workshop I'll be giving on Sunday morning.

32. What will take place at the hotel this weekend?

[8-second pause]

33. What will happen on Saturday night?

[8-second pause]

34. What event will the woman participate in on Sunday morning?

[8-second pause]

Questions 35–37 refer to the following conversation.

Woman: Hi. This is Wanda Williams calling from Wilco. We hired you to take some photos for us last weekend, and I was wondering if they were ready yet.

Man: Right. The Wilco annual meeting and banquet. I'm just finishing them up now. I can e-mail you the files later this afternoon and send the prints on over first thing tomorrow morning.

Woman: Great. I'm putting together the Wilco monthly bulletin now and was planning on using some of the photos for that.

35. Why did the woman make the call?

[8-second pause]

36. What will the man do tomorrow?

[8-second pause]

37. What project is the woman working on now?

[8-second pause]

Questions 38–40 refer to the following conversation.

Man: This is the lease. It's just a standard apartment rental agreement, but if you want to take some time to look it over, you can drop off the signed copy at my office later.

Woman: OK. Thanks.

Man: But I'll need to have it by the end of the week, along with a check for the first month's rent and the security deposit.

Woman: No problem. Oh, I wanted to ask, does the apartment come with parking?

Man: Yes, there's space in the garage for one car per tenant.

Woman: Great. OK, I'll take the lease home with me now and look it over this evening, and then I'll let you know if I have any questions.

38. What is the woman going to rent?

[8-second pause]

39. What does the woman mean when she says, "No problem?"

[8-second pause]

40. What will the woman do next?

[8-second pause]

Questions 41–43 refer to the following conversation.

Woman: You're going to Chicago tomorrow, right? What time does your flight leave?

Man: At eleven. Why?

Woman: Oh, that's great. I have a flight at noon, and I was hoping we could take a taxi to the airport together.

Man: Sure. That'd be fine. Are you going to the conference in Chicago, too?

Woman: No, I'm off to Toronto. I've applied for a position at a firm there, and they've asked me to come up for an interview.

41. What does the woman want to do?

[8-second pause]

42. What time does the man's flight leave?

[8-second pause]

43. Why is the woman going to Toronto?

[8-second pause]

Questions 44–46 refer to the following conversation.

Woman: Your total comes to seventy-five dollars exactly. Are you a member of our frequent buyer's club?
Man: No. What's that?
Woman: It's a free benefit we offer our customers. All you have to do is fill out this form, and we give you a card, which you can use to get ten percent off your entire purchase plus up to twenty-five percent off weekly specials.
Man: I certainly wouldn't mind making my grocery bill a little smaller. So, sure, I'll sign up.

44. Where does this conversation take place?

[8-second pause]

45. How much does membership cost?

[8-second pause]

46. What will the man probably do next?

[8-second pause]

Questions 47–49 refer to the following conversation.

Woman: All set for this afternoon's meeting?
Man 1: Uh huh. I've got my sales presentation all ready to go. And you?
Woman: My budget report is done.
Man 2: Have you seen the agenda? There's quite a lot on it.
Man 1: I know. We've got that new client project to discuss. That'll take a while. And we have to go over the plans for next week's hiring fair.
Man 2: And all those things are on top of the usual agenda items.
Woman: It'll be five o'clock before we get out of here.

47. When will the meeting take place?

[8-second pause]

48. What will the woman report on at the meeting?

[8-second pause]

49. What do the speakers imply about the meeting?

[8-second pause]

Questions 50–52 refer to the following conversation.

Man:    Hi. I'm calling to find out if you've had a chance to review the proposal we
        e-mailed to you yesterday.
Woman:  I'm sorry. Where are you calling from?
Man:    X-Ten Enterprises. We met with you last week to discuss your renovation project,
        and yesterday we sent the promised proposal and preliminary budget.
Woman:  Oh, right. I see it in my in-box now. I've been a bit busy, but I'll look it over and
        get back to you before noon today.

50. How did the man send the proposal?

   [8-second pause]

51. What does the woman mean when she says, "I'm sorry?"

   [8-second pause]

52. What will the woman do this morning?

   [8-second pause]

Questions 53–55 refer to the following conversation.

Woman:  Have you met Mr. Kim yet?
Man:    You mean the new assistant in the marketing department? Yes, he introduced
        himself to me yesterday. He seems very nice.
Woman:  Well, he certainly isn't shy. He's been here only a week and already he's managed
        to learn the names of just about everyone in the office.
Man:    It sure doesn't seem hard for him to talk to people. I think I'd been here at least a
        year before I started getting to know people outside my department.

53. What is Mr. Kim's job?

   [8-second pause]

54. How long has Mr. Kim worked at the company?

   [8-second pause]

55. What do the speakers imply about Mr. Kim?

   [8-second pause]

Questions 56–58 refer to the following conversation.

Woman 1:  I hear the food here is good.
Man:       It is. I've eaten here many times, and it's always great.
Woman 2:  It looks like a good place for a client lunch. In fact, why don't we have our meeting with the Sligo representatives here? We can discuss the contract over lunch.
Man:       Excellent idea. Much better than meeting in our conference room. I'll call their office and make a date for next week.
Woman 1:  And you should make a reservation for a table, too. This place looks crowded.
Man:       You're right. It always fills up at lunch time. A lot of people like to eat here.
Woman 2:  I hope the Sligo reps will like it, too.

56. Where does the conversation take place?

[8-second pause]

57. What is suggested about the place?

[8-second pause]

58. What are the speakers mostly talking about?

[8-second pause]

Questions 59–61 refer to the following conversation.

Man:      I am so looking forward to next week.
Woman:  Are you going to that sales seminar with everyone else?
Man:      No way! I'll be far, far from here, relaxing at my cabin at the lake. I plan to bike up there early Saturday morning.
Woman:  You're kidding! You're gonna ride all the way to the lake over those bumpy roads? And what if it rains?
Man:      I'll get wet. I don't care. I'm just looking forward to a nice, leisurely, relaxing week.
Woman:  Well, while you're taking it easy, think of me stuck behind my desk, writing up reports for clients.

59. Where will the man be next week?

[8-second pause]

60. How will he get there?

[8-second pause]

61. What does the woman suggest about this mode of transportation?

[8-second pause]

Questions 62–64 refer to the following conversation.

Woman: Hi. I bought this sweater here yesterday, but when I got home, I realized it was too small.

Man: I see. Since the sweater was on sale, I can't give you a refund, so I hope store credit will do.

Woman: That's perfect. I'll just get the same sweater but larger. I hope you haven't run out of this style.

Man: We still have plenty, but you'll have to choose a different color. I'm afraid we don't have any more in blue.

62. What does the woman want?

[8-second pause]

63. What is the matter with the sweater?

[8-second pause]

64. What does the man say about the sweater style?

[8-second pause]

Questions 65–67 refer to the following conversation and schedule.

Man: Hi. I have a reservation on the ten twenty to Washington tomorrow afternoon.

Woman: Yes, that train gets in at one forty-five.

Man: Right. So that's exactly my problem. It turns out my client changed the time of the meeting. I have to be there by eleven o'clock.

Woman: I'd be happy to put you on an earlier train. There is a small a fee, though, to do that.

Man: That's not a problem. Just put me on a train that gets me there as close to eleven o'clock as possible.

Woman: Of course. Just give me a minute. And I hope you enjoy your trip. There are so many interesting things to see there.

Man: I wish I had time.

65. Why did the man make the call?

[8-second pause]

66. What will the man do in Washington?

[8-second pause]

67. Look at the graphic. Which train will the man take?

[8-second pause]

Questions 68–70 refer to the following conversation and menu.

Woman: Here's your menu, sir. The lunch specials are on the front.
Man: Wow. These prices are a bit steep. I know I didn't pay this much last time I was here.
Woman: You get a lot with your meal. Most of the specials include salad or soup or both.
Man: Well, I'm not really in the mood for soup. Let me see. Is there anything without meat? Oh, yes, this sandwich special looks good. Bring me that, and can I have a glass of water?
Woman: Of course. Right away.

68. What does the man imply about the prices?

[8-second pause]

69. Look at the graphic. What does the man order?

[8-second pause]

70. What will the woman do next?

[8-second pause]

## PART 4: TALKS

 **Directions:** You will hear a talk given by a single speaker. You will see three questions on each talk, each with four possible answers. Choose the best answer to each question and fill in the corresponding oval on your answer sheet.

Track 25

Questions 71–73 refer to the following talk.

Woman: Good afternoon. I'm Edith Maguire, and I'll be talking with you today about getting organized. I've been in the business for over ten years, helping people get control over the mess in their homes and offices. People often come to me when they're getting their home ready for sale, and they want it to look nice to attract buyers. Or they want some help in developing systems to keep their home and family life organized. And, believe it or not, many of my clients work in business offices, just like yours. Research has shown that a well-organized office leads to higher worker productivity. Before I continue, are there any questions? I am happy to explain anything you want to know, so don't be shy.

71. Who is the speaker?

[8-second pause]

72. How long has she worked in this business?

[8-second pause]

73. What does the speaker mean when she says, "Don't be shy?"

[8-second pause]

Questions 74–76 refer to the following talk.

Man:     Welcome to Starkburg Manor. In addition to once being the Starkburg family home, this five hundred-year-old building has housed a hotel, a girls' school, and even a prison. Now, of course, it is our history museum with displays depicting local life over the past several centuries. We'll begin our tour with a film that gives the background of the museum. That begins shortly, at two thirty, and lasts just about twenty minutes. Then we will view the displays on the first and second floors. After the tour, you are welcome to walk the grounds on your own, enjoy a cup of tea in the garden, or browse our gift shop. Now, if you all will please line up here by the door and show me your tickets, we will begin.

74. Where does this talk take place?

[8-second pause]

75. What will happen at two thirty?

[8-second pause]

76. What are listeners asked to do?

[8-second pause]

Questions 77–79 refer to the following talk.

Woman:   Welcome to today's Health Talk. Health Talk is a free hour-long event sponsored by the hospital. It takes place on the third Tuesday of every month and is open to the public. Our speakers cover a range of health topics from preventative care to new research and procedures. If you would like to receive updates about future programs, you can sign up for our e-mail newsletter using the clipboard by the door. OK. Today's speaker is Gillian Holmes, a registered dietician who teaches regularly at the local community college, as well as seeing patients here at the hospital. She will talk with us today about how food and exercise can help us keep in shape.

77. What is true about the event?

[8-second pause]

78. What can listeners sign up for?

[8-second pause]

79. What will Ms. Holmes talk about?

[8-second pause]

Questions 80–82 refer to the following phone message.

Man:  Hello. This is Roger Briggs calling for Amanda Smith. I got your message inquiring about accounts for small businesses. Yes, we provide that service and would be happy to set you up. Since you already have a personal account with us, that should be no problem. You may also know that we provide loans for small businesses such as yours. If you are just starting out, you will have many upfront costs, such as rent, employee wages, and other costs, which a loan from us would help you cover. You can call our small business office and set up a time to meet with an officer to discuss opening your business account and to go over the other services we can provide you with.

80. Why did the speaker make the call?

[8-second pause]

81. Where does the speaker work?

[8-second pause]

82. What does the speaker ask the listener to do?

[8-second pause]

Questions 83–85 refer to the following weather report.

Woman:  Welcome to the evening weather report. You know, we've been getting a lot of e-mails about the weather we've been having this week. Sorry, folks, I wish it were in my power to change it. "Enough rain already!" is the message most of you are sending, and I have to say that I couldn't have said it better myself. Unfortunately, we are going to have to put up with this for another couple of days, but never fear, Tuesday will see the clouds moving out and we'll have plenty of sunshine through the weekend, with cooler temperatures Saturday afternoon into evening, due to high winds.

83. What does the speaker mean when she says, "I couldn't have said it better myself?"

[8-second pause]

84. When will the weather change?

[8-second pause]

85. What will the weather be like on Saturday?

[8-second pause]

Questions 86–88 refer to the following talk.

Man: Welcome to this evening's meeting of the Architects Club. Our originally scheduled speaker, Matilda Warren, is unfortunately unable to be with us tonight. She has, however, sent over copies of her most recent book, which are available for sale for any who are interested. Instead of our speaker, we'll show a film, *Urban Design for the New Millennium*, which I know you will enjoy. We'll have some time for discussion following the film, and then we'll have our usual cookies and tea and social hour. And don't forget, it's that time of year again— dues-paying time. Our treasurer is coming around now to pick up your checks.

86. What is the purpose of the talk?

[8-second pause]

87. What does the speaker imply about the meeting?

[8-second pause]

88. What will happen next?

[8-second pause]

Questions 89–91 refer to the following announcement.

Woman: Attention, passengers. This is the express train to the airport, making stops at Center City, Overton Mall, and the airport. I repeat, this is an express train. Passengers for University Park, Uptown, City Hall, and other local stops should go downstairs to the east platform and take the local train. This train is scheduled to leave the station in two minutes. Please stand away from the doors to allow other passengers to board. Please have your tickets ready to show the conductor. You must have a blue ticket to ride this train. Yellow tickets are valid on the local train only.

89. What should passengers for City Hall do?

[8-second pause]

90. What will happen in two minutes?

[8-second pause]

91. What is true abut the express train?

[8-second pause]

Questions 92–94 refer to the following news report.

Man:     The Windward Company announced today that it has purchased the old
         Johnson Shoe Factory behind the railroad station. This historic building has
         been empty for several years. Windward spokesperson Rita Hughes said that the
         company plans to use the building to house its main offices. "Although extensive
         renovations are planned," she explained, "we plan to preserve the historic
         character of the building." In addition to three floors of offices, the renovation
         plans include a daycare center and fitness club for use of company employees,
         and a showroom of company products that will be open to the public.
         Renovation work is expected to begin next month and be completed shortly after
         the new year.

92. What will the Windward Company use the building for?

    [8-second pause]

93. Who can use the fitness club?

    [8-second pause]

94. When will the renovations be finished?

    [8-second pause]

Questions 95–97 refer to the following phone message and sign.

Woman:   Hi. I'm calling to find out why my car was towed from the Highland Apartments
         parking lot last Saturday. My office is just across the street from there and I've
         been parking there for years with no problem at all, even though I don't have
         a resident's parking sticker. So I parked in the lot last Saturday because I had a
         tennis game at the nearby courts. It wasn't even six P.M. yet when I got back to
         the lot to find that my car had been towed. I had to pay a towing fee before they
         would give me my car back. Thankfully, it wasn't damaged, but I would like to be
         reimbursed for the towing fee.

95. Look at the graphic. Why was the caller's car towed?

    [8-second pause]

96. Why did the caller use the parking lot last Saturday?

    [8-second pause]

97. What does the caller want the listener to do?

    [8-second pause]

Questions 98–100 refer to the following excerpt from a meeting and agenda.

Man:     Welcome to the bimonthly staff meeting. It looks like almost everybody is here today. That's great. You've all already seen the agenda, but I would like to make a small change and start with the final item because it is so very important, and I would like to avoid having the misunderstandings we had last year as much as possible. Also, Ms. Jones, who will talk to us about an exciting new professional development opportunity, is running a bit behind schedule. So we'll just go ahead and get started without her, and she'll be along soon. So if you will turn your attention to the first slide we have projected on the screen, we'll begin.

98.  How often does the staff meeting take place?

  [8-second pause]

99.  Look at the graphic. Which topic will be discussed first?

  [8-second pause]

100.  What problem does the speaker mention?

  [8-second pause]

# MP3 CD